The State of
Working America
2006/2007

The State of Working America 2006/2007

LAWRENCE MISHEL

JARED BERNSTEIN

SYLVIA ALLEGRETTO

Economic
Policy
Institute

ILR Press
an imprint of Cornell University Press

First published 2007 by Cornell University Press
First printing, Cornell Paperbacks, 2007

ISBN 978-0-8014-4529-3 (cloth: alk. paper)
ISBN 978-0-8014-7355-5 (paper: alk. paper)

Printed in the United States of America

Recommended citation for this book is as follows: Mishel, Lawrence, Jared Bernstein, and Sylvia Allegretto, *The State of Working America 2006/2007*. An Economic Policy Institute Book. Ithaca, N.Y.: ILR Press, an imprint of Cornell University Press, 2007

Cornell University Press strives to use environmentally responsible suppliers and materials to the fullest extent possible in the publishing of its books. Such materials include vegetable-based, low-VOC inks and acid-free papers that are recycled, totally chlorine-free, or partly composed of nonwood fibers. For further information, visit our website at www.cornellpress.cornell.edu.

Cloth printing   10 9 8 7 6 5 4 3 2 1
Paperback printing   10 9 8 7 6 5 4 3 2 1

PRINTED IN U.S.A.

To my bride-to-be, Ellen Brown.
- LAWRENCE MISHEL

To my children, Ellie, Kate, and Sarah.
- JARED BERNSTEIN

To Susan M. Borrello, my wonderfully wacky sister
and a dedicated elementary school teacher for over 20 years.
- SYLVIA ALLEGRETTO

Visit epi.org and StateofWorkingAmerica.org
The Economic Policy Institute's Web sites contain current analysis of issues
addressed in this book. The DataZone section presents up-to-date historical data
series on incomes, wages, employment, poverty, and other topics. It also includes graphic
image files of every figure and table in this volume. The data can be
viewed online or downloaded as spreadsheets.

Acknowledgments

The preparation of this publication requires the intensive work of many people on EPI's staff and many contributions from other researchers on the topics covered in the text.

Yulia Fungard and Rob Gray provided extensive and enormously valuable research assistance in all of the areas covered in this book by collecting and organizing data and creating tables and graphs. Our programming staff, headed by Danielle Gao and including Jin Dai, provided extensive computer programming and data analysis. As this is Ms. Gao's last edition with us, we want to extend our deep gratitude for her invaluable contribution over many past editions.

Among EPI staffers (past and present), Josh Bivens, Lee Price, David Ratner, Monique Morrissey, Liana Fox, and Elise Gould provided extensive insights and guidance in many areas, including outsourcing research, trade and employment, international comparisons, and analysis of capital and labor incomes. We thank all our previous co-authors—Jacqueline Simon, David Frankel, John Schmitt, and Heather Boushey—for their lasting input. Our development staff, headed by Noris Weiss Malvey, provided valuable help in raising funds for this work.

Former EPI economist Jeff Chapman wrote the regional analysis chapter, and it was a pleasure to work with him. His knowledge of regional data and trends has greatly improved the quality of this chapter. We wish Jeff well in his new job in Washington state and we will miss his contribution to this effort in future editions.

Joe Procopio directs the book's production with Ellen Levy, Pat Watson, and Kieran Daly. Their careful editing and layout under considerable time pressure is greatly appreciated. Our readers are the true beneficiaries of their work, as they make us look like far better writers. Nancy Coleman, Karen Conner, and Stephaan Harris work to provide a large audience for our work. We deeply appreciate the energy and creativity they bring to their work.

Many experts were helpful in providing data or their research papers for our use. We are particularly grateful to Ed Wolff, Robert McIntire, Gary Solon, Peter Orzag, and Bhashkar Mazumder, for the provision of special tabulations. Others who provided data, advice, or their analysis include: Elaine Ditsler, Bruce Fallick, Steve Hipple, David Johnson, Chuck Nelson, Wendell Primus, Steven Sabow, Ed Welniak, William Wiatrowski, Michael Lettau, and Jon Sargent.

We are grateful to the Ford Foundation, the Foundation for Child Development, the Joyce Foundation, the John D. & Catherine T. MacArthur Foundation, the Charles Stewart Mott Foundation, the Annie E. Casey Foundation, the Open Society Institute, and the Rockefeller Foundation for providing support for the research and publication of this volume.

Table of Contents

Executive summary

Introduction: Life and times in the new economy

Starting in 1995, a new and important change occurred in the U.S. economy: productivity—the output of goods and services per hour worked—began to grow more quickly. After growing 1.4% per year since the mid-1970s, productivity growth accelerated to 2.5% a year from 1995 to 2000, and then jumped to 3.1% a year from 2000 to 2005. The post-1995 shift in productivity growth, partly attributed to the diffusion and more efficient use of information technology, has sometimes been labeled the "new economy." Because productivity growth provides the basis for rising living standards for everyone, its acceleration is an unequivocally positive development for the economy.

Yet, despite this unequivocally beneficial development, many Americans report dissatisfaction with where the economy seems to be headed, and many worry about their own and their children's well-being. These concerns have led some policy makers and economists to ask: why aren't people happier about the economy? The question seems reasonable to those who follow the top-line numbers of the economy, such as the growth of the total economy (e.g., gross domestic product), the stock market, or corporate profits. The question is easily answered, however, for those who follow and report on the data that fill the chapters in this book.

Our findings show that while faster productivity growth creates the potential for widely shared prosperity, if that potential is to be realized, a number of other factors have to be in place. Those factors include labor market institutions (such as strong collective bargaining), an appropriate minimum wage, and, importantly, a truly tight labor market, all of which are necessary to ensure that the benefits of growth reach everyone, not just those at the top of the wealth scale.

When these institutions are weakened or absent, growth is likely to bypass the majority of working families. The chapters that follow elaborate this story in greater detail by examining trends in incomes, mobility, wages, jobs, wealth, and poverty, and by placing recent developments in their historical, regional, and international context.

Family income: "New economy" drives a wedge between productivity and living standards

A family's income is, of course, one of the most important determinants of their economic well-being. Most working families depend on their income to meet their immediate consumption needs (like food and gas), to finance longer-term investments in goods and services (like housing and education), and to build their savings.

Many families face two separate but related challenges regarding the growth of their real incomes: (1) post-2000 wage stagnation, especially among middle- and lower-income families, and (2) the gap between income and productivity growth. Despite the fact that the most recent economic expansion began in late 2001, the real income of the median family fell each year through 2004, the most recent available data. Between 2000 and 2004, real median family income fell by 3%, or about $1,600 in 2004 dollars.

The post-2000 income trends stand in stark contrast to the extent and pattern of family income growth in the latter 1990s. Then, during a period of uniquely tight job markets, full employment conditions compelled employers to more broadly share the benefits of accelerated productivity growth. Between 1995 and 2000, output per hour grew 2.5% per year, while real median family income grew 2.2% annually. Importantly, the income growth of less-advantaged groups proved to benefit the most from the availability of more and better jobs fostered by the tight labor market. Real median income was up 2.9% per year for African Americans, 4.6% for Hispanic families, 2.3% for young families (family head: 25-34 years old), and 3.1% for single-mother families.

The post-2000 reversal of these favorable trends was a function of diminished employment opportunities, not just during the recession, as we would expect, but over the protracted jobless recovery that followed. This decline in median income during the initial years of expansions appears to be more the norm than the exception in recent recoveries. Over both the 1980s and 1990s recovery, it took seven years for median family income to regain its peak, far longer than in earlier cycles.

In fact, when it comes to income growth over the past generation, the extent of a family's prosperity is largely the result of their placement in the income scale, with the richest families experiencing the fastest income growth. Between 1979 and 2000, for example, the real income of households in the lowest fifth grew 6.1%; the middle fifth was up 12.3%; the top fifth grew 69.6%; and the average income of those in the top 1% grew by 183.7%.

Higher inequality shows up whether we look at consumption or income. Although inequality is not driven by tax changes, lowering the tax burden on the wealthy has demonstrably exacerbated the problem.

Greater inequality has also been generated by an expansion of capital income and an increased concentration of capital income among the very highest income families. Whereas the top 1% received 37.8% of all capital income in 1979, their share rose to 49.1% by 2000 and rose further to 57.5% in 2003 (most recent data). This shift toward greater concentration of capital income reflects an increase in the share of income flowing to corporate profits and that profit rates in 2005 are the highest in 36 years (excepting 1997). If the pre-tax return to capital (i.e., profit rate) in 2005 had remained at its 1979 level, then hourly compensation would have been 5% higher in the corporate sector, equivalent to an annual transfer of $235 billion dollars from labor to capital (measured for 2005).

One way that middle-income families have kept their incomes rising over the past few decades has been for women in general and wives in particular to enter the paid labor market. Among married-couple families with children, for example, middle-income wives added over 500 hours of work to total family work hours between 1979 and 2000. While this has been a positive force for women's economic independence, it has also put a strain on the need to balance work and family.

Income-class mobility: How much is there?

Another important dimension of income and living standards involves income-class mobility. How much progress do families typically make in terms of income growth over their lifetimes? To what extent are children's economic fates determined by the income position of their parents? And is there more or less such mobility in the United States versus other advanced economies?

In fact, we find significant income correlations between parents and their children, implying that income-class mobility is at least partially restricted by a parent's position in the income scale. For example, one recent study finds the correlation between parents and children to be 0.6. One way to view the significance of this finding is to note that it implies that it would take a poor family of four with two children approximately nine to 10 generations—over 200 years—to achieve the income of the typical middle-income four-person family. Were that correlation only half that size—meaning income differences were half as persistent across generations—it would take four to five generations for the poor family to catch up.

In a similar vein, we find that sons of low-earning fathers have slightly less than a 60% chance of reaching above the 20th percentile by adulthood, about a 20% chance of surpassing the median, and a very slight chance—4.5%—of ending up above the 80th percentile.

In other words, the extent of income mobility across generations plays a significant role in the living standards of American families. It is, for example, a key determinant of how many generations a family will be stuck at the low end of the income scale, or snugly ensconced at the high end.

Our folklore often emphasizes the rags-to-riches, Horatio-Alger-like stories that suggest that anyone with the gumption and smarts to prevail can lift themselves up by their bootstraps and transverse the income scale in a single generation. The reality in the United States, however, shows much less mobility than such stories suggest. Surprisingly, international comparisons reveal less mobility in America than other countries with comparably advanced economies. For example, one study reveals the intergenerational income correlations in Finland, Sweden, and Germany to be 0.22, 0.28, and 0.34, respectively, compared to the U.S. correlation of 0.43. Note that these are countries that U.S. economists often criticize for their extensive social protections—each one has universal health coverage, for example—yet their citizens experience greater mobility than do our own.

Another important dimension of the mobility story is the question of how it has evolved over time. One reason this is so important relates back to our findings regarding income inequality. The growth of inequality between two time periods, say between the late 1970s and today, is of less concern if mobility is up, thus offsetting the greater distances between income classes. The evidence reveals, however, that mobility is either flat or diminished over the very period when inequality has been on the rise. For example, one study shows that the intergenerational correlation between fathers' and sons' income has grown from 0.32 to 0.58 (higher correlations imply less mobility). Another study shows that the share of families remaining in the top fifth of the income scale for 10 years went from 49.1% in the 1970s to 53.1% in the 1990s.

What explains the lack of mobility here in the United States? Certainly unequal education opportunities and historical discrimination play a role. As such, opportunities for advancement are limited for those with fewer economic resources. For example, we show that children from wealthy families have much greater access to top-tier universities than kids from low-income families, even once innate skills are taken into account. We also find wealth concentration to be correlated across generations, and this creates another impediment to the upward mobility of the economy's "have-nots." For instance, about two-thirds of children whose parents were in the lowest fifth of the wealth scale ended up in the bottom 40% as adults.

Wages: Growth stalls while productivity and compensation diverge

The major development in the labor market in recent years has been the stunning disconnect between the rapid productivity growth and pay growth, especially given the rapidity of productivity's growth and the how stunted pay growth has been in the past several years.

Also of great concern is the tremendous widening of the wage gap between those at the top of the wage scale, particularly corporate chief executive officers, and other wage earners. The importance of these two developments cannot be overstated because wages and salaries make up about three-fourths of total family income, and as such, are the primary driving force behind income growth and income inequality. Over the 1995-2005 period, productivity grew a remarkable 33.4%, and over half of that growth has occurred since 2001. This pace of productivity growth far exceeded that of the earlier period from 1973 to 1995. However, despite enormous growth in productivity, wages for the typical worker and for those with either a high school or a college degree were about the same in 2005 as in 2001.

By comparison, pay did rise in the earlier period from 1996 to 2001, fueled by the higher productivity and the progressive drop in unemployment to 4.0% by 2000. Moreover, the wage momentum carried forward through 2001 and into 2002, despite rising unemployment. The wage momentum from the late 1990s is important to understand when looking at trends over the 2000-05 period—all of the wage growth from the 2000-05 period occurred within the first two years. The poor job creation during the early 2000s recession and its lackluster recovery eventually knocked wage growth down so that prices rose at least as fast. This was the case even in 2005, when the unemployment rate fell to 5.1%.

In short, historically high productivity growth and historically low unemployment have benefited compensation and wages very little. While productivity grew 33.4% between 1995 and 2005, benefits (health and pension) grew less than half that much and wages for typical workers grew one-third as much as productivity. After 2001, there has been basically no wage improvement for typical workers regardless of significant gains in productivity.

Digging a little deeper into these trends, we find that women are much more likely to earn low wages than men. In 2005, 29.4% of women earned poverty-level wages or less, significantly more than the share of men (19.9%). Women are also much less likely to earn very high wages. In 2005 only 10.1% of women, but 17.6% of men, earned at least three times the poverty-level wage. The proportion of minority workers earning low wages is substantial—33.3% of black workers and 39.3% of Hispanic workers in 2005. Minority women are even more likely to be low earners—37.1% of black women and 45.7% of Hispanic women in 2005.

The trend in the share of workers earning poverty-level wages corresponds to the patterns previously described: momentum in reducing poverty-level work began in the late 1990s, continued until 2002, then dissipated. So, although the share of workers earning poverty-level wages actually fell from 25.1% to 24.5% in the 2000-05 period, this progress came in the first two years of that period and then partially reversed. Among blacks the increase in low-wage work after 2002 was large enough to reverse the progress from 2000 to 2002.

A historical look at wage inequality shows that it has worsened considerably over the past three decades. The deterioration in real wages from 1979 to 1995 was both broad and uneven. Wages were stagnant or fell for the bottom 60% of wage earners over the 1979-95 period and grew modestly for higher-wage workers—over 16 years the growth was just 5.0% at the 80th percentile and 10.9% to 13.9% at the 90th and 95th percentiles, respectively.

More recently, the importance of the late 1990s full-employment labor markets that provided across the board wage increases contrast with the most recent 2000-05 period. Starting in the early 1990s low-wage workers experienced either wage growth more than or comparable to that of middle-wage workers, so that the expanding wage gap between the middle and bottom lessened and then stabilized. Tight labor markets along with increases in the minimum wage in the early and late 1990s, combined with the drop in unemployment in the late 1990s, can explain this trend.

There are three key elements of wage inequality. One is the gap at the "bottom," meaning the difference between median-wage and low-wage workers. Another measure of wage inequality takes into account the "top half" gap, that is, between high-wage (90th or 95th percentile wage earners) and middle-wage earners. The third element is the gap at the very top, i.e., the growth of wages for those in the upper 1%, including chief executive officers (CEOs). These three elements have had differing historical trajectories. The gap at the bottom grew in the 1980s but has been stable or declining ever since, whereas the "top half" wage gap has persistently grown since the late 1970s. The very highest earners have done considerably better than other workers for at least 30 years, but they have done extraordinarily well over the last 10 years.

Explaining these shifts in wage inequality requires attention to several factors that affect low-, middle-, and high-wage workers differently. The experience of the late 1990s is a reminder of the great extent to which a low unemployment rate benefits workers, especially low-wage earners. Correspondingly, the high levels of unemployment in the early and mid-1980s and again in recent years have disempowered wage earners and provided the context in which other forces—specifically, a weakening of labor market institutions and an increase in globalization—could drive up wage inequality. Significant shifts in the labor market, such as the severe drop in the real value of the minimum wage and de-unionization, can explain one-third of the growth in wage inequality. Similarly, the increasing globalization of the economy—immigration, trade, and capital mobility—and the employment shift toward lower-paying service industries (such as retail trade) and away from manufacturing can explain, in combination, another third of the total growth in wage inequality. Macroeconomic factors also played an important role: high unemployment in the early 1980s greatly increased wage inequality, the low unemployment of the late 1990s reduced it, and high unemployment in recent years has renewed it.

The shape of wage inequality shifted in the late 1980s as the gap at the bottom—i.e., the 50/10 gap between middle-wage workers at the 50th percentile and low-wage workers at the 10th—began to shrink. However, over the last few years, this progress against wage inequality at the bottom has been halted among men and wage inequality at the bottom among women has resumed its growth. This reversal is partially the effect of the jobless recovery and the still-remaining shortage of jobs and partially a result of the continued drop in the real value of the minimum wage. The greatest increase in wage inequality at the bottom occurred among women and corresponded to the fall in the minimum wage's value over the 1980s, the high unemployment of the early 1980s, and the expansion of low-wage retail jobs. The positive trend in this wage gap over the 1990s owes much to increases in the minimum wage, low unemployment, and the slight, relative contraction in low-paying retail jobs in the late 1990s. The wage gap at the top half—the 90/50 gap between high- and middle-wage earners—continued its steady growth in the 1990s and early 2000s but at a slightly slower pace than in the 1980s. The continuing influence of globalization, de-unionization, and the shift to lower-paying service industries ("industry shifts") can explain the continued growth of wage inequality at the top.

The erosion of the extent and quality of employer-provided benefits, most notably pensions and health insurance, is an important aspect of the deterioration in job quality for many workers. Employer-provided health care coverage eroded from 1979 until 1993-94, when it stabilized, and then began falling again after 2000 through 2004 (the latest data). In fact, coverage dropped from 69.0% in 1979 to 55.9% in 2004, with a 2.9 percentage-point fall just since 2000. Employees have absorbed half the rise in costs for employer-provided health premiums (not counting any of the higher deductibles or co-pays paid by employees) since 1992, even though their share of costs in that year was just 14%. Employer-provided pension coverage tended to rise in the 1990s but receded by 2.8 percentage points from 2000 to 2004 to 45.5%, 5.1 percentage points below the level in 1979. Pension plan quality also receded, as the share of workers in defined-benefit plans fell from 39% in 1980 to just 19% in 2003. Correspondingly, the share of workers with a defined-contribution plan (and no other plan) rose from 8% to 31%.

Young workers' prospects are another good barometer of the strength of the labor market. Wages actually fell for all entry-level workers since 2000, whether high school or college educated, male or female. This contrasts to the extremely strong wage growth for each of these groups from 1995 to 2000, when wages rose roughly 10% for entry-level high school men and women, 20.9% for entry-level college men, and 11.7% for college women.

Unionized workers earn higher wages than comparable non-union workers and also are 18.3% more likely to have health insurance, 22.5% more likely to have pension coverage, and 3.2% more likely to have paid leave. The erosion of unionization (from 43.1% of blue-collar men in 1978 to just 19.2% in 2005) can account for 65% of the 11.1 percentage-point growth of the blue-collar/white-collar wage gap among men over the 1978-2005 period.

The real value of the minimum wage has been steadily falling in real terms, thereby causing the earnings of low-wage workers to seriously fall behind those of other workers and contributing to the rise in wage inequality. Those affected by the lower minimum wage make important contributions to their family's economic well-being. For instance, minimum wage earners contribute 58% of their family's weekly earnings; in 43% of the affected families the minimum wage earner generated all of the family's earnings. Moreover, there are 7.3 million children living in the families that would benefit from a modest minimum wage increase. While minorities are disproportionately represented among minimum wage workers, 60% are white. These workers also tend to be women (59% of the total) and concentrated in the retail and hospitality industries (46% of all minimum wage earners are employed in those industries, compared to just 21% of all workers).

Conversely, the 1980s, 1990s, and 2000s have been prosperous times for top U.S. executives, especially relative to other wage earners. Over the 1992-2005 period the median CEO saw pay rise by 186.2%, while the median worker saw wages rise by just 7.2%. In 1965, U.S. CEOs in major companies earned 24 times more than an average worker; this ratio grew to 300 at the end of the recovery in 2000. The fall in the stock market reduced CEO stock-related pay (e.g., options), but by 2005 CEO pay had recovered to the point where it was 262 times that of the average worker. The lion's share of the gains for the top 1% in the pay scale accrued to the upper 10% of that elite group (i.e., those in the 99.9th percentile). Of the 3.6 percentage-point gain in the share of all earnings that the top 1% experienced between 1989 and 2000, 3.2 of them accrued to very upper tier.

The jobs of the future will require greater education credentials, but not to any great extent. In 2004, the occupational composition of jobs required that 27.7% of the workforce have a college degree or more. This share will rise by just one percentage point, to 28.7%, by 2014, according to BLS projections.

Jobs: Diminished expectations

Strong job creation that fully utilizes the available workers and skills in our workforce is a critical component to a strong, lasting, and equitable recovery. A robust job market is what is needed to ensure that the proceeds of economic growth are broadly shared. By that measure, the current recovery has fallen short. As is well known, this recovery, which began in late 2001, was a "jobless recovery" well into 2003. That is, real gross domestic product was expanding, but we were losing jobs on net for a year and a half into the expansion (net jobs refer to the number of jobs created minus the number of jobs lost).

Historically, it took just less than two years—21 months—to regain the prior employment peak; in this current cycle, it took almost four years (46 months). Since then, we have consistently added jobs on net, but at a slower rate than in past recoveries. As of this writing the current cycle is five years old and employment is up 1.9% since the last cyclical peak. Comparatively, employment growth for the five year period of the 1990s cycle was 7.1% and the historical average for cycles of this length was 10%.

This record of historically weak job creation is costly for the economy and for workers. Lackluster job creation is partially responsible for the ongoing disjuncture between overall economic growth and the wages and incomes of working families, as shown in earlier chapters. The resulting lower rates of employment and lack of wage pressures translate into lost output and forgone increases in living standards.

Depressed employment rates are usually a sign of weak labor demand. Since the 2001 peak, employment rates are down 1.4 percentage points for men and 1.3 percentage points for women. However, there have been debates as to whether employment rate declines have been a cyclical response to weak demand or if they represented a structural change. Since young college graduates are a group with high attachment to the job market, they make a good test case for whether the low employment rates are related to weak demand as opposed to a voluntary decline in employment (i.e., cyclical vs. structural).

The employment rate of young college graduates fell 3.5 percentage points from 2001 to mid-2003—in step with the recession and jobless recovery. In 2003, when employment started to pick up, this rate also increased significantly. Young college graduates (ages 25 to 35) who had at least a bachelor's degree, and in some cases, an advanced degree, would have been highly motivated to secure employment. Now that employment rates are rebounding, it seems the cyclical responses may have dominated structural ones.

The unemployment rate is, in a historical sense, relatively low—4.8% as of this writing. Unemployment rates that prevailed during the expansion of the late 1990s into 2000— when the annual unemployment rate was 4.0%—were considerably lower. For most of the current recovery, the relatively low unemployment rates have not been particularly good indicators of the actual slack that existed throughout the labor market, particularly in the first several years.

Persistent long-term unemployment has been another problem over this cycle. Shares of those unemployed 27 weeks or longer, as a share of total unemployment, were unusually high, especially given the relatively low unemployment rates that prevailed throughout the 2001 recession and recovery. As of this writing, the unemployment rate varied over the past year between 4.6 and 5.0%, and the average share of long-term unemployment was 18.4%. By comparison, the historical share of long-termers associated with this range of unemployment was just 10.8%.

It is still the case that those with less education disproportionately bear the brunt of economic downturns, but it is also the case that higher levels of education no longer provide the same protection against cyclical forces as in prior downturns. This was evident with depressed employment rates of young college graduates, and it is also evident in long-term unemployment woes associated with this latest cycle. The share of educated long-termers increased 2.8 percentage points from 2000 to 2005, while the share decreased by 5.4 percentage points for those with less than a high school degree.

Job growth has been too tepid to boost living standards for most workers—even as the economy expanded and labor productivity posted some impressive gains over this recovery. Hopefully the economy is poised to generate robust job creation and tight labor markets akin to those in the late 1990s, finally transforming output growth and strong worker productivity into broadly shared prosperity.

Other trends of note regarding jobs:

- Two industrial sectors have been especially hard hit: manufacturing employment, which is off 16%, and the information sector, which includes telecommunications, is down 17% from peak employment levels of 2001.
- Blue-collar workers made up 43.3% of long-term unemployment shares in 1989; in 2005 the share was 33.1%. Corresponding white-collar shares went from 31.0% to 38.9%.
- "Perma-temping," that is, the percent of temporary agency workers who have been on the same work assignment for a year or more, increased from 24.4% in 1995 to 33.7% in 2005.
- Employment rates for men and women at least 55 years old have trended upward since the early 1990s, and the trend even continued over the 2001 recession—the only age cohort to do so.

Wealth: Unrelenting disparities

Wealth and its accumulation are very important to a family's financial stability. Wealth, for example, enables a family to invest in a home, education, and retirement. In the short term, wealth reserves can help a family through difficult times, such as job loss. Wealth accumulation and debt often go hand-in-hand—for example, wealth as well as debt can be generated by home ownership. The ability of families to accumulate wealth and manage their debts is critical. This chapter dissects the two components that make up wealth or net worth—assets and liabilities.

Wealth is unequally distributed, more so than wages or incomes. Moreover, wealth has become more concentrated at the top of the distribution over time. In 2004, those in the top 1% of the wealth scale held over one-third of all wealth. The top fifth controlled 84.7% of all wealth in the United States, while the bottom 80% could claim only 15.3% of the country's total wealth in 2004. Over the 1962-2004 period, the wealth share held by the bottom 80% shrank by 3.8 percentage points, and that 3.8% share of wealth shifted to the top 5% of households. Over time wealth inequality has increased—as measured by the ratio of the wealthiest 1% to median wealth. In the early 1960s, the wealthiest Americans held 125 times that of the median wealth holder; in 2004 the wealthiest held 190 times more. As the wealthiest continue to thrive, many households are left behind with little or nothing in the way of assets and often have significant debt. Approximately one in six households had zero or negative net wealth.

Second, the notion that a vast majority of American households are greatly invested in the stock market is erroneous. Less than half of all households hold stock in any form, including mutual funds and 401(k)–style pension plans. From 2001 to 2004, the share of households holding stock declined—for the first time since 1989—from 51.9% to 48.6%. Moreover, of those households that held stock, just 34.9% had stock holdings of $5,000 or more.

Furthermore, the ownership of stocks was particularly unequal. In 2004, the top 1% of stockowners held 36.9% of all stocks, by value, while the bottom 80% of stockholders owned less than 10%. Additionally, stocks are a bigger part of the asset portfolio for wealthier households. For those in the top 1% of the wealth distribution, stock assets made up over 21% of their total assets, while stocks consisted of just 4.8% of all assets for households in the middle fifth of the wealth distribution. While stock performance is very important, on a daily basis it does not significantly affect average households.

Another key observation is that household debt has consistently trended upward, and it was over 130% of disposable personal income in 2005. As expected, debt-service burdens continued to plague lower-income families disproportionately and they increased from 2001 to 2004. By 2004, a middle-income family spent about a fifth of their income to service their debt. Approximately one in four low-income households had debt-service obligations that exceeded 40% of their income, as did 13.7% of middle-income households.

The opportunity to start anew through fair and reasonable bankruptcy laws is crucial for those who are faced with insurmountable debt. Personal bankruptcy filings soared at the end of 2005 just before new, stricter laws went into effect. For the year, nine out of every 1,000 adults declared personal bankruptcy. Only time will tell how the new laws will affect the number of bankruptcy filings, and ultimately how families will cope with large debt burdens often caused by the loss of employment, unmanageable medical bills, or divorce.

That wealth differs considerably by race is another primary observation of this analysis. Median wealth of white households is 10 times that of black households. Home ownership rates also vary considerably by race. Less than half of black and Hispanic households own their homes, when 72.7% of white households do. While approximately one-in-six households had zero or negative net wealth, broken down by race the numbers diverge considerably—13.0% of white households compared to 29.4% of black households have zero or negative net wealth.

Other key finding from this chapter include:

- Wealth inequality is greater than income inequality: The top 1%, next 9%, and bottom 90% shares of income were 16.9%, 25.6%, and 57.5%, respectively in 2004. Shares of wealth were 34.3%, 36.9%, and 28.7%, respectively.
- Average wealth held by the top 1% was close to $15 million, while it was $81,000 for households in the middle-fifth of the wealth distribution.
- Approximately 30% of households have a net worth of less than $10,000.
- About half of those in the bottom quarter of the income distribution own their homes, while 88.9% in the top quarter of the income distribution own homes.

Poverty: Rising over the recovery as the job market stalls

We next move to the other end of the wealth spectrum and examine the problem of poverty in America.

One of the most important challenges in discussing poverty in America is definitional. What, precisely, characterizes poverty in the U.S. economy? The government has an official definition, but it is widely considered to be an outdated benchmark (the 2005 threshold for a family of four was $19,961). The official thresholds have fallen well behind income growth among middle and higher income families, creating a situation wherein the poor are by definition more economically isolated. For example, the poverty line for a family of four was 48% of median family income in 1960; now it is 29%.

That said, trends in poverty are still revealing of changes in the living standards of our most economically vulnerable families. After falling steeply throughout the latter 1990s, poverty rates increased not only in the recessionary year of 2001, but in each year through 2005 (most recent data available), from 11.3% in 2000 to 12.6% in 2005, when 37 million persons, including 13 million children, were in poverty. This is the first time that poverty rose through each of the first three years of a recovery, another indicator of the narrow distribution of growth over this recovery. If we use a threshold of twice poverty, then the increase over the 2000-05 period went from 29.3% to 31.0% (about 91 million persons were below twice poverty in 2004).

Given their lower incomes, poverty rates for minorities are consistently higher than those of whites. The rate for African Americans, for example, was at least three times that of whites through 1989. However, poverty among blacks and Hispanics was much more responsive than for whites to the faster and more broadly distributed income growth during the 1990s, and by 2000 the poverty rate for blacks was the lowest on record, though even then, more than a fifth of blacks were poor (22.5%).

Tight job markets played a critically important role in poverty reduction in the latter 1990s, as overall poverty fell by 2.5 percentage points, with much larger declines for minorities: 6.8 points for blacks and 8.8 points for Hispanics. Yet, even under the best macroeconomic conditions, many poor families will need extra help to escape poverty. In the latter 1990s, for example, the push of welfare reform and the pull of strong labor demand drew many single mothers into the job market. And for many of these women, full employment conditions helped generate significant wage gains in percentage terms. But even hourly wage gains of about a third, from around $6 to around $8 dollars an hour, do not provide enough income for these families to meet their basic consumption needs. Fortunately, significant work supports—public benefits tied to work—were added or expanded over the 1990s. In the early 1990s, the highest benefit level under the Earned Income Tax Credit for a family with at least two children rose from about $1,700 to about $4,000 in 1995 dollars. The minimum wage was also increased, and more resources were devoted to health and child care subsidies.

The last point is an important one in thinking about the steps policy makers need to take to diminish poverty amid the plenty in the U.S. economy. With both the economy and social policy pushing hard in the same direction, poverty was significantly reduced in the 1990s. The 2000s, by contrast, reveal a different picture. The policy levers from the earlier period were largely still in place, but the absence of full employment meant that a critical piece of the puzzle was missing, and poverty rose over these years.

Regional analysis: Shared experiences, crucial differences

National trends in wages, incomes, poverty, and employment, as well as other economic indicators discussed throughout this book often vary greatly by region and by state. This chapter examines the economy through a regional lens. A regional focus is important because regional data more accurately represent economic circumstances faced by workers in a particular area. While not explicitly discussed in this chapter, state specific analyses and data can be found at www.earncentral.org/swx.htm.

The four Census regions are used throughout this chapter: Northeast, Midwest, South, and West. While the division into these regions for economic purposes is not perfect (dividing such intertwined states as Pennsylvania and Maryland or New Mexico and Texas), the differences between them are notable and thus provide some useful insights regarding regional variation.

This chapter begins by contrasting the early 1990s recession with the 2001 downturn. A regional perspective clearly shows that the early 1990s labor market slump disproportionately affected two areas of the country: the Northeast region and the state of California. The 2001 downturn was more geographically pervasive as there were just a few states that did not experience employment losses over the 2000 to 2003 period.

Job losses in the Northeast and California in the 1990s recession contributed to unemployment rates that rose earlier and faster in those areas compared to the rest of the country. Reflecting widespread job losses over the 2000-03 period, regional increases in unemployment were also prevalent during that time. However, the rates increased the fastest for the Midwest and California and rates increased the most for the Midwest for the latter recession.

In Chapter 4, we examined persistent and worsening long-term unemployment woes from a national perspective. This chapter adds regional perspective to the analysis. Over the current cycle, the growth in long-term unemployment rates by region were very similar at the onset of the recession—2001 to 2002. However, further into the cycle, different regional patterns emerged as long-term unemployment worsened much more in the Midwest relative to the other regions.

This result clearly relates to the regional impact of manufacturing job loss. One of the key factors in the recent recession and jobless recovery was the continued loss of employment in the manufacturing sector—especially for areas that have a heavy reliance on this sector. However, of the 35 states that had fewer jobs in 2003 than in 2000, 20 experienced job growth outside of manufacturing. For example, while Arkansas lost 14.2% of manufacturing jobs, all other industries grew by 2.1%.

Similar to the wage analyses presented in Chapter 3, job loss and increases in unemployment resulted in wage stagnation. In the West North Central division (Midwestern states west of the Mississippi), for example, low wage growth slowed from 3.1% annually from 1995 to 2000 to less than 1% annually from 2000 to 2003. There were some states, primarily in the Northeast, where wage growth was faster in the 2000 to 2003 period than between 1995 and 2000, but the overall picture was one of wage stagnation.

The federal minimum wage—fixed at $5.15—has not been raised since 1997. Tired of waiting for a federal hike, advocates at the state level have taken up the fight to increase state minimum wages. The number of states with minimum wages higher than the federal level has *quadrupled*, from five in 1997 to 21 in 2004, and as of this writing over a quarter of the workforce resides in states with minimum wages above the federal level. More campaigns are on the near horizon.

International comparisons:
How does the United States stack up?

The more market-driven U.S. economic model is often deemed superior to European economic models. The evidence of U.S. supremacy is often made by the singular assertion that the United States is the richest country in the world. While it is true that, in per capita terms, the United States is quite wealthy, a comparative analysis as to how the U.S. economy stacks up to other advanced economies must take into consideration a broader set of criteria.

International comparisons are made between 20 countries all belonging to the Organization for Economic Cooperation and Development (OECD). Comparing the U.S. economy to similar economies facing the same global conditions with respect to trade, investment, technology, and the environment provides an independent yardstick for gauging economic outcomes derived from different economic models. It is important to note that what is commonly referred to as the "European model" is actually many different economic models. Not only is each country unique, but unique occurrences—like the integration of East Germany—need to be taken into account. Many of the countries evaluated here are less market driven and more "interventionist" than the U.S. economic system, and much insight can be drawn from a general comparative analysis.

A main determinant of an economy's standard of living is its productivity, which can be relatively measured by the amount of gross domestic product (GDP) per hour worked. In terms of GDP per hour worked, in 2004 several European countries caught up to or surpassed U.S. levels of productivity. For example, looking at productivity relative to the United States (U.S.=100), five countries are above or equal to U.S. levels—Norway (125), Belgium (113), France (107), Ireland (104), and the Netherlands (100).

The growth rate of productivity is also important, and the United States is currently enjoying an extremely productive economy. In the current cycle (2000-05), U.S. productivity grew at 2.5%, and the United Kingdom came in second at 2.0%. However, as this book's discussion of family income and wages shows, the workforce responsible for this high level of productivity has not been able to enjoy the fruits of their very productive labor. Simply put, earnings have been stagnant for the majority of workers throughout this cycle.

The United States is one of the richest countries in the world. Per capita income in the U.S. was $39,728, but, perhaps surprisingly, that posting was second to Norway's $41,804. Many other economies have very respectable—all above $30,000— per capita incomes, including Ireland, Switzerland, Austria, Canada, Australia, Denmark, Sweden, Netherlands, Finland, Belgium, and the United Kingdom. Many Europeans and Canadians view their social protections as factors that raise their living standards and as such are unmeasured and not captured in income measures. A main reason why per capita incomes in Europe are generally below U.S. levels is because Europeans, relative to those in the U.S., seem to value leisure over the consumption of more goods.

While the United States is one of the wealthiest countries, it also has the highest degree of inequality of the OECD countries analyzed. The gap between richest and poorest is largest in the United States—whether measured in terms of Gini coefficients or the ratio of high earners (90th percentile) to low earners (10th percentile), the United States' inequality stands out. Low-income earners in the United States not only earn relatively lower incomes than their OECD counterparts, but they also are worse off because of limited social policy and safety nets. Access to health care is a good example.

The United States spends more on health care (whether measured as a percentage of gross domestic product or per capita spending) than any of these other countries. The United States spent 15.0% of its GDP on health care in 2003—30% more than the next highest spender (Switzerland at 11.6%). Ireland (7.4%), Austria (7.5%), and Finland (7.5%) spent the lowest percentages of GDP on health care. Even with such high spending, 46 million people in the United States do not have health insurance, and access to health care is much more limited than in the countries of its economic peers. In Canada, Japan, and Europe there is essentially universal health care coverage.

Perhaps surprisingly, the income advantages and high health spending in the United States do not produce better outcomes relative to other developed countries regarding life expectancy, infant mortality, and poverty. The United States has the lowest life expectancy, the highest infant mortality rates, and the highest overall and child poverty rates of all the countries studied. The relatively poor performance of the United States in these categories is symptomatic of the high degree of economic inequality and unequal access to health care in the United States.

Other important insights to come out of this chapter:

- The U.S. unemployment rate in 2004 was above 10 and below nine of the 20 countries examined in this analysis.
- A breakdown in per capita income shows that, while U.S. productivity is an important determinant of relatively higher U.S. incomes, even more significant is that Americans simply work more annual hours.
- European vacation time is mandated, usually four to five weeks worth, while there is no mandated vacation time in the United States.
- U.S. labor costs are not necessarily more prohibitive, as relative U.S. manufacturing labor costs are below that of seven European countries.

Conclusion

America's working families continue to work hard to make ends meet, improve their living standards, and create better opportunities for their children. New economy or old, this remains the case today much as it was a century ago.

Yet there are clearly aspects of today's economy that make it historically unique. Some of these tilt against the bargaining power of American workers: increased global trade, less union membership, and more low-skilled and high-skilled immigration. There are fewer favorable social norms that guide employer behavior or support policies that provide adequate safety nets, pensions, and health care arrangements.

Other new forces in play have the potential to lift the living standards of working families in ways hardly seen in this country for 30 years. Most important of these is a new, stronger productivity growth regime and a brief encounter with full employment in the latter 1990s that showed that, once workers' bargaining power gets a boost, the benefits of this regime shift in productivity growth can be broadly shared.

In other words, the biggest challenge in what many have called the new economy is not growth per se, but rather how growth is distributed. Of course, economists and policy makers will be concerned with whether the economy is growing as fast and efficiently as it can, and they might turn to greater investments in public and private capital stock, more research and development, monetary policy that stresses full employment, and the educational upgrading of the workforce.

Yet, if the findings in the hundreds of tables and figures that follow can be reduced to one observation, it would be that, when it comes to an economy that is working for working families, growth in and of itself is a necessary but not a sufficient condition. The growth has to reach the people: the bakers need to benefit from bread they create each day of their working lives.

The benchmarks by which we judge the economy must reflect these distributional concerns, and we must construct policies and institutions to address them. If we do not—if our enhanced productive capacity continues to benefit mostly the wealthiest Americans—we risk sacrificing bedrock principles that have historically defined the American economic experience.

Introduction
Life and times in the new economy

Starting in 1995, a new and important change occurred in the U.S. economy: productivity —the output of goods and services per hour worked—began to grow more quickly. After growing 1.4% per year since the mid-1970s, productivity accelerated to 2.5% a year from 1995 to 2000 and then jumped to 3.3% a year from 2000 to 2005. The post-1995 shift in productivity growth, partly attributed to the diffusion and more efficient use of information technology, has sometimes been labeled the "new economy." Because productivity growth provides the basis for rising living standards for everyone, its acceleration is an unequivocally positive development for the economy.

In addition, the productivity acceleration has produced ancillary benefits. One key example of such a benefit is the fact that Federal Reserve officials view faster productivity growth as forestalling inflationary pressures, thereby enabling them to pursue more accommodating monetary policy than would otherwise be the case. Research suggests that these dynamics themselves will lead to longer and less volatile business cycles, an obviously positive development.

Yet, despite these clear economic advances, many Americans report dissatisfaction with where the economy seems to be headed, and many worry about their own and their children's well-being. These concerns have led some policy makers and economists to ask: why aren't people getting it? Why are people pessimistic when the economy is growing strongly? The question seems reasonable to those who follow the top-line numbers of the economy such as the growth of the total economy (e.g., gross domestic product), the stock market, or corporate profits. The question is a strange and dissonant one, however, for those who follow trends in living standards and pay attention to the distribution of growth, since the answer is so apparent.

The economic recovery that began in November 2001 set a record not for growth but for hosting the longest "jobless recovery" on record (the government began tracking employment in the 1940s). By 2006, the employment rate (the share of the population at work) was still below its 2000 peak. The weak job market and the lack of policies and institutions that help ensure that growth is broadly shared meant that the living standards of most working families have been stagnant in recent years. In fact, by 2004 (the latest data), the real income of the median or typical family was lower than in 2000, and inflation-adjusted wages, whether for high school or college-educated workers, grew hardly at all since 2000. The number of poor persons grew by 5.4 million between 2000 and 2004, while 6 million were added to the ranks of the uninsured.

If the nation is indeed wealthier in 2006 than at the peak of the last business cycle in 2000, but many families' incomes are lower and the share in poverty has grown, where is all the money going? This answer is fairly obvious as well: wages, income, and wealth are being drawn to the very top earners and families. This redistribution is a continuation of a historic trend that began in the late 1970s, paused for a few years when the financial bubble burst in 2000, and has most recently returned.

In other words, the economist's mantra that faster productivity growth leads to higher living standards needs updating. Such growth creates the *potential* for widely shared prosperity. For that potential to be realized, a number of other factors—labor market institutions such as strong collective bargaining and a minimum wage with some bite, and, importantly, a truly tight labor market—have to be in place to ensure that the benefits of growth reach everyone, not just those at the top of the wealth scale.

A second key ingredient of the new economy, globalization, also has the *potential* to lift living standards by lowering prices and providing much greater supplies of the products and inputs that help keep the economy humming. But its fingerprints are all over the diminished bargaining clout of blue- and white-collar workers who now compete directly with workers from abroad, many of whom are highly skilled but from low-wage countries.

As these disparate economic forces have interacted, we have seen some of the best and worst of what the new economy has to offer. With the late-1990s boom, the United States achieved the first full employment economy in three decades; rising real wages throughout the wage scale; steeply falling poverty rates, especially for the least advantaged; and the narrowing of gaps between most income classes and racial groups (for example, the gap between African American and white median family incomes fell to its lowest level on record).

The 2000s have not been nearly so beneficial. In the absence of the institutional mechanisms that convert overall growth to broadly shared prosperity, and once the recession and jobless recovery did away with the full employment conditions of the latter 1990s, the benefits of productivity growth stopped flowing to the majority of working families.

In this introduction, we highlight current trends as well as some longer-term trends in order to address this fundamental question: to what extent is the economy's growth reaching those largely responsible for its creation, America's working families? The chapters that follow elaborate this story in greater detail by examining trends in incomes, mobility, wages, jobs, wealth, and poverty, and by placing recent developments in their historical, regional, and international context.

Good and bad times in the U.S. economy, 1995-2005

The discussion that follows breaks our usual rule of making historical comparisons at similar points in a business cycle because it is important to examine the unique period that started in the *middle* of the last business cycle. The expansion that began in 1991 and peaked in 2000 includes two distinct periods, one from 1991 to 1995 that had the same sluggish productivity growth that had prevailed since 1973, and one from 1995 to 2000 that was characterized by faster productivity growth. After the recession of 2001 productivity accelerated even further but, unlike in the 1995-2000 period, the high productivity was accompanied by a jobless recovery and then modest employment growth. An interesting question is, how have families fared during the productivity-rich period between 1995 to 2005?

From the perspective of working families, the comparison yields stark and disappointing results. The wage and income growth of middle- and low-income families reversed course sharply, severing the latter-1990s link between productivity growth and living standards. Poverty rose, as did the number of persons without health coverage. Growth in inequality, which slowed markedly following the bust in the capital markets in late 2000, began climbing again by the mid-2000s, as the largest income gains began to accrue to those at the very top of the wealth scale.

Productivity growth and living standards

Table 1 shows the change in a comprehensive set of indicators of living standards between 1995 and 2005 (for some the latest data are 2004). The reversal of fortune between 1995-2000 and 2000-05 is striking.

Productivity grew 13.2% in the second half of the 1990s, and the typical family's income rose at a similar rate of 11.3%. Even more impressive is the fact that the real median income of minority and single-mother families outpaced productivity, a powerful example of who reaps the greatest benefits from a full employment economy.

Productivity rose 4.5% faster in the 2000s, yet income growth has been uniformly negative, with especially large reversals for less-advantaged families. Real median income for African Americans fell by 4.8% in 2000-04, for a swing, or deceleration, of -20.4% between the two periods (meaning their incomes grew about 20% less quickly in the 2000s compared to the latter 1990s). For Hispanic families, the reversal was even larger, from 24.9% to -6.3%. Young families saw a large switch as well.

The number of poor people fell 13.3% from 1995 to 2000, for a decline of 4.8 million people from the poverty rolls, and the number of uninsured fell slightly (-1.9%). These trends reversed in the 2000-04 period, as the number of poor grew by 17.1%, or 5.4 million people, and the number without health coverage grew by 15.1%, adding 6 million to the ranks of the uninsured.

Net worth per household grew by almost 27% from 1995 to 2000, led by housing wealth and financial asset appreciation. Though home ownership kept growing in the 2000s, financial losses were large, and net worth grew 24.7% more slowly in the 2000s than in the latter 1990s.

The main factors behind the slide in family incomes are slower hourly wage growth and fewer available hours of work in the paid job market. As jobs grew 11.1% more slowly

TABLE 1 Productivity growth and living standards, 1995-2005

	Percent changes		
	1995-2000	2000-04/05	Difference
Productivity growth	13.4%	16.6%	3.2
Median family income*			
All	11.3%	-2.9%	-14.2
African American	15.6	-4.8	-20.4
Hispanic	24.9	-6.3	-31.2
Single-mother families	16.4	-4.4	-20.8
Young families (25-34)	12.3	-5.8	-18.1
Poverty and health insurance			
(percent change in number poor and insured)*			
Poverty	-13.3%	17.1%	30.4
No health coverage	-1.9	15.1	17.0
Net worth per household	26.9	2.3	-24.7
Job growth	12.4	1.3	-11.1
Median wage	7.7	3.0	-4.7
High school wage	5.8	1.4	-4.4
College wage (bachelor's degree)	11.3	1.3	-10.0
Annual hours worked, individual workers*	2.7	-0.6	-3.3
Annual hours worked, middle-income families*	5.2	-4.3	-9.5
Employer-provided benefits*			
Health insurance**	0.4%	-2.9%	-3.3
Pension coverage**	2.4	-2.8	-5.2

* Data through 2004. All others are 2005.
** Percentage-point changes.

Source: Various tables throughout *The State of Working America*.

in the 2000s, growth in real median hourly wages decelerated as well for both high school and college graduates. The latter experienced a larger reversal: the real hourly wage for persons with a bachelor's degree rose 11.3% in the 1995-2000 period but only 1.3% over the next five years. The 10% deceleration in wage growth is indicative of a job market that was particularly tough for college-educated workers, due in part to the bursting of bubbles in industries like information technology and financial services that use a lot of these workers. The 2000s have also been a period of greater offshoring of white-collar jobs, and this too puts downward pressure on college wages.

Annual hours worked by both individuals and middle-income families (this latter measure sums hours worked across all family members) rose in the late-1990s but fell after 2000. The share of the workforce with employer-provided health and pension coverage

FIGURE A Real wages and productivity growth, 1995-2006

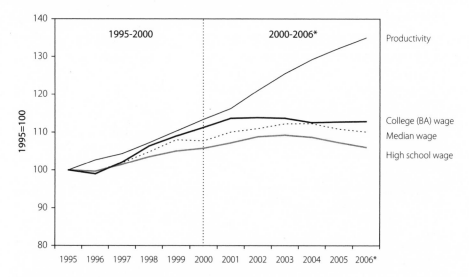

* Wages through first half of 2006; productivity through first quarter of 2006.

Source: Analysis of data drawn from Tables 3.1, 3.4, 3.17.

also contracted in the 2000s. In addition, as shown in Chapter 3, employers have been shifting more of the cost of these fringe benefits onto workers.

Given the different points in the business cycle that we are comparing—the 1995-2000 period had five years of expansion behind it, whereas the 2000-05 period began with a recession—we would expect wages and incomes to perform less well over the early 2000s relative to the latter 1990s. Yet the reversals shown in the last column of the table are economically large and disconcerting, especially given the significant acceleration in productivity growth. Furthermore, yearly trends of some of the key living standards indictors shown in the table reveal movements that have actually worsened as the 2000s business cycle has progressed.

Figure A plots productivity and real hourly wages for the median, high-school-educated, and college-educated worker from 1995 through the first half of 2006, indexed to 100 in 1995. During the latter 1990s, as the job market moved toward full employment, these values all grew together and helped link real wages to overall growth.

After 2000, even as the recession and jobless recovery occurred, the momentum of the latter 1990s boom fueled continued real wage growth through 2003. Since then, real wages have been flat for college-educated workers and falling for median and high-school-educated workers, leading to a historically large gap between wage and productivity growth. In other words, real wages stopped trending along with the business cycle, which was clearly improving when real wages reversed course. By 2006, the fifth year of

FIGURE B Job growth in the current business cycle compared with previous cycles

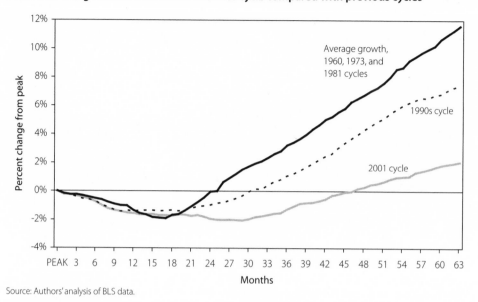

Source: Authors' analysis of BLS data.

a uniquely productivity-rich expansion, with solid GDP growth, one would expect to see a different trend in real wages.

The job market
A tight labor market is an essential element in ensuring that the benefits of growth flow broadly throughout the income scale. Unfortunately, the recession of 2001 and the jobless recovery erased the full employment conditions responsible for the healthy wage growth of the late 1990s. Even by mid-2006 the job market was still failing to generate the number and quality of jobs needed to ameliorate the negative trends that have prevailed thus far in the expansion.

Figure B plots the loss and then growth of jobs over this business cycle compared to the last cycle (the early 1990s) and to the average of the three other previous cycles that lasted at least as long as this one (63 months as of this writing; note that we also performed this analysis including all cycles, and the results were the same). The lines plot the percent change in job growth since the previous business cycle peak.

The unique weakness of the current business cycle in terms of job growth is clear in the figure, even compared to the early 1990s recovery, which was also labeled jobless. By month 63 in the current cycle, employment was up by just 2%, compared to 7% in the 1990s and 12% in the average of the three prior cycles. If this cycle were comparable to the last one at this point, the U.S. economy would have 7 million more jobs, or about 100,000 more per month.

FIGURE C Number of months to regain peak-level employment after a recession, current and prior business cycles

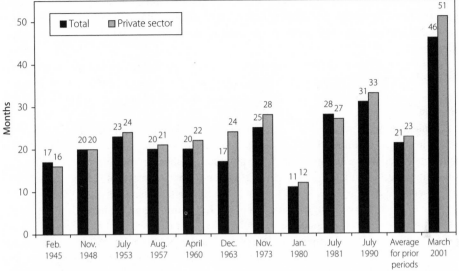

Source: Author's analysis of BLS (2006c) data.

To put this monthly number in context, consider that, since net job growth turned positive in mid-2003, we have added about 170,000 jobs per month, on average (leaving out the impact of the Gulf Coast hurricanes, which lowers the average). Over the comparable period in the last recovery, the one that ultimately led to the full employment job market and the commensurate gains in wages, the economy was adding about 250,000 jobs per month. In other words, another 100,000 jobs per month would have put the economy back on a track similar to the last recovery, helping to rid the post-2000 period of the job market slack that has precluded growth from reaching many working families.

Figure C shows a related dimension of the jobs problem. While it took 21 months for payrolls to regain their peak in the average post-war business cycle, in this case it took more than twice that long: 46 months for total payrolls and even longer for the private sector. These long lags delay the arrival of any job-market-related bargaining power workers need in order to claim a larger share of productivity growth.

A look at current unemployment rates—they have fallen as low as 4.6% in recent months—might suggest that the economy is now at or near full employment. But the unemployment rate was 4.0% in 2000, and there is a significant difference between these values for those groups with the least bargaining power. A sustained unemployment rate of 4.0% is a necessary ingredient for generating broad-based wage and income gains, and the current weak trend in median wages certainly belies any claim that the economy is at full employment. Furthermore, the unemployment rate is artificially reduced if job seekers give up their search. Only those actively seeking work are counted as unemployed, and if, due to a perceived lack of opportunity, enough people give up the job search—they put off entering or they leave the job market—they will not be counted as jobless. This dynamic can serve to lower reported unemployment. In such periods, it is essential to examine labor force participation rates and employment rates to see if they reveal more slack than does the unemployment rate.

In fact, even by mid-2006, the share of the population at work—the employment rate—was 1.6 percentage points below its 2000 peak. This drop implies that literally millions of potential workers have not been looking for work, and their exit from the labor force lowers the jobless rate.

Some analysts object to this comparison of today's employment rates with those of the last cycle's peak, claiming that the 2000 job market was inflated by a market bubble. But the gap between today's employment rate and that of other, pre-bubble years is still large. For example, employment rates in 1997, 1998, and 1999, a period of strong but not obviously speculative demand, were still about one point higher than today's.

One of the key lessons of our analysis of the full employment economy is that we need to aim high when setting employment benchmarks. That is, since it takes a truly tight labor market ("chock-full employment," as late Nobel Laureate economist William Vickery once put it) to ensure widespread gains, we diminish the chance of reaching full employment if we set benchmarks to periods when income and wage growth were stagnant. The speculative demand of the late 1990s may not have been good for the economy overall, but that does not mean one should ignore the success story in the job market. Besides, there are other, non-speculative sources of strong demand, and good economic policy can push back against demand-killers, like the large and growing trade deficit.

A strain of the bubble argument says that demographic change (an older workforce), not a shortage of jobs, is responsible for the decline in both labor force participation and employment rates since 2000. This is a tough case to make, given that job creation was weak over the period when these rates fell, so a decline in labor force participation due to insufficient demand for workers seems to offer a more straightforward interpretation. Moreover, demographic changes usually don't have much impact over the short run.

In fact, as **Figure D** shows, holding employment rates constant for each demographic group at their 1998 level and simply allowing their population shares (by age and gender) to change leads to a simulated rate that falls much less than the actual trend; this suggests a very minor role for demographic change (to stave off the 2000 bubble critique, this simulation starts earlier, in 1998). While the actual employment rate falls 1.4 percentage points over this period, the simulated rate driven solely by the aging of the workforce falls only 0.3 points, indicating that forces other than demography lead to a 1.1 percentage-point drop in employment.

Given the size of the U.S. working-age population in 2005 (226 million), the lower employment rate implies that over 3 million workers were missing from the labor force in that year, and of these, about 675,000 might be explained by the aging of the workforce since 1998. That leaves about 2.4 million persons missing from the job market. It is likely

FIGURE D Changes in the employment rate, 1998-2005

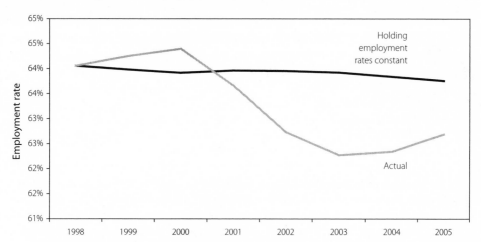

Note: This result differs from that of an influential Federal Reserve Paper (Aaronson et al. 2006, Figure 3). The results of that study, however, appear to stem from the authors' choice to begin the simulation in 1995, well before employment or labor force participation rates peaked. While we prefer employment rates as a measure more indicative of labor demand, they use labor force participation rates (LFPRs). However, our results are the same when using LFPRs.

Source: Authors' analysis of BLS data.

that many of these workers, were they to enter the job market, would be added to the 7 million unemployed in mid-2006, leading to a significantly higher unemployment rate.

The uptick in the actual employment rate trend at the end of the figure coincides with the period when job growth turned positive, and this is another indication that cyclical forces are at work. We pursue this analysis further in Chapter 4 by tracking the employment rates of groups like young college graduates and minorities, who might be expected to be particularly responsive to the availability of jobs. Like this figure, these analyses reveal a clear cyclical response to the deterioration and then improvement in the job market, all of which suggests that the low unemployment rate is, at least for now, an inadequate measure of the true degree of labor market tightness.

Family incomes

Middle-income families derive about three-quarters of their income from the labor market. Thus, weakening labor market trends can explain the income reversals experienced since 2000. **Table 2** summarizes some of the results from Chapter 1, where we examine changes in family income and its components for families by income fifth. Here we focus on middle-income families, whose real income fell 2.1% from 2000 to 2004 after growing almost 12% in the five years prior.

TABLE 2 Changes in real incomes, annual hours, and earnings, 1995-2004, among middle-income families

	Income	Earnings	Hours	Hourly wage
1995-2000	11.7%	14.9%	5.2%	9.2%
2000-04	-2.1%	-3.1%	-4.3%	1.2%
Difference	-13.8	-18.0	-9.5	-8.0

Source: Authors' analysis of March CPS data.

The data clearly suggest that the income loss was a function of labor market contraction. Annual hours worked by all family members fell 4.3%, after rising 5.2% during the 1990s boom. Hourly wages continued to rise (though yearly trends show a real decline in 2004), but by 8.0% less in the 2000s compared to the latter 1990s. Losses in hours worked explain almost 60% of the reversal in income growth, and much slower hourly wage growth explained the rest.

Inequality in income, wealth, and earnings

The gap between productivity, wages, and incomes suggests that inequality is on the rise. The growth embodied in these macro-indicators has to be going somewhere, and if only trace amounts are finding their way into the paychecks of many working families, it stands to reason that the gains are flowing up the wealth scale.

We provide two pieces of supportive evidence. First, **Table 3** examines recent research on income movements among the richest households, including the value of realized capital gains. Between 1995 and 2000, real income grew 12.5% for the bottom 90%, 15.0% for the next highest 5% (the 90-95th percentile), 25.1% for the next highest 4%, and so on, up to the more than doubling of income—up 156.0%—at the very top sliver of the top 1% (the 99.99-100th percentile). So, even as the job market progressed toward full employment, income growth was still skewed toward the top over this period.

The bursting of the financial and investment bubbles led to sharp real declines in the incomes of wealthy households in 2001 and 2002, with the biggest losses among the richest. By 2003, however, the earlier pattern was returning, and in 2004, a year when the economy expanded by 4.2% and productivity grew by 3.4%, the income of the bottom 90% got a mere 1.4% boost. The rest accrued to the top 10%, and the gains were largest at the top of the income scale. The step pattern repeats, with larger percentage gains as we move up to the very top of the income scale. The average income gain at the very top was 27.5% in 2004 alone.

The growth of capital incomes (from corporate profits or, as received directly by individuals, from dividends, interest, and capital gains) has also driven up inequality. First, most capital income is received by the best-off families, so the growth in capital incomes reinforces income inequalities (the decline in capital incomes in 2000-02 actually reduced

TABLE 3 Annual change in income by income group, late 1990s vs. the early 2000s

		Top 10%					
		Next 5%	Next 4%	Next 0.5%	Next 0.4%	Next 0.09%	Top 0.01%
	Bottom 90%	90th-95th	95th-99th	99th-99.5th	99.5th-99.9th	99.9th-99.99th	99.99th-100th
1995-2000	12.5%	15.0%	25.1%	37.9%	52.4%	92.7%	156.0%
2001	-2.0	-3.0	-6.7	-10.9	-15.8	-25.2	-32.1
2002	-3.4	-2.8	-4.7	-6.8	-9.2	-14.7	-19.4
2003	-1.9	-0.5	-0.4	0.2	1.2	3.5	10.4
2004	1.4	2.6	4.7	10.0	12.5	17.8	27.5

Source: Piketty and Saez (2006).

inequality). For 2006, for instance, it is estimated that 84.2% of all capital income will have been received by the upper fifth, with 55.3% received by the top 1% and 36.6% by the top 0.1% alone. In contrast, 3.6% of such income is held by middle-income families. This income landscape implies that fast growth for capital income will disproportionately benefit the best-off income groups.

The rise in inequality caused by the shift toward greater capital income has been compounded by the growing concentration of capital income among the very highest income groups, particularly the top 1%. According to the Congressional Budget Office, the share of capital income received by the top 1% grew by 14.3 percentage points from 1995 to 2003 (the latest data), with proportionately less capital income received by the remaining households in the top fifth (down 7.5 percentage points) and a lesser share received by the bottom 80%.

The shift to greater capital income in the economy can be illustrated by the recent movements in the division of corporate sector income (which excludes proprietorships and other unincorporated businesses but includes more than 75% of the entire private sector) and in the growth of profitability (returns on capital investments). As **Figure E** shows, capital's share of income tumbled in the late 1990s in the context of a tight labor market, but it more than recovered by 2005. This helped boost profitability in 2005 to the highest level reached in 36 years (excepting 1997).

The growth in profitability has left less room for (or, rather, was caused by the muting of) wage growth, and might be considered the consequence of businesses successfully restraining wage growth as sales and profits grew, even in years of seemingly low unemployment. If the pre-tax return to capital in 2005 (11.9%) had been at the 1979 level (9.6%), then hourly compensation would have been 5% higher in the corporate sector. This difference is equivalent to an annual transfer of $235 billion from labor to capital (measured in 2005 dollars), or roughly $1,760 per wage-and-salary employee or $3,032 if this redistribution came from the bottom 80% of workers, who earn just 58% of all hourly earnings.

FIGURE E Share of capital income in the corporate sector, 1995-2005

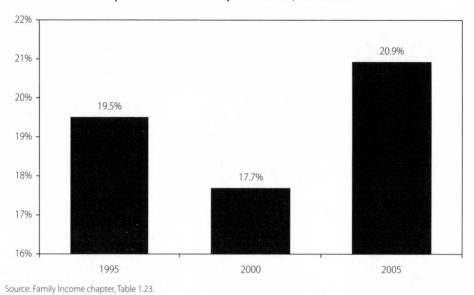

Source: Family Income chapter, Table 1.23.

Even this analysis misses an important part of the picture, since the definition of labor's share includes the pay of chief executive officers and thereby overstates the income share going to typical workers and understates profits, since the bonuses and stock options given CEOs are more akin to profits than wages. The amount of CEO pay relative to corporate profits has grown: in the mid-1990s CEO pay was equivalent to roughly 5% of corporate profits, but that amount rose to roughly 10% of profits by 2003 (unfortunately, more recent data are not available).

The hit on young workers and families

The challenges to living standards that working people and their families have faced over the last few years have been even more pronounced for young workers and their families. When times are good, they are particularly good for young workers, but when times are not so good, they tend to be awful for young workers. Since young workers and their families are at the beginning of their economic life cycle, these differences are important. Those starting off in a down period often suffer losses that will reverberate throughout their careers.

Not surprisingly, the recession, jobless recovery, and then weak job growth of the last five years have sharply reversed the progress that young workers and their families were making in better times. **Table 4** presents indicators of labor market trends (wages, benefit coverage, and employment) and family income and living arrangements that illustrate the hit on young people.

TABLE 4 Employment, wage, benefit, and income trends for young workers and families, 1995-2005

Category	1995	2000	2005	Change* 1995-2000	2000-05	Difference, 2000-05 minus 1995-2000
EMPLOYMENT, WAGES, AND BENEFITS						
High school						
Entry-level wages ($2005)						
Men	$10.15	$11.10	$10.93	9.3%	-1.5%	-10.9
Women	8.65	9.49	9.08	9.8	-4.3	-14.1
*Entry-level benefits coverage***						
Health insurance	38.2%	37.8%	33.7%	-0.4	-4.1	-3.7
Pension	20.6	21.9	18.8	1.4	-3.2	-4.5
*Employment rate***						
All	78.0%	80.0%	75.7%	2.0	-4.2	-6.2
College						
Entry-level wages ($2005)						
Men	$16.97	$20.51	$19.72	20.9%	-3.9%	-24.8
Women	15.59	17.41	17.08	11.7	-1.9	-13.6
*Entry-level benefits coverage***						
Health insurance	69.2%	70.6%	63.5%	1.4	-7.0	-8.4
Pension	45.1	54.6	49.3	9.6	-5.3	-14.9
*Employment rate***						
All	87.8%	87.4%	85.5%	-0.4	-2.0	-1.5
FAMILY INCOME AND LIVING ARRANGEMENTS						
Share living at home (ages 25-34)*						
Male	15.4%	12.9%	13.7%	-2.5	0.8	3.3
Female	8.5	8.3	8.2	-0.2	-0.1	0.1
Median family income (ages 25-34)*						
All	$44,336	$49,769	$46,878	12.3%	-5.8%	-18.1

* Wages and income data are *percent* changes, all others are *percentage-point* chages.
** Data available only through 2004.

Source: Tables 1.7 and 3.21, Figures 3Q and 3R, analysis of CPS ORG and Census Bureau (2006).

One way to illustrate the difficulties faced by young workers in the labor market is to examine the wages and benefit coverage of entry-level workers, both those with a high school degree (and no further education) and those with a four-year college degree. The table presents the trends of the late 1990s and compares them to the latest five-year period in order to illustrate the change in fortunes that has occurred.

The wages earned by entry-level high-school-educated workers (those out of school for one to five years) rose over 9% from 1995 to 2000, then deteriorated over the 2000-05 period. The difference between these two trends was a 10.9% turnaround for men and a 14.1% turnaround for women. Entry-level high school graduates had low rates of benefit coverage from their employers, with only 38.2% receiving health coverage and 20.6% receiving pension coverage in 1995; these rates are substantially down from their levels in 1979 (the health coverage rate was 63.3% that year). Given the declining coverage before 1995, the good news about entry-level high-school-graduate jobs is that employer-provided health and pension benefits fell only a small amount over the late 1990s. However, a sharp erosion of benefits returned from 2000 to 2005, with health coverage falling so that only a third now receives it, roughly half of the coverage in 1979. This leaves young workers joining the growing ranks of the uninsured, unless they are lucky enough to have coverage through a spouse's employer.

The change in fortune was even starker for young college graduates. This group benefited during the late 1990s a great deal, as those graduating then (reflected in the entry-level wages and benefits in 2000) enjoyed far greater pay than those who had graduated in the early 1990s (and measured for 1995). Entry-level wages for male college graduates ballooned 20.9%, and those for women rose 11.7%. Benefit coverage, particularly pensions, improved in the late 1990s for these new workers, but the poor labor market conditions of the 2000-05 period hit college graduates hard, as entry-level wages fell and benefit coverage dropped significantly (for example, health coverage fell from 70.6% to 63.5%). Had the late 1990s trends continued over the 2000-05 period, the entry-level wages of college graduates would have been 24.8% higher for men and 13.6% higher for women, and a much larger share would have been covered by employer-provided health and pensions (a 14.9% coverage rise for pensions and an 8.4% rise for health).

Another reflection of the dramatic turnaround in labor market trends is that employment rates for young (in this case 25-34-year-old) high school graduates grew in the late 1990s (up 2.0%) but then fell 4.2 percentage points from 2000 to 2005, a 6.2 percentage-point turnaround. Even college graduates saw their fortunes turn around as the share employed fell from 2000 to 2005.

Given these faltering labor market trends, it should come as no surprise that families headed by someone age 25-34 had 5.8% lower incomes in 2005 than in 2000. In contrast, this type of family enjoyed incomes 12.3% higher in 2000 than in 1995, amounting to a remarkable 18.1% reversal. Another reflection of these trends is that more young men age 25-34 are living with their parents. The share declined in the late 1990s, from 15.4% in 1995 to 12.9% in 2000, but rose to 13.7% in 2005. Young women's living arrangements have been relatively stable in this period.

Starting lower, growing slower

Thus far, we have examined the productivity gap by comparing, for example, the hourly wages or income of the median worker or the median family in a recent year to that of an earlier year. This is a useful and conventional way of tracking group trends where the median is representative of a group. However, this method does not directly portray how individuals or individual families actually experience the economy. Both dimensions of economic reality are important. Analysts need to track how people experience the economy as they and their cohort age, as well as how groups such as communities, the nation, the working class, or the middle-income family are faring in the economy. The difference arises because the comparisons we have shown thus far inevitably compare different people—for instance, the median worker in 1995 is not likely to be the median worker in 2005.

An illustration reveals the differences between these approaches. How can it be true that the average high-school-educated or non-college-educated worker's wage (inflation-adjusted) can fall over a 10-year period while most individual workers in this group saw their inflation-adjusted wage rise over that same period? As individuals gain experience, change jobs, or get promotions, they usually obtain higher pay, and so it makes sense that the vast majority of workers earn more when they are in their thirties than in their twenties and make further gains into their forties and fifties. Yet it still can be true that the average wage of a group—say, non-college-educated workers—can decline over a decade or two. This is because the average includes workers of all ages and the process by which a group's average wage has declined arises because younger members of the group start out at lower wages and progress more slowly than did their predecessors.

Figure F illustrates this phenomenon. Consider the annual earnings of the group of workers with some college—a group with schooling beyond high school, possibly including an associate's degree, but without a degree from a four-year college. We can illustrate the process of workers raising their wages as they age by following a cohort of "some college" workers over time. For instance, in 1970, when these workers were 20 to 24 years old, they earned an average annual wage of $23,071 (in 2005 dollars). By 1980 this group's earnings had grown to $32,498, a 41% improvement. By ages 40-44 in 1990 their earnings had grown 22% further to $39,488, and by 2000, at ages 50-54, they had grown to $43,809. Overall then, this group saw its earnings grow 90% as it progressed from 1970 to 2000.

Figure G puts this experience of the 1970 cohort into a broader historical context by presenting the annual earnings of particular age groups at each 10-year point from 1950 to 2000. This exercise allows a comparison of how particular age groups in 2000 fared relative to similarly aged workers in the earlier decades. As the figure shows, the $43,809 earnings level that the 1970 cohort attained in 2000 at ages 50-54 was roughly 10% less than the earnings of $48,511 attained by similarly educated workers at the same age 30 years earlier in 1970. Compared to this earlier cohort, the members of the 1970s cohort made far less progress over their working lives. In fact, the earnings of every age group of workers with some college in 2000 were less than what that same age group of some-college workers earned in 1970. So, although the cohort climbed the ladder successfully, the rungs on the ladder were lowered. That is why the average earnings of prime-age earners (ages 25-54) with some college were 11% lower in 2000 than in 1970.

FIGURE F Annual wages of "some college" workers who entered labor force in 1970

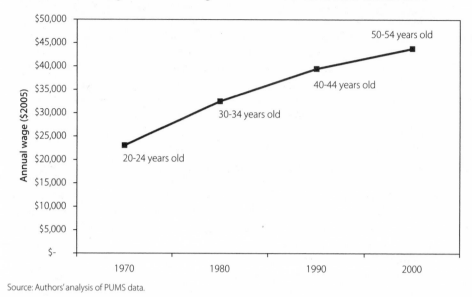

Source: Authors' analysis of PUMS data.

FIGURE G Annual wages of workers with some college attendance (less than a degree) by age, 1950-2000

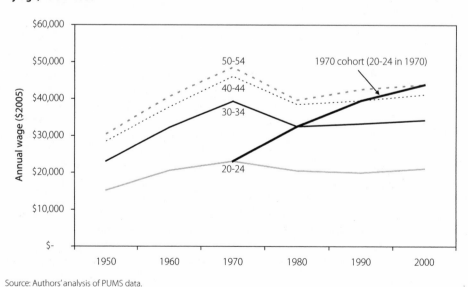

Source: Authors' analysis of PUMS data.

TABLE 5 Annual earnings of 25-29-year-olds, by education, 1950-2000

Education	Annual earnings ($2005)					
	1950	1960	1970	1980	1990	2000
High school	$18,382	$25,242	$30,903	$25,396	$24,873	$25,944
Some college	20,172	27,221	33,550	27,194	27,733	29,180

Source: Authors' analysis of PUMS data.

Another way of viewing this development is to compare the starting earnings of the same age/education group over the decades. As the economy becomes more productive and workers become more educated, we expect new cohorts to start out with higher earnings than their predecessors. **Table 5** illustrates that this process prevailed from 1950 to 1970, as earnings for 25-29-year-olds for both high-school-educated workers and those with some college grew each decade. In this period of fast productivity growth and broadly shared income growth, their starting earnings grew appreciably (about two-thirds more) as each successive cohort started out on a higher rung of the ladder.

However, in the ensuing years, including the rapid growth period in the late 1990s, the starting wage remained below that obtained in 1970. So, despite an economy that was two-thirds more productive in 2000 than in 1970, the beginning earnings of high school workers and workers with some college were actually lower.

Conclusion

Every era's economy seems new to contemporary observers, and our discussion of the historically large gains in productivity is not meant to oversell the notion that today's economy is vastly different from yesterday's. As has always been the case, the majority of families work hard to make ends meet, improve their living standards, and create better opportunities for their children. This remains the case today much as it was a century ago.

Yet there are clearly aspects of today's economy that make it historically unique. Some of these tilt against the bargaining power of American workers: increased global trade, fewer unions, and more low-skilled and high-skilled immigration. There are fewer favorable social norms that guide employer behavior and support public and employer policies that provide adequate safety nets, pensions, and health care arrangements.

Other new forces in play have the potential to lift the living standards of working families in ways hardly seen in this country for 30 years. Most important of these is a new, stronger productivity growth regime and a brief encounter with full employment which showed that, once workers' bargaining power gets a boost, the benefits of this regime shift in productivity growth can be broadly shared.

In other words, the biggest challenge in what many have called the new economy is not growth per se; it's how growth is distributed. Of course, economists and policy makers should be concerned with whether the economy is growing as fast and efficiently as it can, and they might turn to greater investments in public and private capital stock, more research and development, monetary policy that stresses full employment, and the educational upgrading of the workforce.

Yet, if the findings in the hundreds of tables and figures that follow can be reduced to one observation, it would be that, *when it comes to an economy that is working for working families, growth in and of itself is a necessary but not a sufficient condition. The growth has to reach the people: the bakers need to benefit from bread they create each day of their working lives.*

The benchmarks by which we judge the economy must reflect these distributional concerns, and we must construct policies and institutions to address them. If we do not—if our enhanced productive capacity continues to benefit mostly the wealthiest Americans—we risk sacrificing bedrock principles that have historically defined the American economic experience. Such principles include basic fairness—the notion that those who work hard can truly get ahead—as well as the belief that the economy will provide growing opportunities for the least-advantaged while sustaining a large and flourishing middle class.

In the previous version of this book, we wondered whether the distributional problems of the then-young post-2000 expansion would work themselves out. By now, in the fifth year of the recovery, it is clear that they have not. Some commentators urge working Americans to be patient and wait for the lags in the economy to play out. Eventually, we are told, wages and incomes will start rising with productivity.

Except if they don't. In an era with severely weakened distributional institutions, where labor market slack is the norm and full employment is the exception, working families cannot afford to wait for growth to catch up with them. That argument might have some saliency in the second or third quarter of an expansion. But by year five, it is an unacceptable position for policy makers to take. The time for economic growth to be a "spectator sport" for the majority of American families is past.

And even if those urging patience are correct, what about the lost jobs, income, and wages that have already been experienced? What about the years spent in poverty that might have been prevented or at least diminished if more of the growth were flowing widely? These losses can never be made up.

Thus, there is a role for policy makers in reconnecting growth and prosperity. The goal of the chapters that follow is to provide readers with the empirical analysis needed to judge the extent to which the economy is working for working families. In the interest of suggesting ways to reconnect growth and living standards, we have also created an accompanying policy document, available at www.epi.org, to go with this book.

America's working families continue to work harder and smarter. But, while the economy provides them with the potential for prosperity, that potential has yet to be consistently realized. Until that occurs—until living standards can once again be counted on to regularly reflect the benefits of growth—the state of working America will continue to be challenged by inequities that undermine our basic values.

Documentation and methodology

Documentation

The comprehensive portrait presented in this book of changes in incomes, taxes, wages, employment, wealth, poverty, and other indicators of economic performance and well-being relies almost exclusively on data in the tables and figures. Consequently, the documentation of our analysis is essentially the documentation of the tables and figures. For each, an abbreviated source notation appears at the bottom, and complete documentation is contained in the Table Notes and Figure Notes found at the back of the book. (In rare circumstances, however, we incorporate data in the discussion that are not in a table or figure.) This system of documentation allows us to omit distracting footnotes and long citations within the text and tables.

The abbreviated source notation at the bottom of each figure and table is intended to inform the reader of the general source of our data and to give due credit to the authors and agencies whose data we are presenting. We have three categories of designations for these abbreviated sources. In instances where we directly reproduce other people's work, we provide an "author/year" reference to the bibliography. Where we present our own computations based on other people's work, the source line reads "Authors' analysis of *author (year).*" In these instances we have made computations that do not appear in the original work and want to hold the original authors (or agencies) blameless for any errors or interpretations. Our third category is simply "Authors' analysis," which indicates that the data presented are from our original analysis of microdata (such as much of the wage analysis) or our computations from published (usually government) data. We use this source notation when presenting descriptive trends from government income, employment, or other data, since we have made judgments about the appropriate time periods or other matters for the analysis that the source agencies have not made.

Time periods

Economic indicators fluctuate considerably with short-term swings in the business cycle. For example, incomes tend to fall in recessions and rise during expansions. Therefore, economists usually compare business cycle peaks with other peaks and compare troughs with other troughs so as not to mix apples and oranges. In this book, we examine changes between business cycle peaks. The initial year for many tables is 1947, with intermediate years of 1967, 1973, 1979, 1989, and 2000, all of which were business cycle peaks (at least in terms of having low unemployment). We also present data for the latest full year for which data are available (2005, when available) to show the changes over the current business cycle.

In some tables, we also separately present trends for the 1995-2000 period in order to highlight the differences between those years and those of the early 1990s (or, more precisely, 1989-95) and earlier business cycles. This departs from the convention of presenting only business-cycle comparisons (e.g., comparing 1979-89 to 1989-2000 trends) or comparisons of recoveries. We depart from the convention because there was a marked shift in a wide variety of trends after 1995, and it is important to understand and explain these trends.

Growth rates and rounding

Since business cycles differ in length, we usually present the annual growth rates in each period rather than the total growth. We also present compound annual growth rates rather than simple annual rates. Compound annual growth rates are just like compound interest on a bank loan: the rate is compounded continuously rather than yearly. In some circumstances, as noted in the tables, we have used log annual growth rates. This is done to permit decompositions. In presenting the data we round the numbers, usually to one decimal place, but we use unrounded data to compute growth rates, percentage shares, and so on. Therefore, it is not always possible to exactly replicate our calculations by using the data in the table. In some circumstances, this leads to an appearance of errors in the tables. For instance, we frequently present shares of the population (or families) at different points in time and compute changes in these shares. Because our computations are based on the "unrounded" data, the change in shares presented in a table may not match the difference in the actual shares. Such rounding errors are always small, however, and never change the conclusions of the analysis.

Adjusting for inflation

In most popular discussions, the Consumer Price Index for All Urban Consumers (CPI-U), often called simply the consumer price index, is used to adjust dollar values for inflation. However, some analysts hold that the CPI-U overstated inflation in the late 1970s and early 1980s by measuring housing costs inappropriately. The methodology for the CPI-U from 1983 onward was revised to address these objections. Other changes were introduced into the CPI in the mid-1990s but not incorporated into the historical series. Not all agree that these revisions are appropriate. We chose not to use the CPI-U so as to avoid any impression that this report overstates the decline in wages and understates the growth in family incomes over the last few decades.

Instead of the CPI-U, we adjust dollar values for inflation using the CPI-URS index. This index uses the new methodology for housing inflation over the entire 1967-2001 period and incorporates the 1990s changes into the historical series (though not before 1978, which makes economic performance in the years after 1978 falsely look better than the earlier years). The CPI-U-RS is now used by the Census Bureau in its presentations of real income data. Because it is not available for years before 1978, we extrapolate the CPI-U-RS back to earlier years based on inflation as measured by the CPI-U.

In our analysis of poverty in Chapter 6, however, we generally use the CPI-U rather than the CPI-U-RS, since Chapter 6 draws heavily from Census Bureau publications that use the CPI-U. Moreover, the net effect of all of the criticisms of the measurement of poverty is that current methods understate poverty. Switching to the CPI-U-RS without incorporating other revisions (i.e., revising the actual poverty standard) would lead to an even greater understatement and would be a very selective intervention to improve the poverty measurement. (A fuller discussion of these issues appears in Chapter 6.)

Household heads

We often categorize families by the age or the race/ethnic group of the "household head," that is, the person in whose name the home is owned or rented. If the home is owned jointly by a married couple, either spouse may be designated the household head. Every family has a single household head.

Hispanics

Unless specified otherwise, data from published sources employ the Census Bureau's designation of Hispanic persons. That is, Hispanics are included in racial counts (e.g., with blacks and whites) as well as in a separate category. For instance, in government analyses a white person of Hispanic origin is included both in counts of whites *and* in counts of Hispanics. In our original analyses, such as the racial/ethnic wage analysis in Chapter 3, we remove Hispanic persons from other racial (white or black) categories; using this technique, the person described above would appear only in counts of Hispanics.

CHAPTER 1

Family income
"New economy" drives a wedge between productivity and living standards

A family's income is, of course, one of the most important determinants of their economic well-being. Most working families depend on their income to meet their immediate consumption needs (like food and gas), to finance longer-term investments in goods and services (like housing and education), and to build their savings. This chapter begins with an analysis of a key determinant of living standards: family income.

Starting with the most recent period, we find that many families face two separate but related challenges regarding the growth of their real incomes: (1) post-2000 wage stagnation, especially among middle- and lower-income families, and (2) the gap between income and productivity growth. Despite the fact that the most recent economic expansion began in late 2001, the real income of the median family fell each year through 2004. Between 2000 and 2005, real median family income fell by 2.3%, or about $1,300 in 2004 dollars.

The post-2000 income trends stand in stark contrast to the extent and pattern of family income growth in the latter 1990s. Then, during a period of uniquely tight job markets, full employment conditions compelled employers to more broadly share the benefits of accelerated productivity growth. Between 1995 and 2000, output per hour grew 2.5% per year, while real median family income grew 2.2% annually. Importantly, the income growth of less-advantaged groups proved to be particularly responsive to the availability of more and better jobs that tend to accompany full employment. Real median income was up 2.9% per year for African Americans, 4.6% for Hispanic families, 2.3% for young families (family head: 25-34 years old), and 3.1% for single mother families.

As we will show, the post-2000 reversal of these favorable trends was a function of diminished employment opportunities, not just during the recession, as we would expect, but over the protracted jobless recovery that followed. This decline in median income during the initial years of expansions appears to be more the norm than the exception in recent recoveries. Over both the 1980s and 1990s recovery, it took seven years for median family income to regain its peak, far longer than in earlier cycles.

Why should the "new economy" include this unfortunate attribute, wherein economies expand but fail to lift the living standards of many of the working families helping to generate the expansion itself? Certainly, the inequality of economic outcomes plays an important role, and as such, income inequality is a central theme of this chapter. We note, for example, that as real median income has fallen 3% over the recovery thus far, productivity was up a strong 15%. Over the longer term, between 1947 and 1973, productivity and real median family income both doubled, yet since then, output per hour is up 3.5 times as much as the median real income.

In fact, when it comes to income growth over the past generation, the extent of a family's prosperity is largely a function of their placement in the income scale, with the richest families experiencing the fastest income growth. Between 1979 and 2000, for example, the real income of households in the lowest fifth grew 6.1%; the middle fifth was up 12.3%; the top fifth grew 70%; and the average income of those in the top 1% grew by 184%.

Higher inequality shows up whether we look at consumption or income; it is not driven by tax changes, though by lowering the tax burden on the wealthy, such changes have demonstrably exacerbated the problem. It is sometimes argued that greater economic mobility has pushed back against the inequality trends we document throughout the chapter. That is, while the income distribution may be more skewed, one's chances of moving up the income scale have increased over recent decades. In earlier editions of *The State of Working America*, we included a section with evidence that this was not a defensible argument. In this edition, we devote a full chapter—Income-Class Mobility—to elaborating this and related points.

Greater inequality has also shown up as a much-more skewed distribution of national income between labor and non-labor income, as the share of the economy going to capital has grown at historically high rates, leaving a smaller share of the growing income pie to be distributed as compensation to working families. Whereas the top 1% received 37.8% of all capital income in 1979, their share rose to 49.1% by 2000 and rose further to 57.5% in 2003 (most recent data). This shift toward greater wealth concentration has in recent years been exacerbated by an increase in the share of national income flowing to profits, translating into a double-squeeze on labor compensation. If the pre-tax return to capital in 2005 had remained at its 1979 level, then hourly compensation would have been 5.0% higher in the corporate sector. This was equivalent to an annual transfer of $235 billion dollars from labor to capital (measured for 2005).

One mechanism by which middle income families have kept their incomes rising over the past few decades has been the added work in the paid labor market by women in general and wives in particular. We examine the increase in time spent at work among married-couple families with children, and find that middle-income wives in these families added over 500 hours of work between 1979 and 2000. While this has been a positive force for women's economic independence, it has also put a strain on the need to balance work and family.

Virtually all economic commentators waxed enthusiastically about the short and mild recession of 2001. Those same commentators have tended to be extremely bullish on the favorable macroeconomic performance of the economy over the current expansion, especially touting the fast growth of productivity. For many of these pundits, the expansion of the American economy as measured by a few aggregate indicators is enough to assert broadly shared prosperity.

The analysis that follows reveals just how wrong-headed that view can be. Yes, the highly advanced and flexible U.S. economy continues to generate impressive growth with rapidly improving efficiency. But what often gets lost in the economic discussion is the fact that these outcomes by no means ensure that the benefits of growth will be broadly shared. They create the potential for better living standards, but, especially in today's economy, there is simply no guarantee that such a potential will be realized by the broad majority. This chapter will examine to what extent growth in the U.S. economy has or has not reached working families throughout the income scale.

Income growth in the new economy, 1995-2000

The post-1995 period, characterized by a new, faster productivity/growth regime, is often labeled "the new economy." Though digital technology and the Internet were solidly in place before the mid-1990s, it appears that economic actors learned to harness their power in a way that began to show up as greater economic efficiency around then. The result was a significant and lasting increase in productivity growth. Between 1973 and 1995, output per hour grew at an annual rate of 1.4%; since then, it has expanded at 2.9%, twice that annual rate.

This regime shift has important implications for living standards in general, and income growth in particular. Economists often assert that productivity growth is a determining factor of how fast living standards can improve, since more efficient production means more available goods and services per hour worked. However, as we stress throughout, that nugget of conventional wisdom requires an important caveat: faster productivity growth creates the potential for broadly shared prosperity. For that potential to be realized, the benefits of growth must be distributed more equally than has been the case for most of the past few decades and especially over the past few years.

As measured by real gross domestic product, the U.S. economy peaked in early 2001 before entering a brief recession that ended late that year. The current recovery began in November 2001, according to the economists charged with setting the official dates of recessions. This section examines the growth in income and related variables over the current expansion, comparing real income growth from the peak—2000—to the most recent year of available data: 2004. Along the way, we make comparisons between other relevant time periods, to provide important context with which to judge the current recovery.

We find that family incomes have declined in real terms for most families over the course of this recovery, despite even faster productivity growth than in the latter 1990s. Only the wealthiest families—the narrow sliver at the very top of the income scale—began to see significant real gains in the most recent years, signaling a return to a highly unequal pattern of income growth that has prevailed over much of the past few decades.

FIGURE 1A Real income growth: 1990s boom vs. post-2000 expansion

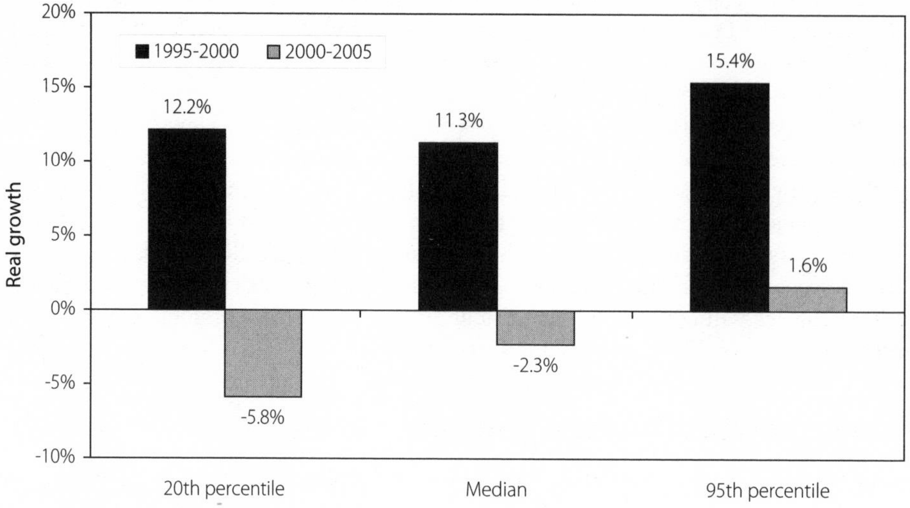

Source: Authors' analysis of U.S. Census Bureau data.

Figure 1A looks at two recent periods with very different underlying economy dynamics, and very different income growth. In contrast to most of the comparisons we make throughout the book, here we compare 1995-2000 with 2000-04, i.e., we contrast income growth over a boom with that over the first part of an expansion, including the recessionary year of 2001. In other words, we depart from our usual "like-to-like" comparisons in terms of the business cycle in order to show the magnitude of the shift in income trajectory that occurred over these years.

Each bar represents the growth in income at the 20th, 50th (median), or 95th percentile of the family income scale. During the second half of the 1990s, a period when the labor market moved toward full employment, incomes grew significantly across the scale, though still faster at the top. A sharp reversal of this trend occurred between 2000 and 2005, when living standards fell by this measure across the board.

The decline was sharpest at the low end (Chapter 6 reveals that poverty increased over this period as well), with real income at the 20th percentile down 5.8%. Median family income fell by 2.3%, representing a loss of about $1,300.

Table 1.1 takes a closer look at the components behind the changes shown in Figure 1A. The top line in each panel provides the percent changes in average real income by family income fifth (note that these are averages within income fifths, not the percentiles themselves as shown in Figure 1A), and the rest of each panel apportions the changes into annual earnings growth and non-labor income (such as government transfers or interest

TABLE 1.1 Real family income growth by income fifth, 1995-2004 (decomposed)

	Income quintiles				
	Lowest	Second	Third	Fourth	Highest
1995-2000					
Income growth	13.2%	10.8%	11.1%	11.9%	13.8%
Earnings	12.7	10.2	11.3	11.1	12.8
Annual hours	7.7	2.4	4.1	2.7	0.6
Hourly wage	5.0	7.8	7.1	8.4	12.3
Other Income	0.5	0.6	-0.2	0.8	1.0
2000-04					
Income loss	-7.1%	-4.4%	-2.1%	-1.2%	-2.2%
Earnings	-6.0	-3.9	-2.6	-1.8	-0.9
Annual hours	-5.2	-3.9	-3.6	-3.2	-1.7
Hourly wage	-0.8	-0.1	1.0	1.4	0.8
Other income	-1.1	-0.4	0.5	0.6	-1.3

Source: Authors' analysis of U.S. Census Bureau data.

income). The annual earnings component is further decomposed into hourly wage growth and annual hours. Note that the overall income growth value is the sum of the earnings and other income values, and that the annual earnings value is the sum of the hours and hourly wage values.

During the latter 1990s, 96% of the 13.2% income growth in the bottom fifth was driven by earnings growth, and that was largely a factor of more hours worked (results shown later in Chapter 6 also emphasize the importance of increased work hours among low-income workers in the 1990s). In the other fifths, increased hourly wages were a larger factor than hours growth.

The reversal in the 2000-04 period was driven by the decline in annual hours and the deceleration in hourly wage growth. In other words, the recession and the ensuing jobless recovery—by leading to the loss of jobs, hours, and wages—drove the family income declines over the period. These differences in the role of labor market income are especially clear in the middle quintile, as shown in **Figure 1B**. The components of the middle-income growth are shown in each bar. Hourly wage growth contributed 7% to the 11% income gain in the middle fifth in the latter half of the 1990s, but only 1% in the 2000-04 period. The growth in annual hours added 4% to income growth in the latter 1990s, and subtracted about that same amount in the 2000s, more than explaining the 2.6% income loss for the middle quintile. Throughout the income scale, much slower wage gains and hours losses led to the sharp reversal in income growth.

FIGURE 1B Components of middle-income changes, 1995-2004

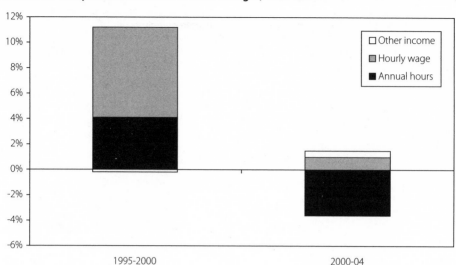

Source: Authors' analysis of March CPS data.

How has income inequality evolved over these recent periods? It too reversed course in the earliest years of the decade, due to very large losses in investment income at the top of the income scale. More recently, however, the pattern of unequal income growth appears to have returned.

The data in **Table 1.2** come from recent research examining income movements among the richest households, including the value of realized capital gains (this income source is not present in Census data shown so far). Between 1995 and 2000, real income grew 12.5% for the bottom 90%, and 40.5% for the top 10%. But when we start calculating the average growth of narrowing slivers among the top 5%, we see ever larger gains. Income grew 75.6% from 1995 to 2000 for the top 1%, and more than doubled for the top 10th and 100th of the top percent.

The bursting of the financial and investment bubbles led to sharp real declines in the incomes of wealthy households in 2001 and 2002, with the biggest losses among the richest. By 2003, however, the earlier pattern was returning, and in 2004, a year when the economy expanded by 4.2% and productivity grew 3.4%, the bottom 90% got a mere 1.4% boost in their income. The rest accrued to the top 10%, and the gains were largest at the top of the income scale.

Though data for 2005 were not available as this book went to press, it is important to recognize that inflation rose 3.4% that year, meaning that family incomes will have to grow at least that much just to stay even with price growth. Reflecting back on the decomposi-

TABLE 1.2 Income inequality, boom and bust

	Bottom 90%	Top 10%	Top 5%	Top 1%	Top 0.5%	Top 0.1%	Top 0.01%
1995-2000	12.5%	40.5%	50.5%	75.6%	87.5%	117.8%	156.0%
2001	-2.0	-12.4	-15.2	-21.2	-23.7	-28.4	-32.1
2002	-3.4	-7.2	-8.8	-12.2	-13.6	-16.8	-19.4
2003	-1.9	1.0	1.5	3.3	4.2	6.5	10.4
2004	1.4	8.7	10.9	16.3	18.0	22.1	27.5

Source: Piketty and Saez, Table A6.

tion in Table 1.1, achieving real family income growth will be challenging in 2005, because hourly wages were flat or falling across much of the wage scale (see Chapter 3 for further analysis). On the other hand, more persons found work in 2005 and family work hours surely rose. Therefore, the question is whether families gained enough hours to offset real hourly wage losses.

Family income probably rose slightly in real terms in 2005, but not nearly enough to make up for the losses since 2000 (e.g., median family income would have to go up by 3% real, or over 6% nominal to regain its prior peak). Thus, it will be at least six years before median family income returns to its pre-recession level. **Figure 1C** shows this to be part of a longer-term pattern, wherein it takes longer in recent years for median family income to recover the losses since the peak. Moreover, we emphasize that "regaining the peak" is a very low benchmark, given that productivity is constantly growing in recoveries. In this regard, the longer time periods shown in Figure 1C are a major factor in the productivity/income split highlighted below.

Income trends over the long term

We next turn to longer-term historical analysis, viewing the evolution of income growth over the post-World War II period. The key observation here is that while incomes at all positions of the income scale have gone up over time—as would be expected in an economy that is generally expanding—the rate of growth has slowed quite significantly in recent decades, particularly for those with lower incomes. A main factor of this slowdown is the less equitable pattern of income growth that has prevailed since the latter 1970s.

Median family income
One of the most important indicators of the living standards of the typical American family is median family income: the income of the family right in the middle of the income scale. In 2004 (the most recent year of available data) the median family's income was $54,061.

FIGURE 1C Years it took for median family income to regain prior peak

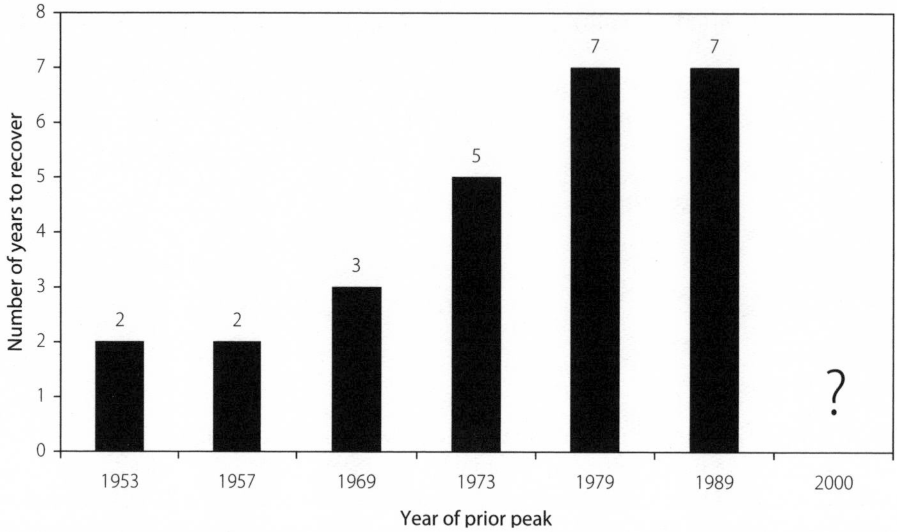

Source: Authors' analysis of U.S. Census Bureau data.

As shown in **Figure 1D**, real median family income usually falls in a recession (shaded areas) and recovers with the upturn in the economy. This is because for most families, especially working families in the middle class, compensation from employment is the main determinant of income growth. In recessions or jobless recoveries, as emphasized in Table 1.1, people are less able to find paid work or are forced to work fewer hours than they would like. Also, if the downturn persists, or, as was the case in the last two recoveries, job creation lags the rest of the recovery, hourly wages may fall behind inflation, and this too dampens income growth.

Along with Figure 1D, **Table 1.3** provides a historical view of median family income since 1947. There are two distinct growth periods. The first, from about 1947 to the early 1970s, was the strongest and by far the most sustained. Over the 26 years from 1947 to 1973, median family income about doubled in real terms. Over the next 27 years, it grew 25%. But this latter period can be subdivided into the period of stagnation (growth never surpassed 1% per year) from the mid-1970s to the mid-1990s, and the short but strong growth period of 1995-2000, when family incomes expanded by 2.2% per year. More recently, as stressed in the first section, income has fallen by 0.5% per year.

Median income and productivity growth

How does this historical record of income growth compare with that of productivity? After all, it is a common mantra among economists that productivity is the main determinant of

FIGURE 1D Real median family income, 1947-2005

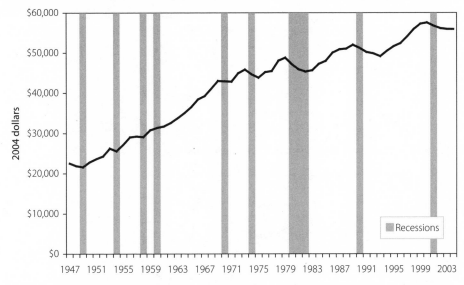

Source: Authors' analysis of U.S. Census Bureau data.

TABLE 1.3 Median family income,* 1947-2005 (2005 dollars)

Year	Median family income*	Changes	Annual growth rates
1947	$22,499	1947-73	2.8%
1973	45,865	1973-79	1.0%
1979	48,804	1979-89	0.6%
1989	52,015	1989-2000	0.9%
1995	51,659	1995-2000	2.2%
2000	57,508	2000-05	-0.5%
2005	56,194		

* Income includes all wage and salary, self-employment, pension, interest, rent, government cash assistance, and other money income.

Source: Authors' analysis of U.S. Census Bureau data.

living standards. But, as **Table 1.4** and **Figure 1E** reveal, while productivity growth handily reached the median family in the generation following World War II, it has not done so since. Between 1947 and 1973, a golden age of growth for both variables, productivity and real median family income grew in just about lockstep, both doubling. Over this era, there is no doubt that the typical family fully benefited from productivity growth.

TABLE 1.4 The growth of real median family income and productivity, 1947-2005

Period	Productivity	Median family income
1947-73	103.7%	103.9%
1973-2004	75.7	21.8
1995-2000	13.2	11.3
2000-05	16.6	-2.3

Source: Authors' analysis of BLS and U.S. Census Bureau data.

FIGURE 1E Productivity and real median family income growth

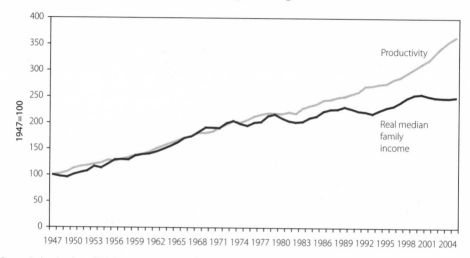

Source: Authors' analysis of U.S. Census Bureau and U.S. Bureau of Labor Statistics data.

Yet starting in the mid-1970s, this close relationship broke down. From 1973 to 2005, median family income grew at less than one-third the rate of productivity. As we discuss in detail below, relative to the earlier years, this was a period of growing income inequality, which served as a wedge between productivity and the living standards of the median family. That is, while faster productivity growth led to a larger economic pie, growing inequality meant that slices were divided up such that some income classes—those at the top of the income scale—claimed most of the income growth (and, as emphasized below, this gap between income and productivity occurred at a time when families were greatly increasing their time spent in the paid labor market).

The last two lines of Table 1.4 reveal a critically important dynamic of the "new economy." Between 1995 and 2000, productivity and median income once again grew at roughly similar rates, as the very tight labor market of this period ensured that the benefits

TABLE 1.5 Annual family income growth for the middle fifth, unadjusted and adjusted for family size, 1967-2004

Period	Unadjusted for family size*	Adjusted for family size**	Difference (adjusted minus unadjusted)
1967-73	2.2%	2.8%	0.6%
1973-79	0.0	0.5	0.5
1979-89	0.2	0.5	0.3
1989-2000	0.6	0.6	0.0
2000-04	-0.6	-0.5	0.1

* Unlike the other tables in the book, we use the CPI-U to deflate income here to be consistent with the size-adjusted measures, which also use that deflator.
** Annualized growth rate of family income of the middle fifth, divided by the poverty line for each family size.

Source: Authors' analysis of U.S. Census Bureau data.

of productivity growth were broadly shared. Yet, once the recession and jobless recovery erased the full employment conditions that prevailed in the latter 1990s, the disconnect between productivity and income growth returned with a vengeance. We return to this essential theme—the importance of full employment to achieving broadly shared prosperity—throughout the book.

Adjusting for family size

One explanation for the slower growth of family income over time is that families are smaller now, and thus have fewer earners and need less income. For this reason, some analysts urge adjusting family income for changes in family size, since the same total family income shared by fewer family members can be interpreted as improved economic well-being for each family member.

Families have grown smaller over time, as family size is down 15% since its mid-1960s peak, driven by a 34% decline in the number of children per family. However, trends in incomes adjusted for family size can be misleading, since smaller families may themselves be a function of slower income growth, as well as of non-economic demographic changes, such as the aging of the baby-boomers (leading to a marked decline in the share of persons in their child-rearing years). Surely, some families feel they cannot afford as many children as they could have if incomes had continued to rise at early postwar rates. As a result, a family deciding to have fewer children or a person putting off starting a family because incomes are down will appear "better off" in size-adjusted, family-income measures. It also seems selective to adjust family incomes for changes in family size and not adjust for other relevant trends such as more hours of work and the resulting loss of leisure.

Nevertheless, even when income growth is adjusted for the shift toward smaller families (**Table 1.5**, column 2), the income growth of the 1980s and 1990s was only slightly higher than the unadjusted measure. In fact, post-1979, the annual growth rates of size-adjusted income are never more than 0.3% higher than the unadjusted numbers. Since 1989, the trends between adjusted and unadjusted income have been virtually identical. Thus, putting aside the critique that income growth and family size are themselves intimately related, these data offer little evidence to support the notion that the shrinking size of families since 1979 has led to greater improvements in economic well-being more than that portrayed by unadjusted income trends.

Family income by race and ethnicity: big gains from full employment, but significant losses since 2000

As with almost every variable measuring living standards, there are persistent gaps between white and African American and Hispanic families. Certainly, discrimination plays a role here, as do the lower levels of educational achievement of minority populations relative to whites. It is also the case that minority families' incomes tend to be more responsive to overall economic trends, both positively and negatively. Thus, in the full employment economy of the latter 1990s, the pace of minority families' income growth surpassed that of white families, and the racial income gap shrunk to historically low levels. In the ensuing downturn, however, some of this valuable ground has been lost.

Table 1.6 shows that during periods of low unemployment, income growth of families headed by African American and Hispanics tended to outpace that of whites, thus helping to narrow the racial income gap. For example, the black/white median income ratio improved by moving from 51.12% to 59.21% between 1947 and 1967, and from 56.18% to 63.50% from 1989 through 2000. The Hispanic gap also closed significantly over the latter 1990s. This last point is also relevant in that the 1990s was a period of fast immigrant inflows, yet the income growth of both African Americans and Hispanics surpassed that of whites, suggesting immigrant competition did not prevent favorable minority income trends. For African Americans, income growth in the 1990s was their fastest in a generation.

These relative minority gains are clear in **Figure 1F**, which plots black and Hispanic median income relative to white. (Hispanic data are available only for 1972 and later; note also that the data for white families include Hispanics who identify their race as white. Data on non-Hispanic whites are available from 1972 forward; using this series for whites does not change the trends shown in the figure.) Throughout the 1960s, the median income of black families increased relative to that of whites, with the ratio peaking in the mid-1970s.

These relative gains for African Americans were partly driven by geographic and industry shifts, as many African American families migrated north and found employment in manufacturing. In fact, by 1970, the share of black men working in manufacturing surpassed that of whites. As manufacturing employment contracted over the 1980s and especially the latter 1990s, this sector ceased to be a venue for relative gains by minorities. Over the 1980s, African American families lost ground relative to whites, but this trend was reversed in the full employment period of the 1990s, when the black/white ratio rose to its highest level of record (63.50% in 2000).

Though the racial income gap compressed in the 1990s, we should not lose track of the magnitude of the gap. Even with this improvement, black median income never reached

TABLE 1.6 Median family income by race/ethnic group, 1947-2005 (2005 dollars)

Year	White	Black*	Hispanic**	Ratio to white family income of:	
				Black	Hispanic
1947	$23,434	$11,981	n.a.	51.12%	n.a.
1967	40,783	24,146	n.a.	59.21	n.a.
1973	47,935	27,665	$33,168	57.71	69.19%
1979	50,927	28,839	35,305	56.63	69.32
1989	54,694	30,724	35,645	56.18	65.17
1995	54,247	33,035	31,254	60.90	57.61
2000	60,112	38,174	39,043	63.50	64.95
2005	59,124	35,594	37,867	60.20	64.05
Annual growth rate					
1947-67	2.8%	3.6%	n.a.		
1967-73	2.7	2.3	n.a.		
1973-79	1.0	0.7	1.0%		
1979-89	0.7	0.6	0.1		
1989-2000	0.9	2.0	0.8		
1995-2000	2.1	2.9	4.6		
2000-05	-0.3	-1.4	-0.6		

*   Prior to 1967, data for blacks include all non-whites.
** Persons of Hispanic origin may be of any race.

Source: Authors' analysis of U.S Census Bureau data.

two-thirds of whites. And even if these favorable (from the perspective of closing the racial gap) trends of the latter 1990s had persisted at the same rate, it would have taken until 2054 for the black/white income gap to close.

But, as the figure reveals, the trend toward smaller race gaps did not persist. Recessionary contractions and the associated increases in unemployment tend to lower minority income more than that of whites, as can be seen in the last row of Table 1.6, which shows black and Hispanic income falling more quickly than that of whites. The post-2000 result was a reversal in the trend in relative incomes and a return to wider racial income gaps. As of 2005, these relative gains were erased for blacks, though the Hispanic/white ratio changed little from its level in 2000. For Hispanics, for example, the relative loss reversed about one-third of the progress they made relative to whites from 1995 to 2000.

Figure 1G shows the result of a simple statistical model that examines the black/white income gap as a function of unemployment. Using the model, we can ask how the black/white ratio would have trended had unemployment stayed at its 2000 level (4.0%) instead of rising over the recession and jobless recovery. Instead of falling, from 63.5% to

FIGURE 1F Ratio of black and Hispanic to white median family income

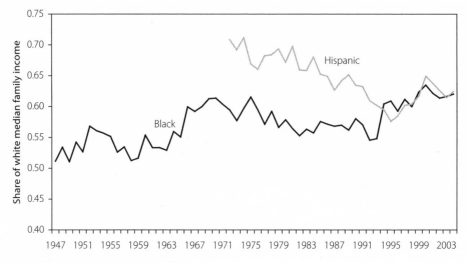

Source: Authors' analysis of U.S. Census Bureau data.

FIGURE 1G Black/white income ratio, actual and simulated holding unemployment constant at 2000 level

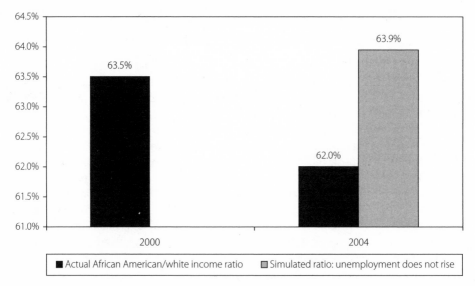

Source: Authors' analysis of U.S. Census Bureau and U.S. Bureau of Labor Statistics data.

TABLE 1.7 Median family income by age of householder, 1947-2005 (2005 dollars)

Year	Under 25	25-34	35-44	45-54	55-64	Over 65	45-54 compared to 25-34 relative incomes
1979	$32,419	$48,109	$57,094	$63,039	$54,605	$28,211	1.31
1989	25,943	46,937	61,120	70,088	57,229	35,094	1.49
1995	23,858	45,819	59,184	69,999	57,577	36,000	1.53
2000	30,557	51,434	65,846	76,904	62,850	37,806	1.50
2005	28,691	48,405	62,944	72,881	65,834	37,765	1.51
Annual growth rate							
1979-89	-2.2%	-0.2%	0.7%	1.1%	0.5%	2.2%	1.3%
1989-2000	1.5	0.8	0.7	0.8	0.9	0.7	0.0
1995-2000	5.1	2.3	2.2	1.9	1.8	1.0	-0.4
2000-05	-1.3	-1.2	-0.9	-1.1	0.9	0.0	0.1

Source: Authors' analysis of U.S. Census Bureau data.

62.0%, it would have continued to trend up. By 2004, the difference between the actual and simulated values was almost two percentage points, a stark reminder of the price minority families pay for weak economies. Moreover, unless the very favorable labor market conditions of the latter 1990s return, racial income gaps are likely to widen further.

Income by age and family type

Along with race and ethnicity, income also varies across the age scale. Young families, just starting out, usually have lower income than older families, who tend to have both higher earning capacity and greater wealth. As families retire and spend down their assets, income tends to decline. In fact, as shown in any year in **Table 1.7**—median income levels by age of the head of the family—the pattern of median family income by age follows an inverted 'U' in any given year.

Starting with the most recent data, Table 1.7 reveals that incomes fell almost across the board between 2000 and 2005, with larger losses for younger families headed by someone under 35. This represents a sharp reversal from the trends in the latter 1990s, when the job and wage opportunities associated with full employment lifted the incomes of young families more quickly than those of older families. Nevertheless, the generational income gap remained well ahead of its 1979 level (see last column).

Note that for younger families, the 1995-2000 period was unique. Between 1979 and 1995, the median income of families headed by young and even middle-age persons was relatively stagnant or falling (real median income for families headed by 35-44 year olds rose only about $2,000 over 16 years). For families headed by someone less than 65, with

FIGURE 1H Impact of a one-point increase in unemployment on median family income, by age

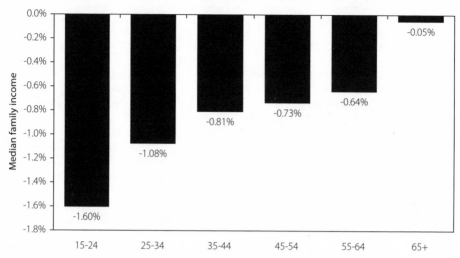

Source: Authors' analysis of U.S. Census Bureau and U.S. Bureau of Labor Statistics data.

one exception, real median income either fell or grew less than 1% over these years (the one exception is the 45-54 group, 1979-89, whose income grew 1.1% per year).

Figure 1H provides some statistical evidence of the relationship between unemployment and income growth by age. The figure plots a simple two-variable relationship between the change in real income by age level and unemployment. Each bar represents the impact on income for families headed by someone that age of a 1 percentage-point increase in the unemployment rate. Thus, an increase in unemployment from, say, 5% to 6% is predicted to lower the growth of family income among the youngest families by 1.6% and among the next oldest families by just over 1%. Note the clear step function of the chart, showing the diminished impact of unemployment by age, until with the oldest families, many of whom are retired, the relationship between the two variables is small and statistically no different from zero.

Some income analysts have discounted the importance of the general trend toward slower income growth by noting that families receive higher real incomes as they age, as shown in Table 1.6. But this fact does not solve the problem of the slower growth of income and wages that has persisted since the mid-1970s. The slower growth of median income means that the living standards of today's working families are improving less quickly as they age compared to the experience of families in earlier periods. We explore these and other related dynamics in the next chapter, which examines the extent of income mobility by persons and families as they grow older.

TABLE 1.8 Median family income by family type, 1973-2004 (2004 dollars)

Year	Total	Married couples Wife in paid labor force	Wife not in paid labor force	Single Male-headed	Female-headed	All families
1973	$47,979	$56,114	$42,049	$39,560	$21,349	$44,381
1979	51,666	59,941	42,690	40,525	23,821	47,225
1989	56,707	66,592	42,290	40,966	24,188	50,332
1995	57,927	68,711	39,849	37,367	24,237	49,987
2000	64,825	75,943	43,856	41,382	28,208	55,647
2004	63,630	76,814	42,221	40,293	26,964	54,061
Annual growth rate						
1973-79	1.2%	1.1%	0.3%	0.4%	1.8%	1.0%
1979-89	0.9	1.1	-0.1	0.1	0.2	0.6
1989-2000	1.2	1.2	0.3	0.1	1.4	0.9
1989-95	0.4	0.5	-1.0	-1.5	0.0	-0.1
1995-2000	2.3	2.0	1.9	2.1	3.1	2.2
2000-04	-0.5	0.3	-0.9	-0.7	-1.1	-0.7
Share of families						
1951*	87.0%	19.9%	67.1%	3.0%	10.0%	100.0%
1979	82.5	40.6	41.9	2.9	14.6	100.0
1989	79.2	45.7	33.5	4.4	16.5	100.0
2000	76.7	47.4	29.4	5.8	17.5	100.0
2004	75.5	45.4	30.0	6.4	18.2	100.0

* Earliest year available for wives' work status.

Source: Authors' analysis of U.S. Census Bureau data.

Income changes by family type

The demographics of the American family are constantly in flux. While most families are still headed by married couples, over the last 50 years there are proportionately fewer married-couple families, and conversely more single-parent families. Among married couples, far more wives have entered the labor force, a topic we devote more analysis to below. This section examines changes in median income among these different family types.

Table 1.8 focuses both on changes in median family income by family type and changes in the shares of different family types in the population. Since 1973, the most consistent income growth has occurred among married couples with both spouses in the paid labor force, as these families (specifically, the wives) have increased their amount of time spent in paid work relative to other families (though single-mother families also made large labor force gains over the 1990s). In 1979, the share of married couples without a wife in the labor force was about equal to that of those with a wife in the labor force (41.9% versus 40.6% of married-couple families). By 2000, married couples with two earners (assuming the husband worked) made up 47.4% of all families, while one-earner married couples were a proportionately fewer 29.4% of the total.

While this shift toward two-earner families has been a major factor in recent income growth, the shift appears to be attenuating, since the rate at which wives have been joining the labor force and increasing their hours of work has slowed in recent years. For example, among married-couple families, the share of families with wives in the paid labor force increased at an annual rate of about 1.0% in the 1960s and 1970s, 0.8% in the 1980s, and 0.4% in the 1989-2000 period. It is difficult to know the causes of this deceleration. It could be that, at 62.0% (47.4%/76.7%), the country is approaching the "ceiling" of the share of wives that are able or willing to spend time in the labor market (we use 2000 as an endpoint here to avoid the cyclical effect of the downturn).

Second, wives' willingness to work has generally been found to be more sensitive to both their own and their spouses' earnings than that of most other groups of workers, meaning that they are more likely to cut back their hours when their earnings or their spouses' earnings rise, as occurred in the latter 1990s. However, while this so-called "cross income effect" has consistently been found to exist, its estimated magnitude is small and has shrunk over time. Thus, it can only explain a small part of the flatter trend in wives' labor force participation. We offer a much more detailed analysis of wives' increased labor supply in the chapter's last section.

We focus more on single-mother families in the Poverty Chapter, since policy changes related to welfare reform had significant effects on this population. Here we note that like other lower income groups, the income of single mothers was highly responsive to the post-1995 boom-and-bust. Their median income grew particularly quickly in the latter 1990s and fell most quickly after the 2000 peak, providing another important example of the benefits of full employment, this time as a necessary complement to welfare reform.

Growing inequality of family income

Clearly, economic inequality is a dominant theme of our times. What, specifically, is its importance regarding our income analysis?

First, growing inequality is one reason for the slowdown in income growth that has beset most working families over the past few decades. True, with the slowdown in productivity in the mid-1970s, we would have expected incomes to slow. But this only explains part of the results discussed so far. The economic pie has grown more slowly in recent decades, at least through 1995, and the slices have been less equitably divided.

Figure 1I shows the pattern of income growth by income fifth using the Census definition of income. While this definition is less complete compared to another used later (e.g., it excludes realized capital gains, an important income component for inequality research), it is historically consistent and widely cited.

The picture of the first two panels is clearly one of growing together/growing apart. In the generation following World War II, real income just about doubled for each quintile

FIGURE 1I Real family income growth by quintile, 1947-2004

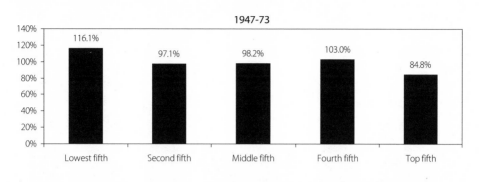

1947-73

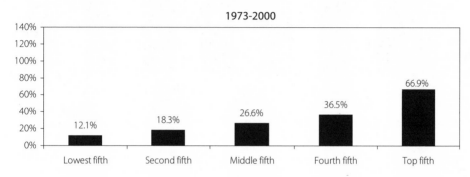

1973-2000

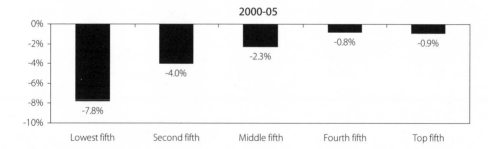

2000-05

Source: Authors' analysis of U.S. Census Bureau data.

along the income scale, though the growth of the lowest income families surpassed that of all others, meaning inequality was diminished over this period.

The 1973-2000 period looks very different: more like a staircase than a picket fence. Real income grew by 12.1% over these years for the poorest families, a rate of 0.4% per

FIGURE 1J Ratio of family income of top 5% to lowest 20%, 1947-2004

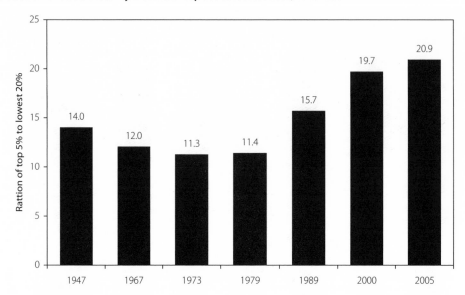

Source: Authors' analysis of U.S. Census Bureau data.

year. And, amazingly, 97% of that growth occurred in the 1995-2000 period, again underscoring the benefits of full employment for the least well-off. In contrast to the 1947-73 period, how fast a family's income grew over the "staircase years" was a function of their position in the income scale.

The final panel shows that while all groups lost income between 2000 and 2005, the losses were largest at the low end, reversing 73% of the gains made in the 1995-2000 period (these share calculations are made using log income changes, which do not precisely match the percent changes in the figures; since log changes are summative over time periods, they lend themselves to this type of comparison).

As shown below, more comprehensive data reveal that large capital losses in the early years of the current decade reversed the trend toward rising inequality. However, as shown in the first section of the chapter, that trend has reasserted itself most recently, but in terms of incomes and shares of national income (analyzed below).

The increase in the income gap between upper- and lower-income groups is illustrated in **Figure 1J**, which shows the ratio of the average incomes of families in the bottom 20% to those of the top 5% from 1947 to 2005. The gap between the top and the bottom incomes fell from 14.0 in 1947 (meaning that the average income of top 5% was 14 times that of the average of the bottom 20%) to 11.3 in 1979. Since then, the gap has grown consistently over cyclical peaks, hitting 20.9 in 2005.

TABLE 1.9 Shares of family income going to income fifths and to the top 5%, 1947-2005

| | | | | | | Breakdown of top fifth | |
| | | | | | | --- | --- |
Year	Lowest fifth	Second fifth	Middle fifth	Fourth fifth	Top fifth	First 15%	Top 5%
1947	5.0%	11.9%	17.0%	23.1%	43.0%	25.5%	17.5%
1973	5.5	11.9	17.5	24.0	41.1	25.6	15.5
1979	5.4	11.6	17.5	24.1	41.4	26.1	15.3
1989	4.6	10.6	16.5	23.7	44.6	26.7	17.9
2000	4.3	9.8	15.4	22.7	47.7	26.6	21.1
2005	4.0	9.6	15.3	22.9	48.1	27.0	21.1
Point change							
1947-73	0.5	0.0	0.5	0.9	-1.9	0.1	-2.0
1973-79	-0.1	-0.3	0.0	0.1	0.3	0.5	-0.2
1979-89	-0.8	-1.0	-1.0	-0.4	3.2	0.6	2.6
1989-2000	-0.3	-0.8	-1.1	-1.0	3.1	-0.1	3.2
2000-05	-0.3	-0.2	-0.1	0.2	0.4	0.4	0.0

Source: Authors' analysis of U.S. Census Bureau data.

Table 1.9 sorts these same Census income data into shares by fifths of families. For example, the 20% of families with the highest incomes claimed 47.7% of all family income in 2000, while the poorest 20% of families held only 4.3%. We further divide the top fifth's share between the 80th to 95th percentile and the top 5%.

In the most recent data, for 2005, the top 5% received about 21% of all income, more than that of the families in the bottom 40% combined (who received just under 14%). In fact, since 2000, the top fifth receive just under half of all income in the entire country.

The bottom panel shows the changes in these shares over time, and reveals a long-term pattern since the early 1970s of shares shifting up the income scale, with large shifts over the 1980s and 1990s. Since 1973, growing inequality resulted in 7% of national income moving from the bottom 80% to the top 20%, with 80% of that shift (5.6/7.0) going to the top 5%.

Another way of viewing the post-1970s surge in income inequality is to compare the "income cutoffs" of families by income group, as in **Table 1.10**. These values, some of which appeared in Figure 1A, represent the income at the top percentile of each fifth, and that at the 95th percentile. Focusing on this measure both allows an examination of income gains and losses for complete groupings of families (e.g., the bottom 40%), and also facilitates a more nuanced view of inequality's evolution, addressing relationships between the top and the bottom, the bottom and the middle, etc. We plot an index of these values for low (20th percentile), middle (median), and top (95th percentile) incomes to show their divergent fortunes over time (**Figure 1K**).

TABLE 1.10 Real family income by income group, 1947-2005, upper limit of each group (2005 dollars)

Year	20th percentile	40th percentile	60th percentile	80th percentile	95th percentile
1947	$11,758	$18,973	$25,728	$36,506	$59,918
1973	23,144	38,188	53,282	73,275	114,234
1979	24,570	40,402	57,239	78,817	126,442
1989	24,330	42,569	62,029	90,535	150,456
1995	24,258	41,958	62,311	91,917	157,295
2000	27,206	46,295	69,516	103,579	181,508
2005	25,616	45,021	68,304	103,100	184,500
Annual growth rate					
1947-73	2.6%	2.7%	2.8%	2.7%	2.5%
1973-79	1.0	0.9	1.2	1.2	1.7
1979-89	-0.1	0.5	0.8	1.4	1.8
1989-2000	1.0	0.8	1.0	1.2	1.7
1989-95	0.0	-0.2	0.1	0.3	0.7
1995-2000	2.3	2.0	2.2	2.4	2.9
2000-05	-1.2	-0.6	-0.4	-0.1	0.3

Source: Authors' analysis of U.S. Census Bureau data.

The annualized percent changes in the bottom panel of the table and the lines in the figure reveal that beginning in the mid-1970s, income growth began to diverge. Over the 1980s, the pattern was "monotonic," meaning the higher the income, the faster the growth. In the 1995-2000 period, however, the bottom slightly outpaced the higher percentiles, though those at the 95th percentile continued to pull away from the rest of the pack. Since 2000, real incomes have receded or stagnated at each cutoff, though most quickly at the lower end.

The next few figures present useful summary measures of inequality over long time periods, and compare the extent of income inequality in our current period relative to those many years back. The Census Bureau calculates the Gini coefficient (**Figure 1L**), an inequality scale that ranges from zero (perfect equality of income across households) to one (all income is concentrated at the very top of the income distribution). The higher the number, the greater the inequality. In 1993, the main survey used by the Census Bureau to measure income changed, inducing a large, one-year jump in the Gini. The new, higher data point that year represents a more accurate measure of the extent of inequality, but the sharp one-year jump is a function of the measurement change, not actual economic developments.

The Gini began to grow in the mid-1970s, and while it slowed in the 1990s, it continued edging up such that each year sets a new record for the highest level of inequality since the series began in 1947. The slower growth in the 1990s relative to the 1980s is due to the fact that the Gini gives greater weight to movements around the middle of the income

FIGURE 1K Low-, middle-, and high-income growth, 1947-2005

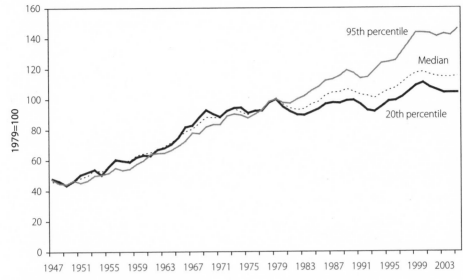

Source: Author's analysis of U.S. Census Bureau data.

FIGURE 1L Family income inequality, Gini coefficient, 1947-2005

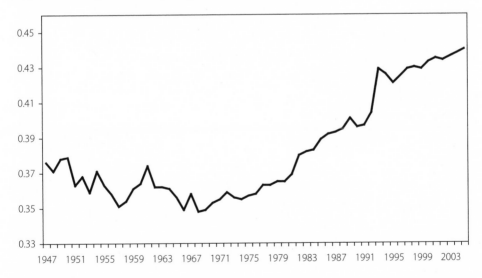

Note: A 1993 survey change led to a one-year jump in inequality.

Source: U.S. Census Bureau.

FIGURE 1M The share of income going to the top 1%, including capital gains, 1913-2004

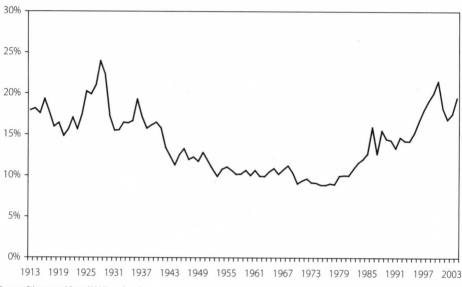

Source: Piketty and Saez (2003) updated.

distribution, whereas the 1990s inequality trend was largely driven by very large gains at the very top of the income scale. Thus, in order to develop a full understanding of trends in income inequality, it is necessary to examine various measures.

For example, we take advantage of a unique historical data set created by the economists Thomas Piketty and Emmanuel Saez (see figure note for more information). While these data, shown in **Figure 1M**, lack detailed information about the lower end of the income distribution, they provide invaluable data on the share and composition of income going to the wealthiest households all the way back to 1913, providing a long view of the evolution of inequality at the top of the income scale. Unlike much of the Census data we use later in this section, the Piketty/Saez data include realized capital gains (the dollar value of asset appreciation or losses claimed by the owner of the asset), and thus capture the contribution of this important component of inequality trends.

Figure 1M plots the share of income going to the top 1% of households over a very long time frame. Note the sharp increase in the share going to the top percentile in the 1990s, followed by a drop with the stock market bust that ended that cycle. At the 2000 peak, the top 1% held 21.5% of household income, a share that was only exceeded by the excesses of the late 1920s, a period of highly unstable economic speculation.

It is important to note that since 2002, the trend toward lesser inequality reversed and the top 1% is again accumulating a greater share of the economy's growth. In fact, between

FIGURE 1N Income share, top 0.01%, by income source, 1917-2004

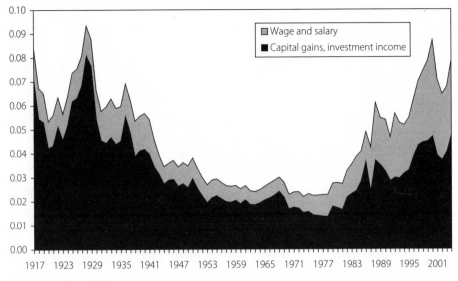

Source: Piketty and Saez (2003) updated.

2002 and 2004, the share of income accruing to the bottom 90% fell by 2.4 percentage points, while the increase shown in the figure is up 2.6 points (implying small share losses above the 90th but below the 99th).

Figure 1N probes even deeper into the upper reaches of the income scale, examining the income shares and composition of the top 0.01%—the very narrow slice representing 1/100th of the top percentile. A similar pattern to the last figure is evident here too, suggesting that the inequality trajectory of the top percentile is closely linked to that of the very top of that group. But the composition of income among this sliver of rich families is also important and revealing: note the increase in both their share of capital income (including capital gains, investment, and self-employment income) and labor income (wages and salaries).

Even holding inequality constant, more labor income flowing to the top of the scale implies less labor income available for the vast majority of the workforce. Add this development to the fact of greater income concentration at the very top of the scale and inequality's squeeze on the earnings of most workers becomes apparent. We return to this theme in Chapter 4 in our discussion of the soaring pay of executives and other high earners.

Another very useful data series for studying the growth of income inequality (as well as the distribution of federal taxes, presented next) is produced by the Congressional Budget Office, covering the years 1979-2003. These data have many advantages over the

FIGURE 10 Growth in real household income, 1979-2003

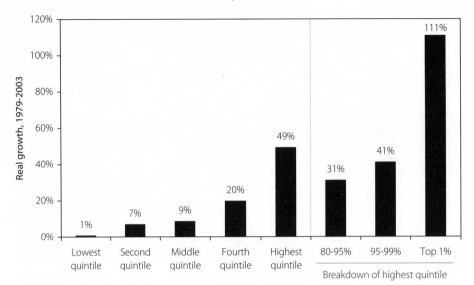

Source: Authors' analysis of CBO data.

Census data for this type of analysis (though they are based largely on those same Census data highlighted above). Most importantly, they are comprehensive, including the value of non-cash benefits like Medicare, Medicaid, employer-paid health insurance premiums, and food stamps, as well as realized capital gains (note that all of the above are left out of Census income). These data also adjust for family size.

Figure 10 shows the growth in real household income by fifth for the full span of the years covered by these data. Once again, the staircase pattern is evident, with minimal growth in the bottom fifth, the middle fifth up by less than 9% (over 24 years), and the top fifth up by 49%. Moreover, the gains at the top were driven by the top 1%, which more than doubled over the period. As shown in **Table 1.11**, were we to compare only cyclical peaks—1979 to 2000—the top 1% was up 184% (the difference is partly driven by the loss of investment income when the stock market bubble burst in late 2000).

The table pulls out selected income classes from these data to evaluate changes over different time periods. Over the 1980s, inequality rose as the bottom fifth lost ground, the middle fifth was stagnant (up 2.1%), and the top fifth was up by about 25%, with larger gains within this highest category. Over the 1990s, the incomes of the bottom and the middle fifths both accelerated significantly, and both grew at about the same rates. The top 1%, however, grew about eight times their rate, up 80.9%. The post-2000 period, as noted, sharply reversed these gains.

TABLE 1.11 Average real income levels, 1979-2003, by income group, and shares of growth accruing to each group (2003 dollars)

	Lowest fifth	Middle fifth	Highest fifth	80-95%	95-99%	Top 1%
1979	$14,700	$47,800	$123,700	$91,800	$153,100	$485,100
1989	14,000	48,800	154,300	105,700	185,000	760,600
2000	15,600	53,700	209,800	125,300	235,200	1,376,300
2003	14,800	51,900	184,500	120,200	216,000	1,022,400
Percent Change						
1979-89	-4.8%	2.1%	24.7%	15.1%	20.8%	56.8%
1989-2000	11.4	10.0	36.0	18.5	27.1	80.9
1979-2000	6.1	12.3	69.6	36.5	53.6	183.7
2000-03	-5.1	-3.4	-12.1	-4.1	-8.2	-25.7
2002-03	-1.3	-0.4	2.3	0.1	3.0	5.9
Addendum: Share of income growth to income group, 1979-2000						
	0.8%	5.3%	77.2%	22.5%	14.7%	40.0%

Source: Authors' analysis of CBO data.

Recall the reversal in trend of the top 1% share series shown in Figure 1M in 2003. We have included a line from these CBO data, 2002-03, to see if they also show a reversal in trend back towards greater inequality. That is, in fact, the case, as real household income fell in 2003 for the lowest fifth, was down slightly (0.4%) for the middle fifth, with significant gains only for the top 5% (3.0% for the 95-99th households, and about 6% for the top percentile). Thus, these data corroborate the earlier figure suggesting that the equalizing effect of the stock market correction appears to have lasted only through 2002. Inequality again appears to be on the rise.

An addendum to the table performs a simple growth analysis on the CBO data over the peak-to-peak period of 1979 to 2000. Of the total income growth over the period, less than 1% accrued to the bottom fifth, about 5% to the middle, and 77.2% was claimed by the top fifth. Among the richest households, the top 1% received 40.0% of the income growth from 1979 to 2000, a stark example of the income concentration over the period.

Some inequality analysts express doubts about measures of income inequality because the incomes of families fluctuate from year to year in response to special circumstances—a layoff, a one-time sale of an asset, and so on. As a result, a family's income may partially reflect transient events and not indicate its economic well-being over the long term. For example, a family experiencing a bad year in terms of income may dip into its savings to continue consuming at the same level as during a better year. In this view, consumption levels of families provide a better measure of inequality, since families typically gear their consumption to their expected incomes over the long term.

TABLE 1.12 Gini coefficients: After-tax income and consumption inequality, 1981-2001

	1981	1986	1990	1994	1999	2001	Percent change 1981-2001
Income	0.342	0.394	0.403	0.396	0.406	0.400	17.0%
Consumption	0.273	0.316	0.314	0.313	0.305	0.307	12.5%

Source: Johnson et al., 2005.

Table 1.12 presents Gini coefficients for consumption along with the Gini ratio for disposable income (basically after-tax income) from the same data source: the Bureau of Labor Statistics' Consumer Expenditure (CE) Survey (once again, the data are adjusted for family size). The income inequality trends from the CPS data—the focus of most of this chapter—are considered more reliable because they come from a larger sample and are based on a more detailed set of questions. Nevertheless, we include the CE income Gini in the table for comparative purposes.

Both inequality measures increased over the 1980s—consumption by about 15% and disposable income by about 18%. Beginning in the early 1990s, disposable income inequality essentially flattened, while consumption inequality drifted down a bit. Over the full period, income inequality by this measure was up 17.0% and consumption was up 12.5%. Thus, both measures are elevated relative to earlier years, though consumption less so, presumably due to some families smoothing over income constraints by spending savings or borrowing. This last point is particularly germane, since, as shown in Chapter 5, household debt increased significantly in recent years. While this may show up as diminished consumption inequality relative to income inequality, a persistent debt burden can be a significant negative factor in family living standards.

Recent research has also revealed a high degree of consumption inequality among children relative to adults and elderly persons. **Figure 1P** plots the share of children in each fifth, using the consumption levels of the overall population to set the quintile breakpoints. By this measure, any bar that is greater than 20% shows the children are over-represented in this fifth, and visa versa.

In each year, children were over-represented in the lowest fifth and under-represented at the top. This means that children consistently had lower levels of relative consumption (i.e., compared to older persons) over these years. Moreover, their relative disadvantage increased over the 1990s, as their share in the bottom consumption fifth grew from 26% to 29%, before sliding back a bit in the 1990s.

These findings imply that relatively fewer of society's consumption goods and services flowed to children as compared to adults. This is worrisome, given the importance of access to basic necessities for children during their formative years. Further research, not shown here, suggests that much larger consumption inequalities exist for children in single-mother families, who, by dint of their low incomes, are likely less able to "smooth

FIGURE 1P Consumption inequality among children, 1981-2001

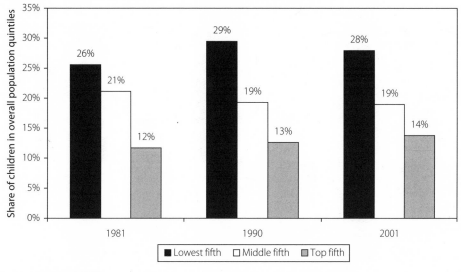

Source: Johnson et al., 2005.

over" periods of disrupted income flows with borrowing or by tapping savings. Such families, and particularly the children in them, suffer significant income and consumption disadvantages with potentially lasting effects.

Federal taxes, living standards, and inequality

Thus far we have looked exclusively at pre-tax income data. This section addresses the role tax policy has played in the trends in income and inequality using the same CBO data source noted above, but accounting for federal income taxes. (A more inclusive analysis would include the impact of state and local taxation, but such distributional data are not available; we do, however, present some information on state tax trends below and in Chapter 7.)

To assess the impact of federal tax policy on inequality, we use the CBO data to compare changes in the share of income accruing to each income class, before and after taxes. This type of comparison should reveal if such changes in income shares are markedly different after taxes—e.g., if taxes offset the inequality growth evident in the skewed income examined thus far.

The data reveal that there is little evidence of any offset over the period covered by the CBO data. In the period between 1979 and 2003, more than 6% of national income shifted from the bottom 80% to the top 20%, with most of the shift—about 5%—accruing

FIGURE 1Q Change in income shares by income percentile, pre- and post-tax, 1979-2003

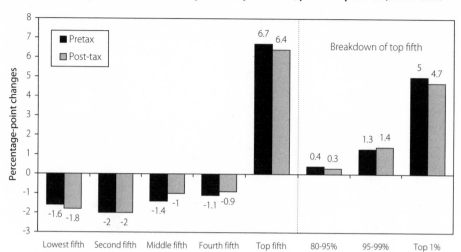

Source: Authors' analysis of CBO data.

to the top 1% (**Figure 1Q**). Importantly, these shifts are virtually equivalent using before- or after-tax income data. After-tax shares are up slightly less from the middle quintile on up, suggesting federal taxes dampened some of the increase in inequality, but the loss of income share in the bottom fifth was slightly larger on an after-tax basis.

Figure 1Q covers many years of tax changes, often pushing the income distribution in different directions. In general terms, over the 1980s, taxes became more regressive—higher-income families saw their tax rates fall relative to lower-income families—and more progressive during the early 1990s—higher-income families saw their tax rates rise relative to lower-income families. Changes in tax policy over the 1980s, then, reinforced the overall trend toward inequality, while changes in tax policy during the early 1990s helped to reduce inequality's growth. As we show below, federal tax changes since 2000 have been regressive.

Table 1.13 presents CBO's estimates of federal effective tax rates (tax payments as a share of income) at three cyclical peaks—1979, 1989, and 2000—as well as the most recent year, 2003. Looking at the "All" category—the average effective rate—shows that there hasn't been much movement on average (the lower effective rate for 2003 is a function both of recent tax changes and income declines since 2000; in a progressive system, tax liabilities often decline faster than incomes, causing effective rates to fall when income goes down).

Significant changes have, however, occurred within and between income classes over these years. Over the 1980s, rates were little changed for the bottom 80%, yet large cuts

TABLE 1.13 Effective federal tax rates for all households, by comprehensive household income quintile, 1979-2003

Income category	1979	1989	2000	2003
Bottom four-fifths				
First	8.0%	7.9%	6.4%	4.8%
Second	14.3	13.9	13.0	9.8
Third	18.6	17.9	16.6	13.6
Fourth	21.2	20.5	20.5	17.7
Top fifth	27.5%	25.2%	28.0%	25.0%
Top 10%	29.6	26.3	29.6	26.8
Top 5%	31.8	27.2	31.0	28.4
Top 1%	37.0	28.9	33.0	31.4
All	22.2%	21.5%	23.0%	19.8%

Source: Congressional Budget Office (2005).

occurred at the top of the income scale. Federal taxes paid as a share of income fell by 3.3 percentage points for the top 10% and 8 points for the top 1%.

Federal taxes at the bottom end of the scale fell over the 1990s, largely due to a significant increase in the Earned Income Tax Credit. This result is due to both the credit being refundable—low income workers receive the credit even if they have no tax liability—and also the fact that employment among low-wage workers surged in this period.

In a progressive tax system, effective rates fall in a recession, enabling post-tax income to fall less than pre-tax income, and providing some income stimulus to the economy. This explains part of the lower rates shown in the 2003 column of Table 1.13. The 2000s also saw significant legislative changes in tax policy, and the effective rates in the table reflect both these economic and tax changes. Below, we take a closer look at these recent changes in the federal tax code.

Table 1.14 shows what some of these changes have meant in terms of actual tax liabilities, i.e., the dollar impact of effective rate changes. The second column of the table simulates tax obligations in later years if the 1979 rate had prevailed. For low- and middle-income families, the changes had a small effect in 1989. Their taxes were $14 and $342 less because of changes in effective rates. By 2000, the changes have a greater impact. But the real story is among the top 1%, who, in dollar terms, saw large declines in the tax payments—about $62,000 in 1989 and $55,000 in 2000. This difference in the dollar amount is expected, since a percent change in liabilities will of course translate into more dollars for wealthier families. But even as a share of pretax income (last column), the lower tax payments are greater (more negative) for those in the top percentile. Thus, even before the

TABLE 1.14 Effective federal tax rates for all households, by comprehensive household income quintile, 1979-2003 (2003 dollars)

	Actual	Using 1979 tax rate	Difference	Share of pretax income
Bottom fifth				
1989	$1,106	$1,120	-$14	-0.1%
2000	998	1,248	-250	-1.6
Middle fifth				
1989	$8,735	$9,077	-$342	-0.7%
2000	8,914	9,988	-1,074	-2.0
Top 1%				
1989	$219,813	$281,422	-$61,609	-8.1%
2000	454,179	509,231	-55,052	-4.0

Source: Authors' analysis of CBO data.

post-2000 tax cuts (discussed below) led to relatively large declines in the liability of those at the top of the income scale, tax payments of the richest households were falling by tens of thousands of dollars.

So far, the analysis of taxes has examined the combined effects of all federal taxes. In fact, federal taxes take a variety of forms, some progressive and some regressive, and the impact of these taxes has changed over time. **Table 1.15** shows the effective tax rate for households at different income levels for the four most important types of federal taxes in 1979, 1989, 2000, and 2003 (we include the most recent year for completeness, but focus on cyclical peaks in the discussion).

The personal income tax is highly progressive, with effective rates rising smoothly with income. As noted, the EITC expansion heightened the progressivity of the income tax by taking the bottom rate from 0% in 1979 to -4.6% in 2000. Thus, while low-income families incurred a zero income-tax burden in 1979, they actually received income through the income-tax system in 2000 ($46 dollars for every $1000 dollars of income, on average).

The payroll tax, which is capped at $94,200 in 2006, is used primarily to finance Social Security and Medicare. All workers pay the payroll tax at the same rate (15.3%, combining the employer and employee's share) from their first dollar of earnings until the point in the year when they reach the cap. With the lowest earners paying the full rate from the first dollar earned and high earners paying no payroll tax on earnings over the cap, the payroll tax is regressive, as borne out by the effective rates in Table 1.15. The rate rises through the bottom, second, middle, and fourth quintiles of households, but falls steeply thereafter. In 2000, for example, households in the middle fifth paid 9.6% of their income in federal payroll taxes, compared to just 1.9% paid by top 1% of households. Comparing rates in 2000 with those in place in 1979 demonstrates that effective rates rose one percentage point

TABLE 1.15 Effective tax rates for selected federal taxes, 1979-2003

Income category	Personal income tax				Payroll tax				Corporate income tax				Excise tax			
	1979	1989	2000	2003	1979	1989	2000	2003	1979	1989	2000	2003	1979	1989	2000	2003
Bottom four-fifths																
First	0.0%	-1.6%	-4.6%	-5.9%	5.3%	7.1%	8.2%	8.1%	1.1%	0.6%	0.5%	0.3%	1.6%	1.8%	2.3%	2.3%
Second	4.1	2.9	1.5	-1.1	7.7	8.9	9.4	9.1	1.2	0.8	0.6	0.4	1.3	1.2	1.4	1.4
Third	7.5	6.0	5.0	2.7	8.6	9.8	9.6	9.2	1.4	1.1	0.9	0.6	1.1	1.0	1.1	1.1
Fourth	10.1	8.3	8.1	5.9	8.5	10.0	10.4	10.3	1.6	1.2	1.0	0.6	0.9	0.9	0.9	0.9
Top fifth	15.7%	14.6%	17.5%	13.9%	5.4%	6.6%	6.3%	7.2%	5.7%	3.5%	3.7%	3.4%	0.7%	0.6%	0.5%	0.5%
Top 10 %	17.4	16.3	19.7	16.0	4.2	5.1	5.0	6.0	7.4	4.4	4.4	4.4	0.7	0.5	0.4	0.4
Top 5 %	19.0	17.7	21.6	17.8	2.8	3.7	3.8	4.7	9.5	5.3	5.2	5.5	0.6	0.4	0.4	0.4
Top 1 %	21.8	19.9	24.2	20.6	0.9	1.4	1.9	2.3	13.8	7.2	6.7	8.2	0.5	0.3	0.2	0.3
All	11.0%	10.2%	11.8%	8.5%	6.9%	8.1%	7.9%	8.4%	3.4%	2.3%	2.4%	2.0%	1.0%	0.8%	0.9%	0.8%

Source: Congressional Budget Office (2005).

TABLE 1.16 Federal and state/local revenue as a share of GDP, 1959-2005

	Federal	State and local	Total
1959	17.1%	6.8%	23.9%
1969	19.2	8.5	27.7
1979	18.5	8.4	27.0
1989	18.2	9.1	27.3
2000	20.4	9.2	29.6
2005	17.6	9.3	26.9

Source: NIPA.

on average as a result of increases in the payroll tax implemented in the 1980s to improve the long-term finances of the Social Security and Medicare systems. Importantly, while the payroll tax is itself regressive, the Social Security and Medicare benefits it funds are progressively distributed, offsetting some of the regressive effects of the full life cycle.

The next set of columns in Table 1.15 display the effective rates from the corporate income tax, which are portioned out to households according to their estimated income from capital. The corporate income tax is progressive, with effective rates rising sharply with income. However, between 1979 and 1989 corporate taxes declined, with particularly large drops in effective rates among the groups in the top fifth. The progressivity of the corporate income tax simply reflects the ownership structure of corporations, with few poor and middle-income households holding any substantial amount of stock (see the chapter on Wealth).

The last set of columns show effective rates of federal excise taxes (such as those on gasoline, alcohol, and cigarettes). While these taxes claim a small share of income—not more than 1% on average in any year in the table—they tend to be highly regressive (this is because the tax rates on these items do not vary by income level). In 2000, for example, the bottom fifth of households spent over four times their income on federal excise taxes compared to the top fifth.

The mix of taxes—federal, state, and local—can have an important impact on how the tax burden is shared and thus on after-tax inequality. Federal taxes are more progressive than state and local taxes, which tend to raise revenue from more regressive sources such as sales and property taxes.

Table 1.16 focuses on the changes over time in government revenues as a share of GDP, again broken down by federal and state/local sectors. Revenue from all levels of government as a share of GDP remained fairly constant over the 1970s and 1980s, from 27.7% in 1969 to 27.3% in 1989. Over the 1990s, the historically sharp rise in high pre-tax incomes (which face the highest marginal income tax rates) caused this share to rise to 29.6% in 2000, the highest level on record. The post-2000 drop in these high-level incomes, in tandem with recent tax cuts, reversed this effect, and the overall revenue share was back down to 26.9% in 2005.

TABLE 1.17 Composition of federal and state/local tax revenue, by progressive and regressive components, 2000 and 2005

Federal	2000	2005
Progressive	60.8%	56.4%
Personal income tax	49.8	42.5
Corporate income tax	10.9	13.9
Regressive	38.9%	43.1%
Excise/customs taxes	4.4	4.4
Contributions for social insurance	34.5	38.7
Other*	0.4%	0.4%

State and local	2000	2005
Progressive	30.1%	28.8%
Personal income tax	26.2	23.7
Corporate income tax	3.9	5.1
Regressive	64.4%	65.0%
Sales	35.0	33.8
Contributions for social insurance	1.2	1.7
Property taxes	28.2	29.5
Other*	5.5%	6.3%

* For federal, this refers to taxes from the rest of the world; for state and local, it refers to other taxes on goods produced or imported.

Source: NIPA.

However, while the overall tax share of GDP has not varied much, there has been somewhat of a shift in composition, with more regressive state and local taxes growing relative to the federal share. Comparing 1979 and 2005, for example, the total tax share was about 27%, but the state and local shares were about 1 point lower in the earlier year, and the federal share was 1 point higher. The decline in federal revenue was largely a result of cuts in most forms of federal taxes in the 2000s, including lower marginal rates in the income tax, and lower taxes on capital gains, dividend income, and inheritances.

Table 1.17 reinforces the above points by breaking federal and state taxes down into progressive and regressive components in two recent years: 2000, the most recent business-cycle peak, and 2005 (the most recent year for complete data). Viewed in tandem with Table 1.16, there are two outstanding facts to note regarding a regressive shift in tax policy. First, by depending more on state tax revenue, we are collecting a larger share through regressive sources. Second, the federal system is less progressive now than it was a few years ago.

TABLE 1.18 Effective tax rates and the impact of the Bush tax changes, 2000 and 2005

	2005 (old law)	2005 (new law)	Impact of law changes
Lowest 20%	8.0%	7.4%	−0.6%
Second 20%	13.0	11.3	−1.7
Middle 20%	18.0	16.3	−1.8
Fourth 20%	21.4	19.7	−1.8
Next 15%	24.7	22.4	−2.2
Next 4%	26.5	24.5	−2.0
Top 1%	29.8	26.8	−2.9
All	23.4	21.3	−2.1

Impact of federal Bush tax cuts, 2006	Average cut	Share of total cut	Share of income
Lowest 20%	-$63	0.8%	−0.6%
Second 20%	-393	5.3	−1.7
Middle 20%	-665	9.0	−1.8
Fourth 20%	-1,113	15.0	−1.8
Next 15%	-2,547	25.8	−2.4
Next 4%	-5,160	13.9	−2.3
Top 1%	-44,477	30.0	−3.6
All	-1,460	100.0	−2.3

Source: ITEP Tax Model, June 2006.

Table 1.17 breaks down taxes to progressive and regressive components. As shown in Table 1.15, federal income and corporate tax rates rise with income; payroll and sales (or excise) taxes do not. The two big changes in the federal system are the decline in the share of federal revenue from income taxes, from just under 50% in 2000 to 42.5% in 2005 (partly offset by an increase in the corporate share), and the increase in social insurance, mostly payroll, taxes. State-level taxes underwent a similar shift, but of a smaller magnitude. In both cases, the progressivity of the system was diminished.

A final table in this section (**Table 1.18**) examines the impact of the many changes in federal tax policy introduced by the Bush Administration and legislated since 2001, including lowering marginal income tax rates, lowering taxes on investment and inheritance income, and other smaller changes. The first panel shows the impact of the changes through 2005 by comparing what effective rates would have been under old law (before any of these changes were made) to rates under current law. Since household incomes are the same in both columns, this type of comparison isolates the impact of the changes in tax law.

The data reveal that while tax cuts occurred throughout the income scale, they were larger (i.e., more negative) at the top. In other words, as shown above regarding revenue

FIGURE 1R The value of the Bush tax cuts by income class, 2006

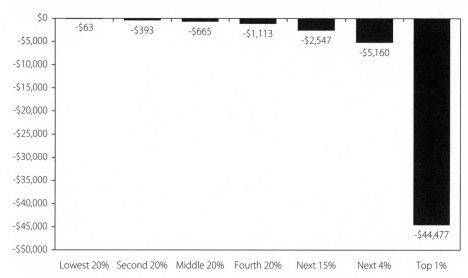

Source: ITEP Tax Model, June 2006.

collection, the federal tax code became less progressive over this period. The 2.9% cut for the top 1% is almost five times the size of the cut for the bottom fifth.

The bottom panel of Table 1.18 and **Figure R** show what these cuts meant in dollar terms in 2006. They lower tax payments at the low end by only $63, the middle by $665, and so on, up to the top value of over $44,000. The highly skewed nature of these cuts is evident in the figure.

Family income changes by income class

Table 1.19 shifts the analysis to the shares of families by constant dollar income brackets, examining the proportion of families with low, middle, and high incomes. We use two measures of family income that facilitate this perspective. The first is an absolute (as opposed to 'relative') measure that looks at the percent of families in a set of real income brackets over time, while the second returns to a more relative approach.

Comparing these two sets of results yields an important insight about the trajectory of income classes over the past few decades: while the growth of average income has led to fewer families with low absolute income levels, income growth of families in these lower brackets has not kept pace with that of higher income families. Moreover, since 2000, only the low-income share has grown, a clear downshifting compared with earlier periods.

The income shares shown in the top panel are the result of two main factors: the rate of growth of average income and changes in income equality. As long as average income

TABLE 1.19 Distribution of families and persons by income level, 1969-2004

Family incomes	1969	1979	1989	1995	2000	2004	Percentage-point change				
							1969-79	1979-89	1989-2000	1995-2000	2000-04
Under $25,000	24.0%	22.0%	21.4%	22.0%	18.4%	20.2%	-2.0	-0.6	-3.0	-3.6	1.8
$25,000 to $50,000	39.5	31.9	28.2	28.3	26.6	25.7	-7.6	-3.7	-1.6	-1.7	-0.9
$50,000 to $100,000	31.4	36.8	35.8	34.4	34.8	34.0	5.4	-1.0	-1.0	0.4	-0.8
Over $100,000	5.0	9.3	14.5	15.4	20.1	20.1	4.3	5.2	5.6	4.7	0.0
Total	100.0	100.0	100.0	100.0	100.0	100.0					

Persons (income relative to the median)	1969	1979	1989	1995	2000	2002*	Percentage-point change			
							1969-79	1979-89	1989-2000	1995-2000
Less than 50% of median	18.0%	20.1%	22.1%	22.2%	22.0%	22.5%	2.1	2.0	-0.1	-0.2
50-200% of median	71.2	68.0	63.2	61.9	61.7	60.7	-3.2	-4.8	-1.5	-0.2
Over 200% of median	10.8	11.9	14.7	15.9	16.3	16.8	1.1	2.8	1.6	0.4
Total	100.0	100.0	100.0	100.0	100.0	100.0				

* Latest data point available.

Source: Authors' analysis of March CPS data.

growth is faster than inflation, as is usually the case, and income inequality is unchanged (which has not been the case in recent decades), there will be a greater proportion of the population at higher income levels over time. For example, the share of families with incomes under $25,000 (adjusted for inflation) will fall under this scenario.

However, if inequality grows such that the low-income population fails to receive much of the income growth and the high-income population obtains an unusually large proportion, then a rise in average income is less likely to translate into a general upward movement of low- and middle-income families to higher income levels.

Table 1.19 reveals that economic growth over time has led to a larger share of families with higher incomes. While some analysts have touted this trend as indicative of balanced growth in an economy that lifts all boats, such a trend is exactly what we would expect to occur. As the U.S. economy becomes more productive and expands year in and year out, the general income level rises, the share of families with low incomes falls, and the share with higher incomes rises. The question is: how steady has this progress been, and have certain income groups benefited less than others from overall growth? In fact, when inequality grew quickly, as in the 1980s, fewer families benefited from growth and the shift toward higher absolute living standards was slowed for many families. Similarly, in the 2000s, slow income growth led to a reversal of the usual upward distribution of families through these brackets.

Between 1969 and 1979, almost 10% of families shifted from lower to higher brackets, as income growth was more broadly shared than in latter decades. For example, in the less equal distributional climate of the 1980s, upward shifts slowed. Over the 20 years, 1969-89, the lowest income share, with incomes below $25,000, fell from 24.0% to 21.4%, while the lower-middle group fell from 39.5% of all families to 28.2%. Since each year's share has to sum to 100%, these changes must be counterbalanced by commensurate growth in the higher brackets. In the top bracket alone, the share of families with incomes above $100,000 almost tripled, from 5.0% to 14.5%.

Shares were relatively stagnant in the first half of the 1990s expansion, but by the latter half of the decade, income gains were particularly large at the bottom of the scale and the less than $25,000 share fell by 3.6 percentage points. The top two shares grew by 5.1 points, most driven by the 4.7 point increase in families with income over $100,000.

As noted, the 2000s have reversed some, though by no means all, of this progress. The top share was unchanged, while the two middle shares contracted, pushing the lowest income share up by 1.8 percentage points. Clearly, the diminished labor market opportunities of the recession and jobless recovery, along with a more porous safety net (see Chapter 6), led to a growth in low-income families, a contraction of middle-income families, and no increase in upper-income families.

The second section of Table 1.19 examines the incomes of individuals—single and in families—according to the per capita incomes of their families (size-adjusted), with single persons given their individual incomes. In this analysis, the income of persons is measured relative to the median. Thus, unlike the top panel of the table, which fixes the income brackets in real dollar terms, the brackets for the income categories in this section move with the median income. This approach provides more important insights into inequality, because it measures the relative, as opposed to the absolute, changes in family incomes.

Thus, in the first section, the absolute income level of a low-income family may grow such that it crosses from the $25,000 category into the middle group. But if its income grows more slowly than that of the median, the family will still fall behind relative to more affluent families.

From 1979 forward, more than one-fifth of the population lived in households with income below half of the median income (we return to a similar measure in the Poverty chapter). Over both the 1970s and 1980s, this share grew by about 2 percentage points, and remained at that level in 2000, climbing slightly over the downturn to 22.5%. The difference in this pattern from that in the above panel provides interesting information about the impact of growing income inequality. Note, for example, the consistent decline in the share of families with incomes less than $25,000, which is about half of the median income in 2002 (about $51,700 in 2002 dollars). Yet the share of persons in families with income less than half the median has grown or remained unchanged since 1969. Thus, while average income growth has helped to diminish the share of low-income families measured in absolute terms, increased inequality has kept them from gaining ground on higher income families. In other words, their incomes have grown in absolute terms, but not relative to that of middle-income or wealthy families.

Meanwhile, the share at the top of the income distribution—above 200% of the median—grew fairly consistently over this period. Since these shares must sum to 100 in each year, and thus the changes in each of the last four columns must sum to zero, this pattern of increased shares on either side of the middle means a declining share in middle-income families (those with incomes from half to twice the median), and this share fell from 71.2% in 1969 to 60.7% in 2002. By this measure, America's broad middle class has been shrinking, with shares shifting upward and downward.

Expanding capital incomes

The fortunes of individual families depend heavily on their reliance upon particular sources of income: labor income, capital income, or government assistance. Since most families receive little or no capital income, their economic well-being is determined by their success in the labor market—getting jobs and higher wages. Capital income, however, is a very important source of income to the top 1% and especially the top 0.1% (who receive more than a third of all capital income). Two significant reasons for the unequal growth in family incomes between 1973 and today are (1) the increased share of capital income (such as rent, dividends, interest payments, and capital gains) and a correspondingly smaller share earned as wages and salaries; and (2) the increased concentration of capital income among the households in the top 1% of the income distribution.

Table 1.20 projects the sources of income for families in each income group in 2006. These data are from a different source than that used for the earlier analysis of income trends, but they are comparable to the CBO data used to analyze tax trends. The table provides two types of breakdowns of income by income group. One shows how reliant an income group is on a particular source (*sources of income by income type*). The other breakdown shows how concentrated a particular type of income is in particular income groups (*distribution of types of income*). The particular incomes identified are: total wage

TABLE 1.20 Sources of income by income group and distribution of income types, 2006

Income group	Sources of household income by income type					Distribution of types of income				
	Wage & salary	Business income	Capital income	Other income	Total	Wage & salary	Business income	Capital income	Other income	Total
Bottom four-fifths	70.3%	2.9%	4.2%	22.6%	100.0%	43.7%	16.1%	15.2%	52.4%	40.0%
Bottom	47.0	5.4	4.5	43.1	100.0	1.8	1.9	1.0	6.1	2.5
Second	61.1	3.3	4.4	31.1	100.0	6.1	3.0	2.6	11.5	6.4
Middle	73.1	2.6	3.5	20.8	100.0	12.9	4.1	3.6	13.7	11.4
Fourth	74.6	2.6	4.5	18.4	100.0	22.9	7.1	8.0	21.0	19.8
Top fifth	60.1%	10.8%	15.4%	13.6%	100.0%	56.2%	91.2%	84.2%	47.5%	60.3%
81–90%	76.0	3.6	5.0	15.4	100.0	18.4	7.8	7.1	13.9	15.6
91–95%	75.2	4.9	6.4	13.5	100.0	13.0	7.7	6.4	8.7	11.2
96–99%	62.8	10.9	11.3	15.0	100.0	14.7	23.0	15.4	13.1	15.1
Top 1%	35.3	20.4	33.2	11.1	100.0	10.1	52.6	55.3	11.8	18.4
All	64.5%	7.1%	11.0%	17.3%	100.0%	100.0%	100.0%	100.0%	100.0%	100.0%
Memo										
Top 0.1%	26.7%	19.5%	48.2%	5.6%	100.0%	3.5%	22.8%	36.6%	2.7%	8.4%
Next 0.4%	38.9	23.1	22.9	15.0	100.0	3.7	19.8	12.7	5.3	6.1

Notes:
(A) Calendar year. Current law.
(B) Tax units with negative cash income are excluded from the lowest quintile but are included in the totals.
(C) Includes both filing and non-filing units. Tax units that are dependents of other taxpayers are excluded from the analysis.
(D) Labor income includes taxable wages and salaries, contributions to tax-deferred retirement accounts, and the employer share of payroll taxes for Social Security and Medicare.
(E) Business income includes income or loss reported on Schedules C, E, and F.
(F) Capital income includes taxable and non-taxable interest income, income from dividends, realized capital gains/losses, and imputed corporate tax liability.
(G) Other income includes total Social Security benefits, taxable and non-taxable pension income, taxable distributions from IRAs, unemployment compensation, TANF, worker's compensation, energy assistance, veteran's benefits, SSI, disability income, child support, and alimony received.

Source: Authors' analysis of Urban-Brookings Tax Policy Center Microsimulation Model (version 0305-3A).

and salary income; capital income (interest, dividends, and capital gains); business income (income from unincorporated businesses, farms); and other income (primarily government transfers, pensions, and child support).

The families in the bottom four-fifths of the income distribution obtain 70.3% of their income from wages and salaries and have very little business income (just 2.9% of their income) or capital income (4.2% of their income). In fact, the same is true for those families in the 80th to 95th percentiles, who obtain 75% of their income from wages and salaries. The only income groups with a particularly different composition of income are the bottom fifth, which receives a substantial 43.1% of its income from other sources (primarily government transfers) and the top 1%, which receives only 35.3% of its income as wages and salaries but obtains over half of its income from capital and business incomes.

The last rows of Table 1.20 present a breakdown of incomes within the upper 0.5%, that of the top 0.1%, and the next 0.4%. The very highest income families, the upper 0.1%, receive nearly half of their income from capital income (48.2%) and another 19.5% from business income: only about a fourth of their income is based on wages and salaries.

Table 1.20 also shows the concentration of particular types of incomes. Most important to note is that 84.2% of all capital income is received by the upper fifth, with 55.3% received by the top 1% and 36.6% by the top 0.1% alone. Business income is similarly concentrated at the top.

This income landscape implies that fast growth for capital income will disproportionately benefit the best-off income groups. Those with less access to capital income depend either on wages (the broad middle) or on government transfers (the bottom) as their primary source of income. As a result, any cutback in government cash assistance primarily affects the income prospects of those in the bottom 40% of the income scale, and particularly the bottom fifth. The income prospects of families in the 20th to 99th percentiles, on the other hand, depend primarily on their wages and salaries (which make up at least 60-76% of their income). Thus, understanding changes in the level and distribution of wages (see Chapter 3) is fundamental to understanding changes in the incomes of the broad middle class.

The shift in the composition of personal income toward greater capital income is shown in **Table 1.21**. Over the 1973-89 period, capital income's share of market-based income (personal income less government transfers) shifted sharply upward, from 13.9% to 20.8%, as interest income expanded. This shift toward capital income was slightly reversed by 2000 as interest rates and, therefore, interest income fell. Interest income fell further between 2000 and 2005 as low interest rates, reflecting low inflation, prevailed. However, dividend income expanded between 1989 and 2005, partially offsetting the decline in interest income. Unfortunately, these data (drawn from the GDP accounts) do not capture realized capital gains as a source of income, and therefore provide only a partial picture of income trends. Adding realized capital gains to the analysis (with data drawn from the Internal Revenue Service shown in the last row) does not affect any conclusions about the 1970s or 1980s, as capital gains were comparably important in 1973, 1979, and in 1989. However, the share of income from capital gains grew to a substantial 7.8% of income in 2000 and was 4.9% of income in 2005. Thus, capital income (inclusive of realized capital gains) was clearly a larger share of personal income in 2005 than in the 1970s, even with the large drop in interest

TABLE 1.21 Shares of market-based personal income by income type, 1959-2005

Income type	Shares of income					
	1959	1973	1979	1989	2000	2005
Total capital income	13.3%	13.9%	15.1%	20.8%	19.1%	16.0%
Rent	4.2	2.3	1.2	1.0	1.9	0.8
Dividends	3.3	2.8	2.9	3.6	4.7	5.3
Interest	5.8	8.8	11.0	16.3	12.6	9.9
Total labor income	73.5%	75.6%	75.8%	71.0%	71.8%	74.2%
Wages & salaries	67.9	66.0	63.4	58.6	60.0	59.6
Fringe benefits	5.5	9.5	12.4	12.4	11.8	14.6
Proprietor's income*	13.3%	10.6%	9.1%	8.2%	9.1%	9.8%
Total market-based personal income **	100.0%	100.0%	100.0%	100.0%	100.0%	100.0%
Realized capital gains	n.a.	3.2%	3.5%	3.3%	7.8%	4.9%

*   Business and farm owners' income.
** Total of listed income types.

Source: Authors' analysis of NIPA and IRS data.

income. Correspondingly, a slightly smaller share of income was paid out as wages and benefits (not counting any impact of capital gains).

This shift away from labor income and toward capital income is unique in the postwar period and is partly responsible for the ongoing growth of inequality since 1979. Since the rich are the primary owners of income-producing property, the fact that the assets they own have commanded an increasing share of total income automatically leads to income growth that is concentrated at the top.

It is difficult to interpret changes in proprietor's income (presented in Table 1.21) because it is a mixture of both labor and capital income. That is, the income that an owner of a business (or farmer) receives results from his or her work effort (labor income) and his or her ownership (capital income) of the business or farm. To the extent that the shrinkage of proprietor's income results from a shift of people out of the proprietary sector (e.g., leaving farming) and into wage and salary employment, there will be a corresponding increase in labor's share of income (e.g., as farm income is replaced by wage income). This shift out of proprietor's income thus helps to explain a rising labor share in some periods, such as from 1959 to 1973. However, there has not been a dramatic shift in proprietor's income over the last few decades (it is roughly equivalent in 1979 and 2005), so it has not been a factor that has shifted the income distribution during that time.

The rise in inequality caused by the shift toward greater capital income is compounded by the growing concentration of capital income among the very highest income groups,

FIGURE 1S Share of capital income, 1979-2003

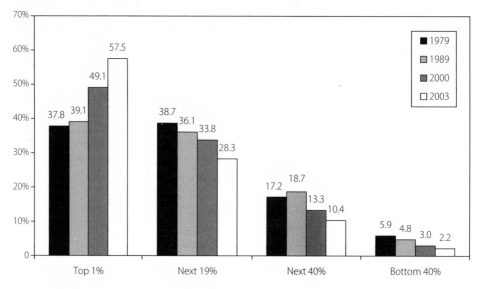

Source: Authors' analysis of CBO data.

particularly the top 1%. This is shown in **Figure 1S**. Whereas the top 1% received 37.8% of all capital income in 1979, their share rose to 49.1% by 2000 and rose further to 57.5% in 2003. All other income groups, including the remainder of the upper fifth, received a much lower share of the economy's capital income in 2003 than in earlier years. For instance, the share of capital income going to the next 19% (those in the 80th to 99th percentile of income) declined from 38.7% in 1979 to just 28.3% in 2003. The bottom 80% received only 12.6% of all capital income in 2003, down from 23.1% in 1979.

From the point of view of the sectors within national income (incomes generated by the corporate, proprietor, and government sectors), one can also discern a clear shift away from labor income toward capital income (**Table 1.22**). As a first cut, one might take the declining share of labor income in *national* income between the 1970s and recent years as evidence of a shift in factor (capital, labor) incomes. For instance, labor's share of national income was 72.7% in 1973 and 73.9% in 1979 but declined to roughly 72.0% in 2000 and 2004 (the last year of data for all sectors). A closer look at the underlying data, however, suggests a somewhat larger shift away from labor income. First, labor's share of national income rose steadily from 1959 to 1979. One reason for the expanding share of labor income in those years was the steady expansion of the government/nonprofit sector. When the government/nonprofit sector expands, there is a tendency for labor's share of income to grow because this sector generates mostly labor income and very little capital income. For example, Table 1.22 shows that the growth of the government/nonprofit sector—from

TABLE 1.22 Shares of income by type and sector, 1959-2004

	Shares of domestic national income						
Sector	1959	1969	1973	1979	1989	2000	2004
National income, all sectors							
Labor	68.3%	72.3%	72.7%	73.9%	71.7%	72.3%	71.8%
Capital	19.3	18.0	17.2	17.3	20.0	18.6	18.7
Proprietor's profit	12.3	9.7	10.2	8.9	8.3	9.1	9.5
Total	100.0	100.0	100.0	100.0	100.0	100.0	100.0
Corporate and business sector							
Labor	43.8%	47.4%	47.8%	50.4%	47.8%	49.4%	47.1%
Capital	12.8	12.1	11.1	11.0	11.1	10.6	11.5
Total	56.6	59.5	58.9	61.4	58.9	60.0	58.6
Non-corporate sector							
Labor	9.4%	6.4%	5.6%	5.1%	4.7%	5.0%	5.3%
Capital	2.3	2.1	2.5	2.8	3.8	2.9	2.2
Proprietor's profit	12.3	9.7	10.2	8.9	8.3	9.1	9.5
Total	24.0	18.2	18.3	16.7	16.7	17.0	17.1
Government/nonprofit sector							
Labor	15.2%	18.5%	19.3%	18.4%	19.2%	17.9%	19.4%
Capital	4.2	3.9	3.6	3.5	5.1	5.1	4.9
Total	19.4	22.4	22.8	21.9	24.3	23.0	24.3
ADDENDUM:							
Shares of corporate sector income*							
Labor	77.3%	79.7%	81.2%	82.1%	81.1%	82.3%	80.3%
Capital	22.7	20.3	18.8	17.9	18.9	17.7	19.7
Total	100.0	100.0	100.0	100.0	100.0	100.0	100.0

* Does not include sole proprietorships, partnerships, and other private non-corporate business. The corporate sector, which includes both financial and non-financial corporations, accounted for 67% of national income in 2004.

Source: Authors' analysis of NIPA data.

19.4% to 24.3% of national income between 1959 and 1989—necessarily added 4.0 percentage points to labor's share of national income (other things remaining equal). On the other
hand, the shrinkage of the government/nonprofit sector over the 1989-2000 period led to a
smaller labor share of income. Thus, the growth of the government sector over the 1980s led
to an understatement of the decline of labor's share in that decade; in the 1990s, the decline
in the government/nonprofit sector had the opposite effect. The seemingly small decline of
labor's share of national income since 1969 is partly due to the slight expansion (roughly 2.0
percentage points of national income) of the size of the government/nonprofit sector.

Labor's share of national income also grows as the non-corporate sector (farm and
non-farm unincorporated businesses) shrinks, as it did from 1959 to 1979, because labor's

share of income in that sector is relatively low (less than a third in 1979). When resources shift from a sector with a low labor share of income (such as the proprietor's sector) to sectors with a higher labor share (all of the other sectors), the share of labor income in the economy necessarily rises. The changing composition of income across organizational sectors (expanding government, shrinking non-corporate) is important to examine when studying particular decades. Changes in the non-corporate sector, however, have not materially affected the aggregate labor share since 1979.

The clearest way to examine the changes in income shares is to focus on the corporate sector, which accounted for 60% of national income. Such an analysis is useful because it is not muddied by income shifts among sectors (such as expanding or shrinking government or non-corporate sectors) or the difficulty in defining proprietor's income as either labor or capital income. The division of incomes in the corporate sector is shown in the bottom section of Table 1.22. Labor's share fell from 82.1% in 1979 to 81.1% in 1989, and then to 80.3% in 2004.

More detailed information (including data for 2005) on labor and capital incomes in the corporate sector are presented in **Table 1.23** and in **Figure 1T,** which charts the share of capital income in total corporate income. Labor's share had dramatically fallen by the mid-1990s, but recovered the lost share in the boom of the late 1990s, gaining two percentage points between 1995 and 2000. This indicator provides further affirmation that low unemployment strengthened workers' hands in the labor market in the late 1990s, although the impact dissipated after the early 2000s recession and jobless recovery knocked down wage growth by 2002, as discussed in Chapter 3. By 2005, labor's share had fallen to levels not seen since the late 1960s. Correspondingly, capital's share of corporate income in 2005—at 20.9%—was the highest in nearly 40 years.

How important is the shift in the shares of labor and capital income? Labor's share in the corporate sector in 2005 was 79.1%, 3.0 percentage points below labor's share in 1979. It would require average hourly compensation to be 3.7% greater (82.1 divided by 79.1, less 1) to return to the previously higher labor share. Thus, the shift toward greater capital income shares has had a non-trivial implication for wage and compensation growth.

An examination of labor and capital income shares, however, cannot fully determine whether there has been a redistribution of income from labor to capital, or vice versa. This type of analysis assumes that, if labor and capital shares remain constant, then there has been no redistribution. Such an analysis is too simple for several reasons. First, in contrast to most topics in economics, such an analysis makes no comparison of actual outcomes relative to what one might have expected to happen given a model of what drives labor and capital income shares. Accomplishing this requires looking at the current period relative to earlier periods, and examining variables that affect income shares. Several trends suggest that, other things being equal, capital's share might have been expected to decline and labor's share to rise over the last two decades. One reason for this expectation is that there has been a rapid growth in education levels and labor quality that would tend to raise labor's share. The primary trend, however, that would tend to lessen capital's share (and increase labor's share) is the rapid decline in the capital-output ratio since the early 1980s (see Table 1.23). For instance, in 1979 there was $1.86 of corporate capital assets (building and equipment) for every dollar of corporate income generated, a ratio that fell to $1.67 by 2000, but rose to $1.76 in 2005. This fall in the ratio of the capital stock to private sec-

TABLE 1.23 Corporate sector profit rates and shares, 1959-2005

	Profit rates*		Income shares			Capital-output ratio
Business cycle peaks	Pre-tax	After-tax	Profit share**	Labor share	Total	
1959	13.3%	7.6%	22.7%	77.3%	100.0%	1.70
1969	13.6	7.9	20.3	79.7	100.0	1.50
1973	11.7	7.0	18.8	81.2	100.0	1.61
1979	9.6	5.7	17.9	82.1	100.0	1.86
1989	10.6	7.0	18.9	81.1	100.0	1.78
1995	11.1	7.6	19.5	80.5	100.0	1.75
2000	10.6	7.1	17.7	82.3	100.0	1.67
2005	11.9	8.6	20.9	79.1	100.0	1.76

* "Profit" is all capital income. This measure, therefore, reflects the returns to capital per dollar of assets.
** "Profit share" is the ratio of capital income to all corporate income.

Source: Authors' analysis of NIPA and BEA data.

FIGURE 1T Capital shares in the corporate sector, 1947-2005

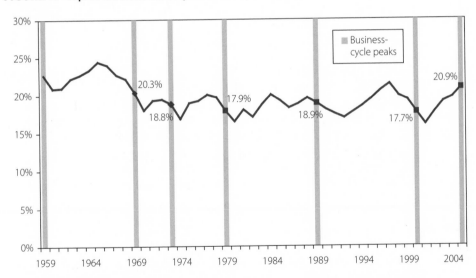

Source: Authors' analysis of NIPA data.

tor output implies that capital's role in production has lessened, suggesting that capital's income share might have been expected to fall in tandem.

Rather than fall, the share of capital income has risen because the return to capital, before and after tax, has risen (**Figure 1U**). That is, the amount of before-tax profit received

FIGURE 1U Before- and after-tax return to capital, 1947-2005

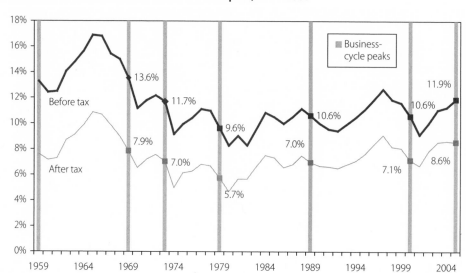

Source: Authors' analysis of NIPA and FRB data.

per dollar of assets (i.e., the capital stock) has grown since the 1970s (which had profit rates below that of the 1960s) and seemed to peak in the late 1990s before the downturn in profits around 2000. By 2005, however, profitability had reached its greatest level in 36 years (excepting 1997). Because of the lowering of taxes on corporate profits, the after-tax return on capital has an even more impressive performance: since 1959, only the booming years of the mid-1960s were comparable in the high after-tax returns on capital attained in 2003, 2004, and 2005 (except, again, 1997). The relationship between the return to capital and capital's share of income is illustrated in *Rising Profit Rates, Constant Profit Share* on the following page.

This analysis misses an important part of the picture since the definition of labor's share includes the pay of CEOs, thereby overstating the income share going to "workers" and understating "profits," since the bonuses and stock options given CEOs are more akin to profits than wages. Moreover, the amount of CEO pay relative to corporate profits has, in fact, grown significantly, as shown in **Figure 1V**. In the mid-1990s, CEO pay was equivalent to roughly 5% of corporate profits. That amount rose to roughly 10% of profits a few years ago (unfortunately, more recent data are not available). This suggests that the growth in corporate profits is understated in our analysis because some of the profits are showing up in CEO paychecks and are counted as worker pay.

This growth in profitability has left less room for wage growth. This might be considered the consequence of businesses successfully restraining wage growth as sales and profits grew in recent years, even in years of seemingly low unemployment. If the pre-tax

Rising profit rates, constant profit share

There has been some confusion as to the difference between a rise in the *profit rate*, or return to capital (which has risen dramatically in the last 15 years), and a rise in *capital's share of income*, which has grown less. The following exercise is designed to show how these two rates differ and how each can rise or fall at its own pace.

Income is the sum of the returns to capital and labor. It can be expressed in the following equation: $(K * r) + (W * L) = Y$ where K is the capital stock, r is the rate of return on capital (the profit rate), W is the average hourly wage, L is the number of labor hours, and Y is income. Capital's share of income can be calculated by dividing capital income, $K * r$, by total income, Y. If the capital share remains constant, then the quantity $(K * r)/Y$ doesn't change (nor does the labor share, $(W * L)/Y$). Capital's share, $(K * r)/Y$, can also be written as $(K/Y) * r$, where the quantity K/Y is equal to the ratio of the capital stock to total income. If K/Y falls, as it has over the last 10 years, then r can rise a great deal, even if capital's share remains constant.

For example, if K = $2,000, r = .05, and Y = $1,000, then the capital share of income would be 10%: $(K * r)/Y = (\$2,000 * .05)/\$1,000 = \$100/\$1,000 = .10$. If the capital stock fell to $1,000 (so that $K' = \$1,000$), the profit rate rose to 10% (so that $r' = .10$), and income remained unchanged ($Y' = \$1,000$), the capital share would still be 10%: $(K' * r')/Y' = (\$1,000 * .10)/\$1,000 = \$100/\$1,000 = .10$. In this example, the profit rate doubles, but the capital share of income remains the same because the capital stock has fallen 50%.

Over the last 15 years, the fall in the capital-output ratio has muted the rise in capital's share of income. From 1979 to 1997 the capital-output ratio fell 25% (from 2.23 to 1.68) while the "profit rate," or return to capital, rose from 6.4% to 10.4% (a 62.5% rise). The combined effect of these two trends was to raise capital's income share from 17.4% to 21.6%.

FIGURE 1V Top-five officers' total pay relative to corporate profits, 1994-2002*

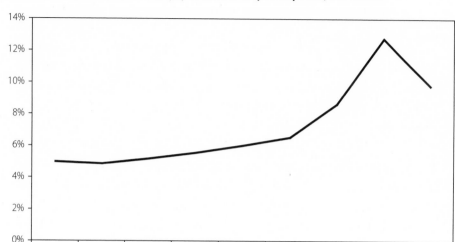

* Data are centered three-year moving averages.

Source: Authors' analysis of Bebchuk and Grinstein (2005).

return to capital in 2005 (11.9%) had been at the 1979 level (9.6%), then hourly compensation would have been 5.0% higher in the corporate sector. This was equivalent to an annual transfer of $235 billion dollars from labor to capital (measured for 2005). This shift in income from labor to capital income is quite large when compared to the size of the loss of wages for the typical worker due to factors such as the shift from manufacturing to services, globalization, the drop in union representation, or any of the other prominent causes of growing wage inequality discussed in Chapter 3.

Family work hours

Though the recession and jobless recovery led to fewer hours worked by many in the workforce, surveys and media accounts suggest that many working Americans experience significant stress in trying to balance the often countervailing demands of work and family. Many of these families report feeling like they are working more hours than their parents did, and spending less time enjoying their families. Such a dynamic potentially engenders feelings of stress and guilt that can erode the quality of family life, even as incomes rise.

Yet, it's often noted that the long-term trend in average hours worked per week is flat if not falling, which seems to contradict the alleged time-squeeze noted above. In fact, as shown in the relatively flat line in **Figure 1W**, the average weekly hours spent in the paid labor market have been flat for all workers (the rising lines in the figure are explained below).

FIGURE 1W Average weekly hours compared to family work hours, 1975-2004

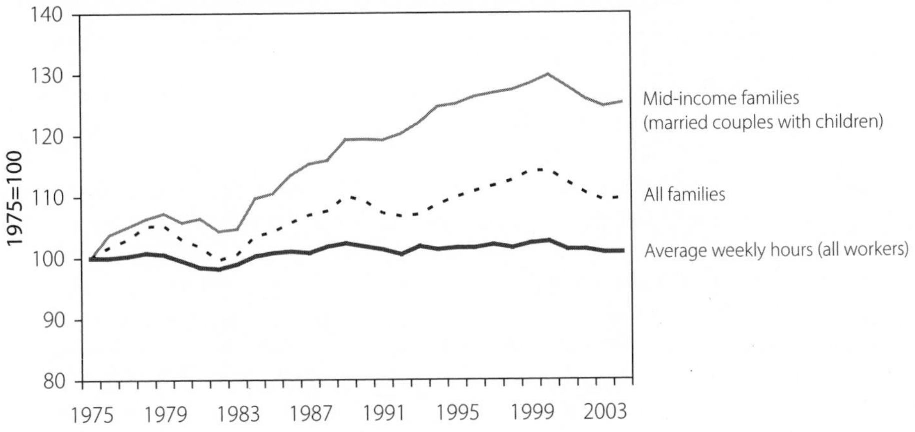

Source: Authors' analysis of March CPS data.

But this trend tells us little about how much families are working, and is even misleading in that regard. The reason has to do with the entry of more women in the paid labor force. That is, one reason for the flat trend in average hours (the lowest line in Figure 1W) is because women are more likely to work part-time and when women increase their share in the labor force, average weekly hours fall despite the fact that more family members are clearly spending more time in the paid labor market.

While more women working may show up as lower weekly average hours, it unequivocally raises the total hours worked by families. That is, consider a married-couple (or cohabiting) family with one spouse working full-time, around 2,000 hours per year. If the other spouse in that family goes to work for half the year, the family's total hours worked rises to 3,000, but average weekly hours could fall due to the addition of a part-time worker.

Figure 1W plots average weekly hours along with total family work hours of all middle-income families and of middle-income married couples with children, with each series indexed to 100 in 1975 (the earliest year for family work hours data). We also add a restriction to the latter group that spouses be between 25 and 54, to remove those less attached to the labor force. This group—middle-income, prime-age married-couple families with children—form the core of our analysis.

In contrast to the flat average weekly hours, family work hours are up significantly, especially for prime-age couples with children, providing ample evidence of a time squeeze. While the average weekly series is up a few percent at the most recent peak of 2000, the series for all families is up about 14% and the prime-age series is up almost 30%. This latter group increased their annual time spent in the paid labor market by about 900 hours between 1975 and the 2000 business cycle peak. This amounts to a net addition of 22 weeks or more than five months of full-time work.

As noted, it is working wives that account for most of the changes in hours worked across families. **Table 1.24** shows husbands and wives hours separately for prime-age married couples with children, by income fifth.

The husbands' panel shows relatively little variance. From the second fifth on up, these husbands tend to work more than full-time, full-year (52 weeks times 40 hours, or 2080 hours), thus there is little room for them to expand work hours (this is known as a "ceiling effect" since the variable under analysis—annual hours—is constrained by the available time in the day). One interesting finding, to which we will return below, is the decline in hours across income quintiles, 2000-04, with larger losses at the low end of the income scale.

Wives, on the other hand, show marked increases, particularly over the 1980s, but in the 1990s as well. Wives in each fifth increased their hours of work by between one-third and one-half between 1979 and 2000. The addendum to the table gives a sense of how much more time these working wives spent in the paid labor market by income fifth. Middle-income wives added the most hours, up 535, the equivalent of over three months of full-time work.

Of course, the increased time spent in the paid labor market by wives in particular, and women in general, represents a challenge in terms of balancing work and family. Yet it is also the result of increased opportunities for women. On the upside, more paid work can mean greater economic independence, and in this sense the greater integration of women into the workforce represents an important advance. But both the lack of "family-friendly" policies in the workplace—such as guaranteed paid leave, or more accessible unemployment insurance—and persistent gender wage differentials (see Chapter 3), contribute to the downside of this long-term trend toward more work.

The importance of wives' labor market contribution to family income is evident in **Table 1.25**. The top row of the table shows the percent change in the real income of these married-couple families, again by income fifth, 1979-2000. Real family income grew for each quintile, from 9.1% at the low end of the income scale, to 24.9% in the middle, to 67.1% at the top fifth. Here again we see the clear evidence of expanding income inequality.

The question, however, for this section, is what role did wives' contributions to family income play in these income trends? This is shown by examining family income growth without wives' earnings. As the second row reveals, family income would have fallen steeply—by almost 10%—in the lowest quintile, and would have grown significantly less quickly in each other income fifth. Instead of increasing by about 25%, 1979-2000, middle-income married-couple families with children would have seen an increase in their average income of only 5.8%.

The difference between the actual and simulated income results give the percent contribution by wives, shown in the last row. For the bottom 60%, wives' contributions raised family income by about one-fifth. Note that wives' contributions added less—13.0%—to family income at the top of the income scale, a result which suggests that wives' had an equalizing effect on family income growth over this period. That is, in the absence of wives' extra earnings, the income distribution of these families would have been even more unequal than was actually the case (tabulations not shown here suggest wives' contributions reduced the growth of the top fifth/bottom fifth ratio by 35%).

TABLE 1.24 Annual hours of work, husbands and wives, age 25-54, with children, 1979-2004, by income fifth

						Percent changes			
	1979	1989	2000	2004	1979-89	1989-2000	2000-04	1979-2004	
Husbands									
Lowest fifth	1,612	1,664	1,732	1,636	3.2%	4.1%	-5.5%	1.5%	
Second fifth	2,042	2,093	2,095	2,044	2.5	0.1	-2.5	0.1	
Middle fifth	2,134	2,196	2,220	2,195	2.9	1.1	-1.1	2.9	
Fourth fifth	2,216	2,248	2,297	2,262	1.4	2.2	-1.5	2.1	
Top fifth	2,331	2,391	2,430	2,408	2.6	1.6	-0.9	3.3	
Wives									
Lowest fifth	456	625	683	598	36.9%	9.3%	-12.3%	31.2%	
Second fifth	722	983	1,140	1,069	36.2	16.0	-6.3	48.1	
Middle fifth	849	1,168	1,385	1,327	37.5	18.6	-4.2	56.2	
Fourth fifth	1,060	1,311	1,437	1,418	23.7	9.6	-1.3	33.8	
Top fifth	1,091	1,345	1,437	1,446	23.3	6.8	0.6	32.5	
Combined									
Lowest fifth	2,068	2,289	2,414	2,235	10.7%	5.5%	-7.4%	8.1%	
Second fifth	2,764	3,076	3,236	3,112	11.3	5.2	-3.8	12.6	
Middle fifth	2,983	3,363	3,605	3,522	12.8	7.2	-2.3	18.1	
Fourth fifth	3,276	3,559	3,734	3,680	8.6	4.9	-1.5	12.3	
Top fifth	3,422	3,736	3,867	3,854	9.2	3.5	-0.3	12.6	

Addendum: Added wives' hours, 1979-2000

	Added hours	As full-time weeks
Lowest fifth	226.3	5.7
Second fifth	418.5	10.5
Middle fifth	535.4	13.4
Fourth fifth	377.1	9.4
Top fifth	346.1	8.7

Source: Authors' analysis of CPS data.

TABLE 1.25 Real income growth of prime-age, married-couple families with children, 1979-2000, and wives' contribution

	Bottom fifth	Second fifth	Middle fifth	Fourth fifth	Top fifth
Percent change	9.1%	16.6%	24.9%	32.8%	67.1%
Without wives' earnings	-9.7	-1.1	5.8	16.2	54.1
Wives' contribution	18.9	17.6	19.1	16.6	13.0

Source: Authors' analysis.

Finally, we reiterate that levels of family work hours, for middle and higher income families, appear to be at or near a ceiling, at least before the cyclical impact of the 2001 recession. In other words, there are only so many hours that husbands, wives, and any other families can work in the job market, and families from the middle of the income scale on up appear to be "topping-out." This has two implications. First, if hourly wages begin to steadily rise again, we may expect to see some evidence of what micro-economists call an "income effect" with family members may take advantage of higher earnings by working a bit less. On the other hand, if real wages were to fall, as was the case for many workers in recent years, it is unlikely that these families could offset such hourly losses by working more hours.

Conclusion

Given the centrality of family income to our study of the economic well-being of working families, our analysis began with a tour through the most important income trends and debates. We found that the allegedly mild recession of 2001 and the productivity-rich recovery that followed were not kind to the real income trends of most families. The real median income fell 3%—or about $1,600 from 2000 to 2004—almost exclusively due to diminished employment opportunities.

Losses were greater for less-advantaged families, and notably, these post-2000 losses represented a sharp reversal from trends that prevailed in the latter 1990s, when full employment conditions in the job market led to much more broadly shared prosperity.

As stressed in the introduction, the gap between the U.S. economy's impressive productivity performance and the real income gains of most families stands as one of its greatest challenges. The findings in this chapter underscore that point. After a pause following the stock market bust in late 2000, inequality is once again on the rise, as would be expected given that the structural forces driving inequality upwards remain in place (see this book's introduction). Whether policy changes or a return to full employment help to offset or even reverse such inequalities is yet to be seen. As we stress above, tax policy has been trending in the other direction, exacerbating the elevated inequalities of our pre-tax distribution. Regarding the job market, unemployment is relatively low, yet wages have not been very responsive. In coming chapters, we investigate each one of these key aspects of the economic lives of working families in great detail.

CHAPTER 2

Income-class mobility
How much is there?

The previous chapter focused on some of the critical income challenges facing working families, including periods of relatively slow income growth, greater inequality, and the stress of increased family work hours. Such analysis is based on tracking income levels—like that of the median family—over time and comparing changes among income classes, such as the average income of different quintiles (i.e., fifths).

Those comparisons essentially take a snapshot of the economy at one point in time and compare it to the same snapshot at a later date. By examining, for example, the inflation-adjusted level of the median income at two points in time, we can learn about changes in the living standards of families in and around the median. These are clearly not, however, the same families; that is, the family in the middle of the income scale in 1997 may be at the 70th percentile 10 years later.

In this chapter we provide analysis that tracks the income progress of the same persons and families over time and examines their progress over their lifetimes. That is, we examine income, wealth, and other aspects of living standards through a lens of income mobility. A closely related part of the analysis examines the extent to which children's fortunes differ from that of their parents. A central dimension of this analysis is the role of intergenerational mobility: the degree to which a child's position in the economy is determined by that of their parents. Essentially, we want to understand the extent to which a child's economic fate is determined by their family's position in the income scale. If this association is relatively high, then the likelihood that a middle-class child will be a rich adult is diminished.

In fact, we find significant income correlations between parents and their children, implying that income mobility is at least partially restricted by a parent's position in the income scale. For example, one recent study finds the correlation between parents and children to be 0.6 (Mazumder 2005). We provide a detailed analysis of the implications of this correlation in this chapter, but one way to view the significance of this finding is to note that it implies that it would take a poor family of four with two children approximately nine to 10 generations—over 200 years—to achieve the income of the typical middle-income four-person family. Were that correlation only half that size—meaning income differences were half as persistent across generations—it would take four to five generations for the poor family to catch up.

In other words, the extent of income mobility across generations plays a determinant role in the living standards of American families. It is, for example, a key determinant of how many generations a family will be stuck at the low end of the income scale, or snuggly ensconced at the high end. Our folklore often emphasizes the "rags-to-riches," Horatio Alger-like stories that suggest that anyone with the gumption and smarts to prevail can lift themselves up by their bootstraps and transverse the income scale in a single generation. The reality in the United States, however, shows much less mobility than such stories suggest. Surprisingly, international comparisons reveal less mobility in America than other countries with comparably advanced economies, such as Germany, Canada, and Scandinavian countries. Note that these are countries that U.S. economists often criticize for their extensive social protections—each one has universal health coverage, for example (see Chapter 8)—yet their citizens experience greater mobility than do our own.

What explains the lack of mobility here? Certainly unequal education opportunities and historical discrimination play a role. In fact, the transmission across generations of these variables appears to be correlated as well, such that opportunities for advancement are limited for those with fewer economic resources. For example, we show that children from wealthy families have much greater access to top-tier universities than kids from low-income families, even once innate skills are taken into account. Though data on the persistence of wealth across generations are less robust, what data that do exist suggest that this too—the tendency of wealth concentration to be correlated across generations—is an important impediment to the upward mobility of the economy's "have-nots."

Intergenerational mobility

The extent of intergenerational mobility is one measure of economic opportunity in a society. If one's position in the earnings, income, or wealth distribution is largely determined at birth, we are left with a rigid society in which even those with prodigious talents will be held back by entrenched class barriers. Conversely, a society with a high level of intergenerational mobility, implying little correlation between parents' economic position and that of their children, is one with more fluidity between classes.

Economists gauge the extent of intergenerational mobility by measuring the correlation in income or earnings between parents and their children in adulthood. **Figure 2A** shows the correlation between the incomes of parents and that of their sons and daughters. The figure shows that about half of the variation in the incomes of children is explained by their parents' position in the income scale.

Does the data in Figure 2A show a relatively high or low level of income persistence? Certainly, a correlation of about half belies any notion of a totally fluid society with no

FIGURE 2A Intergenerational income persistence, sons and daughters, 2000

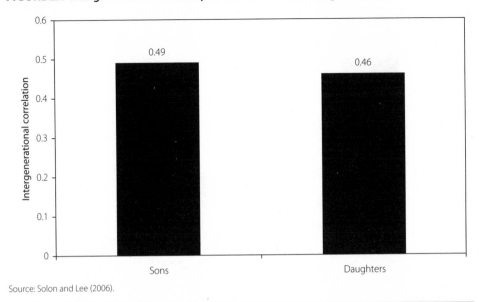

Source: Solon and Lee (2006).

class barriers, yet, without various benchmarks against which to judge these correlations, it is difficult to know what to make of their magnitude. In what follows, we try to present such benchmarks.

Figure 2B (which is based on earnings correlations from mobility expert Gary Solon) shows where sons of low-income fathers (i.e., those in the 10th percentile) would be expected to end up in the earnings scale based on their fathers' position.

Figure 2B also shows that, while income mobility certainly exists, the apple does not end up falling too far from the tree. Sons of low-earning fathers have slightly less than a 60% chance of reaching above the 20th percentile by adulthood, about a 20% chance of surpassing the median, and a very slight chance—4.5%—of ending up above the 80th percentile. To put this in the context of today's earners, a son whose father is at the 10th percentile ($16,000 a year) has a 5% chance of earning over $55,000 per year.

While the discussion so far has focused on the degree of mobility between generations, another question is how stable these values are over time. In other words, has the degree of income mobility between generations increased or fallen in recent years?

Given the rise in cross-sectional inequality shown in Chapter 1, this is a particularly important question. Some analysts have argued that, because the U.S. economy is so dynamic and mobile, we needn't worry about ever larger distances between income classes over time. Greater income mobility, they argue, will counteract these growing income gaps.

In other words, these critics may concede that the distance from the basement to the penthouse has grown further over time, as inequality has increased. But if a family that

FIGURE 2B Likelihood that low-income son ends up above various percentiles

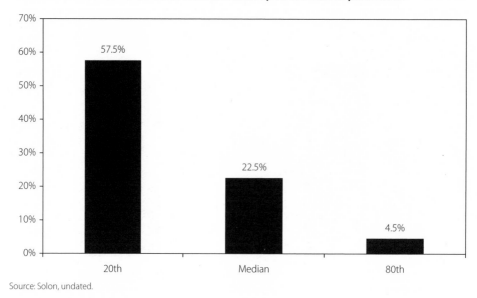

Source: Solon, undated.

starts out in the basement has a better chance these days of making it to the top floor than it used to, then we needn't be so concerned about cross-sectional inequality.

Those who make this mobility argument fail to either articulate or substantiate claims of increased mobility. Instead, these critics simply show evidence of economic mobility and leave it at that, as if mobility in and of itself should lessen the concern about increased inequality. But unless the *rate* of mobility is increasing relative to that of earlier decades, families are no more likely today to span the now-wider income gap. As we will show, there has been no such increase in income mobility, which implies that compared to earlier generations, today's families are truly confronted with greater gaps between income classes over the course of their lifetimes.

For example, one long-term analysis tracks the extent of intergenerational mobility since 1940, finding that, in fact, the rate of mobility has declined significantly in recent decades. As shown in **Figure 2C,** the correlation between the earnings of sons and the income of their families was flat or falling from 1950 to 1980, and then climbed through 2000, implying a trend toward diminished mobility (the relationship between mobility and the intergenerational correlation is inverse—higher correlations mean greater income persistence across generations, and thus less mobility). Note that this trend occurred over the same period when cross-sectional inequality was increasing, as documented in the last chapter. Thus, instead of faster mobility that might have offset the rise in inequality, the opposite trend occurred.

We note, however, that there is disagreement among mobility experts regarding this conclusion. Gary Solon, a premiere expert in this field, has not found evidence of any trend

FIGURE 2C Intergenerational mobility, 1950-2000

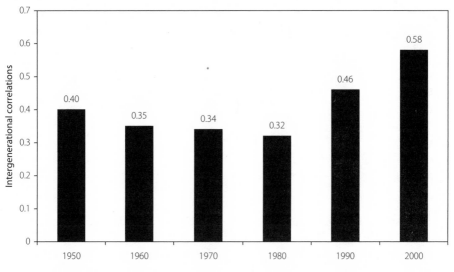

Source: Aaronson and Mazumder (2005).

in intergenerational mobility in his work. Even so, the findings in Figure 2C simply confirm that there has been no increase in mobility that might have offset the clear increases in inequality.

The roles of wealth and education

Mobility experts have investigated the factors that influence mobility across generations, especially education and wealth. Because education is correlated with income, if children of highly educated parents are themselves more likely to be highly educated, then they are also more likely to maintain the income position of their parents. Similarly, we might expect wealth to be a particularly correlated variable across generations, as wealthy parents make bequests to their children. Both factors arguably play a role in the income persistence displayed in Figure 2A.

Table 2.1 uses a transition matrix to show the extent of wealth mobility between children and their parents over the past few decades. The table shows where adult children (in their mid-30s) are positioned along the wealth scale in comparisons to their parents.

For example, 36% of those with parents in the bottom wealth quintile ended up there as adults; only 7% ended up in the top fifth of the scale. Adding the first two rows of the first column, 65% of children with parents in the least wealthy fifth ended up in the bottom 40% of the wealth scale. Moving to the middle fifth, 25% of the children of middle-quintile parents stayed in that middle fifth, while 24% moved up one fifth and 21% moved down

TABLE 2.1 Intergeneration wealth transmission, parents to children

Child's wealth quintile	Parent's wealth quintile				
	Lowest	Second	Middle	Fourth	Top
Lowest	36%	26%	16%	15%	11%
Second	29	24	21	13	16
Middle	16	24	25	20	14
Fourth	12	15	24	26	24
Fifth	7	12	15	26	36
Total	100	100	100	100	100

Source: Charles and Hurst (2003).

one fifth. At the top of the wealth scale, 36% of the children of the wealthiest parents were themselves in the top fifth, and 60% stayed in the top 40%.

Turning to education, researchers have found an "intergenerational elasticity" of about 0.4, meaning that about 40% of the extent of a person's educational attainment is determined by their parents' education level. An interesting corollary to the role of education is the increase in education returns over the last few decades (see Chapter 3), a development that amplifies the impact of education on the persistence of income inequality across generations. That is, a child of a parent who went to college has a greater chance of attending college him or herself. Therefore, that child also has a greater chance of benefiting from the higher relative wages earned by college-educated workers today compared to decades earlier.

There does not appear to have been an increase in the intergenerational educational correlation over the period wherein the earnings correlations between generations has grown (at least according to the data in Figure 2C). It is likely, then, that at least part of the increase is due to increased payoff to higher levels of education.

Figure 2D shows the significant role played by the large wage advantage of more highly educated workers in the United States relative to other countries (here again, the analysis focuses on the correlation between fathers' income and sons' earnings). The lower part of each bar shows the contribution of education to intergenerational mobility in three countries: the United States, United Kingdom, and West Germany. The rest of the bar in Figure 2D is attributable to the myriad other factors that explain intergenerational persistence of earnings. The figure shows that high educational returns in the United States lead to significantly higher levels of earnings immobility here relative to the two other countries in the figure (the other factors are also larger in the United States). In fact, as the last bar shows, were the United States' educational returns more like those in the United Kingdom and West Germany, the mobility correlation would be 24% lower.

Another relevant issue regarding mobility and education involves the quality of education accessible to children from families at different points in the income scale.

FIGURE 2D Intergenerational mobility, role of education

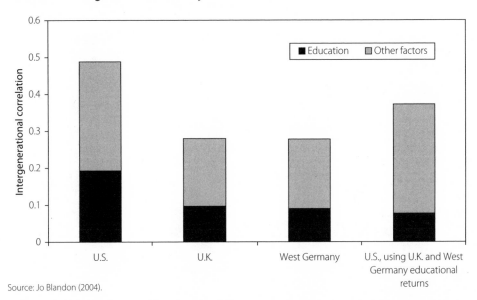

Source: Jo Blandon (2004).

Figure 2E compares the family income of children in the entering classes at top-tier universities and those entering community colleges. Over 70% of those in the top-tier universities come from families with the highest incomes, while less than 10% come from families in the bottom 50% of the income scale. At community colleges, however, the distribution is much more uniform.

Still, one might argue that the findings in Figure 2E simply represent a meritocracy at work, as those from high income families have, perhaps through their privileged positions, acquired the intellectual tools to succeed at the top schools. **Figure 2F** belies this argument, showing that even once we control for academic ability, it remains the case that children from higher income families are more likely to complete college. Each set of bars shows the probability of completing college for children based on income and their math test scores in the eighth grade. For example, the first set of bars, for the students with the lowest test scores, shows that 3% of students with both low scores and low incomes completed college, while 30% of low-scoring children from high-income families managed to complete college.

The fact that each set of bars has an upward gradient is evidence against a system completely driven by merit. The pattern implies that, at every level of test scores, higher income led to higher completion rates. The third set of bars, for example, shows that, even among the highest scoring students in eighth grade, only 29% of those from low-income families finished college, compared with 74% of those from the wealthiest families.

FIGURE 2E Income position of the entering class at top colleges and community colleges

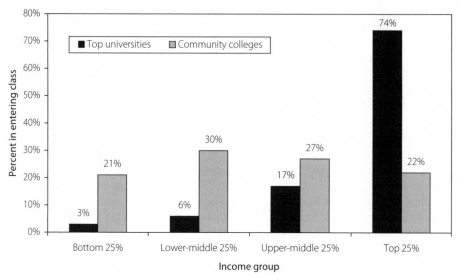

Source: Carnevale and Rose (2004).

FIGURE 2F College completion by income status and test scores

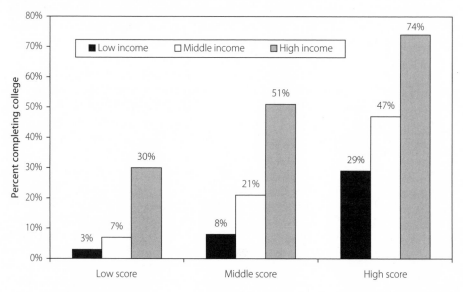

Source: Fox, Connolly, and Snyder (2005).

FIGURE 2G Intergenerational earnings mobility in six countries

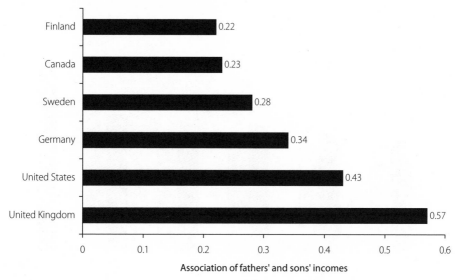

Source: Solon (2002).

Mobility from an international perspective

Though we have not stressed this point, it will surprise many readers to learn from Figure 2D that intergenerational mobility is lower here than in other advanced economies.

A deeply embedded piece of the United States social mythology is the Horatio Alger story: the notion that anyone who's willing and able can "pull themselves up by their bootstraps" and can achieve significant upward mobility. Conventional wisdom also holds that there are many more Mr. Algers in the United States than in Europe or Scandinavia. The idea behind such thinking is that there is a tradeoff between unregulated markets and mobility. Since today's U.S. economic model hews much more closely to the fundamentals of market capitalism—lower tax base, fewer regulations, less union coverage, no universal health care, and a much less comprehensive social contract—one would expect there to be greater mobility here than abroad.

However, as shown in **Figure 2G**, this is not the case, as the correlation between fathers' and sons' earnings are lower in all the comparison countries except the United Kingdom (and note that the results shown in Figure 2F actually find the United Kingdom to have higher mobility, so there is even some disagreement in the research on this point). The Scandinavian countries in Figure 2G—Finland and Sweden—both have significantly lower correlations (and therefore, higher rates of mobility) than that of the United States, as does Canada.

FIGURE 2H Intergenerational mobility: Percent of sons and daughters in lowest fifth, given fathers in lowest fifth

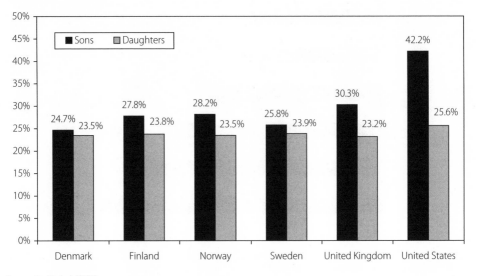

Source: Jantti et al. (2005).

These differences mean that poor families in the United States, for example, have a lesser chance of exiting their low-income status than similarly placed families in other countries. **Figure 2H** shows the probability that sons and daughters with fathers whose earnings placed them in the bottom fifth will themselves end up with low earnings. For sons, the chance of having the same low earnings as their fathers is at or below 30% in each country, with lower probabilities in the Scandinavian countries. The least mobility is for sons in the United States, who face a 42.2% chance of remaining low earners. Daughters have greater earnings mobility, though here, too, the United States is the least mobile country in the comparison.

Note also that these percentages are derived before taxes and transfers, and thus reflect greater mobility generated by market outcomes in these countries. In other words, these mobility rankings do not directly reflect the more extensive social safety nets these countries have compared to the United States. However, it may well be the case that these safety nets serve to diminish class barriers that loom large in the United States. Programs like universal health care (that exists in all the other countries in Figure 2H) and greater child care subsidies for working parents (in Scandinavian countries) may free up some of the less-advantaged members of these societies to better reach their economic potential than is possible in the United States.

FIGURE 2I Real median income growth, cohorts, age 30-50, 1954-2004

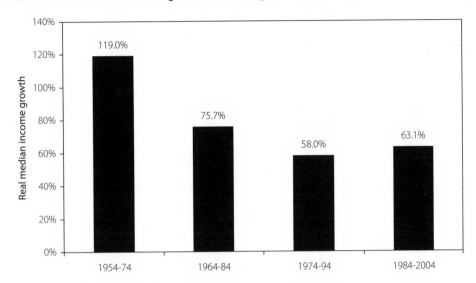

Source: Authors' analysis of U.S. Census Bureau data.

Family income mobility

Another way of viewing the extent of income mobility is to follow persons or families over time, known as a "cohort analysis" in economics parlance. In this section, we offer two examples of such analysis. First, we track the incomes of age cohorts over the past 50 years, showing that, while families surely continue to see their incomes grow as they age, they do so at a diminished rate. Second, we show that, by controlling for the expected growth of income as families age, most families end up in or near the income position in which they started out.

Cohort analysis

Figure 2I shows the percent growth in real family income for families in which the head of the family aged from about 30 to 50 years old (these are "synthetic cohorts"; they don't track the same people, but they track the same age groups). The fact that each bar shows positive real growth confirms the well-known fact that, as families pass through their prime years, their incomes generally rise, primarily due to the higher labor market returns of greater age and experience.

But what is important here is the general decline in the rate at which income grew for these prime-age cohorts over the post-war period. As young families passed through their most important earnings years, their income more than doubled from

TABLE 2.2 Share of young adults remaining in poorest fifth by cohort and race

Income fifth at age 24-26	At age 15-17			
	White		African American	
	Born 1952-59	Born 1962-69	Born 1952-59	Born 1962-69
Lowest fifth	22.0%	26.7%	55.4%	61.2%
Second fifth	26.1	27.6	22.1	12.2
Middle fifth	21.1	18.4	8.3	19.6
Fourth fifth	17.5	19.3	10.0	4.7
Top fifth	13.2	8.0	4.2	2.3
Total	100.0	100.0	100.0	100.0

Source: Corcoran and Matsudaira (2006).

the mid-1950s through the mid-1970s. For cohorts that started out in the mid-1960s, growth decelerated to about 75%, and then slowed further to 58% for the 1974-94 cohort. The cohort that went from ages 30 to 50 from 1984 to 2004 did better, due to the faster real wage growth in the 1990s (see Chapter 3), but only by about 5% (63% compared to 58%).

These falling growth rates make a real difference in living standards. Had the most recent cohort achieved the 75% growth rate of the1964-84 cohort, their median income in 2004 would have been $5,500 higher (about $76,500 instead of $71,000).

Table 2.2 engages in a similar cohort analysis, yet these data are based on following the same persons over time, from childhood until early adulthood. The values in the table show the likelihood that low-income teenagers will become low, middle, or high income adults, comparing a 1950s cohort with a 1960s cohort, by race.

Two important findings can be seen in these data. First, about half of white teenagers and three-quarters of black young adults ended up at or near their start point of the poorest fifth. Looking at the most recent cohort, 54.3% of white children ended up in either the first (lowest) or second fifth; the comparable share for African Americans was 73.4%. Compared to white children, more than twice the share of poor black children remained in the bottom fifth, regardless of cohort.

On the other end of the income scale, only a small share of poor African-American teenagers made it to the top fifth in early adulthood—2.3%—compared to 8.0% for whites.

Second, reflecting the findings from Figure 2C, the latter cohort was less likely to experience upward mobility, especially for African Americans. Whereas 55.4% of black teenagers from the earlier cohort remained in the first quintile by young adulthood, for the later cohort, the share was 61.2%. Across the white cohorts, the increase was smaller: from 22.0% to 26.7%. In other words, we again see the conspicuous absence of evidence that increased mobility offsets growing inequality.

Intragenerational mobility

The analysis so far has examined mobility between generations, and absolute gains for a given cohort over different time periods. Here we turn to mobility within a particular generation as they age—how families progress through the income distribution over time. This research seeks to understand whether families are more or less likely to end up in a higher or lower quintile as they age.

For this research, each person is assigned to an income fifth at the beginning and end of the relevant periods of observation based on his or her family's income. Different income cutoffs are used for each period, meaning that the 20th percentile upper limit in, for example, 1979 will be different than that of 1989. This approach to income mobility examines whether a family becomes better or worse off relative to other families, as opposed to better or worse off in terms of their actual incomes.

In particular, this kind of analysis tracks how families are doing relative to others they started with at the beginning of the periods in the same age cohort and income class. If each family's income grew by the same amount (in percentage terms), there would be no change in mobility, i.e., no changes in the relative positions of families in the income distribution. If, however, a family that starts out in the bottom fifth experiences faster income growth than other low-income families, it may move into a higher fifth, that is, that family experiences upward mobility.

Absolute gains of the type shown in Figure 2I are, of course, important, since higher real incomes enable families to raise their living standards. But inequality researchers have also found that *relative positions* mean a lot to people. Our well-being, along with our sense of accomplishment, is apparently not simply a matter of what we can afford to buy given our income levels, but it is also a matter of how we are faring relative to others from our same generation. Research shows that, if other families in our "cohort" pass us by—that is, if we are downwardly mobile relative to others—then we experience economic stress, even if our buying power has actually increased over time.

Table 2.3 presents three "transition matrices" for three time periods: the 1970s, 1980s, and 1990s (a similar analysis was presented in Table 1.1). Going across each row in the table, the numbers reveal the percent of persons who either stayed in the same quintile or moved to a higher or lower one. For example, the first entry in the top panel shows that just under half—49.4%—of families in the bottom quintile in 1969 were also in the bottom one in 1979 (the family income data are adjusted for family size). About the same share—49.1%—started and ended the 1970s in the richest quintile. The percent of "stayers" (i.e., those who did not move out of the fifth they started out in) are shown in bold.

Note that large transitions are uncommon. In each of the periods covered, the share of families moving from the poorest to the richest fifth never exceeds 4.3%. Conversely, the share moving from the top quintile to the bottom quintile never exceeds 5.0%. Those transitions that do occur are most likely to be a move up or down to the neighboring quintile. For example, in both the 1970s and 1980s, about 25% began and remained in the middle quintile. But close to 50% of those who started in the middle ended up in either the second or fourth quintile (for example, summing the relevant percentages in the 1980s results in 47.9%—23.3% + 24.6%).

Revisiting an earlier point, the extent to which the rate of mobility has changed over time is a critically important aspect of the inequality debate. Inequality analysis, such as

TABLE 2.3 Family income mobility over three decades

	Quintile in 1979				
Quintile in 1969	Lowest	Second	Third	Fourth	Top
Lowest	**49.4%**	24.5%	13.8%	9.1%	3.3%
Second	23.2	**27.8**	25.2	16.2	7.7
Third	10.2	23.4	**24.8**	23.0	18.7
Fourth	9.9	15.0	24.1	**27.4**	23.7
Top	5.0	9.0	13.2	23.7	**49.1**

	Quintile in 1989				
Quintile in 1979	Lowest	Second	Third	Fourth	Top
Lowest	**50.4%**	24.1%	15.0%	7.4%	3.2%
Second	21.3	**31.5**	23.8	15.8	7.6
Third	12.1	23.3	**25.0**	24.6	15.0
Fourth	6.8	16.1	24.3	**27.6**	25.3
Top	4.2	5.4	13.4	26.1	**50.9**

	Quintile in 1998				
Quintile in 1989	Lowest	Second	Third	Fourth	Top
Lowest	**53.3%**	23.6%	12.4%	6.4%	4.3%
Second	25.7	**36.3**	22.6	11.0	4.3
Third	10.9	20.7	**28.3**	27.5	12.6
Fourth	6.5	12.9	23.7	**31.1**	25.8
Top	3.0	5.7	14.9	23.2	**53.2**

Source: Bradbury and Katz (2002).

that in the last chapter, shows that income classes have grown further apart from each other over the last few decades. If the rate at which families move up the income scale has increased over time, then that could serve to offset this development. If anything, the panels in Table 2.3 show the opposite (as did Figure 2C).

In the 1990s, the "stayers," are a larger group than in either of the other two decades. For example, 36.3% started and ended in the second fifth in the 1990s, compared to 27.8% in the 1970s and 31.5% in the 1980s. In terms of upward mobility, when 12.4% moved out of the poorest and up into the fourth or fifth highest quintile in the 1970s, in the 1980s and 1990s that share dropped to 10.6% and 10.7%. Finally, as highlighted in **Figure 2J**, the share of families staying in the top quintile grew slightly over the decade, implying diminished mobility over time.

FIGURE 2J The share of families staying in the top fifth, 1969-98

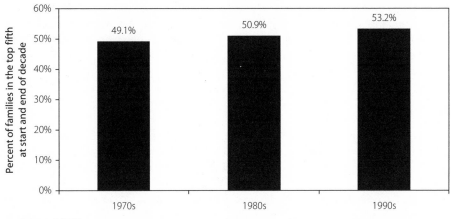

Source: Jantti et al. (2005).

TABLE 2.4 Income mobility for white and black families: Percent moving from the bottom 25% to the top 25% and vice versa

	Bottom to top quartile	Top to bottom quartile
All	7.3%	9.2%
White	10.2	9.0
Black	4.2	18.5
Black-white difference	-6.0%	9.5%

Source: Hertz (2003), Table 9.

Combining all family types masks important differences in mobility by race. Recent work by economist Tom Hertz examines the extent of upward and downward mobility by white and African American families. Some of his findings (presented in **Table 2.4)** reveal far less upward and greater downward mobility among black families relative to whites. The data give the percent of families by race who moved between the bottom and top 25% of the income scale between 1968 and 1998 (income data are adjusted for family size). The share of upwardly mobile families—those moving from the bottom quartile to the top—was 7.3%, slightly lower than the share moving the other direction (9.2%). But this overall measure is quite different by race. For white families, 10.2% were upwardly mobile compared to 4.2% for black families, a statistically significant difference. Note also that far more black families than whites were likely to fall from the top 25% to the bottom quartile:

18.5% compared to 9.0% (though given the small sample size of black families in the top 25%, the difference does not reach statistical significance).

These mobility studies show that, while some degree of family income mobility certainly exists in America, it has not accelerated in such a way as to offset the increase in income inequality discussed in the previous chapter. To the contrary, income mobility appears to have diminished somewhat over the 1990s. In addition, what mobility does exist varies significantly by race, as white families are more than twice as likely as black families to be upwardly mobile.

Conclusion

Chapter 1 revealed a sharp increase in income inequality over time, as income growth at the top of the scale far surpassed that of middle- and low-income families. That analysis, however, depended on snapshots of the U.S. income distribution in different time periods. In this chapter, we reviewed what is known about income mobility. To what extent are children's economic fates tied to their parent's income or wealth? Do most families end up about where they started in the income scale? Is the United States' less-regulated economy characterized by greater economic mobility?

The research on these questions finds that income, wealth, and opportunity are significantly correlated across generations. A son of a low-income father has only a small chance of achieving very high earnings in his adulthood. Almost two-thirds of children of low-wealth parents (those in the bottom 20% of wealth scale) will themselves have wealth levels that place them in the bottom 40% of scale. And while there is some disagreement in the literature, some research shows that the United States has become considerably less mobile over time. This finding is important, because it means there has been no increase in mobility that might serve to offset the higher levels of cross-sectional inequality.

One of the most surprising findings of this research is that the United States has less mobility than other advanced economies, even including those of Scandinavia. Certainly these results run counter to a simplistic story of a favorable tradeoff between less regulation or social protection and greater economic mobility. These other countries manage to provide far more extensive safety nets yet families there appear to face fewer class barriers.

Finding ways to diminish these barriers should be a primary concern of public policy. Clearly, access to higher education is important, but this can't be the sole solution. Such access increased significantly over this period, yet the United States became more immobile (in part due to the rise of educational returns). Other measures are necessary, including programs that help build wealth for those with few assets, and significant improvement in the quality of jobs and career trajectories for those starting out in the workforce.

CHAPTER 3

Wages
Growth stalls while productivity and compensation diverge

Because wages and salaries make up roughly three-fourths of total family income (the proportion is even higher among the broad middle class), wage trends are the driving force behind income growth and income inequality trends. This chapter examines and explains the trends in wage growth and wage inequality during the last few decades up through 2005, with a particular focus on the current business cycle, from 2000 to 2005, and the earlier cycles over the 1979-89 and 1989-2000 periods.

The major development in the labor market in recent years has been the stunning disconnect between the possibilities of improved pay and the reality of stunted pay growth. Productivity growth, which provides the possibility of improved living standards, picked up speed in the mid-1990s and accelerated even further from 2000 through 2005. Yet, despite this enormous growth in productivity, wages for the typical worker were about the same in 2005 as in 2001. Pay rose from 1996 to 2001, fueled by the higher productivity and the progressive lowering of unemployment to 4.0% by 2000. Moreover, the wage momentum carried forward through 2001 and into 2002 despite rising unemployment. The wage momentum from the late 1990s is important to understand when looking at trends over the 2000-05 period; all of the wage growth within that latter period occurred within the first two years. The poor job creation and increased job shortages during the early 2000s recession and lackluster recovery eventually knocked wage growth down so that prices rose at least as fast. This was the case even in 2005, when the unemployment rate fell to 5.1%. The failure of wages to rise for typical workers after 2001 is particularly interesting in light of the fact that half of the productivity growth of the 1995-2005 period occurred since then.

The poor wage performance of the past few years stands in strong contrast to the broad-based wage improvements of the 1995-2000 period, the earlier stage of the "new economy" when productivity growth first accelerated. In that period wages grew strongly across the board, rising at least 7% at every wage level. Remarkably, the fastest growth—11% or more—occurred at the two lowest wage levels (the 10th and 20th percentiles). However, workers with the very highest wages, at the 95th percentile, saw almost comparable wage growth of 10.6%. Since 2000, however, wage growth among lower-wage workers (the 30th percentile or below) has been modest, and the growth at the median, 3.0%, was less than half that of the 1995-2000 period.

There are three key elements of wage inequality. One is the gap at the "bottom," reflected in the difference between middle-wage (median-wage earners) and low-wage workers. Another is the "top half" gap between high-wage (90th or 95th percentile wage earners) and middle-wage earners. The third element is the gap at the very top, i.e., the growth of wages for those in the upper 1%, including CEOs. These three elements have had differing historical trajectories. The gap at the bottom grew in the 1980s but has been stable or declining ever since, whereas the "top half" wage gap has persistently grown since the late 1970s. The very highest earners have done considerably better than other workers for at least 30 years, but they have done extraordinarily well over the last 10 years.

Explaining these shifts in wage inequality requires attention to several factors that affect low-, middle-, and high-wage workers differently. The experience of the late 1990s is a reminder of the great extent to which a low unemployment rate benefits workers, especially low-wage earners. Correspondingly, the high levels of unemployment in the early and mid-1980s and in recent years disempowered wage earners and provided the context in which other forces—specifically, a weakening of labor market institutions and globalization—could drive up wage inequality. Significant shifts in the labor market, such as the severe drop in the minimum wage and deunionization, can explain one-third of growing wage inequality. Similarly, the increasing globalization of the economy—immigration, trade, and capital mobility—and the employment shift toward lower-paying service industries (such as retail trade) and away from manufacturing can explain, in combination, another third of the total growth in wage inequality. Macroeconomic factors also played an important role: high unemployment in the early 1980s greatly increased wage inequality, the low unemployment of the late 1990s reduced it, and high unemployment in recent years has renewed it.

The shape of wage inequality shifted in the late 1980s as the gap at the bottom—i.e., the 50/10 gap between middle-wage workers at the 50th percentile and low-wage workers at the 10th—began to shrink. However, over the last few years, this progress against wage inequality at the bottom has been halted among men and wage inequality at the bottom among women has resumed its growth. This reversal is partially the effect of the jobless recovery and the still-remaining shortage of jobs and partially a result of the continued drop in the real value of the minimum wage. The greatest increase in wage inequality at the bottom occurred among women and corresponded to the fall in the minimum wage over the 1980s, the high unemployment of the early 1980s, and the expansion of low-wage retail jobs. The positive trend in this wage gap over the 1990s owes much to increases in the minimum wage, low unemployment, and the slight, relative contraction in low-paying retail jobs in the late 1990s. The wage gap at the top half—the 90/50 gap between high- and middle-wage earners—continued its steady growth in the 1990s and early 2000s but at a slightly slower pace than in the 1980s. The continuing influence of globalization, deunionization, and the shift to lower-paying service industries ("industry shifts") can explain the continued growth of wage inequality at the top.

The erosion of the extent and quality of employer-provided benefits, most notably pensions and health insurance, is an important aspect of the deterioration in job quality for many workers. Employer-provided health care coverage eroded from 1979 until 1993-94, when it stabilized, and then began falling again after 2000 through 2004 (the latest data): coverage dropped from 69.0% in 1979 to 55.9% in 2004, with a 2.9 percentage-point fall since 2000. Employees have absorbed half the rise in costs for employer-provided health premiums (not counting any of the higher deductibles or co-pays paid by employees) since 1992, even though their share of costs in that year was just 14%. Employer-provided pension coverage tended to rise in the 1990s but receded by 2.8 percentage points from 2000 to 2004 to 45.5%, 5.1 percentage points below the level in 1979. Pension plan quality also receded as the share of workers in defined-benefit plans fell from 39% in 1980 to just 19% in 2003. Correspondingly, the share of workers with a defined-contribution plan (and no other plan) rose from 8% to 31%.

Young workers' prospects are a barometer of the strength of the labor market: when the labor market is strong for workers the prospects for young workers are very strong, and when the labor market is weak their prospects are very weak. Wages actually fell among every entry-level group, both high school and college-educated workers and both men and women in the period of sluggish wage growth since 2000. This contrasts to the extremely strong wage growth for each of these groups from 1995 to 2000, when wages rose roughly 10% for entry-level high school men and women and 20.9% for entry-level college men, 11.7% for college women.

Unionized workers earn higher wages than comparable non-union workers and also are 18.3% more likely to have health insurance, 22.5% more likely to have pension coverage, and 3.2% more likely to have paid leave. The erosion of unionization (from 43.1% in 1978 to just 19.2% in 2005) can account for 65% of the 11.1 percentage-point growth of the blue-collar/white-collar wage gap among men over the 1978-2005 period.

The real value of the minimum wage has been steadily falling in real terms, thereby causing the earnings of low-wage workers to seriously fall behind those of other workers and contributing to rising wage inequality. Those affected by the lower minimum wage make important contributions to their family's economic well-being. For instance, minimum wage earners contribute 58% of their family's weekly earnings; in 43% of the affected families the minimum wage earner contributed all of the family's earnings. Moreover, there are 7.3 million children living in the families that would benefit from a modest minimum wage increase. While minorities are disproportionately represented among minimum wage workers, 60% are white. These workers also tend to be women (59% of the total) and concentrated in the retail and hospitality industries (46% of all minimum wage earners are employed there, compared to just 21% of all workers).

The 1980s, 1990s, and 2000s have been prosperous times for top U.S. executives, especially relative to other wage earners. Over the 1992 to 2005 period the median CEO saw pay rise by 186.2%, while the median worker saw wages rise by just 7.2%. In 1965 U.S. CEOs in major companies earned 24 times more than an average worker; this ratio grew to 300 at the end of the recovery in 2000. The fall in the stock market reduced CEO stock-related pay (e.g., options), but by 2005 CEO pay had recovered to the point where it was 262 times that of the average worker. The lion's share of the gains for the top 1% accrued to the upper 10% of that elite group. Of the 3.6 percentage-point gain in the share of all earnings that the top 1% experienced between 1989 and 2000, 3.2 of them accrued to very upper tier.

The jobs of the future will require greater education credentials, but not to any great extent. In 2004 the occupational composition of jobs required that 27.7% of the workforce have a college degree or more. This share will rise by just one percentage point, to 28.7%, by 2014.

The analysis of wages proceeds as follows. The first half of the chapter documents changes in the various dimensions of the wage structure, i.e., changes in average wages and compensation and changes by occupation, gender, wage level, education level, age, and race and ethnicity. These shifts in the various dimensions of wage inequality are then assessed and explained by focusing on particular factors such as unemployment, industry shifts, deunionization, the value of the minimum wage, globalization and immigration, and technology.

An extraordinary 10 years

Our usual analysis in this book of income, wages, wealth, and the like examines changes at comparable points between business cycles, because it is the underlying movement of the economy, from peak to peak, that is the major force behind changes in income and wages and the standard of living. But a traditional analysis of business cycles—looking at wage growth from 1989 to 2000 and then from 2000 to 2005—would mask a surprising element of the wage story. Understanding the trends in wages and compensation over the 1990s and early 2000s requires an appreciation of the extraordinary characteristics of both the 1995-2000 and the 2000-05 periods.

What has been so extraordinary? First, productivity gained speed in the mid-1990s to rise 2.5% a year, double the rate of the prior 22 years back to 1973. This shift is important because productivity growth means that there is a bigger "economic pie" to provide rising wages and living standards. Second, productivity growth accelerated even further in the early 2000s, to a rate of 3.3% a year. In all, over the 1995-2005 period the output of goods and services per hour of work (productivity) grew a remarkable 33.4%; had pay followed, the annual earnings and incomes for most working people would have risen by a third. This is the third extraordinary fact: despite this enormous growth in productivity, wages for the typical worker were about the same in 2005 as in 2001. Pay rose from 1996 to 2001, fueled by the higher productivity and the progressive lowering of unemployment to 4.0% by 2000. Moreover, the wage momentum carried forward through 2001 and into 2002 despite rising unemployment. The wage momentum from the late 1990s is important to understand when looking at trends over the 2000-05 period; all of the wage growth within that latter period occurred within the first two years. The poor job creation and increased job short-

FIGURE 3A Changes in productivity and hourly wages, benefits, and compensation, 1995-2005

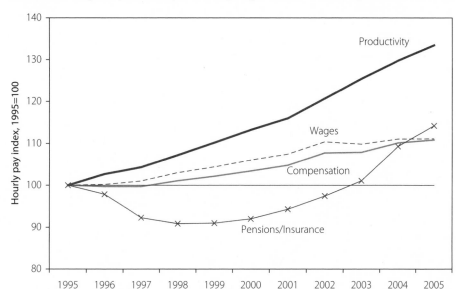

Source: Authors' analysis.

ages during the early 2000s recession and lackluster recovery eventually knocked wage growth down so that prices rose at least as fast. This was the case even in 2005, when the unemployment rate fell to 5.1% (however, as shown in Chapter 4, the unemployment rate does not necessarily reflect the degree of the job shortage).

In short, historically high productivity growth and historically low unemployment have had little if any impact on compensation and wages. The 33.4% increase in productivity between 1995 and 2005 was associated with benefits growth (health and pension) of less than half that much and wage growth for typical workers one-third that much. After 2001 there has been basically no wage improvement for typical workers, even though half of the productivity growth of the 1995-2005 period occurred since then.

The stunning disconnect between the possibilities of improved pay and the reality of stunted pay growth is illustrated in **Figures 3A** and **3B**. Figure 3A shows the disparity since 1995 (the figure is indexed so that 1995=100) between hourly productivity growth and average hourly compensation (wages and benefits plus payroll taxes), hourly wages, and hourly benefits (health and pension coverage). Benefits declined in the late 1990s but grew quickly over the last few years (some of this growth reflects the strong stock market of the late 1990s which allowed employers to make only small contributions to pensions; health care costs were also better under control in the late 1990s). By 2005, benefits exceeded 1995 levels by about 14%. Wages and total compensation per hour grew in tandem, by just

FIGURE 3B Changes in hourly and annual wages and productivity, 1995-2005

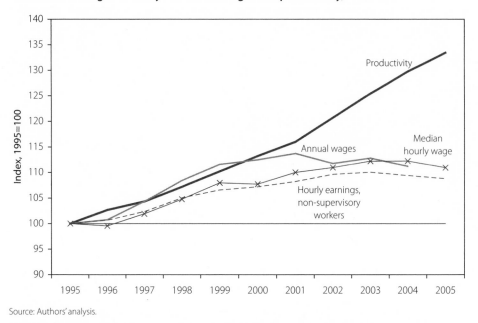

Source: Authors' analysis.

11%, and so the disappointing wage performance probably cannot be blamed on higher benefit costs. By contrast, note the top line, which shows the 33.4% growth in productivity from 1995 to 2005.

Figure 3B focuses on measures for typical workers, i.e., the hourly wage of the median worker and the hourly earnings of production, nonsupervisory workers (about 80% of employment). These measures show wages rising through 2001 and then flattening since, despite lower unemployment and fast productivity growth. The trend in annual wages (a measure that reflects changes in work hours as well as hourly wages) also shows a total lack of improvement in the years past 2001 (the latest data are for 2004).

With this framework in mind, we now turn to an exploration of the various dimensions of the growth of wages, benefits, and compensation.

Contrasting work hours and hourly wage growth

To understand changes in wage trends, it is important to distinguish between trends in annual, weekly, and hourly wages. Trends in annual wages, for instance, are driven by changes in both hourly wages and the amount of time spent working (weeks worked per year and hours worked per week). Likewise, weekly wage trends reflect changes in hourly pay and weekly hours. In this chapter we focus on the hourly pay levels of the workforce

TABLE 3.1 Trends in average wages and average hours, 1967-2004 (2005 dollars)

Year	Productivity per hour (1992=100)	Wage levels			Hours worked		
		Annual wages	Weekly wages	Hourly wages	Annual hours	Weeks per year	Hours per week
1967	65.6	$25,509	$585.68	$14.88	1,716	43.5	39.3
1973	76.3	29,672	683.06	17.70	1,679	43.4	38.6
1979	81.9	29,891	681.67	17.55	1,703	43.8	38.8
1989	94.1	32,718	720.91	18.35	1,783	45.4	39.3
1995	102.0	33,657	732.58	18.43	1,827	45.9	39.8
2000	115.5	37,860	806.45	20.18	1,876	46.9	40.0
2004	132.4	37,424	795.17	20.08	1,864	47.1	39.6
*Annual growth rate**							
1967-73	2.5%	2.5%	2.6%	2.9%	-0.4%	0.0%	-0.3%
1973-79	1.2	0.1	0.0	-0.1	0.2	0.2	0.1
1979-89	1.4	0.9	0.6	0.4	0.5	0.3	0.1
1989-2000	1.9	1.3	1.0	0.9	0.5	0.3	0.2
1989-95	1.3	0.5	0.3	0.1	0.4	0.2	0.2
1995-2000	2.5	2.4	1.9	1.8	0.5	0.4	0.1
2000-04	3.4	-0.3	-0.4	-0.1	-0.2	0.1	-0.2

* Log growth rates.
Source: Authors' analysis of CPS data and Murphy and Welch (1989). For detailed information on table sources, see Table Notes.

and its sub-groups so that we can distinguish changes in earnings resulting from more (or less) pay rather than more (or less) work. Also, the hourly wage can be said to represent the "true" price of labor (exclusive of benefits, which we analyze separately). Moreover, changes in the distribution of annual earnings have been predominantly driven by changes in the distribution of hourly wages and not by changes in work time. Chapter 4 goes on to address employment, unemployment, underemployment, and other issues related to changes in work time and opportunities.

Table 3.1 illustrates the importance of distinguishing between annual, weekly, and hourly wage trends. Over the 2000-04 period (2004 is the latest year of data we have in this series), annual wages declined by 0.3% annually. However, hourly wages, in inflation-adjusted terms, fell by 0.1% annually. The reason for this disparity was the decline in annual work hours, driven by a shorter workweek (weeks worked per year ticked up slightly, but not enough to keep total hours steady). In contrast, the annual wage and salary of the average worker in inflation-adjusted terms grew substantially faster than the average hourly wage in each of the last two decades because of a rise in work hours. Specifically, hourly wages grew 0.4% each year over the 1979-89 period and 0.9% over the 1989-2000 period. Yet annual wages grew at 0.9% and 1.3%, respectively, reflecting hourly wage growth and the 0.5% growth in annual hours worked in each period.

The most remarkable story in Table 3.1, however, is the sharp acceleration in hourly wage growth (to 1.8%) in the 1995-2000 period, a sharp departure from the measly 0.1% growth of the earlier part of the business cycle from 1989 to 1995 and the slow growth (0.4%) of the prior business cycle of 1979-89. As noted in the previous section, this strong hourly wage growth subsided in the early 2000s, as average wages per hour fell 0.1% annually from 2000 to 2004, despite faster productivity growth than in the late 1990s (3.4% vs. 2.5%).

Not surprisingly, trends in family income correspond to the shift from strong annual wage growth in the late 1990s and the decline thereafter. For instance, the strong pickup in wage growth in the late 1990s, along with an even stronger pickup of wage growth at the bottom end of the wage scale (detailed below), is the main factor behind the widespread improvements in family income in the late 1990s, discussed in Chapter 1, and the reductions in poverty, discussed in Chapter 6. Similarly, the fall in annual wages and reduced work hours in recent years has led to falling family incomes and higher poverty.

Faster productivity growth has been considered the main force behind the faster wage growth in the late 1990s. Productivity growth in 1996 and later years (2.5% annual growth from 1995 to 2000) was substantially higher than the productivity growth earlier in the business cycle (1.3% in 1989-95) or in the two prior business cycles (roughly 1.2% to 1.4%). Thus, productivity growth was at least 1% faster each year in the late 1990s than in the prior 22 years and comparable to the growth of the late 1960s (2.5% from 1967 to 1973).

There are two parts to an explanation for the faster wage growth in the late 1990s: first, persistent low unemployment enabled workers to attain a rising wage (through better jobs, better pay offers for new jobs, and greater bargaining power) that more closely reflected productivity growth; second, productivity growth accelerated (which itself requires an explanation, not discussed here). When the low unemployment of the late 1990s yielded to recessionary conditions, the strong hourly wage growth ratcheted down but remained positive (rather than falling in real terms) for a few years before starting to fall in 2002 or so. When the tight labor markets of the late 1990s disappeared, fast productivity growth no longer translated into strong wage growth.

Annual hours of work per worker generally grew over the 1973 to 2000 period, helping to fuel the growth in family income (as discussed in Chapter 1). The decline in work hours in the early 2000s recession had not been reversed by 2004, and whether this business cycle produces a continuation of the long-term trend toward more hours worked (before the next recession is upon us) is yet to be determined.

Contrasting compensation and wage growth

A worker's pay or total compensation is made up of both non-wage payments, referred to as fringe benefits, and wages. Much of our analysis in this chapter focuses on wages because there are no data on workers' hourly compensation, including benefits, that can be analyzed by decile, race, gender, and education. But the available data do allow an examination of overall compensation trends and how they differ from overall wage trends.

TABLE 3.2 Growth in private-sector average hourly wages, benefits, and compensation, 1948-2005 (2005 dollars)

Year	Wages & salaries	Benefits*	Total compensation**	Benefit share of compensation
Hourly pay (NIPA)				
1948	$8.92	$0.48	$9.40	5.1%
1989	18.54	4.21	22.75	18.5
Annual percent change				
1948-73	2.6%	7.3%	3.0%	
1973-79	0.2	5.2	1.0	
1979-89	0.8	1.0	0.8	
Hourly pay (ECEC)*				
1987	$18.23	$4.39	$22.62	19.4%
1989	17.85	4.39	22.24	19.7
1995	17.47	4.34	21.81	19.9
2000	18.52	4.03	22.55	17.9
2005	19.41	4.76	24.17	19.7
Annual percent change				
1989-2000	0.3%	-0.8%	0.1%	
1989-95	-0.4	-0.2	-0.3	
1995-2000	1.2	-1.5	0.7	
2000-05	0.9	3.4	1.4	

* Includes payroll taxes, health, pension, and other non-wage benefits.
** Deflated by CPI for all items except health, with is deflated by CPI medical care index.
*** Data are for March.
Source: Authors' analysis of BLS Employer Costs for Employee Compensation (ECEC) data and BEA National Income and Products Accounts (NIPA) data.

Table 3.2 examines the growth of compensation using the only two available data series. We employ the wage and compensation data that are part of the National Income and Product Accounts (NIPA) to track the historical trends from 1948 to 1989. These NIPA data are the Commerce Department's effort to measure the size of the national economy, termed the gross domestic product. Compensation levels exceed wage levels because they include employer payments for health insurance, pensions, and payroll taxes (primarily payments toward Social Security and unemployment insurance). We track more recent trends with data drawn from the Bureau of Labor Statistics' Employer Costs for Employee Compensation (ECEC) survey, which provides the value of wages and employer-provided benefits for each year since 1987. These data vary from those in NIPA because they describe only the private sector (government employment is excluded) and because the definition of "hours worked" is different.

Measured over the long term, benefits have become a more important part of the total compensation package. In 1948 only 5.1% of compensation comprised payroll taxes and health and pension programs. By 1989 the share had risen to 18.5%. But the benefits share of compensation has remained flat for about 20 years and even fell in the late 1990s (it regained ground in recent years). We examine trends of specific benefits, such as health, in a later section.

In the 2000-05 period benefits grew much faster than average wages, 3.4% vs. 0.9%, but since benefits make up only about 20% of compensation the rise in total compensation was just 1.4% a year. A different trend prevailed in the late 1990s, when benefits declined by 1.5% annually while wages rose 1.2%. Over the entire 1995-2005 period, as well as during the longer 1989-2005 period (and for 1979-89), the growth of wages and compensation was comparable. Thus, although compensation and wage trends may diverge during particular sub-periods, this has not generally been the case since 1979. One implication of compensation and wages growing roughly in tandem is that analyses (such as the one below) that focus on wage trends are using an appropriate proxy for compensation, at least on average. However, analyses of wage growth sometimes overstate the corresponding growth of compensation, as in the late 1990s, and sometimes understate compensation growth, as in recent years. If benefits inequality has grown faster than wage inequality, as a few studies have suggested, then our analysis of wage trends understates the growth of compensation inequality.

We return to a discussion of benefits growth below when we examine specific benefits, such as health insurance and pensions.

Wages for production and nonsupervisory workers

We now turn to the pattern of growth or decline in wages for the various segments of the workforce since 1973. Again, there are at least two distinct "wage regimes" over the last 30 years, one from 1973-95 that consisted of stagnant average wage growth and real wage reductions for the vast majority, and one from 1995 to the present that consists of faster real wage growth in the late 1990s followed by slower growth and then declining wages for typical workers in the 2000s. In general, the workers who experienced the greatest fall in real wages in the 1973-95 period were likely to be men, workers who initially had lower wages, workers without a college degree, blue-collar or service workers, or younger workers. In the early 1990s, however, wages also stagnated among male white-collar and college-educated workers. In the late 1990s real wages grew most rapidly among low-wage workers, the very highest-paid workers, and younger workers. The recession of the early 2000s knocked down wage growth, although the highest-wage earners fared best.

The data in **Table 3.3** and **Figure 3C** show wage trends for the 80% of the workforce who are production workers in manufacturing and nonsupervisory workers in other sectors. This category includes factory workers, construction workers, and a wide variety of service-sector workers ranging from restaurant and clerical workers to nurses and teachers; it leaves out higher-paid managers and supervisors. From 2000 to 2005 the hourly wage of production/nonsupervisory workers grew 0.3% per year, though in the last year (2004-05) it didn't grow at all (see Figure 3C). The momentum of the strong wage growth of the

TABLE 3.3 Hourly and weekly earnings of private production and nonsupervisory workers,* 1947-2005 (2005 dollars)

Year	Real average hourly earnings	Real average weekly earnings
1947	$9.00	$361.02
1967	14.12	535.25
1973	15.76	581.67
1979	15.78	561.74
1989	14.91	514.24
1995	14.81	508.43
2000	15.88	544.81
2005	16.11	543.65

Business cycles	Annual growth rate	
1947-67	2.3%	2.0%
1967-73	1.8	1.4
1973-79	0.0	-0.6
1979-89	-0.6	-0.9
1989-2000	0.6	0.5
1989-95	-0.1	-0.2
1995-2000	1.4	1.4
2000-05	0.3	0.0
1979-2005	0.1	-0.1

* Production and nonsupervisory workers account for more than 80% of wage and salary employment.
Source: Authors' analysis.

late 1990s was offset by the recession, but it took a few years for the recession's impact to be felt; this delay reflects the fact that macroeconomic conditions affect the labor market with a long lag. As we have discussed above, wage growth over the 2000-05 period was substantially less than the 1.4% growth over the 1995-2000 period.

The differences in trends between the early and latter part of the 1989-2000 period are striking: hourly wages fell 0.1% a year from 1989 to 1995 and then grew 1.4% a year from 1995 to 2000, a turnaround of 1.5 percentage points. Over the longer term, from 1979 to 2005, wages are up only slightly, from $15.78 in 1979 to $16.11 in 2005, a growth of just 0.1% per year—virtually stagnant. Figure 3C also tracks the hourly compensation of production/nonsupervisory workers; with the exception of the 1970s, when compensation grew far faster than wages as wages stagnated (see the divergence between the two lines arising in the 1970s), compensation and wage growth show similar trends.

The trend in weekly earnings corresponds closely to that of hourly earnings, with a decline in the 1980s and early 1990s and a shift to strong positive growth after 1995. The

FIGURE 3C Hourly wage and compensation growth for production/non-supervisory workers, 1959-2005

Source: Authors' analysis.

fall in weekly hours in 2000 and after meant that growth in weekly wages dropped to zero, even while hourly wages increased 0.3% annually. The weekly earnings of production and nonsupervisory workers in 2005 were $543.56 per week (in 2005 dollars), nearly $20 less than in 1979 and almost $40 less than in 1973.

Wage trends by wage level

For any given trend in average wages, particular groups of workers will experience different outcomes if wage inequality grows, as it has throughout the last 26 years: it grew pervasively in the 1980s, and grew at the top and fell or was stable at the bottom through most of the 1990s and 2000s. Wage trends can be described by examining groups of workers by occupation, education level, and so on, but doing so omits the impact of changes such as increasing inequality within occupation or education groups. The advantage of an analysis of wage trends by wage level or percentile (the 60th percentile, for instance, is the wage at which a worker earns more than 60% of all earners but less than 40% of all earners) is that it captures all of the changes in the wage structure.

Table 3.4 provides data on wage trends for workers at different percentiles (or levels) in the wage distribution, thus allowing an examination of wage growth for low-, middle-, and high-wage earners. The data are presented for the cyclical peak years 1973, 1979,

TABLE 3.4 Wages for all workers by wage percentile, 1973-2005 (2005 dollars)

Year	Wage by percentile*									
	10	20	30	40	50	60	70	80	90	95
Real hourly wage										
1973	$6.79	$8.20	$9.74	$11.33	$12.99	$14.91	$17.31	$19.80	$24.88	$31.21
1979	7.37	8.40	9.86	11.60	13.13	15.22	17.99	20.96	25.64	31.31
1989	6.33	7.88	9.45	11.29	13.13	15.33	18.24	21.81	27.54	33.85
1995	6.44	7.87	9.41	11.07	12.89	15.25	18.18	22.01	28.44	35.67
2000	7.15	8.81	10.29	11.90	13.88	16.42	19.47	23.66	30.92	39.44
2005	7.20	8.84	10.21	12.12	14.29	16.82	19.86	24.44	32.49	41.70
Percent change										
1973-79	8.4%	2.4%	1.2%	2.4%	1.0%	2.1%	3.9%	5.9%	3.1%	0.3%
1979-89	-14.1	-6.2	-4.2	-2.7	0.0	0.7	1.4	4.0	7.4	8.1
1989-2000	13.0	11.8	8.9	5.4	5.7	7.1	6.7	8.5	12.3	16.5
1989-95	1.8	-0.1	-0.5	-2.0	-1.8	-0.5	-0.3	0.9	3.3	5.4
1995-2000	11.1	11.9	9.4	7.5	7.7	7.7	7.1	7.5	8.7	10.6
2000-05	0.6	0.3	-0.8	1.8	3.0	2.4	2.0	3.3	5.1	5.7
1979-2005	-2.3	5.2	3.5	4.4	8.9	10.5	10.4	16.6	26.7	33.2

* The Xth percentile wage is the wage at which X% of the wage earners earn less and (100-X)% earn more.
Source: Authors' analysis of CPS ORG.

1989, and 2000, and for the most recent year for which we have a complete year of data, 2005, as well as for 1995-2000 (so we can examine the character of the rebound in wage growth over this period and since this period).

Wage growth slowed between the 1995-2000 period and the 2000-05 period, though wage growth has remained better than that of the 1979-95 period of relatively stagnant wages. Wages grew strongly across the board from 1995 to 2000, rising at least 7% at every wage level. Remarkably, the fastest growth was at the two lowest wage levels (10th and 20th), where wage growth was at least 11%. However, workers with the very highest wages, at the 95th percentile, saw almost comparable wage growth of 10.6%. Since 2000, however, wage growth among lower wage workers (30th percentile or below) has been modest, and the growth at the median, 3.0%, was less than half that of the 1995-2000 period. Wage growth among higher-wage workers was also much slower in recent years than in the 1995-2000 period. This wage deceleration, thus, has been pervasive. The deterioration in wage growth is even stronger than Table 3.4 shows because the momentum of the late 1990s carried wage growth into 2002 but was absent in the 2002-05 period (as seen in the earlier Figures 3A and 3B).

The deterioration in real wages from 1979 to 1995 was both broad and uneven. Wages were stagnant or fell for the bottom 60% of wage earners over the 1979-95 period and grew

TABLE 3.5 Wages for male workers by wage percentile, 1973-2005 (2005 dollars)

Year	Wage by percentile*									
	10	20	30	40	50	60	70	80	90	95
Real hourly wage										
1973	$8.02	$10.29	$12.13	$13.90	$15.76	$17.87	$19.67	$22.63	$28.83	$34.74
1979	8.11	10.31	12.40	14.43	16.51	18.75	21.03	24.43	29.74	35.67
1989	7.25	9.08	11.14	13.19	15.35	18.07	20.90	24.49	30.67	38.08
1995	6.98	8.82	10.49	12.61	14.79	17.28	20.30	24.28	31.66	39.59
2000	7.78	9.54	11.40	13.51	15.81	18.39	21.64	26.26	34.98	43.80
2005	7.79	9.64	11.24	13.37	15.64	18.33	21.79	26.71	36.08	46.40
Percent change										
1973-79	1.1%	0.1%	2.2%	3.8%	4.7%	4.9%	7.0%	7.9%	3.2%	2.7%
1979-89	-10.6	-11.9	-10.2	-8.6	-7.0	-3.6	-0.7	0.2	3.1	6.8
1989-2000	7.4	5.2	2.4	2.4	2.9	1.8	3.6	7.2	14.0	15.0
1989-95	-3.6	-2.8	-5.8	-4.4	-3.7	-4.4	-2.8	-0.8	3.2	3.9
1995-2000	11.4	8.2	8.7	7.1	6.9	6.4	6.6	8.1	10.5	10.6
2000-05	0.1	1.0	-1.5	-1.1	-1.1	-0.3	0.7	1.7	3.1	5.9
1979-2005	-3.9	-6.5	-9.4	-7.4	-5.3	-2.2	3.6	9.3	21.3	30.1

* The Xth percentile wage is the wage at which X% of the wage earners earn less and (100-X)% earn more.
Source: Authors' analysis of CPS ORG.

modestly for higher-wage workers—over 16 years the growth was just 5.0% at the 80th percentile and 10.9-13.9% at the 90th and 95th percentiles. Starting in the early 1990s low-wage workers experienced either more or comparable wage growth to that of middle-wage workers, so that the expanding wage gap between the middle and bottom lessened and then stabilized. Increases in the minimum wage in the early and late 1990s and the drop in unemployment in the late 1990s can explain this trend.

This overall picture, however, masks different outcomes for men and women. Among men over the 2000-05 period, wages declined slightly or were relatively stagnant for the bottom 70%, grew 3.1% at the 90th decile, and 5.9% for the highest-wage earners (**Table 3.5**). Thus, the wage gap between the top and the middle continued to grow strongly in the 2000-05 period. This trend contrasts with the strong broad-based wage growth of the latter 1990s, when low-wage workers fared better than middle-wage workers. Over the preceding 1979-95 period, the wage declines were substantial, exceeding 10% for the median male worker (Table 3.5 and **Figure 3D**). Between 1979 and 1989, the median male hourly wage fell 7.0%, and low-wage men lost 10.6%. In the early 1990s, across-the-board wage declines of roughly 3-5% affected the bottom 70% of male earners. Even high-wage men at the 90th percentile, who earned about $30 per hour in 1979, did well only in relative terms, since their wage was only about 6% higher in 1995 than in 1979.

FIGURE 3D Change in real hourly wages for men by wage percentile, 1973-2005

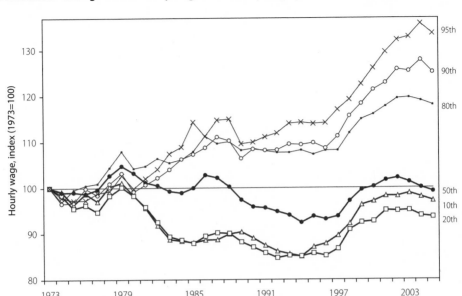

Source: Authors' analysis of CPS ORG.

As with the overall trend, the pattern of male wage deterioration shifted between the 1980s and the early 1990s. In the 1980s, wages fell most at the lower levels, while in the 1990s wages eroded in the middle and at the bottom. Thus, the wage gap between middle- and low-wage men was stable in the early 1990s, although the gap between high-wage men (at the 90th percentile) and middle- and low-wage men continued to grow.

Over the longer term (1979-2005), the 95th percentile male wage grew faster than any other, at 30.1%, while wages at the middle and lower end fell. The median male wage in 2005, for instance, was still 5.3% below its 1979 level and was $0.12 less than its level in 1973.

Wages grew more among women than men over the 2000-05 period; they rose from about 2-5% for the middle 40% and just about 1% for the lowest-wage women (**Table 3.6**). The highest-wage women, those at the 95th percentile, enjoyed 8.3% wage growth in this period.

As with men, women's wages rose strongly across the board in the 1995-2000 period. It is remarkable that this wage growth was fairly even among all women, from about 8% to 10.5%. But the recessionary conditions and weak recovery in recent years knocked down wage growth for women, as it did for men.

The most persistent wage growth between 1979 and 1995 was among the highest-wage women (Table 3.6 and **Figure 3E**). For instance, wages grew 22.2% for women at the 95th percentile from 1979 to 1989 and another 10.7% over 1989-95. In contrast,

TABLE 3.6 Wages for female workers by wage percentile, 1973-2005 (2005 dollars)

Year	Wage by percentile*									
	10	20	30	40	50	60	70	80	90	95
Real hourly wage										
1973	$5.65	$7.02	$7.90	$8.83	$9.95	$11.20	$12.62	$14.55	$17.99	$21.26
1979	7.03	7.62	8.27	9.22	10.35	11.76	13.10	15.24	18.97	22.42
1989	5.89	7.26	8.40	9.65	11.22	12.82	15.10	18.09	22.71	27.39
1995	6.16	7.35	8.59	9.88	11.35	13.07	15.53	18.98	24.39	30.31
2000	6.80	8.09	9.32	10.80	12.32	14.25	16.88	20.51	26.95	33.10
2005	6.88	8.17	9.75	11.04	12.82	14.99	17.80	21.78	28.86	35.84
Percent change										
1973-79	24.5%	8.5%	4.7%	4.4%	4.0%	5.0%	3.8%	4.8%	5.4%	5.5%
1979-89	-16.2	-4.7	1.6	4.7	8.4	9.0	15.2	18.7	19.7	22.2
1989-2000	15.4	11.5	10.9	11.9	9.8	11.1	11.8	13.4	18.7	20.9
1989-95	4.6	1.2	2.2	2.4	1.1	2.0	2.9	4.9	7.4	10.7
1995-2000	10.3	10.1	8.5	9.3	8.6	9.0	8.7	8.0	10.5	9.2
2000-05	1.2	1.0	4.7	2.2	4.0	5.2	5.5	6.2	7.1	8.3
1979-2005	-2.1	7.3	18.0	19.7	23.9	27.5	35.9	42.9	52.2	59.9

* The Xth percentile wage is the wage at which X% of the wage earners earn less and (100-X)% earn more.
Source: Authors' analysis of CPS ORG.

FIGURE 3E Change in real hourly wages for women by wage percentile, 1973-2005

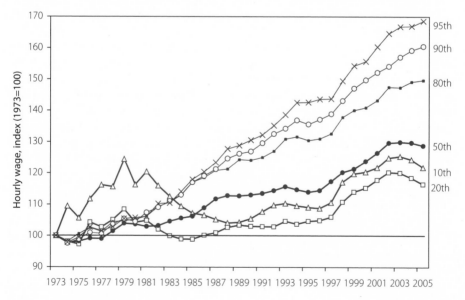

Source: Authors' analysis of CPS ORG.

low-wage women saw their wages fall in the 1980s; the lowest paid at the 10th percentile experienced a decline of 16.2%. In the early 1990s women's wages at the 40th percentile and above grew more slowly than in the 1980s, with the wages in the middle dropping to a stagnant 1.1% growth over the six years (they grew 8.4% from 1979 to 1989). A very positive development of the early 1990s was the fact that wages for 10th percentile women rose, a marked contrast to the sharp decline in the 1980s. As we will discuss below, minimum wage trends—falling in real value in the 1980s and rising in the 1990s—can explain this pattern.

Over the entire 1979-2005 period the wages of the highest-earning women at the 95th percentile grew by 59.9%, more than double the 23.9% wage growth for the median woman over the same period.

Shifts in low-wage jobs

Another useful way of characterizing changes in the wage structure is to examine the trend in the proportion of workers earning low, middle, and high wages. These trends are presented in **Table 3.7** and **Figure 3F** for all workers and for men and women. The workforce is divided into six wage groups based on multiples of the "poverty-level wage," or the hourly wage that a full-time, year-round worker must earn to sustain a family of four at the poverty threshold, which was $9.60 in 2005 (in 2005 dollars), equal to two-thirds of the median hourly wage. Thus, workers are assigned to a wage group according to the degree to which they earned more (or less) than poverty-level wages.

Women are much more likely to earn low wages than men. In 2005, 29.4% of women earned poverty-level wages or less, significantly more than the share of men (19.9%). Women are also much less likely to earn very high wages. In 2005 only 10.1% of women, but 17.6% of men, earned at least three times the poverty-level wage.

The trend in the share of workers earning poverty-level wages corresponds to the story outlined at the start of this chapter: momentum in reducing poverty-level work began in the late 1990s, continued until 2002, then dissipated. This is evident in Figure 3F and **Figure 3G**, which shows trends by race/ethnicity. So, although the share of workers earning poverty-level wages actually fell from 2000 to 2005, from 25.1% to 24.5%, this progress came in the first two years of that period and then partially reversed. Among blacks the increase in low-wage work after 2002 was large enough to reverse the progress from 2000 to 2002.

In the 1989-2000 period the share of workers earning poverty-level wages fell from 30.5% to 25.1%, reversing the trend of the 1980s toward more poverty-level jobs. As Figures 3F and 3G show, the erosion of poverty-wage jobs in the 1990s came in the latter part of the decade, which saw falling unemployment and broad-based real wage growth. The turnaround toward more poverty-level jobs in 2003 thus represents a reversal of a seven-year trend.

The share of workers earning at least 25% below the poverty-level wage (labeled "0-75") expanded significantly between 1979 and 1989, from 4.9% to 13.9% of the workforce. The group earning poverty-level wages (the "total" group) rose from 27.1% in 1979 to 30.5% in 1989. Thus, over the 1979-89 period there was not only a sizable growth (3.3% of the workforce) in the proportion of workers earning poverty-level wages, but also a shift within this group to those earning very low wages.

TABLE 3.7 Distribution of total employment by wage level, 1973-2005

Year	Share of employment by wage multiple of poverty wage*							
	Poverty level wages:							
	0-75	75-100	Total**	100-125	125-200	200-300	300+	Total
All								
1973	11.7%	18.2%	29.9%	13.8%	35.0%	14.9%	6.4%	100%
1979	4.9	22.2	27.1	14.2	33.0	18.5	7.1	100
1989	13.9	16.5	30.5	12.6	30.9	17.2	8.9	100
2000	9.8	15.3	25.1	15.5	28.4	19.1	11.9	100
2005	10.0	14.5	24.5	16.0	27.2	18.3	14.0	100
Change								
1979-89	9.0	-5.7	3.3	-1.6	-2.1	-1.4	1.8	
1989-2000	-4.1	-1.3	-5.3	2.8	-2.4	1.9	3.0	
2000-05	0.1	-0.7	-0.6	0.5	-1.2	-0.7	2.1	
Men								
1973	5.6%	11.9%	17.4%	11.2%	40.2%	21.5%	9.7%	100%
1979	2.8	12.9	15.7	10.8	35.5	26.8	11.2	100
1989	9.5	13.2	22.7	10.7	31.8	21.7	13.1	100
2000	7.3	12.4	19.6	13.7	28.6	22.3	15.7	100
2005	7.6	12.3	19.9	14.7	27.5	20.2	17.6	100
Change								
1979-89	6.7	0.3	7.0	-0.1	-3.7	-5.1	1.9	
1989-2000	-2.2	-0.8	-3.0	3.0	-3.2	0.6	2.7	
2000-05	0.4	-0.1	0.3	1.0	-1.1	-2.1	1.8	
Women								
1973	20.5%	27.5%	48.0%	17.6%	27.5%	5.4%	1.6%	100%
1979	7.8	34.4	42.1	18.6	29.8	7.7	1.8	100
1989	19.0	20.3	39.2	14.8	29.8	12.0	4.2	100
2000	12.7	18.4	31.1	17.4	28.2	15.5	7.7	100
2005	12.5	16.9	29.4	17.3	26.8	16.3	10.1	100
Change								
1979-89	11.2	-14.1	-2.9	-3.8	0.1	4.3	2.4	
1989-2000	-6.3	-1.8	-8.1	2.6	-1.6	3.6	3.5	
2000-05	-0.2	-1.5	-1.7	-0.1	-1.4	0.7	2.4	

*   The wage ranges are equivalent in 2005 dollars to: $7.20 and below (0-75), $7.20-9.60 (75-100), $9.60-12.00 (100-125), $12.00-19.19 (125-200), $19.19-28.79 (200-300), and $28.79 and above (300+).

** Combines lowest two categories and represents the share of wage earners earning poverty-level wages.

Source: Authors' analysis of CPS ORG.

FIGURE 3F Share of workers earning poverty-level wages by gender 1973-2005

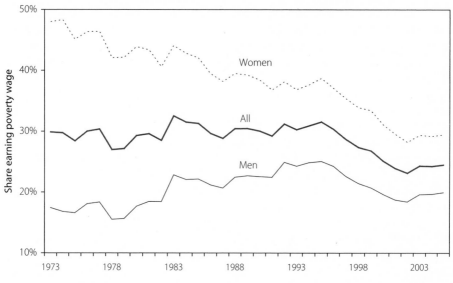

Source: Authors' analysis of CPS ORG.

FIGURE 3G Share of workers earning poverty-level wages by race/ethnicity, 1973-2005

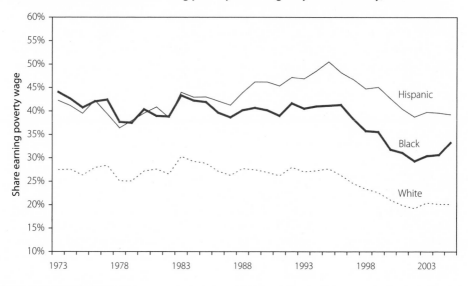

Source: Authors' analysis of CPS ORG.

The share of workers earning poverty-level wages continued to expand, though more slowly, in the 1989-95 period, but then, not surprisingly given wage trends at the bottom, contracted in the 1995-2000 period (Figure 3F). The result was a fall in the poverty-wage employment share to 25.1% in 2000, down 5.4 percentage points from 1989 and the lowest level since 1973. Those earning very low wages still represented 9.8% of the workforce in 2000, twice the share as in 1979 but significantly less than the share in 1989. The real wage growth at the bottom of the wage scale in the latter 1990s thus rapidly diminished the share of workers earning poverty-level wages and offset the growth in poverty-wage shares over the 1979-95 period. However, a large share of the workforce, roughly a fourth, still earns poverty-level wages.

Over the 1979-89 period, the entire wage structure shifted downward, with proportionately fewer workers in the middle- and high-wage groups in 1989 than in 1979. The only exception is the modest expansion of the share of the workforce at the very highest earnings level (exceeding three times the poverty-level wage). In the 1989-2000 period there was a larger shift to the two highest-wage categories and a shift upward into lower-middle-wage jobs paying $9.60 to $12.00.

Overall trends in the share of workers earning poverty-level wages are primarily driven by trends among women, since women are disproportionately the ones earning these low wages. The share of women earning poverty-level wages declined modestly during the 2000-05 period, from 31.1% to 29.4%; all of the drop took place by 2002 and was slightly reversed by 2005 (Figure 3F). In the 1989-2000 period, the very bottom of the wage structure shrank as the proportion of women earning poverty-level wages, including the share earning very low wages, diminished. At the same time, the top two wage categories grew. The improvements, as Figure 3F shows, accelerated in the 1995-2000 period.

Among women workers, 11.2% shifted into the very-low-wage category during the 1979-89 period, while at the same time the two highest-wage groups grew by 6.7 percentage points. The shift downward among women appears to be an enlargement of the workforce earning very low wages, even though the proportion earning poverty-level wages overall fell from 42.1% to 39.2%.

Among men, the overall changes in the wage structure between 1979 and 1989 meant proportionately fewer middle-wage workers and more low-wage workers, with little growth in the share of very high earners. For instance, 7.0% of the male workforce shifted into the group earning less than the poverty-level wage, and the proportion of men in the other wage groups (except the highest) contracted. Over the 1989-2000 period the share of men earning poverty-level wages declined by 3.0%. Regardless of the recent trends, the share of poverty-level earners among men was 19.9% in 2005, still 4.2% more than in 1979.

Tables 3.8, **3.9**, and **3.10** (and Figure 3G) present an analysis similar to the one in Table 3.7 for white, black, and Hispanic employment. The proportion of minority workers earning low wages is substantial—33.3% of black workers and 39.3% of Hispanic workers in 2005. Minority women are even more likely to be low earners—37.1% of black women and 45.7% of Hispanic women in 2005. The wage structure for each race/gender group has shifted over the last few decades.

Figure 3G shows the decline in white workers earning poverty-level wages from 1996 to 2002 and the bump up since then, ending with 20.1% earning low wages. This prog-

TABLE 3.8 Distribution of white employment by wage level, 1973-2005

| | Share of employment by wage multiple of poverty wage* | | | | | | | |
| | Poverty-level wages: | | | | | | | |
Year	0-75	75-100	Total**	100-125	125-200	200-300	300+	Total
All								
1973	10.3%	17.1%	27.5%	13.6%	35.8%	16.1%	7.1%	100%
1979	4.5	20.6	25.1	13.9	33.5	19.6	7.9	100
1989	12.3	15.1	27.5	12.3	31.6	18.5	10.1	100
2000	8.0	13.0	21.1	14.4	29.4	21.2	13.9	100
2005	8.2	12.0	20.1	14.6	28.4	20.6	16.4	100
Change								
1979-89	7.8	-5.4	2.4	-1.5	-1.9	-1.1	2.2	
1989-2000	-4.3	-2.1	-6.4	2.1	-2.2	2.7	3.9	
2000-05	0.1	-1.0	-0.9	0.2	-1.1	-0.6	2.4	
Men								
1973	4.6%	10.3%	14.9%	10.7%	40.4%	23.1%	10.8%	100%
1979	2.4	11.0	13.4	10.0	35.7	28.4	12.4	100
1989	7.7	11.2	18.9	10.1	32.3	23.7	15.0	100
2000	5.4	9.6	15.0	11.7	29.3	25.2	18.8	100
2005	5.7	9.4	15.2	12.5	28.4	23.0	21.0	100
Change								
1979-89	5.3	0.2	5.5	0.0	-3.4	-4.7	2.6	
1989-2000	-2.3	-1.6	-3.9	1.6	-3.0	1.5	3.7	
2000-05	0.3	-0.2	0.2	0.8	-1.0	-2.2	2.2	
Women								
1973	18.9%	27.2%	46.1%	17.9%	28.9%	5.6%	1.6%	100%
1979	7.4	33.2	40.6	18.9	30.7	8.0	1.9	100
1989	17.6	19.5	37.1	14.9	30.8	12.7	4.5	100
2000	10.9	16.7	27.6	17.3	29.5	16.9	8.7	100
2005	10.8	14.7	25.5	16.7	28.3	18.1	11.4	100
Change								
1979-89	10.2	-13.6	-3.4	-4.1	0.2	4.7	2.6	
1989-2000	-6.7	-2.9	-9.5	2.4	-1.4	4.2	4.2	
2000-05	-0.2	-2.0	-2.1	-0.6	-1.1	1.1	2.7	

* The wage ranges are equivalent in 2005 dollars to: $7.20 and below (0-75), $7.20-9.60 (75-100), $9.60-12.00 (100-125), $12.00-19.19 (125-200), $19.19-28.79 (200-300), and $28.79 and above (300+).

** Combines lowest two categories and represents the share of wage earners earning poverty-level wages.

Source: Authors' analysis of CPS ORG.

TABLE 3.9 Distribution of black employment by wage level, 1973-2005

	Share of employment by wage multiple of poverty wage*							
	Poverty-level wages:							
Year	0-75	75-100	Total**	100-125	125-200	200-300	300+	Total
All								
1973	20.2%	23.9%	44.1%	14.2%	31.1%	8.1%	2.4%	100%
1979	7.3	30.2	37.5	15.6	31.0	13.0	3.0	100
1989	19.8	20.9	40.7	14.6	28.3	12.6	3.8	100
2000	12.3	19.5	31.8	18.9	28.8	15.0	5.5	100
2005	13.0	20.3	33.3	19.3	26.1	14.1	7.1	100
Change								
1979-89	12.6	-9.4	3.2	-1.0	-2.7	-0.4	0.9	
1989-2000	-7.5	-1.3	-8.9	4.3	0.5	2.4	1.7	
2000-05	0.7	0.8	1.5	0.4	-2.6	-0.9	1.6	
Men								
1973	11.8%	20.2%	31.9%	13.4%	40.3%	11.4%	3.0%	100%
1979	4.9	22.3	27.2	14.6	35.2	18.5	4.5	100
1989	15.5	19.8	35.3	14.2	30.4	15.4	4.7	100
2000	10.0	16.3	26.3	19.4	30.5	17.2	6.6	100
2005	11.3	17.4	28.7	19.5	28.2	15.3	8.2	100
Change								
1979-89	10.6	-2.5	8.1	-0.4	-4.8	-3.1	0.2	
1989-00	-5.4	-3.5	-8.9	5.2	0.0	1.8	1.9	
2000-05	1.3	1.1	2.4	0.1	-2.2	-1.9	1.6	
Women								
1973	30.1%	28.1%	58.2%	15.2%	20.5%	4.4%	1.7%	100%
1979	9.8	38.7	48.5	16.6	26.5	7.1	1.4	100
1989	24.0	21.8	45.9	14.9	26.2	10.0	3.0	100
2000	14.3	22.2	36.5	18.4	27.3	13.2	4.6	100
2005	14.3	22.8	37.1	19.1	24.4	13.1	6.3	100
Change								
1979-89	14.2	-16.9	-2.7	-1.6	-0.2	2.9	1.7	
1989-00	-9.8	0.4	-9.4	3.5	1.1	3.3	1.6	
2000-05	0.1	0.6	0.7	0.7	-3.0	-0.1	1.7	

* The wage ranges are equivalent in 2005 dollars to: $7.20 and below (0-75), $7.20-9.60 (75-100), $9.60-12.00 (100-125), $12.00-19.19 (125-200), $19.19-28.79 (200-300), and $28.79 and above (300+).

** Combines lowest two categories and represents the share of wage earners earning poverty-level wages.

Source: Authors' analysis of CPS ORG.

TABLE 3.10 Distribution of Hispanic employment by wage level, 1973-2005

| | Share of employment by wage multiple of poverty wage* | | | | | | | |
| | Poverty-level wages: | | | | | | | |
Year	0-75	75-100	Total**	100-125	125-200	200-300	300+	Total
All								
1973	16.8%	25.4%	42.3%	17.4%	30.4%	7.7%	2.1%	100%
1979	6.4	31.5	37.9	16.4	30.0	12.7	3.0	100
1989	21.8	24.4	46.2	13.0	27.2	10.0	3.6	100
2000	17.8	24.9	42.7	19.2	23.3	10.4	4.5	100
2005	16.6	22.7	39.3	20.9	23.5	10.5	5.7	100
Change								
1979-89	15.4	-7.1	8.3	-3.4	-2.8	-2.7	0.6	
1989-2000	-4.0	0.5	-3.5	6.2	-3.9	0.4	0.9	
2000-05	-1.2	-2.2	-3.4	1.7	0.2	0.1	1.3	
Men								
1973	10.6%	21.0%	31.7%	16.7%	38.0%	10.6%	2.9%	100%
1979	4.3	22.8	27.1	15.9	35.0	17.8	4.1	100
1989	18.1	23.0	41.1	12.9	29.0	12.5	4.5	100
2000	14.5	23.7	38.2	20.2	24.6	11.9	5.2	100
2005	13.2	21.9	35.0	21.9	24.9	11.5	6.7	100
Change								
1979-89	13.8	0.1	14.0	-3.0	-6.1	-5.3	0.4	
1989-2000	-3.6	0.7	-2.9	7.2	-4.4	-0.6	0.7	
2000-05	-1.3	-1.8	-3.1	1.7	0.3	-0.4	1.5	
Women								
1973	27.6%	33.0%	60.6%	18.7%	17.2%	2.8%	0.7%	100%
1979	9.6	44.8	54.5	17.3	22.2	4.8	1.2	100
1989	27.2	26.6	53.8	13.2	24.6	6.3	2.1	100
2000	22.6	26.7	49.3	17.8	21.3	8.2	3.4	100
2005	21.7	24.0	45.7	19.5	21.4	9.1	4.3	100
Change								
1979-89	17.6	-18.3	-0.7	-4.1	2.4	1.5	0.9	
1989-2000	-4.6	0.1	-4.4	4.6	-3.3	1.9	1.2	
2000-05	-0.9	-2.7	-3.6	1.8	0.1	0.9	0.9	

* The wage ranges are equivalent in 2005 dollars to: $7.20 and below (0-75), $7.20-9.60 (75-100), $9.60-12.00 (100-125), $12.00-19.19 (125-200), $19.19-28.79 (200-300), and $28.79 and above (300+).

** Combines lowest two categories and represents the share of wage earners earning poverty-level wages.

Source: Authors' analysis of CPS ORG.

ress was solely among white women, whose low-wage share fell from 27.6% to 25.5%. Among white men over the 2000-05 period the share in low-wage work rose slightly; the share with the highest earnings grew; and the share in the middle, from 125% to three times the poverty wage, declined—in other words, men were pushed both up and down out of the middle.

The wage structure shifted downward for whites in the 1979-89 period, but in 1989-2000 whites moved from poverty-level to low- to middle-wage jobs and into very high wage jobs. By 2000, the poverty-wage share among white workers had fallen to 21.1%, 4% below its 1979 level, all due to progress in the late 1990s. The white male and white female wage structures have moved in different directions. In the 1980s, white women shifted substantially into the lowest and highest earnings groups. In contrast, the share of white men eroded in the middle-wage range in the 1980s, grew in the very high wage category, and shifted (although less than for women) to the very bottom. Similarly, the improvements in the 1990s were far greater for white women than for white men. Over the longer term, in fact, white women have seen their share of poverty-level earners decline remarkably, from 46.1% in 1973 to 25.5% in 2005. The share of high and very high earners also grew strongly among white women. In the 2000-05 period white women shifted up the wage scale, with fewer at low earnings and more in the higher-earning categories.

Blacks (Table 3.9) were the only race/ethnic group to see a growth in poverty-level wage earners over the 2000-05 period, despite the progress from 1996 to 2002. This growth in low-wage work occurred among both men and women. Among black men there was also a slight shift to the highest-paying jobs, but the predominant shift was from middle-wage jobs to lower-paying ones. The same pattern is true in this period for the shifts in the wage structure among black women.

In the 1980s blacks experienced a dramatic shift out of middle-wage employment into both very low wage employment and higher-wage employment. The shift out of poverty-level jobs in the 1990s reversed the 1980s expansion of the group of very low earners. By 2000, the share of poverty-wage earners among black men, 26.3%, was about the same as in 1979, but the 36.5% share among women was a historic low. Still, though, in 2000, 31.8% of black workers were in jobs paying less than poverty-level wages. The post-1979 trends, despite the improvement in the late 1990s, have left black men with fewer middle-wage jobs and more very low earning and very high earning jobs. Among black women, the share of very low earners grew (from 9.8% in 1979 to 14.3% in both 2000 and 2005), but otherwise they saw a general movement up the wage structure.

Hispanics, as other groups, saw a shrinkage of low-wage work from the mid-1990s to 2002 (Figure 3G), but no further progress since then. This trend was the case for both Hispanic men and women. While the share of Hispanic women in low-wage work has declined over the long term (down to a still high 45.7% in 2005 from 60.6% in 1973), the share of Hispanic men in low-wage work has risen (up to 35.0% in 2005, from 31.7% in 1973). These trends could be due to a change in the composition of the Hispanic workforce—a larger share of immigrants—as well as a shift in the overall job structure, but we are unable to distinguish between the two factors in this analysis. It is noteworthy, though, that immigration of low-wage Hispanic workers cannot explain why low-wage work grew among Hispanic men but not among women.

Both Hispanic women and men shifted in large numbers into the lowest-wage jobs between 1979 and 1989 and saw modest improvement over the 1990s. The growth in the percentage of Hispanic males earning poverty-level wages was substantial, up from 27.1% in 1979 to 38.2% in 2000. Roughly half (49.3%) of Hispanic women earned poverty-level wages in 2000, a decline from the 54.5% who did so in 1979. Among Hispanic men the share holding jobs over 125% of the poverty wage declined after 1979, but among Hispanic women those shares increased overall. Both Hispanic men and women saw their jobs shift to higher-wage categories in the 2000-05 period, although that upward shift ended in 2002.

Trends in benefit growth and inequality

The analysis on the preceding pages shows that real wages declined for a wide array of workers over both the 1980s and the early 1990s, rose strongly between 1995 and 2002, then fell flat or declined through 2005. Also, total compensation, the real value of both wages and fringe benefits, grew at the same pace as wages over the 1979-2005 period, though sometimes wages grew faster than compensation (the late 1990s) and sometimes more slowly (e.g., 2000-05). Benefits grew faster than wages during much of that time, but since they make up a small share of compensation (15-20%), their growth did not generate fast compensation growth overall. But fast growth in health care costs and pensions helped benefit growth exceed wage growth after 2000, and total compensation grew. In this section, we explore these issues further and examine changes in benefits by type of benefit and changes in health and pension coverage for different groups of workers. **Table 3.11** provides a breakdown of the growth in non-wage compensation, or benefits, using the BLS Employer Costs for Employee Compensation data (the aggregate amounts appeared in Table 3.2). These data, based on a survey of employers, show that total non-wage compensation, including health, pensions, and payroll taxes, were maintained at about $4.40 per hour over the 1987-95 period. Following a 1.6% annual fall in the late 1990s, costs for health and pensions grew in the 2000-05 period, with a net increase of $0.33 per hour from 1995 to 2005. Note, however, that this small rise in benefits costs occurred at the same time that productivity grew 33.3%.

The data in Table 3.11 show average benefit costs. Given the rapid growth of wage inequality in recent years, it should not be surprising to find a growing inequality of benefits. **Tables 3.12** and **3.13** examine changes in health insurance and pension coverage for different demographic groups between 1979 and 2005. The share of workers covered by employer-provided health care plans dropped a steep 13.0 percentage points, from 69.0% in 1979 to 55.9%, in 2004 (Table 3.12). As **Figure 3H** illustrates, health care coverage eroded from 1979 until 1993-94, when it stabilized, and then began falling again after 2000 through 2004 (the latest data). We examine an indicator of the quality of coverage below.

Over the 1979-2005 period, health care coverage has declined twice as much among men (down 16.7 percentage points) than among women (down 6.9 percentage points), and slightly more among whites (10.5 percentage points) than among blacks (9.0 percentage points); Hispanics, though, suffered by far the largest drop—20.6 percentage points.

TABLE 3.11 Growth of specific fringe benefits, 1948-2005 (2005 dollars)

Year*	Voluntary benefits			Payroll taxes	Total benefits and non-wage compensation
	Pension	Health**	Subtotal		
Hourly pay					
1987	$0.79	$1.75	$2.53	$1.86	$4.39
1989	0.64	1.82	2.46	1.93	4.39
1995	0.66	1.67	2.33	2.01	4.34
2000	0.67	1.48	2.14	1.89	4.03
2005	0.90	1.76	2.66	2.10	4.76
Annual dollar change					
1989-2000	$0.00	-$0.03	-$0.03	$0.00	-$0.03
1989-95	0.00	-0.02	-0.02	0.01	-0.01
1995-2000	0.00	-0.04	-0.04	-0.02	-0.06
2000-05	0.05	0.06	0.10	0.04	0.15
Annual percent change					
1989-2000	0.4%	-1.9%	-1.2%	-0.2%	-0.8%
1989-95	0.5	-1.4	-0.9	0.6	-0.2
1995-2000	0.3	-2.5	-1.6	-1.2	-1.5
2000-05	6.2	3.6	4.4	2.2	3.4

* Data are for March.
** Deflated by medical care price index.

Source: Authors' analysis of BLS ECEC data.

The pattern in the erosion of health insurance coverage by wage level shows a growth in inequality in the 1980s, with greater erosion the lower the wage. The 1990s, however, saw modest extensions of coverage for the bottom 20%, while erosion continued for middle- and high-wage workers. Health insurance coverage eroded for all wage groups in the 2000-04 period. Consequently, over the longer period, 1979-2004, health insurance coverage declined sizably, and comparably, across the wage spectrum. Along education lines, however, there is evidence of growing inequality: employer-provided health insurance coverage fell 17.1 percentage points among high school graduates but by a lesser, though large, 11.2 percentage points among college graduates.

Table 3.13 uses information from the National Compensation Survey to examine an important aspect of employer-provided coverage: whether and to what extent the employee must contribute. The top panel shows the trends, for both single and family coverage, in whether employees are required to contribute to the insurance premium. In 1993 about half (54%) of workers in the private sector with single coverage were required to make con-

TABLE 3.12 Change in private-sector employer-provided health insurance coverage, 1979-2004

Group*	Health insurance coverage (%)					Percentage-point change			
	1979	1989	1995	2000	2004	1979-89	1989-2000	2000-04	1979-2004
All workers	69.0%	61.5%	58.5%	58.9%	55.9%	-7.4	-2.7	-2.9	-13.0
Gender									
Men	75.4%	66.8%	62.6%	63.2%	58.7%	-8.7	-3.6	-4.4	-16.7
Women	59.4	54.9	53.3	53.6	52.5	-4.5	-1.3	-1.1	-6.9
Race									
White	70.3%	64.0%	61.7%	62.7%	59.8%	-6.3	-1.2	-3.0	-10.5
Black	63.1	56.3	53.0	55.4	54.1	-6.8	-0.9	-1.3	-9.0
Hispanic	60.4	46.0	42.1	41.8	39.7	-14.3	-4.3	-2.0	-20.6
Education									
High school	69.6%	61.2%	56.3%	56.2%	52.5%	-8.4	-5.0	-3.7	-17.1
College	79.6	75.0	72.1	71.3	68.5	-4.6	-3.8	-2.8	-11.2
Wage fifth									
Lowest	37.9%	26.4%	26.0%	27.4%	24.4%	-11.5	1.0	-2.9	-13.4
Second	60.5	51.7	49.5	50.9	46.0	-8.8	-0.8	-4.9	-14.5
Middle	74.7	67.5	62.9	63.9	61.5	-7.2	-3.6	-2.3	-13.2
Fourth	83.5	78.0	74.0	73.7	70.6	-5.5	-4.3	-3.0	-12.8
Top	89.5	84.7	81.5	79.9	77.5	-4.7	-4.8	-2.4	-12.0

* Private-sector, wage and salary workers age 18-64, who worked at least 20 hours per week and 26 weeks per year.

Source: Authors' analysis of March CPS.

tributions; by 2005 that share had risen to 76%. Almost all workers with family coverage, 88%, are required to pay some of the insurance premium.

How much more employees pay now than in the past for health insurance premiums is answered in the bottom panel of Table 3.13. Unfortunately, data relating to type of coverage are available only for years starting in 2003. In 2005, employers were paying 82% for single coverage and 71% for family coverage, about the same as in 2003. Another survey, sponsored by the Kaiser Family Foundation, confirms these data.

Data on cost sharing for *all* coverage are available for 1992 and 2003. The employer share fell from 86.0% in 1992 to 77.9% in 2003 (a share unlikely to be much different in 2005, given the stability of shared costs for single and family coverage). This shift in cost-sharing caused employees to pay the equivalent of $0.25 more per hour worked in 2005 than if employers had maintained their 86.0% share of premium costs (the $0.25 figure is calculated using the employer cost of $1.76 per hour from Table 3.11, which implies a total employee and employer cost of $2.26). The total cost in 1992, adjusted for overall inflation,

TABLE 3.13 Employee health insurance contribution requirements and employee cost shares, 1992-2005

	Single coverage		Family coverage		All coverage	
	Contribution:		Contribution:		Contribution:	
	Not required	Required	Not required	Required	Not required	Required
NCS						
1993	46%	54%	26%	74%	n.a.	n.a.
2000	32	68	19	81	n.a.	n.a.
2005	24	76	12	88	n.a.	n.a.
	Share of costs		Share of costs		Share of costs	
	Employer	Employee	Employer	Employee	Employer	Employee
NCS						
1992	n.a.	n.a.	n.a.	n.a.	86.0%	14.0%
2003	82%	18%	70%	30%	77.9	22.1
2005	82	18	71	29	n.a.	n.a.
Kaiser						
2005	84%	16%	74%	26%	n.a.	n.a.

Source: Authors' analysis of National Compensation Survey data, Wiatrowski (2004), Lettau (2004), and Kaiser Family Foundation.

FIGURE 3H Private-sector employer-provided health insurance coverage, 1979-2004

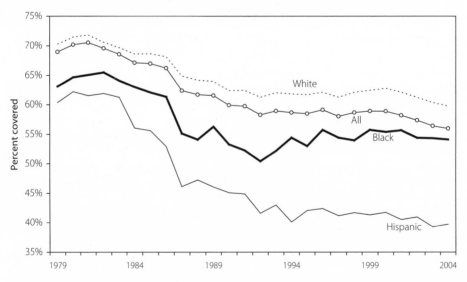

Source: Authors' analysis of March CPS.

was $1.76, with an employer share of $1.52. Thus, total insurance costs increased $0.50 per hour worked from 1992 to 2005, and half of the increase was paid by employers and half by employees. If employee cost-sharing had held to its 1992 rate, then employees would have paid $0.18 less and employers would have paid $0.18 more per hour worked. This shift onto employees for basic premium costs does not count any of the higher deductibles or co-pays paid by employees that have occurred in this time period.

Inequalities in the coverage and quality of employer-provided health insurance are illustrated in **Table 3.14**, which shows participation and costs in private sector employment for workers according to their wage "fourth." Only 19% of workers with the lowest wages participated in their employers' health insurance plan, far less than the 72% participation rate of the highest-wage workers. This difference in participation helps explain why employer costs for health insurance are much higher per hour for the highest-wage workers ($2.28) and the upper-middle fourth ($1.49) than for the lowest-wage workers, for whom employers spend just $0.29 per hour. Differences in participation are not the only reason for this inequality in health care costs. The last column shows that employers spend twice as much per participant for the highest-wage workers ($3.18) than for the lowest-wage workers ($1.54). The gap reflects differences in the quality of insurance coverage and the degree to which employees must share premium costs.

Pension plan coverage (**Table 3.15**) declined as quickly as health care coverage in the 1980s: it dropped from 50.6% in 1979 to 43.7% in 1989. This decline is one of the reasons for the lessening of pension costs for employers over that period. In the 1989-95 period, however, pension coverage expanded slightly to 45.8%, and by 2000 coverage had grown to 48.3%, just 2.3% shy of 1979's level. Pension coverage receded, however, in the 2000-04 period (the latest data), down to 45.5%, 5.1 percentage points less than in 1979. This means that less than half the workforce is covered by employer-provided pensions.

Over the entire 1979-2004 period, pension coverage declined primarily among men, from 56.9% to 46.4%. Women's pension coverage, on the other hand, rose slightly, from 41.3% to 44.3%. Pension coverage eroded in the 1980s and then again between 2000 and 2004 for both men and women. By 2004, women workers were slightly less likely (44.3% versus 46.4%) than men to be covered by an employer's pension plan. Both black and white workers saw pension coverage erode in the 1980s, but Hispanics experienced a large decline—an 11.9 percentage-point drop from 1979 to 1989. In the late 1990s, however, whites expanded their pension coverage and attained a level of 53.7%, 1.5 percentage points above the 1979 level of 52.2%. Hispanics also increased their share in the 1990s but still had coverage—27.5% in 2000—far below the 1979 level. Black workers saw only a modest 0.7 percentage-point increase in coverage in the 1990s. Surprisingly, black workers saw pension coverage erode during the late 1990s recovery. Over the entire 1979-2004 period pension coverage eroded dramatically among all racial/ethnic groups: down 1.5 percentage points among whites, 3.6 percentage points among blacks, and 13.1 percentage points among Hispanics.

The pattern of decline in pension coverage by wage level shows coverage dropping relatively evenly across wage groups in the 1980s and broadening across the board in the 1990s, with coverage expanding the most in the middle. Coverage declined across each wage fifth during the 1980s, between 2000 and 2004, and over the entire 1979-2004

TABLE 3.14 Inequality of employer-provided health insurance participation and cost, 2003

Wage fourth	Employer cost per hour	Participation rate	Cost per participant
Lowest	$0.29	19%	$1.54
Low-middle	0.93	49	1.91
High-middle	1.49	65	2.28
Highest	2.28	72	3.18

Source: Authors' analysis of Lettau (2004).

TABLE 3.15 Change in private-sector employer-provided pension coverage, 1979-2004

Group*	Pension coverage (%)					Percentage-point change			
	1979	1989	1995	2000	2004	1979-89	1989-2000	2000-04	1979-2004
All workers	50.6%	43.7%	45.8%	48.3%	45.5%	-7.0	4.6	-2.8	-5.1
Gender									
Men	56.9%	46.9%	48.6%	50.3%	46.4%	-10.1	3.4	-3.8	-10.5
Women	41.3	39.6	42.5	45.8	44.3	-1.7	6.2	-1.5	3.0
Race									
White	52.2%	46.1%	49.5%	53.7%	50.6%	-6.1	7.6	-3.1	-1.5
Black	45.8	40.7	42.6	41.3	42.2	-5.1	0.7	0.9	-3.6
Hispanic	38.2	26.3	24.7	27.5	25.0	-11.9	1.2	-2.4	-13.1
Education									
High school	51.2%	42.9%	43.2%	43.8%	40.3%	-8.3	0.9	-3.5	-11.0
College	61.0	55.4	58.8	63.7	60.7	-5.6	8.3	-3.0	-0.3
Wage fifth									
Lowest	18.4%	12.7%	13.7%	16.3%	14.3%	-5.7	3.6	-2.0	-4.1
Second	36.8	29.0	32.0	35.8	31.9	-7.7	6.8	-3.9	-4.8
Middle	52.3	44.5	47.0	50.9	47.5	-7.8	6.4	-3.4	-4.8
Fourth	68.4	60.0	63.2	64.8	62.5	-8.3	4.8	-2.4	-5.9
Top	78.5	72.8	74.8	74.8	71.8	-5.8	2.1	-3.1	-6.8

* Private-sector, wage and salary workers age 18-64, who worked at least 20 hours per week and 26 weeks per year.

Source: Authors' analysis of March CPS.

period. Lower-wage workers are very unlikely to have jobs with employer-provided pension plans (14.3% were covered in 2004), and less than half of middle-wage workers have pension coverage. It should be noted that there was little coverage for low-wage workers to lose—just 18.4% for the lowest fifth and 36.8% for the second-lowest fifth in 1979. In

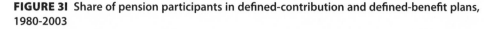

FIGURE 3I Share of pension participants in defined-contribution and defined-benefit plans, 1980-2003

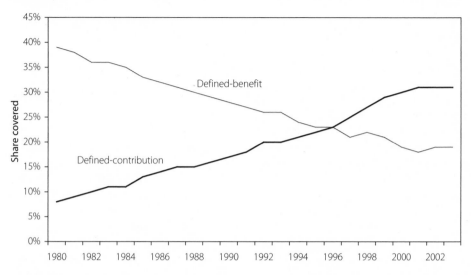

Source: Center for Retirement Research (2006).

2004, the highest-wage workers were nearly five times as likely to have pension coverage as the lowest-wage workers (71.8% versus 14.3%). Changes in pension coverage by education show a growing inequality: over the 1979-2004 period pension coverage fell 11.0 percentage points among high school graduates but only 0.3 percentage points among college graduates. However, each educational group, both high school and college, had declines in health care coverage in the 2000-04 period.

The widening coverage of employer-provided pension plans in the 1990s was most likely due to the expansion of 401(k) and other defined-contribution pension plans. These plans differ from defined-benefit plans, which are generally considered the best plans from a workers' perspective because they guarantee a fixed payment in retirement based on pre-retirement wages and years of service regardless of stock market performance. Yet, as shown in **Figure 3I**, a larger share of workers are now covered by defined-contribution plans, in which employers make contributions (to which employees often can add) each year. With this type of plan, a worker's retirement income depends on his or her success in investing these funds, and investment risks are borne by the employee rather than the employer. Therefore, the shift from traditional defined-benefit plans to defined-contribution plans represents an erosion of pension quality. Chapter 5 provides further discussion of pensions and retirement assets and income.

Explaining wage inequality

In this section we shift the discussion from a descriptive presentation of wage and benefit trends overall and for sub-groups to an examination of explanations for the pattern of recent wage growth. It is important to understand the average performance of wage growth and why particular groups fared well or poorly compared to others.

The data presented up to this point have shown the stagnation of wages and overall compensation between 1973 and 1995 and strong wage growth in the late 1990s. The momentum of the strong wage growth from the latter 1990s carried into the first few years of the early 2000s recession and prolonged labor slump, with wages starting to falter in 2002. **Table 3.16** presents indicators of a variety of dimensions (excluding race and gender differentials, discussed below) of the wage structure that have grown more unequal over the 1973-2005 period. Any explanation of growing wage inequality must be able to explain the movement of these indicators. (These inequality indicators are computed from our analysis of the Current Population Survey (CPS) outgoing rotation group (ORG) data series. These trends, however, parallel those in the other major data series, the March CPS.)

The top section of Table 3.16 shows the trends, by gender, in the 90/10 wage differential and its two components, the 90/50 and 50/10 wage differential (whose annual values are shown in **Figures 3J** and **3K**), over the 1973-2005 period. These differentials reflect the growth in overall wage inequality. The 90/10 wage gap, for instance, shows the degree to which 90th percentile workers—"high-wage" workers who earn more than 90% but less than 10% of the workforce—fared better than "low-wage" workers, who earn at the 10th percentile. The 90/50 wage gap shows how high earners fared relative to middle earners, and the 50/10 wage gap how middle earners fared relative to low earners.

Wage inequalities have been growing continuously since 1979, although the pattern differs across time periods. For instance, among both men and women the shape of growing inequality differed in the 1980s (through about 1987-88) and thereafter. Over the 1979-89 period (as we saw above in the analysis of wage deciles in Tables 3.4 through 3.6), there was a dramatic across-the-board widening of the wage structure, with the top pulling away from the middle and the middle pulling away from the bottom. In the late 1980s, however, the wage inequality in the bottom half of the wage structure, as reflected in the 50/10 differential, began shrinking and continued to shrink through 1999, then stabilized and then fell a bit among men but rose a bit among women. On the other hand, the 90/50 differential continued to widen in the 1980s and 1990s and through to 2005 (except the last year for men). This widening of the wage gap at the top is even stronger in the 95/50 differential, shown **Figure 3L**. (The 95th percentile is the highest wage we feel can be tracked in our data with technical precision. We use other data in a later section to track the growing wage gap between the very highest earners and other workers). These disparate trends between high- versus middle-wage growth and middle- versus low-wage growth should motivate explanations that focus on how causal factors affect particular portions of the wage structure—top, middle, or bottom—rather than on how causal factors affect inequality generally.

The trends in the later years, 2000-05, may signal a return to the 1980s pattern of an across-the-board widening of wage inequality. The 50/10 wage gap started growing again

TABLE 3.16 Dimensions of wage inequality, 1973-2005

	Log wage differentials						Percentage-point change			
	1973	1979	1989	1995	2000	2005	1973-79	1979-89	1989-2000	2000-05
Total wage inequality										
90/10										
Men	128.0%	130.0%	144.3%	151.1%	150.3%	153.3%	2.0	14.3	6.0	3.0
Women	115.9	103.2	134.9	137.6	137.7	143.4	-12.7	31.8	2.8	5.7
90/50										
Men	60.3%	58.8%	69.2%	76.1%	79.5%	83.6%	-1.5	10.4	10.2	4.1
Women	59.2	60.6	70.5	76.5	78.2	81.2	1.4	9.9	7.7	3.0
50/10										
Men	67.6%	71.1%	75.1%	75.0%	70.8%	69.7%	3.5	3.9	-4.2	-1.1
Women	56.7	42.5	64.4	61.1	59.5	62.2	-14.2	21.9	-4.9	2.7
Between group inequality*										
College/high school										
Men	25.3%	20.1%	33.9%	37.1%	42.0%	43.1%	-5.2	13.9	8.1	1.1
Women	37.7	26.5	41.0	46.7	47.9	47.1	-11.2	14.5	6.9	-0.8
H.S./Less than high school										
Men	22.3%	22.0%	22.1%	26.5%	26.0%	23.9%	-0.3	0.1	3.9	-2.1
Women	26.2	21.3	26.4	29.8	29.5	28.9	-4.9	5.1	3.0	-0.6
*Experience***										
Middle/young										
Men	22.0%	21.5%	25.7%	27.0%	22.9%	25.9%	-0.5	4.1	-2.8	3.1
Women	8.0	9.5	17.8	21.8	18.4	21.6	1.5	8.3	0.6	3.2
Old/middle										
Men	3.4%	8.2%	12.4%	12.7%	8.8%	8.1%	4.7	4.3	-3.6	-0.7
Women	-2.0	0.4	2.1	5.4	4.6	6.4	2.4	1.7	2.5	1.8
Within group inequality*										
Men	42.3%	42.8%	46.7%	47.8%	48.1%	49.3%	1.4%	9.0%	3.0%	3.2%
Women	41.8	40.2	44.7	46.7	45.8	47.6	-3.8	11.4	2.4	2.1

* Differentials based on a simple human capital regression of log wages on five education categorical variables, age as a quartic, race, marital status, region, and ethnicity (Hispanic).
** Age differentials between 25- and 35-year-olds and 35- and 50-year-olds.
*** Mean square error from same regressions used to estimate experience and education differentials. Changes measured as percent change.

Source: Authors' analysis of CPS ORG.

among women after 1999, which corresponds to the earlier pattern—rising inequality at the top and the bottom of the wage distribution. However, among men there was falling inequality at the bottom (50/10 ratio). At the top, the wage gap (95/50 or 90/50) spiked upward sharply among men and grew moderately among women (especially the 95/50 ratio). Overall wage inequality, measured by the 90/10 ratio, grew among men and women over the 2000-05 period at about the same pace as in the 1990s for men and at an even greater pace than in the 1990s among women.

FIGURE 3J Men's wage inequality, 1973-2005

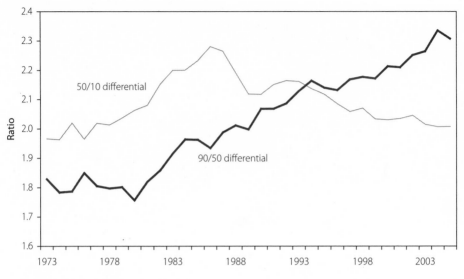

Source: Authors' analysis of CPS ORG.

FIGURE 3K Women's wage inequality, 1973-2005

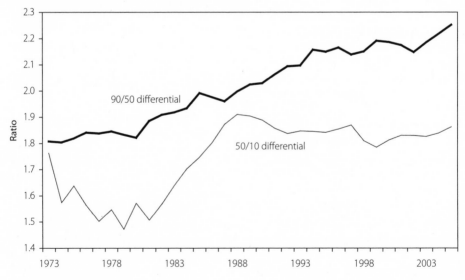

Source: Authors' analysis of CPS ORG.

FIGURE 3L 95/50 percentile wage inequality, 1973-2005

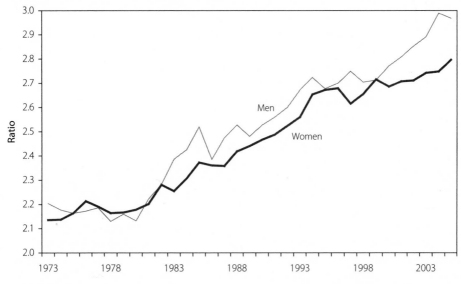

Source: Authors' analysis of CPS ORG.

Among men, wage inequality grew dramatically at the top and bottom in the 1979-89 period, and the growth in the 90/50 differential continued as quickly through the 1989-2000 period (Table 3.16 and Figure 3J). Specifically, the 90/50 wage gap grew roughly 10 (log) percentage points in both periods. As discussed above, the character of this growing male wage inequality shifted in the most recent period. In the 1980s the separation between both the top and the middle and the middle and the bottom grew (seen in the 50/10 differential). However, in the 1989-2000 period, all of the growing wage inequality was generated by a divergence between the top and everyone else: the 90/50 differential grew while the 50/10 differential actually fell. The drop in the 50/10 wage gap among men actually began in 1986 (Figure 3J). After 2000, the 90/50 wage gap continued to grow, and the 50/10 wage gap declined slightly.

Among women, the wage inequality trends across time periods correspond to those of men. The 90/10 ratio dropped significantly between 1973 and the late 1970s, primarily because of the strong equalization in the 50/10 wage gap. In the 1980s, however, the 50/10 wage gap grew tremendously (up 21.9 percentage points), reversing the 1970s compression and increasing the gap another 8 percentage points over 1973. One conclusion that can be reached about women's wage inequality is that it has been driven much more by what happened at the bottom—the 10th percentile—than was the change for men. This is likely due to the importance of the legal minimum wage to low-wage women, as we will discuss in a later section. Among women, the growth of the 90/50 differential was comparable to that of men in the 1980s but somewhat less in the 1990s. As with men, the 50/10 wage gap declined in the 1990s (Figure 3K shows the drop starting in about 1987). As mentioned above, the wage gap at the bottom among women started rising again after 1999.

The 95/50 wage gap among women followed approximately the same track as for men (Figure 3L). Wage inequality between the very top earners and those in the middle has been growing strongly, and steadily, since about 1980, confirming the continuous widening of wages at the top over the last two decades. The only exception is the flattening of the 95/50 gap among women since 1999.

Analysts decompose, or break down, growing wage inequality into two types of in-equality—"between group" and "within group." The former is illustrated in Table 3.16 in two ways: the growing wage differentials between groups of workers defined either by their education levels or by their labor market experience. The most frequently dis-cussed differential is the "college wage premium"—the wage gap between college and high school graduates—which fell in the 1970s among both men and women but exploded in the 1980s, growing about 14 percentage points for each. Growth then slowed after 1989. The pattern of growth of this key education differential in the 1990s, however, differed be-tween men and women (see **Figure 3M**). Among men there was only modest growth in the education premium in the early 1990s—year-by-year trends (discussed below) show it to be relatively flat between 1987 and 1996—but it grew strongly thereafter. Thus, the 1990s growth in the male education premium primarily occurred in the last few years. Among women, however, the college wage premium grew steadily but modestly in the early 1990s and then evened out starting around 1995. The college wage premium declined a bit in the early 2000s before perking up in 2005.

Table 3.16 also presents the trends in another education differential—between those completing high school and those without high school degrees; this differential would be expected to affect the wage distribution in the bottom half, as about 10% of the work-force has less than a high school education, and high school graduates make up about a third of the workforce (see discussion of Tables 3.17 through 3.19). In 1973 as in 2005, those with a high school degree earned about 25% more than those without a degree. One reason for the stability of this differential is that, even as having a high school degree was becoming more valuable, the share of workers without a high school degree dramatically declined. This wage differential has been fairly stable among men over the last 30 years, suggesting that education differentials have not been a driving force behind the changes in the 50/10 wage gap (up in the 1980s and declining thereafter). Among women, the wage gap between middle- and low-wage workers is far higher in 2005 than in 1973, yet the high school/less than high school differential is roughly the same. This suggests that changing wage differentials at the bottom among women have had only a weak relation-ship to changing education differentials.

Experience, or age, is another way of categorizing "skill." The growth of experience dif-ferentials reflects the wage gap between older and middle-age and younger workers. The wage gap between middle-age and younger workers grew in the 1980s but not in the 1990s, particu-larly because the 1995-2000 wage boom, characterized by relatively faster wage growth among younger workers, markedly reduced this differential. The wage gap between older and middle-

FIGURE 3M College/high school wage premium, 1973-2005

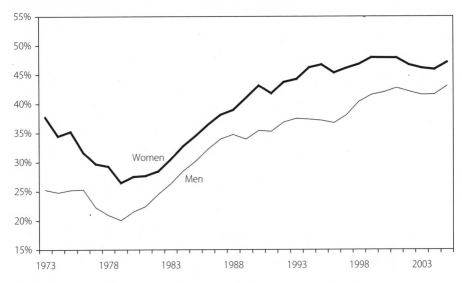

Source: Authors' analysis of CPS ORG.

age women workers grew over the 1973-95 period and was relatively flat thereafter; it grew as well for men until 1995, and then declined by 2000 and was flat in the early 2000s.

Within-group wage inequality—wage dispersion among workers with comparable education and experience—has been a major dimension of growing wage inequality. Unfortunately, most discussions of wage inequality focus exclusively on the between-group dimensions of wage inequality discussed above, even though within-group wage inequality is by far the most important dimension of wage inequality's growth. The growth of within-group wage inequality is presented in the last section of Table 3.16, with changes measured in percent. These data show that within-group inequality grew slightly among men in the 1970s and 1990s but grew strongly, by 9.0%, over the 1980s. Among women, within-group inequality fell in the 1970s, grew by 11.4% in the 1980s, and then grew a modest 2.4% in the 1990s. However, within-group wage inequality fell among women in the 1995-2000 period, while rising slightly among men. Growth in within-group wage inequality returned in the 2000-05 period among both men and women; it grew as much in five years as it had over the 11 years from 1989 to 2000.

This measure of within-group wage inequality is a "summary measure" describing changes across the entire wage distribution. Unfortunately, such a measure does not help us understand changes in particular measures of wage inequality, such as the 90/50 and 50/10 differentials presented in Table 3.16. This shortcoming is particularly troublesome for an analysis of the 1989-2000 period in which inequalities were expanding at the top (i.e., the 90/50) but shrinking at the bottom (i.e., the 50/10). A summary measure of inequality by definition reflects the net effect of the two disparate shifts in wage inequality in the 1990s, and explains the small change of within-group wage inequality from 1989 to 2000.

Since changes in within-group wage inequality have been a significant factor in various periods, it is important to be able to explain and interpret these trends. In a later section, we show that about half of the growth of wage inequality since 1979 has been from growing within-group wage inequality. Unfortunately, the interpretation of growing wage inequality among workers with similar "human capital" has not been the subject of much research. Some analysts suggest it reflects growing premiums for skills that are not captured by traditional human capital measures available in government surveys. Others suggest that changing "wage norms," employer practices, and institutions are responsible.

We now turn to a more detailed examination of between-group wage differentials such as education, experience, and race/ethnicity as well as an examination of within-group wage inequality.

Productivity and the compensation/productivity gap

Productivity growth, which is the growth of the output of goods and services per hour worked, provides the basis for the growth of living standards. However, for the vast majority productivity growth actually provides only the *potential* for rising living standards: recent history, especially since 2000, has shown that wages, compensation, and income growth for the typical worker or family have lagged tremendously behind the nation's fast productivity growth. In contrast, between 1995 and 2000 wage growth accelerated along with productivity growth. It seems important, therefore, to understand why productivity growth was better shared in the late 1990s than in the years since.

The relationship between hourly productivity and hourly compensation growth is portrayed in **Figure 3N**, which shows the growth of each relative to 1973 (i.e., each is indexed so that 1973 equals 100). As the figure illustrates, productivity grew 81% from 1973 to 2005, enough to generate large advances in living standards and wages if productivity gains were broadly shared. As Figures 3A and 3B showed at the start of this chapter, huge differences emerged between productivity and wages or compensation in the 2000-05 period.

There are two important gaps displayed in Figure 3N. First, the growth in average compensation—which includes the pay of CEOs and day laborers alike—lagged behind productivity growth. Second, median hourly compensation grew far less than average compensation, reflecting growing wage and benefit inequality. Thus, there have been two wedges between the typical or median worker's compensation and overall productivity growth: one is that workers, on average, have not seen their pay keep up with productivity (partly reflecting the shift from wage to capital income described in Chapter 1), and the other is that median workers have not enjoyed growth in compensation as fast as higher-wage workers, especially the very highest paid (as explored in a later section). This wedge reflects growing wage and benefit inequality.

There are several possible interpretations of the gap between average compensation and productivity. A benign explanation is that prices for national output have grown more slowly

FIGURE 3N Productivity and hourly compensation growth, 1973-2004

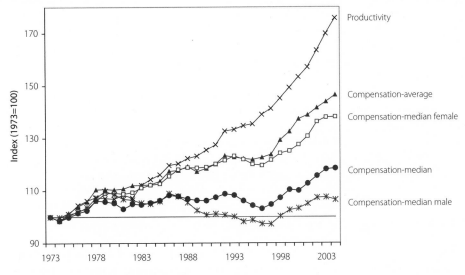

Source: Authors' analysis of NIPA, CPS ORG, and BLS productivity data.

than prices for consumer purchases. Therefore, the same growth in nominal, or current dollar, wages and output yields faster growth in real (inflation-adjusted) output (which is adjusted for changes in the prices of investment goods, exports, and consumer purchases) than in real wages (which is adjusted for changes in consumer purchases only). That is, workers have suffered worsening "terms of trade," in which the prices of things they buy (i.e., consumer goods) have risen faster than the items they produce (consumer goods but also capital goods). Thus, if workers consumed microprocessors and machine tools as well as groceries, their real wage growth would have been better and in line with productivity growth.

This terms-of-trade scenario is actually more of a description than an explanation. A growing gap between output and consumer prices has not been a persistent characteristic of the U.S. economy or other economies, and the emergence of this gap requires an exploration of what economic forces are driving it. Once the causes of the price gap are known (not simply accounted for), it can be interpreted. In the meantime, there are two ways to look at the divergence of compensation and productivity created by the terms-of-trade shift of prices. One is to note that, regardless of cause, the implication is that the "average" worker is not benefiting fully from productivity growth. Another is to note that the price divergence does not simply or solely reflect a shift in income from labor to capital; the gap between compensation and productivity growth reflects, at least in part, differences in price trends rather than a larger share of productivity growth going to capital incomes.

A cursory look at the data gives a sense of the relative contribution of the two components of the productivity-compensation gap, the price divergence and the shift in "factor incomes" (capital's profits and labor's compensation). The gap between productivity and average hourly compensation over the 1979-2005 period was 0.9%, of which divergent price trends (gross domestic product or "output prices" versus consumer prices) could explain roughly 43%. This time period, however, includes some different dynamics in certain sub-periods, particularly over the last 10 years. From 1995 to 2000 productivity grew just slightly faster than real hourly compensation, 2.5% versus 2.4% annually. In this period the divergence between output price inflation and consumer inflation more than explains the divergence, indicating that, in this boom period compensation growth exceeded the growth of profitability. However, in the most recent five year period, 2000-05, productivity grew twice as fast as real hourly compensation, 3.30% versus 1.65%, reflecting a productivity-compensation gap growing 1.65% each year. In this period, price divergence can explain only 13% of the growth of the productivity-compensation gap, suggesting that the rapidly widening gap in recent years reflects a giant-scale shift from wages to profits. Over the entire period from 1979 to 2005 roughly 44% of the growth in the productivity-compensation gap can be explained by the relatively faster inflation in consumer purchases than in the inflation of overall output.

The issue of whether the growth in rates of profit (defined broadly as profits and interest per dollar of assets) has meant that wages have grown less than they would have otherwise was examined directly in Chapter 1. There, we saw that the share of income going to capital has grown significantly, and the trend was driven by a large increase in "profitability," or the return to capital per dollar of plant and equipment. This growth has been especially strong since 2000. Labor's share of corporate-sector income has dropped correspondingly, thus providing evidence of a redistribution of wages to capital incomes. Specifically, capital's share of corporate income in 2005, at 20.9%, was the highest in nearly 40 years. Had the capital share of income stayed at the level of 1979, 17.9%, then compensation could have been 3.7% greater. The rise in profitability (pre-tax profits per dollar of assets) had an even larger impact: if the pre-tax return to capital in 2005 (11.9%) had been at the 1979 level (9.6%), then hourly compensation would have been 5% higher in the corporate sector, equivalent to reversing an annual transfer of $235 billion from labor to capital (measured for 2005). The shift that has occurred in income from labor to capital has been large when compared to the size of the loss of wages for the typical worker due to factors such as the shift to services, globalization, the drop in union representation, or any of the other prominent causes of growing wage inequality discussed in this chapter.

Rising education/wage differentials

Changes in the economic returns to education affect the structure of wages by changing the wage gaps between different educational groups. The growth in "education/wage differentials" led to greater wage inequality in the 1980s and 1990s (see Table 3.16 and Figure 3M) and helps explain the relatively faster wage growth among high-wage workers. This section examines wage trends among workers at different levels of education and begins the discussion, carried on through the remainder of the chapter, of the causes of rising education/wage differentials and of overall wage inequality.

Table 3.17 presents the wage trends and employment shares (percentage of the work-force) for workers at various education levels over the 1973-2005 period. It is common to point out that the wages of "more-educated" workers have grown faster than the wages of "less-educated" workers since 1979, with the real wages of less-educated workers falling sharply (or rising more slowly in the 1995-2000 period). This pattern of wage growth is frequently described in terms of a rising differential, or "premium," between the wages of the college-educated and high-school-educated workforces (as shown earlier in Table 3.16).

The frequent categorizing of workers as either "less educated" (those who are faring relatively poorly) or "more educated" (those faring relatively better) is potentially misleading. As we will show shortly, in some periods the better-educated workers do not fare so well. Moreover, the group labeled "less educated" actually comprises about 70-75% of the workforce and has skills and education that exceed those of most workers in the world. Only about 10% of the U.S. workforce, age 18-64, does not have a high school or equivalent degree. Last, it is notable that the "college-educated" group consists of two groups: one with just four years of college, and another more-educated ("advanced degree") group; the wage trends for these two groups have frequently diverged so it makes sense to treat them separately.

Over the entire 1979-2005 period the simple story is that wages rose more the greater the education level of the group. This trend played out differently in various time periods. From 1979 to 1995 the wages of those with less than a college degree actually declined while those of college-educated workers rose modestly (Table 3.17). In the most recent period, 2000-05, wages grew a modest 0.3% annually for college-educated workers and for those with a high school degree or less. Those with "some college" saw no rise in wages (though the 0.3% annual wage growth of other workers can also be described as relatively stagnant). In contrast, wages grew rapidly for each education group from 1995 to 2000. One interesting pattern to note is that those with advanced degrees (master's degrees, professional degrees in law, medicine, and so on) sometimes saw their wages grow faster than those with just a college degree (1979-89, 1989-95) but sometimes saw lower wage growth (1995-2000) and sometimes comparable growth (2000-05).

The increased wage differential between college-educated and other workers is frequently ascribed to a relative increase in employer demand for workers with greater skills and education. This interpretation follows from the fact that the wages of college-educated workers increased relative to others despite an increase in their relative supply, from 12.7% of the workforce in 1979 to 19.8% in 2005. That is, given the increased supply of college-educated workers, the fact that their relative wages went up implies a strong growth in employer demand for more-educated workers, presumably reflecting technological and other workplace trends.

Yet an increased relative demand for educated workers is only a partial explanation, especially if it is credited to a benign process of technology or other factors leading to a higher value for education and thus bidding up the wages of more-educated workers. Note, for instance, that the primary reason for an increased wage gap between college-educated and other workers is the precipitous decline of wages among the non-college-educated workforce in the 1979-95 period and not any strong growth in the college wage (it was

TABLE 3.17 Real hourly wage for all by education, 1973-2005 (2005 dollars)

Year	Less than high school	High school	Some college	College	Advanced degree
Hourly wage					
1973	$12.56	$14.39	$15.50	$21.00	$25.38
1979	12.82	14.38	15.38	20.17	24.62
1989	11.02	13.43	15.08	21.15	27.26
1995	9.97	13.18	14.75	21.88	28.87
2000	10.36	13.94	15.85	24.35	30.79
2005	10.53	14.14	15.89	24.67	31.49
Annualized percentage change					
1973-79	0.3%	0.0%	-0.1%	-0.7%	-0.5%
1979-89	-1.5	-0.7	-0.2	0.5	1.0
1989-2000	-0.6	0.3	0.5	1.3	1.1
1989-95	-1.6	-0.3	-0.4	0.6	1.0
1995-2000	0.8	1.1	1.5	2.2	1.3
1979-2000	-1.0	-0.1	0.1	0.9	1.1
2000-05	0.3	0.3	0.0	0.3	0.5
Share of employment					
1973	28.5%	38.3%	18.5%	10.1%	4.5%
1979	20.1	38.5	22.8	12.7	6.0
1989	13.7	36.9	26.0	15.6	7.9
2000	11.1	31.8	29.6	18.8	8.8
2005	10.4	30.1	29.9	19.8	9.8

Source: Authors' analysis of CPS ORG.

rising a modest 0.5% annually in this time period). Moreover, as discussed below, there are many important factors that may not reflect changes in the relative demand for skill; these might include high unemployment, the shift to low-wage industries, deunionization, a falling minimum wage, and import competition, that can also lead to a wage gap between workers with more and less education. Below, we argue that technological change has not been the driving force behind growing wage inequality.

Tables 3.18 and **3.19** present trends in wage and employment shares for each education group for men and women. Among men, wage growth in the most recent 2000-05 period has been relatively stagnant, up or down very modestly, for workers with college degrees and each education group of non-college-educated workers. This follows a period of exceptionally strong growth in the late 1990s, a period that stands apart from the long-term trend over the 26 years from 1979 to 2005. In the early part of this long period, from 1979 to 1995, wages fell strongly among non-college-educated men. The decline was sizable even among men with "some college"—8.0% from 1979 to 1995. The wage of the

TABLE 3.18 Real hourly wage for men by education, 1973-2005 (2005 dollars)

Year	Less than high school	High school	Some college	College	Advanced degree
Hourly wage					
1973	$14.68	$17.41	$17.79	$24.01	$26.67
1979	14.79	17.33	18.03	23.56	26.80
1989	12.49	15.59	17.19	24.25	30.15
1995	10.98	14.88	16.60	24.61	32.01
2000	11.38	15.74	17.95	27.64	34.54
2005	11.48	15.65	17.76	28.06	35.67
Annualized percentage change					
1973-79	0.1%	-0.1%	0.2%	-0.3%	0.1%
1979-89	-1.7	-1.1	-0.5	0.3	1.2
1989-2000	-0.8	0.1	0.4	1.2	1.2
1989-95	-2.1	-0.8	-0.6	0.2	1.0
1995-2000	0.7	1.1	1.6	2.4	1.5
1979-2000	-1.2	-0.5	0.0	0.8	1.2
2000-05	0.2	-0.1	-0.2	0.3	0.6
Share of employment					
1973	30.6%	34.4%	19.2%	10.3%	5.4%
1979	22.3	35.0	22.4	13.2	7.1
1989	15.9	35.2	24.4	15.7	8.8
2000	13.1	32.0	27.5	18.4	9.1
2005	12.6	31.4	27.4	18.9	9.6

Source: Authors' analysis of CPS ORG.

average high-school-educated male fell more, 14.1%, from 1979 to 1995, while the wages of those without a high school degree fell 25.8%. By contrast, the wages of male college graduates rose, but more modestly than commonly thought—just 2.9% from 1979 to 1989 and an additional 1.4% over the 1989-95 period. Year-by-year data show that male college wages in the 1979-95 period peaked in 1987. The period from 1995 to 2000 was one of strong real wage growth among college-educated men, 2.4% annually, even stronger than among those with an advanced degree.

Over the entire 1979-2005 period the pattern of growing wages for college-educated males (almost entirely due to the 1995-2000 period) and declining or stagnant wages for non-college-educated males meant a rise in the relative wage, or wage premium, for male college graduates. As shown in Table 3.16, the estimated college/high school wage premium (where experience, race, and other characteristics are controlled for) grew from 20.1% in 1979 to 33.9% in 1989 and to 43.1% by 2005. As Figure 3M shows, however, there was a flattening of the male college/high school premium over the 1988-96 period, particularly

TABLE 3.19 Real hourly wage for women by education, 1973-2005 (2005 dollars)

Year	Less than high school	High school	Some college	College	Advanced degree
Hourly wage					
1973	$8.85	$10.96	$11.84	$16.40	$21.72
1979	9.49	11.25	12.09	15.30	19.60
1989	8.67	11.21	12.99	17.57	22.90
1995	8.37	11.33	12.98	18.88	24.85
2000	8.73	11.96	13.88	20.90	26.36
2005	8.88	12.34	14.18	21.30	27.08
Annualized percentage change					
1973-79	1.2%	0.4%	0.3%	-1.1%	-1.7%
1979-89	-0.9	0.0	0.7	1.4	1.6
1989-2000	0.1	0.6	0.6	1.6	1.3
1989-95	-0.6	0.2	0.0	1.2	1.4
1995-2000	0.9	1.1	1.3	2.0	1.2
1979-2000	-0.4	0.3	0.7	1.5	1.4
2000-2005	0.3	0.6	0.4	0.4	0.5
Share of employment					
1973	25.6%	44.0%	17.5%	9.9%	3.1%
1979	17.2	43.0	23.4	12.0	4.4
1989	11.2	38.8	27.8	15.4	6.8
2000	8.9	31.7	31.9	19.2	8.4
2005	7.9	28.7	32.6	20.8	9.9

Source: Authors' analysis of CPS ORG.

in the early 1990s. Since there has not been an acceleration of the supply of college-educated men (as shown in a later section), this slower wage growth implies, within a conventional demand-supply framework, that growth in the relative demand for college workers slowed in that period. From 1996 to 2000, however, this key education differential among men jumped again, followed by a decline and modest recovery by 2005. Thus, the growth in the college wage premium was relatively modest after 1988 with the exception of the late 1990s.

As we have seen in our earlier examinations of the wage structure, women's wages have grown faster than men's in nearly every category (deciles, poverty-level wages, etc). However, the same general pattern of relative wages—i.e., who does better—prevails among women as among men (Table 3.19). From 2000 to 2005, wage growth among women of all education groups rose comparably, from 0.6% for high school women to 0.4% or 0.5% for those with college or advanced degrees. In contrast, men's wage growth was more differentiated in recent years. In the late 1990s wages grew strongly among women in each

TABLE 3.20 Educational attainment of workforce employment, 2005

| Highest degree attained | Percent of employment | | | | |
	Men	Women	All	Natives only	Immigrants only
Less than high school	12.6%	7.9%	10.4%	6.8%	30.1%
High school/GED	31.4	28.7	30.1	31.0	25.2
Some college	18.8	21.5	20.1	21.7	11.3
Assoc. college	8.6	11.1	9.8	10.6	5.7
College B.A.	18.9	20.8	19.8	20.3	17.2
Advanced degree*	9.6	9.9	9.8	9.6	10.6
Total	100.0	100.0	100.0	100.0	100.0
Memo					
High school or less	44.0%	36.6%	40.5%	37.8%	55.3%
Less than B.A. degree	71.5	69.3	70.4	70.1	72.3
College B.A. or more	28.5	30.7	29.6	29.9	27.7
Advanced degree*	9.6	9.9	9.8	9.6	10.6

* Includes law degrees, Ph.D.s, M.B.A.s, and similar degrees.

Source: Authors' analysis of CPS ORG.

education group, with the familiar pattern of greatest growth among college graduates (even greater than those with advanced degrees). In the 1979-89 and 1989-95 periods wages were stagnant among high-school-educated women but fell significantly among those without a high school degree (11.9% overall). Women with some college saw significant wage gains in the 1980s (unlike their male counterparts), but not in the early 1990s. College-educated women saw strong wage growth throughout the 1979-95 period (23.4% overall), faring by far the best among all gender-education categories. This pattern of wage growth resulted in growth of the college/high school wage differential comparable to that of men (Table 3.16), from 26.5% in 1979 to 41.0% in 1989 and to 46.7% in 1995 (the increase up to 1995 being higher than among men). However, the college wage premium among women has barely budged over the last 10 years, only rising to 47.1% by 2005. Thus, the education/wage gap grew more among women than among men in the 1979-95 period and then stagnated while it rose somewhat among men. The relative losers among women—the non-college-educated—saw relatively stagnant wages, whereas among men wages fell.

Even though the wages of college-educated women have grown rapidly since 1979, a female college graduate in 2005 still earned $6.76 less, or 24%, than a male college graduate in 2005.

Table 3.20 shows a breakdown of employment in 2005 by the highest degree attained and by gender and immigrant/native status. Some 29.6% of the workforce had at least a four-year college degree (19.8% have a college degree only and 9.8% also have a graduate or professional degree). Correspondingly, 70.4% of the workforce has less than a college degree, with 10.4% never completing high school; 30.1% completing high school or obtaining a GED; another 20.1% attending college but earning no degree beyond high school; and 9.8% holding associate degrees. These data reinforce the earlier discussion that the poor wage performance experienced by the "less educated" (frequently defined by economists as those without a college degree) between 1979 and 1995 and then from 2000 to 2005 affected a very large share of the workforce. This is important to note because the language used in public discussion asserts that the "less-educated" have done poorly, leaving the impression that they are a small part of the population. But "less-educated" implicitly corresponds to those without a four-year college degree, their share of the workforce, at 70.4%, is huge.

It is also interesting to note that the group of workers with more than a high school degree but less than a four-year college degree now make up a group equivalent in size (29.9%) to groups of high school graduates (30.1%) and bachelor's degree holders (29.6%). Among women, those with some college or an associate's degree (32.6%) now exceed those holding at most a high school degree (28.7%).

Young workers' wages

Young workers' prospects seem to be an apt barometer of the strength of the labor market—when the labor market is strong for workers the prospects for young workers are very strong, and when the labor market is weak their prospects are very weak. For instance, the most dramatic erosion of wages over the 1973-95 period was among young workers. However, young workers also experienced the fastest wage growth over the 1995-2000 period. As a result, there have been significant changes—up and down—in wage differentials between younger and older workers, as shown earlier in Table 3.16.

Table 3.21 presents trends in wages for entry-level (one to five years of experience) high school and college graduates by gender. It is interesting to note that in the recent period of sluggish wage growth, wages actually fell among every entry-level group, both high school and college and both men and women. This contrasts to the extremely strong wage growth for each of these groups from 1995-2000, when wages rose roughly 10% for entry-level high school men and women and 20.9% for entry-level college men, 11.7% for college women. This change illustrates the vast swing in wages for entry-level workers between a period of strong wages and stagnant wages.

The generally poor wage performance of non-college-educated workers has been magnified among young entry-level workers (**Figure 3O**). Since the wages of both younger and non-college-educated workers fell most rapidly in the 1979-95 period and fared more poorly from 2000 to 2005, it should not be surprising that entry-level wages for men and women high school graduates in 2005 were still below their levels of 1979 or 1973. For instance, the entry-level hourly wage of a young male high school graduate in 2005 was 19.0% less than that for the equivalent worker in 1979, a drop of $2.57 per hour. Among women, the entry-level high school wage fell 9.0% in this period. Entry-level wages for high school graduates grew rapidly, over 9%, between 1995 and 2005 for both men and women, and this growth ameliorated the long-term decline in their wages. Note that wages in entry-level jobs held by high-school-educated women are still less than those for their male counterparts, though the gap is not as wide as in the 1970s.

TABLE 3.21 Hourly wages of entry-level and experienced workers by education, 1973-2005 (2005 dollars)

Education/experience	Hourly wage						Percent change				
	1973	1979	1989	1995	2000	2005	1973-79	1979-89	1989-2000	1995-2000	2000-05
High school											
Men											
Entry*	$13.39	$13.50	$10.93	$10.15	$11.10	$10.93	0.8%	-19.0%	1.5%	9.3%	-1.5%
34-40	19.14	19.32	16.91	16.22	16.88	16.77	1.0	-12.5	-0.2	4.1	-0.6
49-55	20.17	20.61	19.07	18.32	18.13	18.22	2.2	-7.5	-4.9	-1.0	0.5
Women											
Entry*	$9.81	$9.98	$8.95	$8.65	$9.49	$9.08	1.7%	-10.3%	6.1%	9.8%	-4.3%
34-40	11.26	11.65	11.73	11.87	12.59	12.62	3.5	0.6	7.3	6.1	0.3
49-55	11.73	11.99	12.34	12.44	13.23	13.92	2.2	2.9	7.2	6.3	5.2
College											
Men											
Entry**	$17.76	$17.79	$18.29	$16.97	$20.51	$19.72	0.2%	2.8%	12.1%	20.9%	-3.9%
34-40	28.66	27.64	27.06	27.74	30.72	31.44	-3.6	-2.1	13.5	10.8	2.3
49-55	29.54	30.64	30.43	30.75	31.64	30.70	3.7	-0.7	4.0	2.9	-3.0
Women											
Entry**	$14.88	$14.07	$15.92	$15.59	$17.41	$17.08	-5.5%	13.2%	9.3%	11.7%	-1.9%
34-40	17.75	16.13	18.39	20.73	22.63	23.75	-9.2	14.0	23.1	9.2	4.9
49-55	16.94	16.32	17.85	20.91	21.83	21.95	-3.7	9.4	22.3	4.4	0.6

* Entry-level wage measured as wage of those from 19 to 25 years of age.
** Entry-level wage measured as wage of those from 23 to 29 years of age.

Source: Authors' analysis of CPS ORG.

FIGURE 3O Entry-level wages of male and female high school graduates, 1973-2005

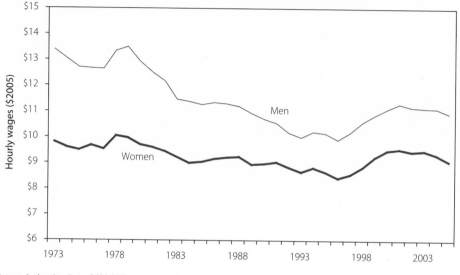

Source: Authors' analysis of CPS ORG.

Entry-level wages among male college graduates were stagnant over the 1973-89 period, fell 7.3% from 1989 to 1995, and then escalated rapidly in the late 1990s (**Figure 3P**). Much ground was lost for new college graduates from 2000 to 2005, as wages fell 3.9% among men and 1.9% among women. Thus, new male college graduates earned $0.79 less per hour in 2005 than their counterparts did in 2000. Wages among women college graduates have grown more strongly than among any other group of women, and this strength is reflected in the long-term trend among entry-level women college graduates; their wages grew 21.4%, or $3.01, from 1979 to 2005. Still, wages for new women college graduates in 2005 were 13.4%, or $2.64, less than that of their male counterparts and 1.9%, or $0.33, less than in 2000. So far in this business cycle, the better-educated workers with the newest skills are not faring so well in the "new economy."

The erosion of job quality for young workers can also be seen in the lower likelihood of their receiving employer-provided health insurance or pensions. **Figures 3Q** and **3R** show the rate of employer-provided health insurance and pension coverage in entry-level jobs for, respectively, high school graduates and college graduates. Employer-provided health insurance among these recent high school graduates fell by roughly half, from 63.3% to 33.7%, between 1979 and 2004 (the latest data). Pension coverage fell over this period as well, from an already low 36.0% in 1979 to an even lower 18.8% in 2004.

Health insurance coverage also fell among recent college graduates, but not as drastically as among recent high school graduates. The share covered was 77.7% in 1979 and

FIGURE 3P Entry-level wages of male and female college graduates, 1973-2005

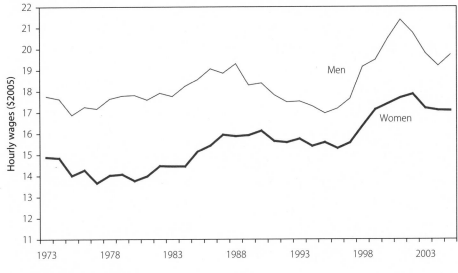

Source: Authors' analysis of CPS ORG.

FIGURE 3Q Health and pension coverage for recent high school graduates, 1979-2004

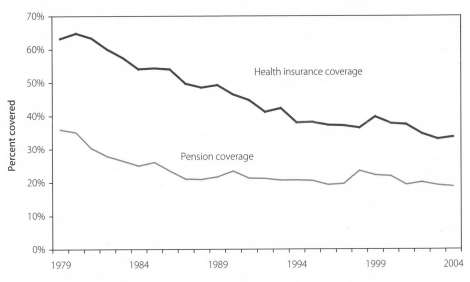

Source: Authors' analysis of March CPS.

FIGURE 3R Health and pension coverage for recent college graduates, 1979-2004

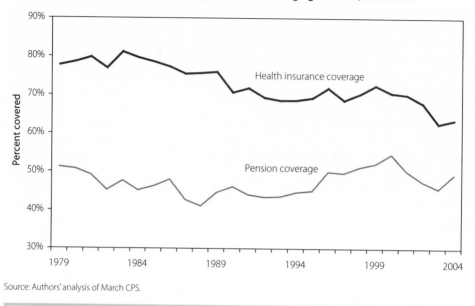

Source: Authors' analysis of March CPS.

63.5% in 2004, with roughly half the decline resulting from the precipitous 7 percentage-point drop between 2000 and 2004. Pension coverage among young college graduates follows the overall pattern discussed in an earlier section. It fell between 1979 and the late 1980s and then regained its earlier level by 1998. However, this group's pension coverage fell over the 2000-04 period by 5.3 percentage points, from 54.6% to 49.3%. This sharp reduction in both health and pension benefits for young college graduates over the last few years indicates a substantial job quality problem even for those with the highest educational attainment.

The growth of within-group wage inequality

The data presented so far illustrate the various dimensions of wage inequality. The "between-group" inequality for workers by both education and experience (or age) can be characterized as a growth in differentials in education and experience, which are sometimes labeled as an increase in the "returns to education and experience" or as a shift in the rewards or price of "skill." We now examine in greater depth the growth of "within-group" wage inequality, the inequality among workers with similar education and experience.

This growth in within-group wage inequality was shown earlier in Table 3.16. The analysis in **Table 3.22** illustrates the growth of this type of inequality by presenting wage trends of high-, middle-, and low-wage workers among high school and college graduates. In other words, the data track the wages of 90th, 50th (median), and 10th percentile high-school-educated and college-educated workers by gender and show a growing wage gap among college graduates and high school graduates.

Because of rising within-group inequality, the wage growth of the median or "typical" worker within each group has been less than that of the average worker. For instance, the median wage of the male high school graduate fell 13.8% over the 1973-2005 period, compared to a 10.1% drop in the average wage (Table 3.18). Similarly, the wage growth of male college graduates in the 1973-2005 period was 16.8% at the average (Table 3.18) but only 12.8% at the median (Table 3.22).

The growing disparity of wages within groups is demonstrated in Table 3.22. While the high (90th percentile) wage among female college graduates grew 55.9% from 1973 to 2005, the low (10th percentile) wage in this group rose 11.2%, a 44 percentage-point disparity. Similarly, wage trends at the top of the college male wage ladder (24.9% growth) and the bottom (a 3.2% decline) diverged dramatically over the 1973-2005 period.

The question remains, however, as to how much the growth in overall wage inequality in particular time periods has been driven by changes in between-group versus within-group wage inequality. It would also be useful to know the role of the growth of between- and within-group inequality on growing wage inequality at the top (the 90/50 differential) versus the bottom (the 50/10 differential), but measurement techniques for answering this question are not readily available.

Table 3.23 presents the trends in overall wage inequality, as measured by the standard deviation of log hourly wages, and the trends in within-group wage inequality. These measures allow an examination of how much of the change in overall wage inequality in particular periods was due to changes in within-group wage inequality and between-group wage inequality (primarily changes in the differentials for education and experience).

The data in Table 3.23 indicate that roughly 60% of the growth of wage inequality since 1979 has been driven by the growth of within-group wage inequality. Among women, for instance, overall wage inequality grew 0.132 over the 1979-2005 period, of which 0.075 was due to growth of within-group inequality. Similarly, 0.064 of the 0.108 increase in overall male wage inequality over the 1979-2005 period was due to growing within-group inequality.

The growth of wage inequality in the 2000-05 period is a departure from the prior five years of the late 1990s wage boom, when wage inequality was stable. For men, this shift to a renewed growth of wage inequality is about equally due to a renewed growth of within-group wage inequality (up from .003 to .012 among men compared to a within-group change from -.003 to .007). However, among women the renewed growth of wage inequality is much more due to growing within-group inequality than rising age or education differentials.

Wage inequality over the 1995-2000 period was essentially unchanged among men and declined among women, the latter a result of a decline in within-group wage inequality. Thus, Table 3.23 makes clear that any explanation of growing wage inequality must go beyond explaining changes in skill, education, experience, or other wage differentials and be able to explain growing inequalities within each of these categories.

It is also noteworthy that between-group wage inequality did not rise in the 1995-2000 technology-related productivity and wage boom, nor did it rise much during the fast

TABLE 3.22 Hourly wages by decile within education groups, 1973-2005 (2005 dollars)

Education/gender decile	Hourly wage						Percent change				
	1973	1979	1989	1995	2000	2005	1973-79	1979-89	1989-2000	2000-05	1973-2005
High school											
Men											
Low*	$8.89	$8.45	$7.31	$7.10	$7.75	$7.76	-5.0%	-13.5%	6.1%	0.1%	-12.7%
Median	16.03	16.11	14.19	13.09	13.77	13.82	0.5	-11.9	-3.0	0.4	-13.8
High	26.19	26.30	25.01	24.07	25.22	25.21	0.4	-4.9	0.8	-0.1	-3.8
Women											
Low	$6.02	$7.05	$5.80	$6.05	$6.64	$6.58	17.0%	-17.7%	14.4%	-0.9%	9.2%
Median	9.95	9.97	10.03	9.89	10.58	10.69	0.2	0.6	5.4	1.1	7.4
High	16.47	17.03	18.08	18.26	18.99	19.78	3.4	6.2	5.0	4.2	20.1
College											
Men											
Low	$10.98	$10.90	$10.36	$9.90	$11.30	$10.62	-0.7%	-5.0%	9.1%	-6.0%	-3.2%
Median	20.61	20.55	21.48	21.21	23.37	23.24	-0.3	4.5	8.8	-0.6	12.8
High	38.43	37.75	38.94	41.43	45.31	48.01	-1.8	3.2	16.3	6.0	24.9
Women											
Low	$8.44	$7.83	$8.17	$8.34	$9.24	$9.39	-7.2%	4.3%	13.1%	1.6%	11.2%
Median	14.58	13.60	15.79	16.79	18.17	18.35	-6.8	16.1	15.1	0.9	25.8
High	23.04	23.11	27.50	31.15	34.84	35.93	0.3	19.0	26.7	3.1	55.9

* Low, median, and high earners refer to, respectively, the 10th, 50th, and 90th percentile wage.

Source: Authors' analysis of CPS ORG.

TABLE 3.23 Decomposition of total and within-group wage inequality, 1973-2005

	Women				Men			
Year	Overall wage inequality* (1)	Between-group inequality** (2)	Within-group inequality*** (3)	Contribution of within-group inequality (3)/(1)	Overall wage inequality* (1)	Between-group inequality** (2)	Within-group inequality*** (3)	Contribution of within-group inequality (3)/(1)
1973	0.478	0.061	0.418		0.506	0.083	0.423	
1979	0.446	0.044	0.402		0.506	0.078	0.428	
1989	0.529	0.082	0.447		0.579	0.112	0.467	
1995	0.562	0.095	0.467		0.595	0.118	0.478	
2000	0.552	0.094	0.458		0.595	0.114	0.481	
2005	0.578	0.101	0.476		0.614	0.121	0.493	
Change								
1973-79	-0.033	-0.017	-0.016	49.1%	0.000	-0.005	0.006	n.a.****
1979-89	0.083	0.038	0.046	54.7	0.073	0.034	0.038	52.8%
1989-2000	0.023	0.012	0.011	46.6	0.016	0.002	0.014	86.3
1989-95	0.033	0.013	0.019	59.5	0.016	0.006	0.011	65.5
1995-2000	-0.009	-0.001	-0.009	91.8	0.000	-0.003	0.003	n.a.****
2000-05	0.026	0.007	0.018	72.1	0.019	0.007	0.012	63.7
1979-2005	0.132	0.057	0.075	56.7	0.108	0.043	0.064	59.8
1973-2005	0.099	0.041	0.059	59.2	0.108	0.038	0.070	64.9

*   Measured as standard deviation of log wages.
**   Reflects changes in education, experience, race/ethnicity, marital status, and regional differentials.
***   Measured as mean square error from a standard (log) wage regression.
**** Not applicable because denominator is zero or too small.

Source: Authors' analysis of CPS ORG.

productivity period from 2000 to 2005 (.007 among both men and women). This finding is inconsistent with a story that technology (or the "new economy") has generated greater wage inequalities by expanding the economic return to skills—primarily education and experience. These data reflect that, while it is true that the college/high school wage differential grew in the 1995-2000 period, experience differentials fell and education differentials between high-school-educated workers and workers without a high school education were stable (see Table 3.16).

Wage growth by race and ethnicity

Race and ethnicity have long played an important role in shaping employment opportunities and labor market outcomes, and **Table 3.24** examines changes in those dimensions of the wage structure. Wage trends are presented by gender for two indicators of the middle of the wage structure (the median wage and the high school wage) for four populations: white, black, Hispanic, and Asian. (A finer breakdown of groups (e.g., sub-populations of Hispanics) is not possible because of sample-size limitations and, for the same reason, the trends for the 1980s are not available. Also, note that our definitions of race/ethnicity categories exclude Hispanics from the white, black, and Asian groups.)

Over the recent 2000-05 period the male median wage was stagnant for whites and Hispanics and fell 1.3% for blacks. The 7.6% rise among Asian men is a standout exception. The wage trends among male high school graduates tell a similar story of stagnant wages for each race/ethnic group in recent years. In contrast wages rose rapidly for every race/ethnic group in the boom years from 1995 to 2000 but declined, especially among Hispanics, in the early 1990s.

Wage growth among women was stronger than that for men in recent years, at least as measured by median wages. White women fared best with a 6.4% rise, and Asians and Hispanics saw roughly 4% growth. The slight 0.9% decline of the median black woman's wage is the exception to the trend. In contrast, the median wage for black women grew faster than that for whites and Hispanics in the late 1990s (as with men, Asian women's wages soared faster than that of any other ethnic group). The wage trend among women high school graduates mirrors that of the median wage, although growth was slower both in the recent period and in the late 1990s by this measure.

The gender wage gap

As discussed in several earlier sections, women's wages have generally fared better than men's over the last few decades. For instance, in 1973 the ratio of the median woman's wage to the male median wage was 63.1% but rose to 82.0% by 2005 (see **Table 3.25** and **Figure 3S**). The rapid closing of the gender gap occurred primarily between 1979 and 1995, mostly as the result of a steady fall in the male median wage and modest growth of the female median wage. Figure 3S also shows the gender wage gaps at other points in the wage distribution—e.g., comparing the wages of low-wage men and low-wage women (looking at the 20th percentile) and doing likewise for high-wage men and women (looking at the 90th percentiles). The gender wage gap between low-wage men

TABLE 3.24 Hourly wage growth by gender, race/ethnicity, 1989-2005 (2005 dollars)

Demographic group	Hourly wage				Percent change			
	1989	1995	2000	2005	1989-2000	1989-95	1995-2000	2000-05
Men								
Medians								
White	$16.51	$15.88	$17.28	$17.42	4.7%	-3.8%	8.8%	0.8%
Black	11.94	11.61	12.64	12.48	5.8	-2.8	8.9	-1.3
Hispanic	11.10	10.12	11.09	11.14	-0.1	-8.9	9.6	0.5
Asian	15.42	15.29	17.18	18.49	11.4	-0.9	12.4	7.6
By education								
High school*								
White	$16.21	$15.56	$16.66	$16.64	2.8%	-4.0%	7.1%	-0.1%
Black	12.95	12.45	13.34	13.22	3.0	-3.9	7.2	-0.9
Hispanic	13.43	12.84	13.32	13.61	-0.9	-4.4	3.7	2.2
Asian	14.18	13.85	14.73	14.36	3.9	-2.3	6.4	-2.5
Women								
Medians								
White	$11.56	$11.84	$12.96	$13.78	12.1%	2.4%	9.5%	6.4%
Black	10.30	10.18	11.33	11.22	10.0	-1.1	11.2	-0.9
Hispanic	9.19	9.00	9.58	9.99	4.2	-2.0	6.4	4.3
Asian	11.96	12.18	13.81	14.49	15.4	1.8	13.4	4.9
By education								
High school*								
White	$11.38	$11.57	$12.24	$12.78	7.6%	1.6%	5.8%	4.3%
Black	10.50	10.45	11.25	11.38	7.1	-0.5	7.7	1.2
Hispanic	10.56	10.64	11.07	11.30	4.8	0.8	4.0	2.1
Asian	10.83	10.96	11.78	12.00	8.7	1.1	7.5	1.9

* Average wage

Source: Authors' analysis of CPS ORG.

and women as well as between high-wage men and women was fairly stable from the mid-1990s to 2001 or 2002. Over the last few years there was a spurt of wage growth among high-wage women relative to high-wage men, closing the gender gap further. However, low-wage women have not closed the wage gap any further with their male counterparts in recent years.

Unfortunately, there is no research that explains these trends or examines how shifts in skills, the gender composition of work, and other factors have contributed to the closing and then flattening of the gender gap.

TABLE 3.25 The gender wage ratio, 1973-2005 (2005 dollars)

	Median wage		
	Women	Men	Ratio: Women/Men
1973	$9.95	$15.76	63.1%
1979	10.35	16.51	62.7
1989	11.22	15.35	73.1
1995	11.35	14.79	76.7
2000	12.32	15.81	78.0
2005	12.82	15.64	82.0

Source: Authors' analysis of CPS ORG.

FIGURE 3S Gender wage ratio by percentile, 1973-2005

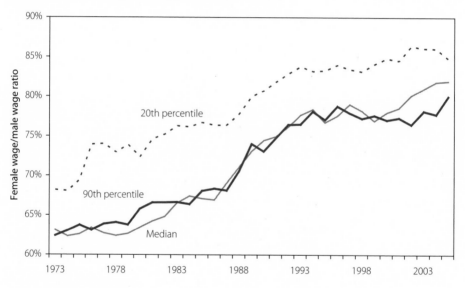

Source: Authors' analysis of CPS ORG.

Unemployment and wage growth

One category of factors shaping wage growth can be labeled macroeconomic. These factors reflect the overall health of the economy and determine whether it is producing less than it has the capacity to do, as indicated by high unemployment and excess production capacity. Generally, slack in the economy is driven by monetary policy (the growth of the money supply, interest rates), fiscal policy (the size of the government surplus/deficits, with increasing deficits adding to demand and thereby lessening slack), and the U.S. international position (trade deficits, the flow of investment dollars abroad or from abroad to the United States). Factors that affect growth include those that limit or generate slack but also those that shape productive potential, such as public and private investment, technological change, workforce skills, and work organization (how factors of production are combined).

Macroeconomic conditions greatly affect wage growth and wage inequality. The issue of productivity and wage growth was discussed in an earlier section, so here we focus on other macroeconomic factors, particularly the extent of unemployment and underemployment (trends in these factors are explored in detail in Chapter 4). The burdens of an underperforming economy and high employment are not equally shared; lower- and middle-income families are more likely to experience unemployment, underemployment, and slower wage growth because of a weak economy. For many years, until recently, white-collar workers and high-wage workers were relatively unaffected by unemployment and recessions. Not surprisingly, therefore, high unemployment is a factor that widens wage and income inequality.

There are a number of mechanisms through which high unemployment affects wages and, especially, affects them differently for different groups of workers. The wages of groups that have lower wages, less education or skill, and less power in the labor market are generally more adversely affected by high unemployment and underemployment. In other words, those already disadvantaged in the labor market become even more disadvantaged in a recession or in a weak economy. Conversely, as unemployment falls in a recovery and stays low, the greatest benefit accrues to those with the least power in the labor market—non-college-educated, blue-collar, minority, and low-wage workers.

How does this happen? First, these groups experience the greatest employment decline in a downturn and the greatest employment growth in a recovery. This greater-than-average gain in employment reflects higher demand for these workers and consequently provides them with a greater increase in leverage with employers, a position that generates higher wages. Second, as unemployment drops, more opportunities arise for upward mobility for these workers, as they switch jobs either to a new employer or within the same firm. Third, unions are able to bargain higher wages when unemployment is low. Fourth, macroeconomic conditions and institutional and structural factors interact in important ways. For instance, the early 1980s saw a surge of imports and a growing trade deficit, a decline in manufacturing, a weakening of unions, and a large erosion of the minimum wage that coincided with (and in some cases partly caused, as was the case with the trade and manufacturing problems) the rising unemployment at that time. The impact of these factors on wage inequality was probably greater because of high unemployment. So, for example, the impact of trade on wages (discussed below) was greater because the recession had already induced a scarcity of good jobs. It should not be surprising that the most radical restructuring of wages (a tremendous growth in wage inequities) and the substantial real wage reductions for non-college-educated workers occurred during the period of very high unemployment from 1979 to 1985.

The impact of rising unemployment and falling unemployment can be illustrated by examining the effect on wages of increases in unemployment in the 1979-85 period and

TABLE 3.26 Impact of rising and falling unemployment on wage levels and wage ratios, 1979-2000

	1979-85		1995-2000	
	Men	Women	Men	Women
Actual changes				
Unemployment rate	1.4	1.4	-1.6	-1.6
50/10 (log)	9.6	17.0	-3.9	-1.8
90/50 (log)	8.7	8.0	3.8	1.1
Simulated effect of change in unemployment on:				
Hourly wages				
10th percentile	-15.2%	-17.2%	10.2%	7.0%
50th percentile	-9.4	-8.0	4.1	2.3
90th percentile	-8.9	-8.3	3.1	3.7
Wage ratios (log)				
50/10	6.6	10.5	-5.7	-4.5
90/50	0.6	-0.3	-0.9	1.4
Unemployment contribution to change				
50/10 (log)	68%	62%	145%	257%
90/50 (log)	6	-4	-25	131

Source: Authors' analysis.

decreases in unemployment in the 1995-2000 period, as shown in **Table 3.26**. These estimates focus on the effect of unemployment trends on the 10th, 50th, and 90th percentile wages and the 90/50 and 50/10 wage ratios for each gender.

Figure 3T shows the course of unemployment in these two periods—the sharp rise in unemployment in the early 1980s and the persistent drop in unemployment to roughly 4% in the late 1990s. During the 1980s recession wage inequality rose sharply, both at the top (the 90/50 ratio) and the bottom (the 50/10 ratio), with low-wage women being most adversely affected. Correspondingly, during the 1995-2000 boom the 50/10 wage ratios became smaller among both men and women while the 90/50 ratio among women continued to grow.

How much of these shifts in wage inequality were due to unemployment trends? Table 3.26 presents the results of simulations that estimate the effect of unemployment trends during the 1979-85 and 1995-2000 periods on the wages in the final year of each period—1985 and 2000, respectively. For instance, the early 1980s recession lowered the wages (relative to what they otherwise would have been) of workers at the 10th percentile in 1985 by 15.2% among men and 17.2% among women. The drop in unemployment in

FIGURE 3T Unemployment, 1973-2005

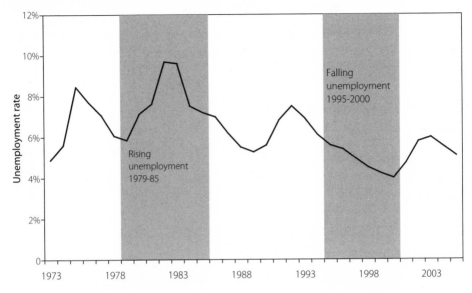

Source: Bureau of Labor Statistics.

the 1995-2000 period raised wages for low-wage (10th percentile) men and women by 10.2% and 7.0%, respectively. Unemployment had a sizable but lesser effect on the wages of middle- and high-wage workers; surprisingly, unemployment seems to affect middle- and high-wage workers to the same extent—about an 8-9% reduction in the 1980s and a 3-4% improvement in the late 1990s. Thus, unemployment did not greatly affect the 90/50 wage ratio, which grew overall in both periods. However, the very large impact of unemployment on the wages at the bottom led to large changes in the 50/10 wage ratio—a roughly 5 percentage-point reduction in the late 1990s and a 6.6 percentage-point increase for men and a 10.5 percentage-point increase for women in the early 1980s. Consequently, the higher unemployment in the early 1980s can account for over 60% of the growth in the 50/10 wage ratio in that period, while lower unemployment can account for more than all of the diminution of wage inequality at the bottom in the late 1990s. In the latter period, then, unemployment likely offset other factors (such as immigration, trade, and so on, as discussed below) that otherwise would have generated growth in wage inequality.

The higher unemployment and overall labor slack in the early 2000s (documented in Chapter 4) clearly took their toll on wage growth and exacerbated wage inequality. Simulations comparable to those presented in Table 3.26 show that the yearly growth of real median wages was slowed by 1.5% among men and 1.0% among women. The persistently high unemployment had an even greater effect on the wage growth of low-wage (10th percentile) workers, knocking growth of their wages down 2.2% and 1.5% per year, respectively, among men and women. As a result, wage inequality was higher at the bottom—as reflected in the 50/10 wage gap—than it would have been if low unemployment had been maintained: the 50/10 wage gap would have fallen slightly among women (0.7 percentage points) rather than risen slightly and fallen much faster among men (2.5 percentage points) than the slight fall (by 0.7 percentage points) that actually occurred. Since wage growth for high-wage workers was affected to the same extent as that for middle-wage workers, higher unemployment did not fuel the continuing growth of the wage gap at the top.

The shift to low-paying industries

One factor that contributes to growing inequality and lower pay, especially for non-college-educated workers, is a changing mix of industries in the economy. Such changes include the continued shift from goods-producing to service-producing industries and at times to lower-paying service industries. The shift in the industry mix of employment matters because some industries pay more than others for workers of comparable skill.

These industry employment shifts result from trade deficits and deindustrialization as well as from differential patterns of productivity growth across industries. (Industries facing the same growth in demand for their goods and services will generate more jobs the slower their productivity growth.) This section examines the significant erosion of wages and compensation for workers resulting from the employment shift to low-paying industries since the 1980s.

Despite a common perception, this industry-shift effect is not the simple consequence of some natural evolution from an agricultural to a manufacturing to a service economy. For one thing, a significant part of the shrinkage of manufacturing is trade-related. More important, industry shifts would not provide a downward pressure on wages if service-sector wages were more closely aligned with manufacturing wages, as is the case in other countries. Moreover, since health coverage, vacations, and pensions in this country are related to the specific job or sector in which a worker is employed, the industry distribution of employment matters more in the United States than in other countries. An alternative institutional arrangement found in other advanced countries sets health, pensions, vacation, and other benefits through legislation in a universal manner regardless of sector or firm. Therefore, the downward pressure of industry shifts on pay can be said, in part, to be the consequence of the absence of institutional structures that lessen inter-industry pay differences.

Trends in employment growth by major industry sector and the annual compensation and "college intensity" (the share of workers with a college degree) in 2005 for each sector are presented in **Table 3.27**. Over the 2000 to 2005 period payroll employment rose by a very modest 1,678,000 (the sluggish job growth is explored in detail in Chapter 4). Many jobs were lost in this period in the highest-paying sectors, including manufacturing (down 3,031,000) and especially durable manufacturing (down 1,923,000), with jobs also lost in other highly paid industries, such as information, that had grown rapidly in the 1989-2000 period. Thus, industry shifts in the current business cycle have put downward pressure on compensation.

The extent of adverse industry shifts in the past is best examined in an analysis of changes in the shares of the workforce in various sectors (Table 3.27). When industries

TABLE 3.27 Employment growth by sector, 1979-2005

Industry sector	Employment shares				Change 2000-05		Hourly compensation 2005	Percent college graduates
	1979	1989	2000	2005	Shares	Level (000)		
Goods producing	27.8%	22.3%	18.7%	16.6%	-2.1	-2,516	$29.37	19%
Mining	1.1	0.7	0.5	0.5	0.0	26	37.07	16
Construction	5.1	4.9	5.2	5.5	0.3	490	28.48	10
Manufacturing	21.6	16.7	13.1	10.7	-2.4	-3,031	29.47	23
Durable goods	13.6	10.2	8.3	6.7	-1.5	-1,923	30.98	25
Nondurable goods	8.0	6.5	4.8	4.0	-0.9	-1,110	26.96	21
Service producing	72.2%	77.7%	81.3%	83.4%	2.1	4,194	$23.58	32%
Trans., utilities	4.0	3.8	3.8	3.7	-0.1	-107	20.48	17
Wholesale trade	5.0	4.9	4.5	4.3	-0.2	-184	27.44	25
Retail trade	11.3	12.1	11.6	11.4	-0.2	-25	15.23	16
Information	2.6	2.4	2.8	2.3	-0.5	-565	36.38	42
Fin., ins., real estate	5.4	6.1	5.8	6.1	0.3	454	32.80	39
Services	26.0	31.8	37.0	39.3	2.2	3,607	22.86	37
Government	17.9%	16.6%	15.8%	16.3%	0.6	1,013	n.a.	50%
Federal	3.2	2.9	2.2	2.0	-0.1	-141	n.a.	40
State and local	14.6	13.7	13.6	14.3	0.7	1,154	$36.55	51
Total	100.0%	100.0%	100.0%	100.0%		1,678	$26.61	30%

Source: Authors' analysis of BLS payroll data and Employer Costs for Employee Compensation and CPS.

TABLE 3.28 Annual pay of expanding and contracting industries, 1979-2005

Annual pay	Industries		Difference		Annual impact
	Contracting	Expanding	$	%	
Compensation (000)					
2000-05	$62.2	$47.7	-$1,453	-23.4%	-0.2%
1989-2000	47.7	37.3	-1,047	-21.9	-0.2
1979-89	48.3	33.1	-1,518	-31.4	-0.3
Wages and salaries (000)					
2000-05	$51.6	$41.0	-$1,066	-20.6%	-0.2%
1989-2000	39.5	32.0	-748	-19.0	-0.1
1979-89	39.4	30.3	-907	-23.0	-0.2

Source: Authors' analysis of BLS payroll employment data and NIPA compensation data for roughly 60 industries in each time period.

with above (or below) average pay levels expand employment share they raise (or lower) the average pay. The 1979-89 period saw significant downward pressure on pay due to industry shifts: the share of the workforce in low-paying services and in retail trade was 6.4 percentage points higher in 1989 than in 1979. The parallel trend was the roughly 7 percentage-point drop in the share of the workforce in high-paying industries such as manufacturing, construction, mining, government, transportation, and utilities.

The data in Table 3.27 illustrate the different, and less adverse, shifts in industry employment in the 1990s relative to the 1980s. Although durable manufacturing's share of employment declined in the 1990s (by 1.9 percentage points), this was less than the decline of the 1980s (3.4 percentage points). The low-wage retail trade sector expanded by 0.8 percentage points in the 1980s but shrank in the 1990s. Similarly, higher-wage sectors such as construction and transportation/utilities expanded or were stable in the 1990s but contracted in the 1980s. In general, high-wage sectors fared better in terms of employment growth in the 1990s than in the 1980s. Correspondingly, the 1990s contraction of retail trade, by far the lowest-wage sector, helped wages grow. Thus, one reason that median wages eroded less and low wages did better in the early 1990s than in the 1980s might be related to this different pattern of industry employment growth.

The annual wages and compensation of the expanding and contracting industries in each business cycle since 1979 are presented in **Table 3.28**. The wages and compensation of "expanding" industries, for instance, reflect the pay levels of each industry that experienced a rise in the share of total employment, weighted by the extent of the expansion in employment shares. These calculations show that expanding industries have paid annual wages roughly 20% lower than the industries that were contracting. The gap in pay between expanding and contracting industries has been somewhat larger for compensation than wages, indicating that the benefits gap is wider than the wage gap. The last column shows how much the shift toward lower pay has meant in terms of lower growth in wages and compensation: generally, wages and compensation grew 0.2% less each year, or at least 2.0% less over 10 years, as a result of industry shifts.

Trade and wages

The process of globalization since the 1980s has been an important factor in both slowing the growth rate of average wages and reducing the wage levels of workers with less than a college degree. In more recent years trade and globalization have begun to affect white-collar and college-educated workers to a great extent as well. The increase in international trade and investment flows affects wages through several channels. First, increases in imports of finished manufactured goods, especially from countries where workers earn only a fraction of what U.S. workers earn, reduces manufacturing employment in the United States. While increases in exports create employment opportunities for some domestic workers, imports mean job losses for many others. Large, chronic trade deficits over the last 27 years suggest that the jobs lost to import competition have outnumbered the jobs gained from increasing exports. Given that export industries tend to be less labor intensive than import-competing industries, even growth in "balanced trade" (where exports and imports both increase by the same dollar amount) would lead to a decline in manufacturing jobs.

Second, imports of intermediate manufactured goods (used as inputs in the production of final goods) also help to lower domestic manufacturing employment, especially for production workers and others with less than a college education. The expansion of export platforms in low-wage countries has induced many U.S. manufacturing firms to purchase part of their production processes from low-wage countries. Since firms generally find it most profitable to purchase the most labor-intensive processes, the increase in intermediate inputs from abroad has hit non-college-educated production workers hardest. The growth in imports of intermediate inputs is shown in **Figure 3U** for the years 1979 to 2005. For all of manufacturing, the share of intermediate inputs into the production process that were imported rose from 7.7% in 1979 to 19.9% in 2005. In transportation equipment, the imported intermediate inputs share rose from 10.7% in 1979 to 20.1% by 2005.

Third, low wages and greater world capacity for producing manufactured goods can lower the prices of many international goods. Since workers' pay is tied to the value of the goods they produce, lower prices from international competition, despite possible lower inflation, can lead to a reduction in the earnings of U.S. workers, even if imports themselves do not increase.

Fourth, in many cases the mere threat of direct foreign competition or of the relocation of part or all of a production facility can lead workers to grant wage concessions to their employers. This is referred to as the "threat effect."

Fifth, the large increases in direct investment flows (i.e., plant and equipment) to other countries have meant reduced investment in the domestic manufacturing base and significant growth in the foreign manufacturing capacity capable of competing directly with U.S.-based manufacturers.

FIGURE 3U Share of imported intermediate inputs

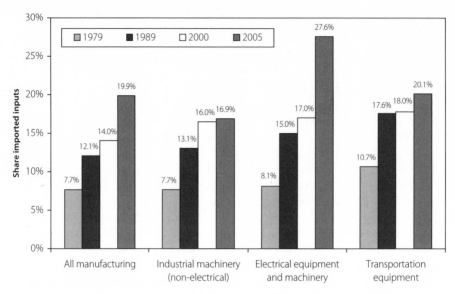

Source: Bivens (2006).

Sixth, the effects of globalization go beyond those workers exposed directly to foreign competition. As trade drives workers out of manufacturing and into lower-paying service jobs, not only do their own wages fall, but the new supply of workers to the service sector (from displaced workers plus young workers not able to find manufacturing jobs) helps to lower the wages of similarly skilled workers already employed in service jobs.

Last, trade in services has gained prominence in recent years as call center operations, computer programming, doctor support services (reading X-rays, for instance), research and development, and other white-collar services have been transferred or purchased abroad, sometimes to countries with far lower wages than those in the United States (most notably India and China). Less is known about this recent phenomenon, sometimes called "offshoring," but it seems to be a mechanism through which globalization is now adversely affecting white-collar jobs and wages (and will increasingly continue to do so). Not only are jobs directly displaced, but also the wage growth of still-employed white-collar workers threatened by offshoring is constrained.

This section briefly examines the role of international trade and investment in recent changes in the U.S. wage structure. Since even the preceding list of channels through which globalization affects wages is not complete and not yet quantified, this analysis understates the impact of globalization on wages in the 1980s, 1990s, and the 2000s.

Table 3.29 provides information on the growth of the manufacturing trade deficit (the excess of manufactured imports over exports) from 1979 to 2005 by region and type of industry—industries that heavily use unskilled labor, skilled labor, or capital. The manufacturing trade deficit grew to $586 billion in 2005, or to 4.6% of GDP, from a position of balance in 1979. This growing trade deficit reflects the far faster growth of imports and the much slower growth of exports since 1979.

The growth of the manufacturing trade imbalance was greater in the 1980s (up 2.3% of GDP) than in the 1990s (up 1.6% of GDP). The pace quickened between 2000 and 2005, however, as the imbalance grew by 0.9% of GDP in just five years (compared to 1.6% of GDP over 11 years).

Trade with developing countries (the "non-OECD" row in Table 3.29) has been increasingly important in driving up the trade deficit. It was responsible for 33.2% of the growth in the 1980s but 51.4% and 64.3% in the following periods. Much of the growing importance of developing-country trade is due to trade with China, which accounted for 58.2% of the higher trade deficit in the 2000-05 period and about a third of the higher deficit in the 1990s. The increased trade imbalance with China arises more from trade in skilled-intensive products (contributing 34.0% of the total growth) than unskilled-intensive (up 21.2% of total growth). Trade with Mexico contributed about 10% of the higher deficit between 2000 and 2005 and over the 1990s.

Table 3.29 also provides a breakdown of the growth in the manufacturing trade deficit by the skill-intensity and capital-intensity of the product. Deficits have grown in each of the three product types, both skilled-intensive and unskilled-intensive as well as capital-intensive products. It is important to note that the growth in the trade deficit since 2000 has been more from trade in skilled-intensive industries (44.7% of total growth) than industries relying on unskilled workers (accounting for 35.9% of the growth). These data do not include trade in primarily white-collar sectors, but it is clear that even in manufacturing trade is leading to increased global pressure for U.S. white-collar workers.

These data suggest not only a large increase in the trade deficit but a growing exposure of a broad range of industries to foreign competition from the most advanced countries and from lower-wage developing countries. This growth in the trade deficit and increased global competition can, and would be expected to, adversely affect the wages of non-college-educated workers relative to others, as we will explore below. In fact, any potential gains from trade would be created precisely through such a mechanism—a redeployment of workers and capital into more highly skilled or capital-intensive industries, a movement that lessens the need for non-college-educated workers. The offshoring trend is a mechanism whereby workers with high levels of education are being replaced, but this is still a smaller phenomenon than the more usual trade impact on middle- and low-wage workers.

We now turn to an examination of the types of jobs that were lost as the trade deficit grew and as job losses in import-sensitive industries exceeded job gains in export industries. In periods of low unemployment, it may be the case that a trade deficit does not cause actual job loss because workers displaced by rising imports have found employment in non-traded sectors such as services. Nevertheless, even with low unemployment a trade deficit will affect the composition of jobs (less manufacturing, more services), thereby affecting wage inequality. In this light, **Table 3.30** indicates how trade flows affect the composition of employment by wage level and education relative to a situation in which the ratios of imports and exports to output remained at 1979 levels. Specifically, Table 3.30

TABLE 3.29 Source of rising manufacturing trade deficit by country/region and factor intensity, 1979-2005

Region	Skilled intensive			Unskilled intensive			Capital intensive			Total		
	1979-89	1989-2000	2000-05	1979-89	1989-2000	2000-05	1979-89	1989-2000	2000-05	1979-89	1989-2000	2000-2005
OECD	17.8%	12.7%	15.5%	14.9%	7.4%	4.9%	34.1%	28.4%	15.3%	66.8%	48.6%	35.7%
Latin America	-0.3	-4.3	17.2	1.5	4.3	6.0	1.4	-2.1	0.4	2.6	-2.1	23.6
Asia - 4 Tigers*	9.4	4.1	-5.3	12.9	-2.8	-1.9	-0.5	1.1	1.9	21.8	2.4	-5.3
Japan	21.8	6.1	-3.9	0.4	0.3	-0.1	16.0	6.2	2.8	38.3	12.6	-1.2
Mexico	1.7	6.5	8.9	0.4	1.9	1.5	0.5	2.9	-1.7	2.6	11.3	8.8
China	0.4	12.8	34.0	5.4	16.2	21.2	-0.2	2.1	3.0	5.5	31.0	58.2
Non-OECD	10.0	16.9	29.2	23.1	31.1	31.0	0.1	3.4	4.1	33.2	51.4	64.3
World	27.8	29.7	44.7	38.0	38.5	35.9	34.2	31.8	19.4	100.0	100.0	100.0

Change in manufacturing trade deficit ($billion)

Region	Skilled intensive			Unskilled intensive			Capital intensive			Total		
World	-$34.1	-$74.1	-$94.6	-$46.7	-$96.2	-$76.0	-$42.0	-$79.3	-$41.0	-$122.8	-$249.6	-$211.6

* Singapore, Taiwan, South Korea, and Hong Kong.

Source: Bivens (2006) update of Cline (1997) using data from Feenstra (2002) and the University of California-Davis Center for International Data.

TABLE 3.30 Trade-deficit-induced job loss by wage and education level, 1979-2004

	1979-89	1989-2000	2000-04	Share of total employment, 2000
Total job displacement (thousands)	1,766	3,431	1,915	n.a.
Share of displacement				
College graduate*	12.2%	21.2%	21.3%	25.6%
Non-college	87.8	78.9	78.7	74.4
Some college	22.8	26.2	29.2	32.9
High school	37.0	36.5	35.9	30.8
Less than high school	28.0	16.1	13.5	10.7
Wage level**				
Highest wage	9.2%	13.3%	16.5%	14.2%
High wage	10.5	12.1	15.4	14.7
Upper-middle	15.2	21.8	27.5	26.3
Lower-middle	27.1	26.0	26.5	27.0
Lowest wage	37.9	26.8	14.2	17.7
Total	100.0	100.0	100.0	100.0

* Four years of college or more
** Corresponding to jobs that paid in the following wage percentile in 1979: 90-100, 75-89, 50-74, 21-49, and 0-20.

Source: Scott et al. (1997), Tables 1 and 2 and analysis of Census and BLS data in Bivens (2006).

shows the number of jobs lost because of the growing trade deficit in recent periods and the share of jobs lost in particular education and wage categories. This analysis relies on information on the types of jobs in each industry and the changes in the trade deficit by industry. By using an input-output model, the analysis can examine how jobs across the economy are affected, including jobs that feed into other industries (e.g., showing how steel workers are affected by fewer car sales).

To examine the historical shifts of the effect of globalization, it is worthwhile to first examine the 1980s, a period where large trade imbalances and job-related losses became important and very visible to the public. In the 1980s, 87.8% of the 1,766,000 trade-related job losses were jobs held by non-college-educated workers. In contrast, 74.4% of all jobs in 2000 were held by workers without college degrees. Therefore, trade disproportionately impacted the non-college-educated workforce. Moreover, workers with lesser education credentials were generally more intensely affected by trade; those without high school degrees were disproportionately affected relative to those with high school degrees, and those with no college were affected more than those with some college. Likewise, trade-deficit-related job losses in the 1980s fell disproportionately on the lowest-wage workers and lower-middle-wage workers. The 44.7% of the workforce in the two lowest pay categories (as of 2000) suffered 65.0% of the trade-related job losses. Consequently, non-college-educated and middle- and lower-wage workers disproportionately bore the costs and pressures of trade deficits and global competition in the 1980s.

Interestingly, trade-related job losses were more evenly spread across wage and education levels in the 1990s and since 2000 than in the 1980s. After 1989, about 21% of the trade-related job losses have been borne by college graduates, a share not much below their 25.6% share of the workforce in 2000 and an impact nearly twice as large as in the 1980s. Likewise, trade after 1989 cost high-wage jobs roughly in proportion to their presence in the workforce (see the two highest wage categories contributing 25.4% of the losses in the 1990s and 31.9% of the losses since 2000, comparable to their workforce share of 28.9%). This pattern suggests that the effect of growing trade imbalances since 1989 may have been more evenly spread over the workforce; thus, trade may have had a lesser effect on inequality between education or wage-level groups in the last decade and a half than in the 1980s (creating a more broad-based loss of worker bargaining power in the economy). This analysis probably overstates the adverse trade impact on the higher wage and education groups because one of its underlying assumptions is that, when an industry loses jobs, it does so proportionately across types of jobs (e.g., a 10% loss of jobs means 10% fewer jobs in each category within the industry). Since the response to lost export opportunities or displacements from greater imports has almost surely fallen disproportionately on the non-college-educated workforce of each industry (rather than the white-collar or technical workers), this analysis understates the degree to which trade and globalization affect non-college-educated workers relative to those with college degrees. Nevertheless, this analysis does show that the industries adversely affected recently by trade are higher-paying and employ more college-educated workers than the trade-impacted industries of the 1980s.

Taken together, Tables 3.29 and 3.30 suggest that trade, particularly with low-wage developing countries, accelerated the long-term decline in manufacturing employment. The data also suggest that the fall in employment opportunities was especially severe for non-college-educated manufacturing production workers in the 1980s, with broader but more even impacts in the 1990s. Since production (and white-collar) workers in manufacturing earn, on average, substantially more than workers with similar skills in non-manufacturing jobs, these trade-induced job losses contributed directly to the deterioration in the wage structure, particularly for middle-wage and lower-wage workers. And since millions of trade-displaced workers sought jobs in non-manufacturing sectors, trade also worked to depress the wages of comparable workers employed outside manufacturing. The result is to weaken the wages of middle- and low-wage workers relative to those of high-earning workers.

It is difficult to quantify the other channels discussed at the beginning of this section—the "threat effect" of imports and plant relocation on U.S. manufacturing wages and the reality of large-scale international direct investment flows. Nevertheless, these effects are likely to be as large as or larger than those that are more readily quantifiable.

In the early 2000s globalization's adverse impacts seemed to be moving upscale, affecting so-called knowledge workers such as computer programmers, scientists, and doctors as work previously done in the United States was located in or relocated to other countries. This phenomenon of offshoring high-tech, white-collar work is noteworthy because the workers affected, especially computer-related professionals, are frequently discussed as the winners in the globalization process. If the jobs of such highly educated workers are now at risk in the global economy, it makes one wonder which jobs cannot be moved offshore. Two factors seem to have made offshoring of white-collar work a potentially significant phenomenon. One is that technology, particularly fast Internet and other communications technology, makes coordination and transmission of work worldwide much easier. A second factor is what could be called a "supply shock" arising from the availability of millions of highly educated workers in places such as China, India, Eastern Europe, Russia, and elsewhere who are willing to do the work for a lower wage than U.S. workers.

Hard data that could inform us of the extent of offshoring and how much more to expect in the future are not available because our data systems are not well suited to measuring trade in services (including that which is transferred over the Internet) as opposed to goods. Even if the current level of offshoring is modest, the high public profile of this practice and the statements from firms of their intentions to intensify their offshoring is sufficient to depress wage expectations in the relevant labor markets.

Outsourcing also emerged as a concern for many workers at a time when the labor market for college-educated workers, especially new college graduates, was faring poorly. As discussed above, wages for entry-level college graduates have fallen since 2000. The review of unemployment and employment trends in Chapter 4 shows that the college graduate unemployment rate increased more in this than in earlier recessions and that the employment rates of college graduates declined in recent years, a highly unusual development. The data in the next chapter also point to high unemployment among software programmers and engineers. In this light, offshoring is affecting a group that has already been experiencing unusual labor market distress.

There is some evidence to suggest that the increased global sourcing of software work is not just a future possibility but an ongoing development. **Figure 3V** examines trends in information technology (IT) software *employment* relative to *demand* for IT software. Some analysts have pointed to the bursting of the IT investment bubble as a major source of the labor market distress for IT professionals; however, the burst bubble has not been the sole source of IT labor market woes.

While the lesser investment in IT software following the bursting of the IT investment bubble surely led to declining IT employment, by early 2004 real (inflation-adjusted) spending on IT software had actually exceeded its 2000 peak, and by the end of 2005 it had considerably grown further. Yet, employment in IT software industries remains well below its peak level. One interpretation is that this employment gap is due to the movement of IT software work offshore. The experiences of the United States and India offer some persuasive, though indirect, evidence.

Another aspect of globalization is immigration. The percentage of the labor force that are immigrants declined in the United States over the first half of the last century but began to grow in the 1970s and started to grow faster in the 1980s, as seen in **Table 3.31** (which shows the immigrant share of the workforce from 1940 to 2005 for all immigrants and for those from Mexico, the largest single source country). These data indicate that the growth in the number of immigrant workers, relative to native labor force growth, has doubled in each decade starting in 1970: the immigrant share grew 1.3 percentage points in the 1970s, followed by 2.3 percentage points in the 1980s and 4.4 percentage points in the 1990s. Roughly

FIGURE 3V Employment in software and computer services and real software investment, 1990-2005

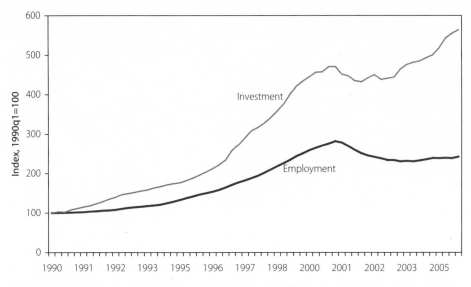

Source: Bivens (2006).

half the growth in immigration as a share of the workforce has resulted from Mexican immigration, especially among men. Whereas immigrants made up 5.2% of the workforce in 1970 they now constitute roughly 15%, almost three times as important a presence.

Holding all else constant, a rise in immigration increases the available labor supply in the United States and thus tends to reduce wages. If one workforce group—say, those without a high school degree—experiences the largest growth in immigration, then that group will have wage growth inferior to (or real wage declines greater than) that of other less-affected groups. Since the largest share of immigrants is found among those without a high school degree, it would be that group of native workers most affected by immigration. (Recall from Table 3.20 that 6.8% of the native-born workforce had less than a high school education, compared with 30.1% of immigrant workers.) **Table 3.32** shows that a majority of Mexican immigrants, 63.0% of men and 57.0% of women, do not have a high school education. Among non-Mexican immigrants the share without a high school degree (15.5% of women and 17.0% of men) is larger than among native workers (6.8% overall). Thus, immigration disproportionately adds to the supply of "less than high school" or "dropout" workers relative to other education levels.

At the other end of the education spectrum, Table 3.20 shows a greater share of immigrants than native workers with advanced degrees, 10.6% versus 9.6%, and a not dissimilar share of those with just a college degree, 17.2% versus 20.3%. Therefore, the impact of

TABLE 3.31 Share of Mexican and other immigrants in workforce, 1940–2005

	Share of workforce (decennial Census)							Share of workforce (CPS)		Change		
	1940	1950	1960	1970	1980	1990	2000	2000	2005	1980-90	1990-2000	2000-05
Total												
All immigrants	9.8%	7.3%	6.0%	5.2%	6.5%	8.8%	13.2%	13.4%	14.9%	2.3	4.4	1.5
Mexican immigrants	0.3	0.4	0.4	0.4	1.1	2.0	4.0	3.9	4.6	0.9	2.0	0.8
Other immigrants	9.5	6.9	5.6	4.8	5.4	6.8	9.2	9.6	10.3	1.4	2.4	0.7
Male												
All immigrants	10.9%	7.8%	6.1%	5.0%	6.4%	9.4%	14.5%	15.0%	16.8%	3.0	5.1	1.8
Mexican immigrants	0.4	0.4	0.4	0.5	1.3	2.5	5.1	5.0	6.1	1.2	2.6	1.0
Other immigrants	10.5	7.4	5.7	4.5	5.1	6.9	9.4	10.0	10.7	1.8	2.5	0.7
Female												
All immigrants	6.9%	6.0%	5.9%	5.4%	6.5%	8.2%	11.7%	11.6%	12.8%	1.7	3.5	1.2
Mexican immigrants	0.2	0.2	0.3	0.3	0.9	1.4	2.8	2.5	3.0	0.5	1.4	0.5
Other immigrants	6.7	5.8	5.6	5.1	5.6	6.8	8.9	9.1	9.8	1.2	2.1	0.7

Source: Borjas and Katz (2006) and authors' analysis of CPS ORG.

TABLE 3.32 Percent distribution of educational attainment of immigrants, 1940-2000

	1940	1950	1960	1970	1980	1990	2000
Male workers							
Mexican immigrants							
High school dropouts	94.6%	91.2%	88.3%	82.6%	77.2%	70.4%	63.0%
High school graduates	3.0	6.7	6.7	11.7	14.3	19.0	25.1
Some college	1.0	1.5	2.7	3.6	5.7	7.8	8.5
College graduates	1.4	0.6	2.4	2.2	2.9	2.8	3.4
Non-Mexican immigrants							
High school dropouts	84.4%	76.4%	64.5%	45.5%	30.2%	21.0%	17.0%
High school graduates	9.2	14.5	16.8	23.9	26.7	26.0	25.8
Some college	2.8	4.0	8.3	11.7	15.2	21.3	20.9
College graduates	3.7	5.1	10.4	18.9	27.9	31.7	36.3
Female workers							
Mexican immigrants							
High school dropouts	84.5%	82.4%	83.9%	77.3%	72.9%	64.7%	57.0%
High school graduates	12.5	10.3	11.4	16.9	17.7	21.9	26.6
Some college	2.1	4.4	2.7	4.5	7.0	10.5	11.8
College graduates	0.9	2.9	2.0	1.4	2.4	3.0	4.5
Non-Mexican immigrants							
High school dropouts	79.2%	68.5%	59.3%	43.9%	30.1%	20.0%	15.5%
High school graduates	15.8	22.3	25.5	33.7	35.2	31.1	27.6
Some college	2.8	5.0	9.6	12.6	16.8	24.0	24.4
College graduates	2.2	4.2	5.7	9.9	17.9	24.9	32.6

Source: Borjas and Katz (2006) Table 2.

growing immigration has been broadly felt, including among those with college or advanced degrees. These numbers suggest that immigrants compete disproportionately with the least-skilled U.S. workers and therefore have generated pressure to lower wages for those without a high school degree, particularly since the end of the 1970s. On the other hand, immigration has probably not been associated with growing wage inequality between high- and middle-wage earners and may have lessened the growth in inequality. This might be the case because immigration has added more workers relative to native workers in the college and advanced degree categories than it has added among the high school educated or among those with some college or an associate's degree.

The degree to which immigration adversely affects the wages of workers is a matter of some dispute among economists. The answer heavily depends on how much employers see immigrants as substitutes for native workers and, related to this, whether immigrants are working in somewhat distinct markets. A particular concern is whether new immigrants adversely affect the employment and wages of other populations (e.g., the black workforce, native Hispanics, and Hispanics who immigrated some time ago) with a disproportionate share of workers lacking a high school degree.

Given this downward pressure on the wages of low-wage workers from increased immigration, it is surprising that wages at the bottom did better in the 1990s than in the 1980s and that the 50/10 wage gap has been stable or declining since the late 1980s. However, two sets of increases in the minimum wage and many years of persistent low unemployment in the late 1990s may have offset the impact of immigration. In the early 2000s there was no low unemployment or minimum wage increases to boost low wages, and the 50/10 wage gap stopped its strong descent and instead grew slightly among women and fell more slowly among men (see Table 3.16). Immigration may be asserting an adverse impact under these conditions.

The union dimension

The percentage of the workforce represented by unions was stable in the 1970s but fell rapidly in the 1980s and continued to fall in the 1990s and the early 2000s, as shown in **Figure 3W**. This falling rate of unionization has lowered wages, not only because some workers no longer receive the higher union wage but also because there is less pressure on non-union employers to raise wages (a "spillover" or "threat effect" of unionism). There are also reasons to believe that union bargaining power has weakened, adding a qualitative shift to the quantitative decline. This erosion of bargaining power is partially related to a harsher economic context for unions because of trade pressures, the shift to services, and ongoing technological change. However, analysts have also pointed to other factors, such as employer militancy and changes in the application and administration of labor law, that have helped to weaken unions and their ability to raise wages.

Table 3.33 shows the union wage premium—the degree to which union wages exceed non-union wages—by type of pay (benefits or wages) for all workers (useful occupational breakdowns are no longer available) in 2005. The union premium is larger for total compensation (43.7%) than for wages alone (28.1%), reflecting the fact that unionized workers are provided insurance and pension benefits that are more than double those of non-union workers.

Table 3.34, using a different data source and methodology, presents another set of estimates of the union wage premium. Specifically, the premium is computed so as to reflect differences in hourly wages between union and non-union workers who are otherwise comparable in experience, education, region, industry, occupation, and marital status. The union premium is presented as the extra dollars per hour and the percentage higher wage earned by those covered by a collective bargaining contract. This methodology yields a lower but still sizable union premium of 14.7% overall—18.4% for men and 10.5% for women.

There are sizable differences in union wage premiums across demographic groups, with blacks and Hispanics having union premiums of 20.3% and 21.9%, respectively, far higher than the 13.1% union premium for whites. Consequently, unions raise the wages

FIGURE 3W Union coverage rate in the United States, 1977-2005*

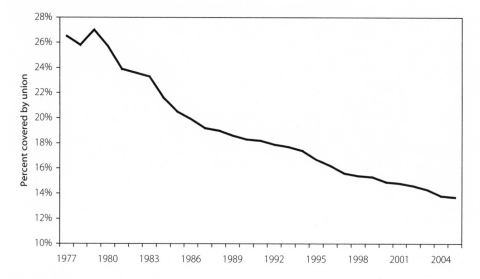

* Covered by a collective bargaining agreement.

Source: Hirsch and Macpherson (1997) and BLS.

TABLE 3.33 Union wage and benefit premium, March 2005 (2005 dollars)

	Hourly pay			
	Wages	Insurance	Pension	Compensation
All workers				
Union	$24.10	$3.63	$2.39	$33.17
Non-union	18.81	1.54	0.72	23.09
Union premium				
Dollars	$5.29	$2.09	$1.67	$10.08
Percent	28.1%	135.7%	231.9%	43.7%

Source: Authors' analysis of BLS data.

of minorities more than of whites (the wage effect of unionism on a group is calculated as the unionism rate times the union premium), helping to close racial/ethnic wage gaps. Hispanic and black men tend to reap the greatest wage advantage from unionism, though minority women have roughly double the union premiums that their white counterparts enjoy. Unionized Asians have a wage premium somewhat higher than that of whites, with Asian women obtaining a premium on par with that of other minority women.

TABLE 3.34 Union wage premium by demographic group, 2005 (2005 dollars)

Demographic group	Percent union*	Union premium**	
		Dollars	Percent
Total	14.3%	$1.52	14.7%
Men	15.6	2.32	18.4
Women	12.9	0.97	10.5
Whites	14.2%	$1.27	13.1%
Men	15.9	2.14	17.0
Women	12.4	0.61	8.2
Blacks	18.2%	$2.31	20.3%
Men	19.9	2.46	22.0
Women	16.8	2.24	18.6
Hispanics	11.9%	$3.02	21.9%
Men	12.1	4.16	26.8
Women	11.6	1.75	15.9
Asians	12.8%	$2.02	16.7%
Men	12.6	1.72	16.0
Women	13.1	2.53	17.5
New immigrants (less than 10 years)			
Men		$1.28	14.6%
Women		1.74	14.6
Other immigrants (more than 10 years)			
Men		$2.25	17.8%
Women		0.91	10.2

* Union member or covered by a collective bargaining agreement.
** Regression-adjusted union premium advantage controlling for experience, education, region, industry, occupation, and marital status.

Source: Authors' analysis of CPS ORG.

Unionized immigrant workers obtain a premium comparable to other workers, whether they have immigrated relatively recently (within 10 years) or further back in time.

Table 3.35 provides information on the union premium for various non-wage dimensions of compensation related to health insurance, pensions, and paid time off. The second and third columns present the characteristics of compensation in union and non-union settings. The difference between the union and non-union compensation packages are presented in two ways, unadjusted (simply the difference between columns two and three) and adjusted (for differences in characteristics other than union status such as industry, occupation, and

TABLE 3.35 Union premiums for health, retirement, and paid leave

| Benefit | Union | Non-union | Difference | | Union premium |
			Unadjusted	Adjusted*	
Health insurance					
Percent covered	83.5%	62.0%	21.5%	17.5%	28.2%
Employer share (%)					
Single	88.3%	81.8%	6.5%	9.1%	11.1%
Family	76.3%	64.9%	11.4%	10.1%	15.6%
Deductible ($)	$200	$300	-$100	-$54	-18.0%
Retiree health coverage	76.6%	59.8%	16.7%	14.6%	24.4%
Pension					
Percent covered	71.9%	43.8%	28.1%	23.6%	53.9%
Employer costs (per hour)					
Defined benefit	—	—	—	$0.39	36.1%
Defined contribution	—	—	—	-0.11	-17.7
Time off					
Vacation weeks	2.98	2.35	0.63	—	26.6%
Paid holiday/vacation (hours)	—	—	—	22.2	14.3

* Adjusted for establishment size, occupation, industry, and other factors.

Source: Buchmueller, DiNardo, and Valletta (2001) and Mishel et al. (2003).

establishment size). The last column presents the union premium, the percentage difference between union and non-union compensation, calculated using the "adjusted" difference.

These data show that a union premium exists in every dimension of the compensation package. Unionized workers are 28.2% more likely to be covered by employer-provided health insurance. Unionized employers also provide better health insurance, paying an 11.1% higher share of single-worker coverage and a 15.6% higher share of family coverage. Moreover, deductibles are $54, or 18.0%, less for union workers. Finally, union workers are 24.4% more likely to receive health insurance coverage in their retirement.

Similarly, 71.9% of union workers have employer-provided pensions, compared to only 43.8% of non-union workers. Thus, union workers are 53.9% more likely to have pension coverage. Union employers spend 36.1% more on defined-benefit plans but 17.7% less on defined-contribution plans. As defined-benefit plans are preferable, as discussed earlier, these data indicate that union workers are more likely to have the better form of pension plans.

TABLE 3.36 Union impact on paid leave, pension, and health benefits

Benefit	Paid leave	Pension and retirement	Health insurance
Union impact on benefit incidence	3.2%	22.5%	18.3%
Union impact on benefit cost per hour			
Total impact	11.4%	56.0%	77.4%
From greater incidence	3.4	28.4	24.7
From better benefit	8.0	27.7	52.7

Source: Pierce (1999), Tables 4, 5, and 6.

Union workers also get more paid time off. Their three weeks of vacation amount to about three days (0.63 weeks) more than non-union workers receive. Including both vacations and holidays, union workers enjoy 14.3% more paid time off.

Table 3.36 provides a more refined analysis of the union wage premium by comparing the employer costs in unionized settings to non-union settings in comparable occupations and establishments (factories or offices). Specifically, the estimated union premium controls for the sector (public or private) in which the establishment is located, the establishment's size, full-time or part-time status of its employees, and its detailed industry and region. Unionized workers are 18.3% more likely to have health insurance, 22.5% more likely to have pension coverage, and 3.2% more likely to have paid leave. Unionized employers pay more for these benefits because the benefits they provide are better than those offered by non-union employers and because unionized employers are more likely to provide these benefits. For instance, unionized employers pay 77.4% more in health insurance costs per hour, 24.7% more because of the greater incidence and 52.7% because of the better benefit.

This analysis also shows that unionized employers pay 56.0% more per hour for pension plans, 28.4% from a greater incidence of providing pensions and 27.7% from providing better pensions. Similarly, unionized workers have 11.4% greater costs for their paid leave, mostly because of the more extensive paid leave (the 8.0% "better benefit" effect).

The effect of the erosion of unionization on the wages of a segment of the workforce depends on the degree to which deunionization has taken place and the degree to which the union wage premium among that segment of the workforce has declined. **Table 3.37** shows both the degree to which unionization and the union wage premium have declined by occupation and education level over the 1978-2005 period (1979 data were not available). These data, which are for men only, are used to calculate the effect of weakened unions (less representation and a weaker wage effect) over the period on the wages of particular groups and the effect of deunionization on occupation and education/wage differentials.

Union representation fell dramatically among blue-collar and high-school-educated male workers from 1978 to 2005. Among the high-school-graduate workforce, unionization fell from 37.9% in 1978 to 19.0% in 2005, or by about half. This decline obviously

TABLE 3.37 Effect of declining union power on male wage differentials, 1978-2005

A. Unionization and effect of union decline on wages

	Percent union				Union effect*			
	1978	1989	2000	2005	1978	1989	2000	2005
By occupation								
White collar	14.7%	12.1%	11.2%	10.7%	0.2%	0.0%	-0.2%	-0.2%
Blue collar	43.1	28.9	23.1	19.2	11.5	6.7	4.3	3.8
Difference	-28.4	-16.7	-11.9	-8.5	-11.3	-6.8	-4.5	-4.1
By education								
College	14.3%	11.9%	13.1%	11.0%	0.9%	0.5%	0.9%	0.4%
High school	37.9	25.5	20.4	19.0	8.2	5.5	3.1	3.3
Difference	-23.6	-13.6	-7.4	-8.0	-7.3	-5.0	-2.3	-2.8

B. Contribution of union decline on wage differentials

	Change in wage differential**				Change in union effect				Deunionization contribution			
	1978-89	1989-2000	2000-05	1978-2005	1978-89	1989-2000	2000-05	1978-2005	1978-89	1989-2000	2000-05	1978-2005
White collar/blue collar	5.0%	4.2%	1.9%	11.1%	-4.6%	-2.3%	-0.5%	-7.3%	-90.5%	-55.2%	-23.5%	-65.3%
College/high school	3.0	8.1	1.1	22.1	-2.3	-2.5	0.6	-4.4	-17.8	-30.6	53.6	-20.1

* Premium estimated with simple human capital model plus industry and occupational controls. Union effect is premium times union coverage.
** Estimated with a simple human capital model.

Source: Authors' update of Freeman (1991).

weakened the effect of unions on the wages of both union and non-union high-school-educated workers. Because unionized high school graduates earned about 17% more than equivalent non-union workers (a premium that declined from roughly 22% in 1978, not shown in table), unionization raised the wage of the average high school graduate by 8.2% in 1978 (the "union effect"). Unions had a 0.9% impact on male college graduate wages in 1978, leaving the net effect of unions on narrowing the college/high school gap by 7.3 percentage points in that year. The decline in union representation from 1978 to 2005, however, reduced the union effect for high school male workers to just 3.3% in 2005 while hardly affecting college graduates; thus, unions closed the college/high school wage gap by only 2.8 percentage points in 2005. The lessened ability of unions to narrow this wage gap (from a 7.3% to a 2.8% narrowing effect) contributed to a 4.4 percentage-point rise in the college/high school wage differential from 1978 to 2005, an amount equal to 20.1% of the total rise in this wage gap. In other words, deunionization can explain a fifth of the growth in the college/high school wage gap among men between 1978 and 2005.

The weakening of unionism's wage impact had an even larger effect on blue-collar workers and on the wage gap between blue-collar and white-collar workers. The 43.1% unionization rate among blue-collar workers in 1978 and their 26.6% union wage premium boosted blue-collar wages by 11.5%, thereby closing the blue-collar/white-collar wage gap by 11.3 percentage points in that year. The union impact on this differential declined as unionization and the union wage premium declined, such that unionism reduced the blue-collar/white-collar differential by 4.1 rather than 11.3 percentage points in 2005, a 7.2 percentage-point weakening. This lessened effect of unionism can account for 65% of the 11.1 percentage-point growth of the blue-collar/white-collar wage gap over the 1978-2005 period. It was primarily driven by the enormous decline of unionism among blue-collar men, from 43.1% in 1978 to just 19.2% in 2005. In that nearly 30-year period unionism among blue-collar workers lost much of its ability to set wage patterns.

Unions reduce wage inequalities because they raise wages more at the bottom and in the middle of the wage scale than at the top. Lower-wage, middle-wage, blue-collar, and high-school-educated workers are also more likely than high-wage, white-collar, and college-educated workers to be represented by unions. These two factors—the greater union representation and the larger union wage impact for low- and mid-wage workers—are key to unionization's role in reducing wage inequalities.

The larger union wage premium for those with low wages, in lower-paid occupations, and with less education is shown in **Table 3.38**. For instance, the union wage premium for blue-collar workers in 1997, 23.3%, was far larger than the 2.2% union wage premium for white-collar workers. Likewise, the 1997 union wage premium for high school graduates, 20.8%, was much higher than the 5.1% premium for college graduates. The union wage premium for those with a high school degree or less, at 35.5%, is significantly greater than the 24.5% premium for all workers.

Table 3.38 presents a comprehensive picture of the impact of unions on employees by showing the union wage premiums by the wage distribution. The sample is split into five equal groups of workers from the lowest wage to the highest. The union wage premium was far greater among low-wage workers (27.9%) than among middle-wage (18.0%) or the

TABLE 3.38 Union wage premium for sub-groups

Benefit	Union wage premiums	Percent union
Occupation		
White collar (1997)	2.2%	11.6%
Blue collar (1997)	23.3	20.8
Education		
College (1997)	5.1%	10.4%
High school (1997)	20.8	23.6
All (1992, 1993, 1996)	24.5	n.a.
High school or less	35.5%	n.a.
Wage distribution (1989)		
Lowest fifth	27.9%	23.5%
Second fifth	16.2	30.3
Middle fifth	18.0	33.1
Fourth fifth	0.9	24.7
Top fifth	10.5	17.7

Source: Mishel et al. (2003), Table 2.3a; Gundersen (2003), Table 5.1 and Appendix C; and Card (1991).

highest-wage (10.5%) workers. The table also shows the greater unionization rates in the middle of the wage distribution and the greater unionization at the bottom than the top.

There are several ways that unionization's impact on wages goes beyond the workers covered by collective bargaining to affect non-union wages and labor practices. For example, in industries and occupations where a strong core of workplaces are unionized, non-union employers will frequently meet union standards or, at least, improve their compensation and labor practices beyond what they would have provided if there were no union presence. This dynamic is sometimes called the union threat effect, the degree to which non-union workers get paid more because their employers are trying to forestall unionization.

There is a more general mechanism (without any specific "threat") in which unions have affected non-union pay and practices: unions have set norms and established practices that become more generalized throughout the economy, thereby improving pay and working conditions for the entire workforce. This has been especially true for the 75% of workers who are not college educated. Many fringe benefits, such as pensions and health insurance, were first provided in the union sector and then became more generalized—though, as we have seen, not universal. Union grievance procedures, which provide due process in the workplace, have been adapted to many non-union workplaces. Union wage-setting, which has gained exposure through media coverage, has frequently established standards of what

TABLE 3.39 Impact of unions on average wages of high school graduates

	Share of workforce	Union wage impact	Union contribution to higher average wage
Non-union	75.0%	5.0%	3.8%
Union	25.0	20.0	5.0
Total	100.0	8.8	8.8

Source: Authors' analysis.

workers generally expect from their employers. Until the mid-1980s, in fact, many sectors of the economy followed the patterns set in collective bargaining agreements. As unions have weakened, especially in the manufacturing sector, their ability to set broader patterns has diminished. However, unions remain a source of innovation in work practices (e.g., training, worker participation) and in benefits (e.g., child care, work-time flexibility, sick leave).

The impact of unions on wage dynamics and the overall wage structure is not easily measurable. The only dimension that has been subject to quantification is the threat effect. The union effect on total non-union wages is nearly comparable to the effect of unions on total union wages. **Table 3.39** illustrates the union impact on union, non-union, and average wages among workers with a high school education. Assuming that unions have raised the wages of union workers by 20.0%, the average high school wage would be raised by 5.0% (25% of 20%). The total effect of unions on the average high school wage in this example is an 8.8% wage increase, 3.8 percentage points of which are due to the higher wages earned by non-union workers and 5.0 percentage points of which are due to the union wage premium enjoyed by unionized workers.

Two conclusions can be reached based on these studies. First, unions have a positive impact on the wages of non-union workers in industries and markets in which unions have a strong presence. Second, because the non-union sector is large, the union effect on the overall aggregate wage comes almost as much from the impact of unions on non-union workers as on union workers.

The decline of union coverage and power affects men more than women and adversely affects middle-wage men more than lower-wage men. Consequently, deunionization has its greatest impact on the growth of the 90/50 wage gap among men. In this light, it is not surprising that the period of rapid decline of union coverage from 1979 to 1984 (during a deep recession, and at a time that the manufacturing sector was battered by the trade deficit) was also one where the male 90/50 wage gap grew the most. Recall from Table 3.37 that male blue-collar unionization fell from 43.1% in 1978 to just 28.9% in 1989, contributing to the rapid growth of male wage inequality in the 1980s. The decline of unionization in the 1990s and 2000s put continued downward pressure on middle-wage men and contributed to the continued growth of the 90/50 wage gap between middle- and high-wage men.

FIGURE 3X Real value of the minimum wage, 1960-2005

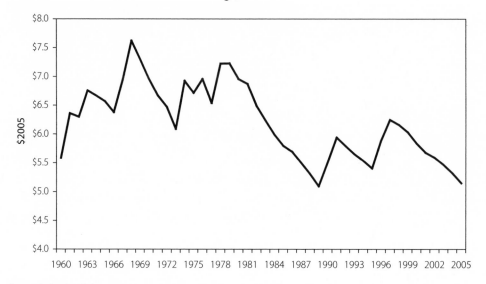

Source: Authors' analysis.

An eroded minimum wage

The real value of the minimum wage has fallen considerably since its high point in the late 1960s (**Figure 3X**). The decline was particularly steep and steady between 1979 and 1989, when inflation whittled it down from $7.23 to $5.09 (in 2005 dollars), a fall of 29.5% (**Table 3.40**). Despite the legislated increases in the minimum wage in 1990 and 1991 and again in 1996 and 1997, the value of the minimum wage in 2005 was still 25.7% less than in 1967. The increases in the 1990s raised its 2000 value 14.6% over 1989.

Another way to illustrate the historically low level of the current minimum wage is to examine the ratio of the minimum wage to the average workers' wage (as measured by the average hourly earnings of production/nonsupervisory workers), as shown in **Figure 3Y**. In 2005, the minimum wage was worth just 32% of what an average worker earned per hour, the lowest point in 40 years. In contrast, the ratio of the minimum wage to the average wage was about 50% in the late 1960s, about 45% in the mid-1970s, and about 40% in the early 1990s. This analysis shows that the earnings of low-wage workers have fallen seriously behind those of other workers, and this decline is a causal factor in rising wage inequality.

It has been argued that the minimum wage primarily affects teenagers and others with no family responsibilities. In earlier versions of this book we presented the demographic composition of those who benefited from the last minimum wage increases in 1996-97 and found that they were disproportionately working women, particularly minorities. **Table 3.41**

TABLE 3.40 Value of the minimum wage, 1960-2005

| Year | Minimum wage | |
	Current dollars	2005 dollars
1960	$1.00	$5.59
1967	1.40	6.93
1973	1.60	6.09
1979	2.90	7.23
1989	3.35	5.09
1990	3.80	5.50
1991	4.25	5.94
1996	4.75	5.88
1997	5.15	6.25
2000	5.15	5.84
2005	5.15	5.15
Period averages		
1960s	$1.29	$6.65
1970s	2.07	6.78
1980s	3.33	5.99
1990s	4.53	5.82
1979-2005	4.16	5.87
Percent change		
1979-89		-29.5%
1989-2000		14.6%
2000-05		-11.8%
1967-2005		-25.7%

Source: Authors' analysis.

examines the demographic composition of the workforce that would benefit from a potential increase in the minimum wage to $7.25 by 2008. An analysis of only those earning between the old and the new minimum wage would be too narrow, since a higher minimum wage affects workers who earn more than but close to the minimum; they will receive increases when the minimum wage rises. For these reasons, Table 3.41 also includes other low-wage workers who would gain from the "spillover effect" of a higher minimum wage. This more broadly defined minimum wage workforce includes an additional 8.3 million workers, or an additional 6% of the total workforce. Thus, the change in the minimum wage to $7.25 would affect a substantial group, 14.9 million workers or 11% of the workforce.

Those affected make important contributions to their family's economic well-being. For instance, the information at the bottom of the table shows that minimum wage earners

FIGURE 3Y Minimum wage as percentage of average hourly earnings, 1964-2005

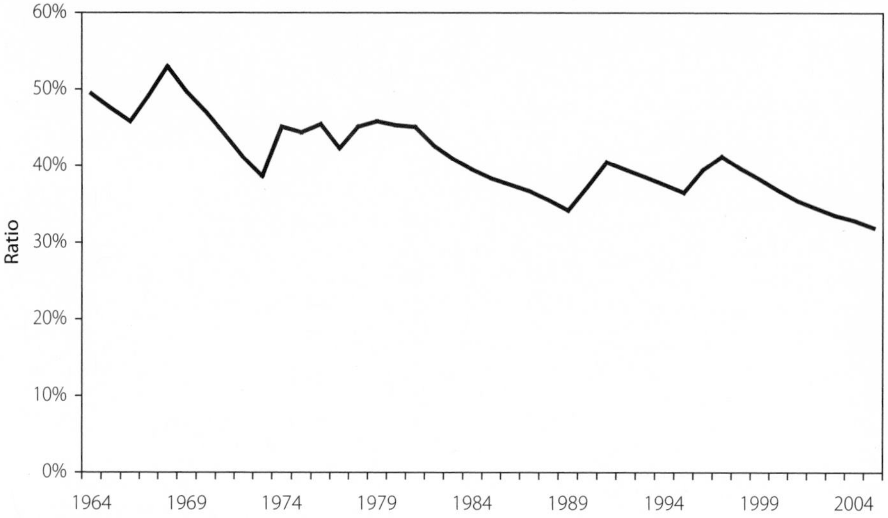

Source: Authors' analysis.

contribute 58% of their family's weekly earnings; in 43% of the affected families the minimum wage earner contributed all of the family's earnings. Moreover, there are expected to be 7,315,000 children living in the families benefiting from a minimum wage increase.

A slight majority, 54%, work full time (more than 35 hours weekly), and another 30% worked more than 20 hours each week. While minorities are disproportionately represented among minimum wage workers, 60% are white. These workers also tend to be women (59% of the total). Table 3.41 also shows that minimum wage earners are concentrated in the retail and hospitality industries (46% of all minimum wage earners are employed there, compared to just 21% of all workers) but are underrepresented in other industries.

The demographic breakdown of those affected by the spillover effects of a minimum wage increase is more inclusive of full-time and adult workers but has a similar gender and racial/ethnic breakdown as the group of directly affected minimum wage earners.

Table 3.42 assesses the impact of the erosion of the real value of the minimum wage on key wage differentials over the 1980s and 1990s. The analysis is limited to women, who are affected most by the minimum wage. As the bottom of Table 3.42 shows, 20.1% of women workers in 1989 earned less than the real 1979 value of the minimum wage; in other words, they were directly affected by its erosion in value after 1979. Women without a high school degree were hit hardest, with 43.4% and 53.7% earning below the 1979 minimum wage level in 1989 and 1997, respectively.

The analysis in Table 3.42 of the impact of a lower minimum wage on the wage structure is based on a simple simulation. Data on individual workers' wages in recent years are

TABLE 3.41 Characteristics of workers affected by potential federal minimum wage increase to $7.25 by 2008*

	Total workers affected by minimum wage increase	Workers directly affected by increase**	Workers affected by spillover***	All workers****
Number of workers (in millions)	14.9	6.6	8.3	130.3
Percent of workforce	11%	5%	6%	100%
Demographics				
Gender				
Male	41%	39%	43%	52%
Female	59	61	57	48
Race / ethnicity				
White	60%	59%	61%	69%
Black	16	16	16	11
Hispanic	19	21	18	14
Asian	2	2	2	4
Family status				
Parent	26%	25%	28%	36%
Married parent	17	16	18	29
Single parent	9	9	10	7
Age				
Teens (16-19)	21%	29%	14%	5%
Adults (20+)	80	71	86	95
Work hours				
1-19 hours	16%	21%	12%	5%
20-34 hours	30	35	26	13
Full time (35 + hrs)	54	44	62	82
Industry				
Retail trade	23%	24%	23%	12%
Leisure and hospitality	23	29	18	9
Other	54	48	60	79

Share of weekly earnings contributed by minimum wage workers

	Average share of earnings from affected workers	Share of families with 100% of earnings from affected workers
All families with an affected worker	58%	43%
Excluding families without children	59	46

Number of children with parents affected by minimum wage increase: 7,315,000

* Assuming a phase-in with the final step in 2008.

** These are the workers earning between the state minimum wage and $7.25.

*** These are workers currently earning above $7.25, likely to be affected by "spillover effects."

**** Includes workers not covered by minimum wage.

Source: EPI analysis of 2005 CPS ORG data.

Table 3.42 Impact of lower minimum wage on key wage differentials among women, 1979-97

Wage differential	Actual wage differentials			Simulated wage differentials at 1979 minimum wage		1979-89				1979-97			
						Change in wage differential			Minimum wage effect	Change in wage differential			Minimum wage effect
	1979	1989	1997	1989	1997	Actual	Simulated	Difference		Actual	Simulated	Difference	
Wage ratios (logs)													
50/10	0.39	0.64	0.63	0.41	0.41	0.26	0.02	0.23	91.1%	0.24	0.02	0.21	89.5%
90/10	1.00	1.35	1.39	1.12	1.18	0.35	0.12	0.23	66.4	0.39	0.18	0.21	54.3
Education differentials													
College/high school	0.31	0.46	0.51	0.42	0.48	0.15	0.11	0.04	28.1%	0.20	0.17	0.03	15.8%
College/less than high school	0.49	0.69	0.75	0.60	0.67	0.20	0.11	0.09	44.2%	0.26	0.18	0.08	29.4%
Addendum:													
Percent earning less than 1979 minimum													
Less than high school		43.4%	53.7%										
High school		23.6	26.2										
College		6.1	7.0										
All		20.1	21.5										

Source: Authors' analysis.

used to construct what the wage structure would have been in 1989 and 1997 if the 1979 minimum wage (again, inflation adjusted) had prevailed. Drawing on these scenarios, the analysis compares the actual growth in wage differentials to the growth that would have occurred if the 1979 minimum wage had been maintained. The difference between "actual" and "simulated" is a measure of the impact of the lowering of the real value of the minimum wage on particular wage differentials.

The minimum wage most affects women at the 10th percentile and women with the least education, so it should not be surprising that wage differentials between middle- and low-wage women (the 50/10 differential) and college/less-than-high-school wage differentials are greatly affected by a decline in the minimum wage. For instance, the 50/10 differentials (in logs, which approximate percentage differences) would have grown from 0.39 in 1979 to only 0.41, rather than to 0.64, in 1989 had the minimum wage been maintained. Thus, 0.23 of the 0.26 rise in the 50/10 differential in the 1980s among women, or 91.1% of the increase, can be attributed to the declining real value of the minimum wage. Similarly, the devaluing of the minimum wage can explain 44.2% of the growth in the college/less-than-high-school wage gap among women in the 1980s. A lower minimum wage also greatly affected the college/high school wage gap, explaining 28.1% of its growth in the 1980s. This analysis confirms the importance of the erosion of a key labor market institution, the minimum wage, on the growth of women's wage inequality at the bottom of the wage scale.

Because there is substantial evidence (with some controversy, of course) that a moderately higher minimum wage does not significantly lower employment (or reduce it at all), there has been an increased focus on which groups of low-wage workers benefit from a higher minimum wage. In other words, because a higher minimum may not have much of an effect on efficiency or output, the merit of such a policy will depend greatly on its fairness as well as on the need for a wage floor.

Table 3.43 presents a computation of which families would benefit from a minimum wage at the $7.25 level in 2008. The analysis calculates the annual gain to each worker based on the amount of his or her new wage and annual hours worked. Given this information, it is possible to calculate the share of the aggregate wage gain generated from the higher minimum wage that accrues to each household earnings fifth. As the table shows, 38% of the gains generated by this higher minimum wage would be received by the poorest 20% of working households; 57% of the gains would be received by the lowest-earning 40% of households. Since these lower-earning households take in just 15% of all earnings, it follows that a higher minimum wage generates the most help to those with the least income. Correspondingly, the highest-earning fifth takes in 45% of all earnings but receives only 12% of the benefits of the higher minimum wage, i.e., those with the most income get the least help.

The level of the minimum wage strongly affects the wage gains of low-wage workers, particularly low-wage women whose wage is essentially set by the legislated minimum. Thus, the erosion of the minimum wage's value led to a precipitous drop in the wages of low-wage women in the 1980s and to a large increase in the 50/10 wage gap. The level of women's low wages (i.e., the 10th percentile) stabilized in the late 1980s when the wage level descended to its lowest possible level (at which employers could still hire) and as unemployment dropped. Thereafter, the 50/10 gap was flat or declined as unemployment fell to low levels in the late 1990s and as the federal government implemented two increases in the minimum wage. Be-

TABLE 3.43 Distribution of potential minimum wage gains and income shares by fifth for a proposed federal increase to $7.25 by 2008

Weekly earnings fifth	Share of gain from increase	Share of total earnings	Average weekly earnings
Lowest	38%	5%	$315
Second	19	10	635
Middle	18	16	978
Fourth	14	24	1,446
Highest	12	45	2,762

Source: EPI analysis of 2005 CPS ORG data.

tween 1999 and 2005, as the value of the minimum wage eroded and unemployment rose, the wages of low-wage women once again weakened and the 50/10 wage gap grew.

It is important to note that the federal minimum wage is now so low, $5.15 ($10,712 a year for a full-time worker), that 22 states and the District of Columbia have raised their minimum wage above the federal standard (as of July 2006). These jurisdictions have nearly half the U.S. population.

The technology story of wage inequality

Technological change can affect the wage structure by displacing some types of workers and by increasing demand for others. Many analysts have considered technological change a major factor in the recent increase in wage inequality. Unfortunately, because it is difficult to measure the extent of technological change and its overall character (whether it requires less skill from workers or more, and how much), it is difficult to identify the role of technological change on recent wage trends. More than a few analysts, in fact, have simply assumed that whatever portion of wage inequality is unexplained by measurable factors can be considered to be the consequence of technological change. This type of analysis, however, only puts a name to our ignorance.

What is the technology story?

It is easy to understand why people might consider technology to be a major factor in explaining recent wage and employment trends. We are often told that the pace of change in the workplace is accelerating, and there is a widespread visibility of incredible new communications, entertainment, Internet, and other technologies. Given these advances, it is not surprising that many non-economists readily accept that technology is transforming the wage structure. It needs to be noted, however, that technological advances in consumer products are not in and of themselves related to changes in labor market outcomes—it is the way goods and services are produced and consequent changes in the relative demand for different types of workers that affect wage trends. Since many high-tech products are made with low-tech methods, there is no close correspondence between advanced consumer products and an increased need for skilled workers. Similarly, ordering a book over the Internet rather than at a downtown bookstore may change the type of jobs in an industry—we might have fewer retail workers in bookselling and more truckers and warehouse workers—but it does not necessarily change the skill mix.

The economic intuition for a large role for technology in the growth of wage inequality is that the growth of wage inequality and the employment shift to more-educated workers has occurred within industries and has not been caused primarily by shifts across industries (i.e., more service jobs, fewer manufacturing jobs). Research has also shown that technological change has traditionally been associated with an increased demand for more-educated or "skilled" workers. As we have noted, the wage premium for "more-educated" workers, exemplified by college graduates, has risen over the last two decades. This pattern of change suggests, to some analysts, an increase in what is called "skill-biased technological change" that is thought to be generating greater wage inequality.

Because wages have risen the most for groups whose supply expanded the fastest (e.g., college graduates), most economists have concluded that non-supply factors (i.e., shifts in demand or institutional factors, such as those discussed in earlier sections) are the driving force behind growing wage inequality. These economists reason that those groups with the relatively fastest growth in supply would be expected to see their wages depressed relative to other groups unless there were other factors working strongly in their favor, such as rapid expansion in demand. Rapid technological change favoring more-educated groups could logically explain demand-side shifts leading to wider wage differences.

One complication in assessing any technology explanation is that technology's impact can vary in different periods, sometimes adversely affecting the least-educated and sometimes mid-level skilled workers the most. This means that almost any pattern or change in the pattern of wage inequality can be explained by technological change or some change in how technology affects different types of skills. The challenge is to empirically trace how technology affects the demand for different types of skills in different periods.

Computers and wage inequality

One common version of the technology story of wage inequality is that the increased use of computers at work by some groups (e.g., the college-educated) has led them to be more skilled and productive relative to other groups (e.g., the non-college-educated), thereby enlarging the wage gap between these groups. **Table 3.44** presents data on trends from 1984 to 1997 in the use of computers at work both overall and by gender, race, age, and education. These data permit an assessment of this particular technology story by comparing the change in wage gaps by education, gender, race, and age to see whether they correspond to changes in the intensity of computer use. The data reveal that trends in computer use are generally poor predictors of wage trends.

The use of computers at work doubled from 1984 to 1997, rising from 24.5% to 49.9% of the workforce. Computer use grew more rapidly (looking annually) in the 1984-89 period than in the 1989-97 period. The faster pace of technological change in the 1980s corresponds to the faster growth of wage inequality in that period compared to the 1990s.

TABLE 3.44 Use of computers at work (1984-97)

	1984	1989	1993	1997
All workers	24.5%	36.8%	46.0%	49.9%
By education				
Less than high school	4.8%	7.4%	8.9%	11.3%
High school	19.8	29.2	34.0	36.1
Some college	31.9	46.4	53.5	56.3
College or more	41.5	57.9	69.1	75.2
Ratio high school/college	47.7%	50.5%	49.1%	48.1%
Men	30.2	34.2	34.2	35.5
Women	69.4	69.3	66.9	62.7
By gender				
Men	21.1%	31.6%	40.3%	44.1%
Women	29.0	43.2	52.7	56.7
Ratio male/female	73.0%	73.2%	76.5%	77.8%
By race				
Whites	25.3%	37.9%	47.3%	51.3%
Blacks	18.2	27.2	36.2	39.9
Other	23.7	36.0	42.3	48.2
Ratio black/white	72.1%	71.7%	76.7%	77.7%
By age				
Under 30	24.7%	34.9%	41.4%	44.5%
30-39	29.5	42.0	50.5	53.8
40-49	24.6	40.6	51.3	54.9
50 and older	17.6	27.6	38.6	45.3

Note: Entries display percentage of employed individuals who answer that that they "directly use a computer at work."

Source: Card and DiNardo (2002).

Table 3.44 also shows that computer use is greater among those with more education. However, the relative use of computers did not change much, with high-school-educated workers half as likely to use computers as college graduates in both 1984 and in 1997 (47.7% and 48.1%, respectively). Of course, this pattern does not accord with the trends in the college/high school wage premium, which rose a great deal in the 1980s and rose modestly in the 1990s. Among women, the relative rate of computer use between high school and college graduates fell from 69.4% in 1984 to 62.7% in 1997, moving opposite to the upward shift in the college wage premium among women.

Women use computers at work more than men, a fact that does not, of course, accord with the higher level of men's wages. This gender computer gap, however, closed modestly in the 1990s, as use of computers by men grew more rapidly. The opposite occurred with wages, however, with women's wages faring better than men's (Table 3.25). Likewise, the black/white gap in computer use narrowed in the 1990s, yet the racial wage gap changed little (Table 3.24). So neither gender nor racial wage gaps correspond well to technology trends.

The change in computer use by age in the 1980s does accord with changes in the wage gap by age (or by experience—see Table 3.16). For instance, in the 1984-89 period computer use rose more among those in their 30s or 40s than among younger workers, a time when younger workers also fared worse in wage growth. Nevertheless, the far-better wage growth by younger rather than older workers in the 1990s is not associated with any catch-up in computer use—in fact, younger workers fell further behind. As was the case with wage trends by race and gender, computer use trends do not help much in understanding changes in the wage gap by age.

It may be the case that a large increase in overall computer use at work corresponds to the growth of overall wage inequality in the 1980s. However, when one examines what happened for particular subgroups by gender, education, race, or age, no strong link emerges between the increase in computer use and the growth of the associated dimensions of wage inequality.

Reasons for skepticism about the technology story

There are many reasons to be skeptical of a technology-led increase in demand for "skill" as an explanation for growing wage inequality. Unfortunately, the "skills/technology" hypothesis frequently is presented as if evidence that technological change is associated with a greater need for skills or education is sufficient to show that technological change has led to the growth in wage inequality since 1979. This is not the case. Technological change certainly has generated the need for a more-educated workforce. However, the workforce has become far more educated: the share of the workforce without a high school degree has fallen sharply and many more workers have college degrees (as Table 3.17 shows, 29.6% of workforce now has a four-year or advanced college degrees, up from 14.6% in 1973). It is generally true that investment and technological change are associated with the need for more workforce skill and education—but this was true for the entire 20th century, and it therefore does not explain why wage inequality began to grow two decades ago. A convincing technology story must show that the impact of technology "accelerated" relative to earlier periods in order to explain why wage inequality started to grow in the 1980s, 1990s, and 2000s and did not grow in the prior decades.

Explaining education/wage gaps

The skills/technology story is frequently reduced to a tale about the growth of education wage gaps, particularly the gap between college and high school wages. In this scenario, technology causes education wage gaps to grow, and in turn wage inequality grows. It is easy to see that this particular tale is not valid. First, we have shown in earlier sections that changes in labor market institutions such as the minimum wage and unionization are responsible for some of the rise in education/wage differentials. Other factors, such as trade and industry shifts, also affect education and other skill differentials, and so there is not a complete correspondence of technology with skill differentials.

Second, the pattern of growth in the two key education differentials does not match this story. Since 2000 the wage gap between high- and middle-wage earners has continued to rise sharply, as reflected in the 90/50 and 95/50 wage gaps presented in Figures 3J, 3K, and 3L and the data shown in Table 3.16. Yet the college/high school wage gap hardly grew at all in this period and even fell among women (see Table 3.16 and Figure 3M). What is true in recent years is also true in other periods: the growth of the wage gaps in the upper half of the wage scale rose continuously over the 1980s and 1990s even though the college wage premium shot up sharply in the 1980s but much less so in the 1990s.

The behavior of the education/wage gap between high school graduates and those without a high school degree is the one most in conflict with a technology story. This wage gap (Table 3.16) has been relatively stable over the entire 1973-2005 period. Thus, if those without a high school degree can be considered "unskilled," then the wage structure has not shifted much against these unskilled workers. This is probably because the lesser need for those without a high school degree was accompanied by a shrinkage in their share of the workforce, from 28.5% to 10.4% of the workforce between 1973 and 2005 (Table 3.17). It is apparent, therefore, that shifts in education differentials do not drive the changes in wage inequality at the bottom, since the 50/10 wage gap (shown in Table 3.16 and Figures 3J and 3K) rose markedly in the 1980s and has fallen ever since, all while the education gap at the bottom was relatively stable.

Within-group wage inequality

As we discussed above, there are two dimensions of wage inequality—between-group wage differentials, such as those relating to education and experience, and within-group wage inequality that occurs among workers of similar education and experience. We have already seen that the key education/wage differentials do not readily support a technology story. The same is true for the growth of within-group inequality, which accounts for roughly 60% of the growth of overall wage inequality since 1973 (see Table 3.23). The connection between growing wage gaps among workers with similar education and experience is not easily related to technological change unless interpreted as a reflection of growing economic returns to worker skills (motivation, aptitudes for math, etc.) that are not easily measured (that is, the regressions used to estimate education differentials cannot estimate these kinds of differentials). However, there are no signs that the growth of within-group wage inequality has been fastest in those industries where the use of technology grew the most. It is also unclear why the economic returns for measurable skills (e.g., education) and unmeasured skills (e.g., motivation) should not grow in tandem. In fact, between-group and within-group inequality have not moved together in the various sub-periods since 1973.

The timing of the growth of within-group wage inequality does not easily correspond to the technology story (see Table 3.23). For instance, consider what happened during the 1995-2000 period associated with a technology-led productivity boom: within-group wage inequality actually declined among women and was essentially flat among men. In the early

1990s, the so-called early stages of the new economy, within-group wage inequality grew moderately, whereas it grew rapidly in the low-productivity 1980s. Within-group wage inequality did, however, start growing again as productivity accelerated further after 2000 but still lags far behind the 1980s pace. All in all, changes in within-group wage inequality do not seem to mirror the periods of rapid productivity growth or technological change.

Has there been a shift in the types of technologies deployed?

The experience since the mid- to late 1980s does not accord with the conventional technology story, whose imagery is of computer-driven technology bidding up the wages of workers who have the most education and skills. In this picture the more-skilled do better than the middle-skilled and the middle-skilled do better than those with the least skills. It is certainly not the case that technology is leaving behind only a small group of unskilled workers with inadequate abilities—we have seen the continued wage gap between middle- and high-wage workers grow and have seen the faltering wage growth in the middle of the wage scale except during the late 1990s. If technology were most adverse for unskilled or less-educated workers, then we would expect a continued expansion of the wage differential between middle-wage and low-wage workers (the 50/10 differential) and high-school-educated workers and "dropouts." Yet, the 50/10 differential has been stable or declining among both men and women from 1986 or 1987 to 2005 and the high school/dropout wage differential has been flat. Instead, we are seeing the top earners steadily pulling away from nearly all other earners—reflected in the 90/50 and 95/50 wage gaps. Therefore, there seem to be factors driving a wedge between the top 10% and everyone else, rather than a skill-biased technological change aiding the vast majority but leaving a small group of unskilled workers behind. Further confirmation of the breadth of those left behind is that over the 1979-95 period wages were stable or in decline for the bottom 80% of men and the bottom 70% of women, and wages fell for the entire non-college-educated workforce (roughly 70-75% of workers).

These inconsistencies can be resolved if one believes that technology started having an adverse impact on middle-wage workers more than the least-skilled workers starting at the end of the 1980s: the decline in the 50/10 wage ratio thereafter, in this view, is the result of harsher technological displacement of middle-wage than low-wage jobs. At this point the research is not available to allow a determination of whether the "bias" of technology sharply shifted in the late 1980s. Our own analysis of year-to-year occupation shifts does not accord with this view; we do not find any sharp break in the impact of occupational shifts on the need for high-level workers, mid-level workers (high school or some college), or dropouts in the late 1980s or early 1990s that seems associated with the shift to a falling 50/10 wage gap.

Nevertheless, it is important to understand the implications of the hypothesized shift in "bias" such that middle-wage workers are most adversely affected by technological change and that technology only favors those in the very top of the education and wage distribution (perhaps the upper 10% or the upper fifth of workers ranked by education levels). If so, then the policy response of making less-skilled workers into middle-skilled workers and middle-skilled workers into college graduates does not make sense, since this story suggests we have too many middle-skilled workers already. This bias shift story basically implies that the bottom 80-90% of the workforce is technologically disadvantaged and needs to become very highly educated. Perhaps if enough of the workforce makes that education transition, wage inequality will stop growing or even decline. However, given that the wages of entry-level college workers and those of all college graduates have declined or been flat over this business cycle (Tables 3.17-3.19 and 3.21), a strategy of vastly increasing the number of college graduates seems certain to drive down the wages of current and future college graduates. The possibility of increased offshoring of white-collar work may make such a strategy even more untenable in the future.

Executive pay and the very highest earners

One distinct aspect of growing wage inequality is the gap between the very highest earners—those in the upper 1% or even upper 0.1%—and other high-wage earners at, say, the 90th percentile (who earn more than 90% of all workers). In this light, overall wage inequality has three gaps, that between the very highest earners and high earners, that between high earners (90th or 95th percentile) and middle-wage workers (median earners), and that between middle-wage earners and low-earners (10th or 20th percentiles). This section addresses the growth of pay at the top.

The tremendous growth of pay among the very highest earners is closely linked to the enormous pay increases received by CEOs and the spillover effects (the pay of other executives and managers rising in tandem with CEO pay) of these increases. These large pay raises go far beyond those received by other white-collar workers.

The 1980s, 1990s, and 2000s have been prosperous times for top U.S. executives, especially relative to other wage earners. This can be seen by examining the increased divergence between CEO pay and an average worker's pay over time, as shown in **Figure 3Z**. In 1965, U.S. CEOs in major companies earned 24 times more than an average worker; this ratio grew to 35 in 1978 and to 71 in 1989. The ratio surged in the 1990s and hit 300 at the end of the recovery in 2000. The fall in the stock market reduced CEO stock-related pay (e.g., options), causing CEO pay to tumble to 143 times that of the average worker's in 2002. Since then, however, CEO pay has recovered and by 2005 was 262 times that of the average worker. In other words, in 2005 a CEO earned more in one workday (there are 260 in a year) than what the average worker earned in 52 weeks.

Table 3.45 presents more detail on the trends in CEO pay over the 1989-2003 period. CEO pay is based on a survey of 350 large publicly owned (i.e., they sell stock on the open market) industrial and service firms. CEO pay in this survey includes all of the components of direct compensation: salaries, bonuses, incentive awards, stock options exercised, stock granted, and so on. The data go back furthest for the "average" CEO, and they show a 309% increase in CEO compensation between 1989 and 2005 despite a small setback of 7.6% from 2000 to 2005. Apparently, the very high pay for the average CEO in 2000 was driven by pay at the very highest end: from 2000 to 2005 average CEO pay fell while pay for the 75th percentile CEO (one who makes more than 75% but less than 25% of his or her peers) actually rose 64.7%.

Pay for the typical, or median, CEO grew 186.2% from 1992 (the earliest year) to 2005. This includes 139% growth in the late 1990s and a further 83.8% growth from 2000

FIGURE 3Z Ratio of CEO to average worker pay, 1965-2005

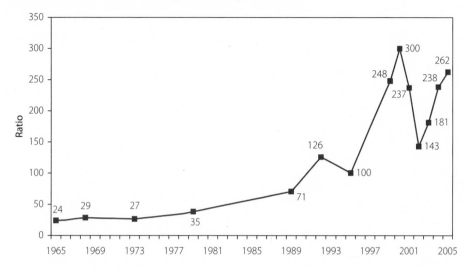

Source: Authors' analysis of *Wall Street Journal*/Mercer (2006).

to 2005. In contrast, the median hourly wage for all workers grew just 4.2% from 1992 to 2000 and another 3.0% from 2000 to 2005. So, over the 1992 to 2005 period the median CEO saw pay rise by 186.2%, while the median worker saw wages rise by 7.2%.

The breakdown in Table 3.45 for CEOs at the 25th, median (50th), and 75th percentiles allows an assessment of pay inequalities among CEOs. From 1992 to 2005 the pay for a high-paid CEO (at the 75th percentile) grew faster than that for the median CEO. Pay for a lower-paid CEO (25th percentile) grew the least but was still 105.7% higher in 2005 than in 1992.

The data in **Table 3.46** expands our analysis in a few directions. First, the data separate CEOs according to the size of their firms, as reflected in whether the firm is listed in the S&P 500 or is in the MidCap 400 or SmallCap 600. The second innovation is that pay trends for the next highest-paid four managers in each firm are also presented (unfortunately, the data are available only through 2003). These data show an even steeper increase in CEO pay in the 1990s, as the top S&P 500 CEO saw compensation rise 371% from 1993 to 2000. However, these data also show a steep decline of top CEO pay of 47.6% between 2000 and 2003, leaving pay 147.0% over its 1993 level. Top CEOs from smaller companies received lesser but still substantial increases in pay in the 1990s and experienced smaller declines in pay between 2000 and 2003: still, top CEO pay for the smaller firms was up 50.0% or 80.0% from 1993 to 2003. Given that the survey data in Table 3.45 show CEO pay rising more than 50% between 2003 and 2005, one can be assured that top CEO pay in the firms represented in Table 3.46 have also grown substantially since 2003.

TABLE 3.45 Executive annual pay, 1989-2005 (2005 dollars)

Pay category and percentile	Annual pay ($thousands)*					1992-2005		Percent change		
	1989	1992	1995	2000	2005	($000)	%	1989-2005	1995-2005	2000-05
Realized direct compensation*										
25	n.a.	$1,311	$1,545	$1,812	$2,697	$1,386	105.7%	n.a.	75.0%	48.8%
Median	n.a.	2,114	2,536	3,292	6,050	3,936	186.2	n.a.	139.0	83.8
75	n.a.	4,032	4,548	8,110	13,360	9,328	231.4	n.a.	194.0	64.7
Average	$2,687	4,760	3,795	11,886	10,982	6,222	130.7	309%	189.0	-7.6

* Sum of salary, bonus, gains from options exercised, value of restricted stock at grant, and other long-term incentive award payments.

Source: Authors' analysis of Wall Street Journal/Mercer (2006).

TABLE 3.46 Average CEO compensation, 1993-2003 (2005 dollars)

	Annual compensation ($millions)						Percent change		
	1993	1995	2000	2001	2002	2003	1993-2000	2000-03	1993-2003
Top CEO									
S&P 500	$4.00	$5.25	$18.86	$15.52	$11.15	$9.89	371.0%	-47.6%	147.0%
MidCap 400	2.42	3.13	5.48	5.09	5.07	4.35	127.0	-20.7	80.0
SmallCap 600	1.46	1.68	2.67	2.79	2.39	2.19	83.0	-18.1	50.0
Next highest four managers									
S&P 500	$1.58	$1.93	$5.23	$4.77	$3.61	$3.34	232.0%	-36.1%	112.0%
MidCap 400	0.96	1.06	1.91	1.59	1.52	1.45	98.0	-23.7	51.0
SmallCap 600	0.50	0.67	0.93	0.86	0.82	0.73	84.0	-21.4	45.0

Source: Authors' analysis of Bebchuk and Grinstein (2005), Table 1.

The pay of other highly paid managers also grew substantially but not by as much as that for top CEOs. In S&P 500 firms the "next highest four" saw their pay grow 112.0% from 1993 to 2003, and those in the smaller firms had smaller pay increases of 51.0% and 45.0%. These data suggest that the very rapid growth of top CEO pay spills over to other managers, but not on a one-to-one basis: the gap between the pay of top CEOs and other highly paid managers grew over this period. How much the rapid growth of pay for these managers, top CEO or otherwise, spills over to the remainder of the management and white-collar workforce is an interesting research question yet to be answered.

Not only are U.S. executives paid far better than U.S. workers, they also earn substantially more than CEOs in other advanced countries. **Table 3.47** shows CEO pay in 13 other countries in 1988, 2003, and 2005 and an index (in the last two columns) that sets U.S. compensation equal to 100 (any index value less than 100 implies that that country's CEOs earn less than U.S. CEOs). The index shows that U.S. CEOs earn two and a quarter times the average of the 13 other advanced countries for which there are comparable data (note the non-U.S. average of 44%). In fact, there is only one country, Switzerland, whose CEOs are paid even as much as 60% that of U.S. CEOs. This international pattern does not hold true for the pay of manufacturing workers; these jobs in other advanced countries pay 85% of what U.S. workers earn. Not surprisingly, the ratio of CEO to worker pay was far larger in the United States in 2005 than in other countries, 39.0 versus 20.5. (Note that these cross-country comparisons employ different data, and definitions, than those used for historical U.S. trends in Table 3.45 and Figure 3Z and therefore yield a different CEO/worker pay ratio.) Last, Table 3.47 shows that CEO pay in other countries has tended to grow rapidly over the 1988-2005 period; in many countries CEO pay rose as fast as or faster than in the U.S.

Figure 3AA looks at the growth of top earners' earnings (not just CEOs) in terms of the shares of all earnings that went to the top 1% and groups within the top 1%: the top 0.01% (the top one of 10,000 earners), the next 0.09%; the next 0.4%; and the next 0.5% of earners. In 1989, the top 1% of earners took in 10.5% of all earnings. This share boomed in the 1990s, peaking at 14.1% in 2000, but then fell to 12.1% in 2003 (reflecting fewer stock options, bonuses, and so on corresponding to the drop in the stock market). Despite the drop over the 2000-03 period, the earnings share of the top 1% was still 1.6 percentage points higher than the 1989 share. It is likely the case that the top 1%'s share has substantially increased further since 2003, given that median CEO pay grew more than 50% from 2003 to 2005.

The lion's share of the gains for the top 1% accrued to the upper 10% of the top 1%, shown as the top 0.01% and the next 0.09%. Of the 3.6 percentage-point gain in earnings share for the top 1% between 1989 and 2000, 3.2 percentage points accrued to this upper tier. Even after the relative erosion of earnings at the top between 2000 and 2003, the 1.6 percentage-point increase in earnings share since 1989 went almost entirely (1.3 of the 1.6 percentage-point gain) to the very top tier. Trends for and among the top 1% reveal a pattern—wage inequality has grown between every tier of earners. The gap has widened between high-wage earners and middle-wage earners, as seen in the growing wage ratio between the 95th percentile and the median, discussed above; it has widened between the top 1% and other high earners, such as those at the 95th

TABLE 3.47 CEO pay in advanced countries, 1988-2005 (2005 dollars)

Country	CEO compensation ($000)			Percent change 1988-2005	Ratio of CEO to worker pay, 2005*	Foreign pay relative to U.S. pay, 2005 U.S. = 100	
	1988	2003	2005			CEO	Worker
Australia	$180,760	$737,162	$707,747	292%	15.6	33%	82%
Belgium	383,718	739,700	987,387	157	18.0	46	99
Canada	423,358	944,375	1,068,964	152	23.1	49	83
France	404,331	780,380	1,202,145	197	22.8	56	95
Germany	412,259	1,013,171	1,181,292	187	20.1	55	106
Italy	342,492	893,035	1,137,326	232	25.9	53	79
Japan	502,639	484,909	543,564	8	10.8	25	91
Netherlands	396,403	716,387	862,711	118	17.8	40	87
New Zealand		476,926	396,456		24.9	18	29
Spain	352,006	658,039	697,691	98	17.2	32	73
Sweden	234,670	743,160	948,990	304	19.2	44	89
Switzerland	510,567	1,263,450	1,390,899	172	19.3	64	130
United Kingdom	453,485	881,047	1,184,936	161	31.8	55	67
United States	**805,490**	**2,386,762**	**2,164,952**	**169**	**39.0**	**100**	**100**
Non-U.S. average	383,057	794,749	946,931	173	20.5	44	85

* Ratio of CEO compensation to the compensation of manufacturing production workers.

Source: Authors' analysis of Towers Perrin (1988, 2003, and 2005).

FIGURE 3AA Shares of earnings among top 1% of earners, 1989-2003

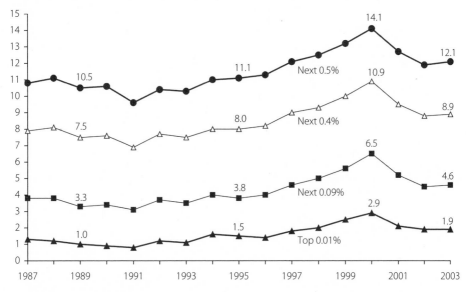

Source: Authors' analysis of Schwabish (2006).

percentile; and it has widened between the upper 10% of the top 1% and the rest of the very high earners among the top 1%.

Jobs of the future

This section presents an analysis of the pay levels and education requirements of the jobs that are projected by the Bureau of Labor Statistics to be created over the next 10 years. Some analysts examine which occupations are expected to grow at the fastest (and slowest) rates, while others examine which occupations will create the most (or least) absolute number of jobs. Our purpose here is to assess whether the types of jobs that are expected to be created will significantly change the wages that workers earn or significantly raise the quality of work or the skill/education requirements needed to fill tomorrow's jobs. This exercise requires an analysis of how the composition of jobs will change, i.e., which occupations will expand or contract their share of overall employment.

Table 3.48 presents such an analysis of the 754 occupations for which the Bureau of Labor Statistics provides projections from 2004 to 2014. Through a shift-share analysis (weighting each occupation's characteristic, such as wage level, by its share of total employment) we can see what the characteristics of jobs are in 2004 and what they will be in 2014 if the projections are realized.

TABLE 3.48 Effect of changing occupational composition on education

Job characteristic	Change		
	2004	2014	2004-14
Annual earnings	$34,694	$35,088	1.1%
Education level	·		
High school or less	43.5%	42.6%	-0.9%
Some college	28.7	28.7	0.0
College or more	27.7	28.7	1.0
	100.0	100.0	
Education/training			
Work experience in a related occupation	7.6%	7.4%	-0.2%
Short-term on-the-job training	35.6	35.1	-0.5
Moderate-term on-the-job training	19.9	19.1	-0.8
Long-term on-the-job training	7.6	7.3	-0.3
Postsecondary vocational award	5.4	5.7	0.2
Associate's degree	3.7	4.1	0.4
Bachelor's degree	11.7	12.4	0.7
Bachelor's or higher degree, plus work experience	4.5	4.6	0.1
Doctoral degree	1.3	1.5	0.2
First professional degree	1.3	1.3	0.1
Master's degree	1.5	1.6	0.1
Total	100.0	100.0	

Source: Authors' analysis of BLS data.

There are a few drawbacks to this analysis. One is that it does not take into account how the jobs of a particular occupation (one of the 754 we analyze) will change over the next 10 years. (For example, will the education requirements of a loan officer or a parking lot attendant grow?) In other words, the changing "content" of particular jobs is a dimension of future skill requirements not captured by our analysis. Second, we have no point of historical comparison (for lack of data availability owing to changing occupational definitions) for judging whether what is expected in the future is fast or slow relative to the past. However, there is still much to learn from how occupational composition shifts will affect the job and wage structure.

Table 3.48 shows that employment will be shifting to occupations with higher median annual wages, but the effect will be to raise annual wages by 1.1% over 10 years (or about 0.1% per year). This is not a large change compared to the real wage growth that occurs each year or to the composition effects evaluated in earlier years (using a different occupation coding system). The jobs of the future will require greater education credentials but not to any great extent. In 2004, according to these data, the occupational composition of jobs requires that 27.7% of the workforce have a college degree or more. This share will rise by one percentage point to 28.7% by 2014. The jobs will entail no need to expand the share of the workforce with only some college, a group roughly the same size as the required college-educated workforce. The demand for workers with a high school degree or less will fall slightly, from 43.5% to 42.6% over the 2004-14 period.

Table 3.48 also provides a detailed assessment of the education or training needed to be employed in an occupation. The results suggest a somewhat sharper shift to the occupations that require the most education or training (those requiring a bachelor's degree or more increase their employment share by 1.2 percentage points) and, correspondingly, a sharper shift from those occupations that require the least education and training (the bottom three categories lose a 1.5 percentage-point share of employment). Nevertheless, this method of gauging occupational skill requirements yields a lower estimate of the share of jobs requiring a college degree or more, just 21.4% in 2014; the other method, based on actual education in those occupations today, suggests a higher 28.7% of college graduates needed. So, using assessments of skill requirements in each occupation suggests a faster growth in skill requirements but to a lesser level in 2014.

These projections show that there will continue to be an occupational upgrading in the future in which the jobs created will be in occupations with somewhat higher wages and educational and training requirements. This trend has been evident over the last century, and the developments in the future do not appear to be extraordinary in any sense. Whether workers earn substantially more in the future than now will be determined primarily by how much earnings in particular occupations rise rather than by any change in the occupational composition of jobs.

Conclusion

The period since 2000 encompasses a few years in which the momentum from the late 1990s carried forward and brought real wage gains. However, real wages stopped growing when the recession took hold and unemployment and underemployment rose. Because of weak employment growth in the recovery, wage growth never picked up steam. Consequently, this period has seen a wide divergence between productivity and the wage or compensation of the typical worker. Wage inequality has continued to grow between those at the very top and other very high earners and between all the very high earners and other wage earners such as those earning high (90th percentile) wages or median wages.

Structural factors such as the shift to lower-paying industries, increased trade competition, and deunionization have generated wage inequities and eroding job quality. The eroding value of the minimum wage, sluggish job creation, and immigration have taken their toll on low-wage earners. Young workers' wages and benefits have faltered the most. Even young college graduates are facing disappointing prospects.

CHAPTER 4

Jobs
Diminished expectations

The job market is the primary mechanism through which economic growth is distributed to working families. So in the aftermath of a recession, a robust job market, that is to say one with enough job creation to fully utilize the workforce's workers and their skills, is a critical component to a strong, lasting, and equitable recovery.

By that measure, the current recovery has fallen short. As is well known, this recovery, which began in late 2001, was a "jobless recovery" well into 2003—that is, real GDP was expanding, but the economy was losing jobs on net for a year and a half into the expansion (net jobs refers to the number of jobs created minus the number of jobs lost). Historically, it took less than two years—21 months—to regain the prior employment peak; in the case of this recovery, it took almost four years (46 months). Since the end of the jobless recovery in mid-2003, we have consistently added jobs on net, although at a much slower rate than in past recoveries.

This record of historically weak job creation is costly. The resulting lower rates of employment and thus lack of upward pressure on wages translates into lost output and forgone increases in living standards. Poor job growth is one of the main reasons for the ongoing disjuncture between overall economic growth and the wages and incomes of working families, as shown in earlier chapters.

What factors are responsible for the current lackluster record? The strength of job growth is determined to a great extent by the speed at which the economy grows out of recession. The 2001 recession was mild in terms of gross domestic product, but that also meant there was not much of a "bounce back" coming out of the trough as the expansion got underway. As of this writing, the current cycle is over five years old and employment is up 1.9% since the last cyclical peak in 2001. Comparatively, employment growth for the same five-year period of the 1990s cycle was 7.1%, and the historical average for cycles of this length is 10%.

The recovery was also accompanied by large and growing trade imbalances that hurt labor demand as well, especially in the manufacturing sector, which is 16% below the peak employment levels of 2001. The investment bubble in Internet technology (IT) led to a retrenchment in business investment, and hiring also played a role in dampening job growth. Employment in the information sector—which includes telecommunications—is down 17%. Finally, increased outsourcing and the adoption of "just-in-time" inventory approaches to hiring and firing, which allowed firms to ratchet up (or down) employment whenever necessary, also had an effect on U.S. employment growth.

Unlike most past recoveries, for most of the current one, the relatively low unemployment rates have not been particularly good indicators of slack in the labor market, especially in the first several years of this recovery. And, though the unemployment rate is, in a historical sense, relatively low (4.8% as of this writing), it is not as low as the rates that prevailed during the expansion of the late 1990s into 2000—when the annual unemployment rate was 4.0%.

It is important to note that the current recovery has been hampered by the lackluster performance of other relevant economic indicators. For example, the share of the population employed has lagged considerably behind the shares attained over the course of the last expansion. Depressed employment rates are usually a sign of weak labor demand. However, there have been debates as to whether employment rate declines have been a temporary cyclical response to weak labor demand or if they represent a permanent structural change—or voluntary change not related to labor market conditions. Since young college graduates are a group with high attachment to the job market, they make a good test case for whether the low employment rates are related to weak demand as opposed to a voluntary decline in employment (i.e., cyclical vs. structural). In fact, the employment rate of this group fell approximately 3.5 percentage points from 2000 to mid-2003—in step with the recession and jobless recovery. In 2003, when employment started to pick up, this rate also increased significantly. Young college graduates aged 25 to 35 who had at least a bachelor's degree, and in some cases, an advanced degree—would have been highly motivated to secure employment. Now that employment rates are rebounding it seems the cyclical responses may have dominated structural ones.

Another indicator to examine in conjunction with the unemployment rate is the share of workers unemployed for long stretches of time (i.e., long-term unemployment). The percent of the unemployed who were without a job for 27 weeks or longer was unusually high especially given the relatively low unemployment rates that prevailed throughout the 2001 recession and recovery. For the past year or so the unemployment rate varied from 4.6% to 5.0%, and the average share of long-term unemployment was 18.4%; historically when unemployment rates have been in this range the long-term unemployment share was just 10.8%.

Education, once a bulwark against economic downturns, provided less protection in this last recession. The employment rates of young college graduates, and long-term unemployment rates of educated workers clearly demonstrate that education offered less protection from economic woes in this latest cycle. The share of educated long-termers increased 2.8 percentage points from 2000 to 2005, while the share decreased by 5.4 percentage points for those with less than a high school degree. It is still the case that those with less education disproportionably bear the brunt of economic downturns, but it is also the case that higher levels of education no longer provide the same protection against cyclical forces that they did in prior downturns.

FIGURE 4A Number of months to regain peak-level employment after a recession, current and prior business cycles

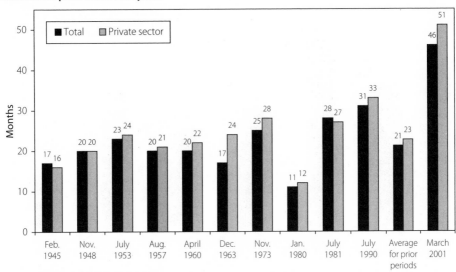

Source: Authors' analysis of BLS (2006c) data.

Jobs

The following tables and figures document the jobless recovery that began in late 2001 and lasted until mid-2003. This section documents the extent of the jobless recovery—by far the longest on record—as well as some of the dynamics responsible. The picture painted by these data is one that complements the results discussed in previous chapters: slack labor markets have led to diminished bargaining power of most in the workforce, helping to explain the coexistence of strong productivity gains yet stagnant living standards.

The first figures underscore the weakness of job growth in this recovery by comparing it to past ones. **Figure 4A** shows it took an unprecedented 46 months to regain peak-level employment from March 2001. Peak-level employment was regained following the 1990s jobless recovery in 31 months, and the average time it took to recoup peak-level employment for all recessions prior to 2001 was 21 months.

Unsurprisingly, given this result, job growth in percentage terms over this cycle has been about one-fifth that of the average of past cycles of comparable length. April 2006 marked 61 months—just over five years—since the last business cycle peak, and in those 61 months employment grew 1.9%, or by about 2.5 million jobs. To put this growth into perspective, **Figure 4B** gives employment growth for all past cycles that have lasted at least 61 months. The average rate of employment growth (the current cycle excluded) was 10.0%. Even in the early 1990s, the only other jobless recovery, employment growth was 7.1%, which corresponded to an employment increase of approximately 7.7 million.

FIGURE 4B Employment growth 61 months after peak

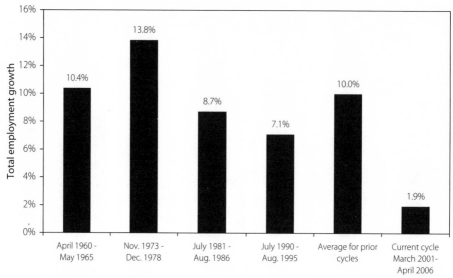

Source: Author's analysis of BLS (2006c) data.

FIGURE 4C Gross job gains and losses, 1990q2 to 2005q3

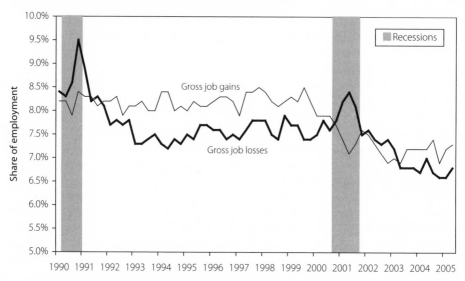

Source: Authors' analysis of Faberman (2004) and BLS (2006a) data.

If the current recovery generated the same amount of jobs as the 1990s recovery (7.7 million), job growth in this recovery would have been 5.8%, or about 4% higher than it was at the 61-month mark. Even in the early 1960s recovery, with a much smaller economy, employment growth was 5.6 million jobs—twice as many as generated by this recovery.

One of the main reasons for this sub-par net job growth was not gross job destruction as much as historically weak gross job creation, that is, a weak demand for labor. **Figure 4C** shows the trajectory of data on gross job gains and gross job losses expressed as rates. Gross job gains include the sum of all jobs added at either opening or expanding establishments. Gross job losses include the sum of all jobs lost in either closing or shrinking establishments. The net change in employment is the difference between gross job gains and gross job losses, and it is tracked from the second quarter of 1990 to the third quarter of 2005 (the latest data available).

As expected, during each recession job losses outweighed job gains, and a net loss of jobs resulted. While both of these recessions were followed by jobless recoveries, the data presented in Figure 4C show that they were different in several ways. Although the two jobless recoveries are similar in that job losses slowed quickly and considerably after each recession, following the 1990 recession, job gains were quickly back on track and consistent within a short period of time after the recession. In contrast, job gains started to slip in the fourth quarter of 1999 and continued to trend downward over the recession and the ensuing recovery. By the third quarter of 2005 they had yet to regain pre-recessionary rates.

During the 1990 recession/recovery, job losses lasted five quarters, were slightly positive one quarter, and then negative for another quarter. But in short order, a long stretch of net gains occurred between the first quarter of 1992 and the first quarter of 2001. On average, net job gains were about 0.6%, or 614,000 jobs, per quarter during this period. The most striking contrast between these two recessions was that, in the 1990 recession, job gains ticked down to a low of 7.9% in the fourth quarter of 1990 but jumped up to 8.4% the very next quarter—hence job gains rebounded very quickly and remained fairly constant until the late 1990s. From the fourth quarter of 1999, job gains fell precipitously through the third quarter of 2001, when they fell to 7.1%, rebounded for two quarters (to 7.6%), and then continued their decline through the third quarter of 2003, when they reached a low of 6.9%.

The figure illustrates that the 2001 jobless recovery was plagued not by increasing job losses but by a persistent failure to produce gross job gains that persisted into mid-2003. The 2001 recession/recovery produced net job losses for six quarters, then a zero gain for one quarter, followed by three more quarters of net job losses. Since 2003, job gains have outstripped job losses but at a much lower rate than was typical in the recovery of the 1990s.

Industry sectors

The industrial make-up of the U.S. economy has been shifting away from producing goods to becoming a more intensive service-producing economy. This shift can be seen in **Figure 4D**, which shows employment growth by industry over the last three business cycles that have lasted just over five years. The figure again reflects the meager job growth of the current cycle compared to the earlier 1980s and 1990s cycles. It also shows growth in the ser-

FIGURE 4D Percent change in employment 61 months after business cycle peak, by industry

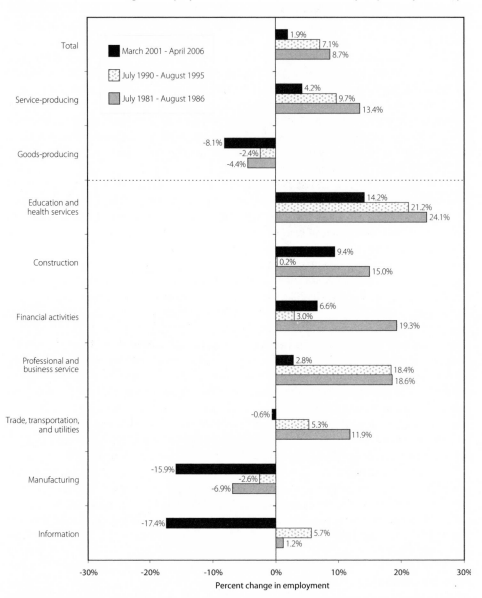

Source: Authors' analysis of BLS (2006b) data.

FIGURE 4E Employment changes for all private-sector industries and IT-producing industries

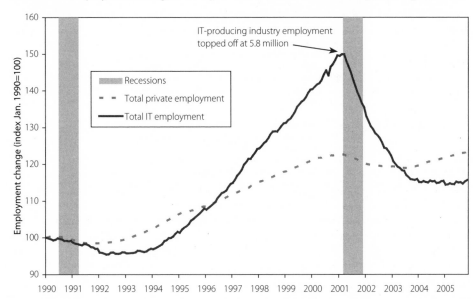

Source: Allegretto (2005).

vice-producing sector and contracting growth in the goods-producing sector. The bottom two-thirds of the figure breaks out job growth among several industrial sectors.

The most recent cycle has had strong job growth in the education and health services, construction, and financial activities sectors. Education and health services remained strong even throughout the 2001 recession and subsequent jobless recovery. Two sectors that continue to struggle are manufacturing (down 15.9%) and information (down 17.4%). The largest subsector of the information sector is telecommunications; other subsectors include Internet service providers, Web search portals, other industries dealing with information services, and Internet publishing/broadcasting.

Technological advances, sharp price declines, and the rapid adoption and widespread use of information technologies resulted in unprecedented growth in IT-producing industries from the mid-1990s into 2001. **Figure 4E** illustrates IT-producing employment across industries. The figure reflects the ubiquitous expansion and integration of information technology throughout the economy that created a swell in demand for IT workers. Ultimately, speculative demand led to over-investment in IT workers and contributed to the inflation of the tech bubble. When that bubble burst in mid-2000, it served as a prelude to the 2001 recession, a combination of blows that hit IT workers especially hard. In fact, employment in IT-producing industries has yet to recover significantly.

Job quality

Job quality over the long-run is an important part of labor market dynamics. As mentioned earlier, net employment or net job creation is comprised of jobs created and jobs destroyed in the economy; it helps to remember that the labor market is constantly flowing and churning. For instance, the current economy has less of a supply of manufacturing jobs compared to a few decades ago, but it also has many new jobs today—such as many IT jobs—that did not exist just a short time ago. So, a fair question to ask is whether over the long run, have increases in gross domestic product and productivity translated into a higher share of good jobs on net?

The following analysis shows that the economy in 2004 produced about the same share of good jobs as it had 25 years ago—24.6% in 1979 and about 25.2%, in 2004. However, the share of good jobs held steady over this time frame only because demographic changes in the population produced a better labor force. If demographic changes in age and educational attainment are taken into account, the ability of the economy to generate good jobs has declined 25% to 30% over the last 25 years.

Table 4.1 presents results from research that addresses this issue. These results are based on an analysis that examined the share of "good" jobs in the economy in 1979 and in 2004. A good job was defined as one that paid at least $16 per hour (the median male wage in 1979, adjusted for inflation) or approximately $32,000 per year, had some amount of employer-paid health insurance, and had a pension. Compared to 1979, the workforce in 2004 was, on average, much better educated and older (these changes are addressed in Table 4.1).

Table 4.1 is broken down into 12 age and education cohorts. The 1st and 3rd columns give the shares of the workforce for the 12 age/education cohorts for 1979 and 2004. The 2nd and 4th columns in Table 4.1 give the share of good jobs within each cohort for 1979 and 2004, respectively. In general, in 1979 the shares of good jobs were more evenly distributed across the cohorts, although, as in 2004, the cohort with the highest share of good jobs was those with a college degree or more education. A worker with a high school degree or less had a much better chance of having a good job in 1979 than in 2004. Overall, in 11 of the 12 age/education cohorts, the share of workers with a good job fell between 1979 and 2004. During this time frame, those with a high school degree or less also became a much smaller share of the total workforce—falling from 57.7% to 40.8%. "Skills upgrading" also occurred during this period as the share of the workforce with a college degree or more increased from 18.3% in 1979 to 29.6% in 2004.

The bottom part of Table 4.1 imposes counterfactual simulations to account for demographic changes that took place over the last 25 years. In other words, the data in the bottom part of Table 4.1 attempts to create a comparison by taking into account the fact that the average level of education and the average age of the workforce in 2004 were substantially higher than in 1979. So what would the share of good jobs in the economy look like in 2004 if workers more closely resembled their 1979 counterparts and vice versa?

The results are clearly seen in **Figure 4F.** The first two bars of the figure show the actual share of good jobs in 1979 and 2004, respectively. The third bar represents a coun-

TABLE 4.1 Effects of aging population and educational upgrading on share of good jobs, 1979-2004

Education	Age	1979		2004	
		Share of total workforce	Share with good jobs	Share of total workforce	Share with good jobs
Less than high school	18-34	8.2%	6.5%	4.2%	1.8%
Less than high school	35-54	8.4	22.0	4.0	6.1
Less than high school	55-64	3.9	22.9	1.1	8.6
High school	18-34	19.1%	14.9%	11.5%	6.8%
High school	35-54	13.7	30.2	16.0	20.5
High school	55-64	4.4	31.3	4.0	22.9
Some college	18-34	15.8%	14.6%	12.2%	11.0%
Some college	35-54	6.3	37.1	14.0	32.0
Some college	55-64	1.8	38.6	3.5	32.0
College graduates	18-34	9.3%	30.4%	9.0%	33.3%
College graduates	35-54	7.3	52.9	16.2	47.8
College graduates	55-64	1.7	56	4.4	48.8
Total (actual)		100%	24.6%	100%	25.2%
Simulations					
1979 pop.; 2004 rates					17.9%
2004 pop.; 1979 rates			31.3%		
Difference			6.1		-7.3

Source: Schmitt (2005).

terfactual that imposes the make up of the labor force in 1979 along with the 2004 good job rates. This process can be imposed because the overall averages (i.e., the first two bars) are a simple weighted average of the shares of good jobs for each of the cohorts. This counterfactual exercise has the share of good jobs at 17.9%—meaning that if demographic skills upgrading for the workforce in 2004 were not taken into account, then actual good jobs would have been much lower in 2004 (17.9% versus 25.2%). Conversely, if the 2004 age/education shares were used in conjunction with the 1979 good job rates, good job shares would have been 31.3% or 6.1 percentage-points higher than actual. This exercise illustrates that extensive upgrading of skills by today's workers has masked a substantial decline in the ability of the economy to produce good jobs, on the order of approximately 25% to 30%.

FIGURE 4F Actual and simulated shares of good jobs, 1979 and 2004

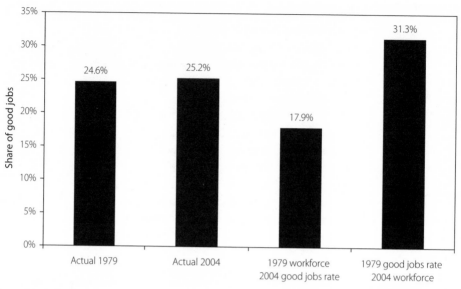

Source: Schmitt (2005).

Unemployment

As expected, the unemployment rate increased throughout the 2001 recession. What was unexpected was that it steadily increased well beyond the recession's end to its 6.3% peak in mid-2003—an unprecedented length of time for unemployment to finally peak in the aftermath of a recession. Unprecedented weak labor demand propelled unemployment rates to continue rising for such a long stretch of time. **Figure 4G** illustrates annual unemployment rates and their historical trend from 1948 to 2005. While the 4.8% unemployment rate as of this writing is relatively low, it is well above the 4.0% annual rate of 2000. Like so many economic indicators, the overall unemployment rate masks differences in the rate by demographic characteristics, including, but not limited to, race and ethnicity, gender, and educational attainment.

Table 4.2 looks at peak unemployment rates by gender and by race. Generally, peak unemployment rates for women were higher than for men—although the difference between rates by gender has been shrinking over time. In 2005, unemployment rates by gender were the same, and there was only a 0.1 percentage-point difference in rates by gender for the first quarter of 2006. The convergence of unemployment rates by gender is due, at least in part, to the increased participation of women in the workforce as well as the changing composition of jobs in the workforce, with historically female-dominated sectors—such as education and health services—seeing growth while male-dominated sectors, like manufacturing, have been on the wane.

FIGURE 4G Unemployment rate and its trend, 1948-2005

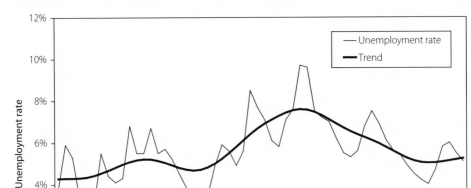

Source: Authors' analysis of BLS (2006c) data.

Unemployment rates were highest for blacks, followed by Hispanics and then whites. Table 4.2 shows that the tight labor markets of the late 1990s helped greatly to bring down all unemployment rates, but especially for blacks.

At this point in the early 1990s recovery, or 20 quarters from peak, the unemployment rates for some races/ethnicities were lower than the previous peak, and some were higher. Notably, the rates for blacks were much improved by this time in the last recovery. But throughout this current cycle, which started in March 2001, unemployment rates have been higher by comparison for all groups—except Hispanics—as shown in **Table 4.3**, and blacks had the largest increase. Even as overall unemployment rates recently hit a four-year low, the rates for blacks have been relatively static, remaining 1.1 percentage-points above their rate in the first quarter of 2001.

Blacks with some college experience have unemployment rates that are significantly higher than whites, regardless of educational attainment. Educational attainment and race heavily influence labor market outcomes, and the juncture between the two is telling. Unemployment rates by educational categories within racial grouping have important differences, as illustrated in **Table 4.4**. This table gives rates for the last peak year (2000), the last recessionary year (2001), the end of the jobless recovery (2003), and for the most recent annual data (2005). The first thing to note in this table is the vast differences in unemployment rates by educational attainment—this held regardless of gender or race.

TABLE 4.2 Unemployment rates, 1947-2005

Business cycle peaks	Total	Female	White	Black	Hispanic*	Asian
1947	3.9%	3.7%	n.a.	n.a.	n.a.	n.a.
1967	3.8	5.2	4.3%	n.a.	n.a.	n.a.
1973	4.9	6.0	5.1	9.4%	7.5%	n.a.
1979	5.8	6.8	6.2	12.3	8.3	n.a.
1989	5.3	5.4	4.9	11.4	8.0	n.a.
2000	4.0	4.1	3.5	7.6	5.7	3.6%
2005	5.1	5.1	4.4	10.0	6.0	4.0
2006**	4.7	4.8	4.1	9.2	5.6	n.a.
Annual averages						
1947-67	4.7%	5.3%	n.a.	n.a.	n.a.	n.a.
1967-73	4.6	5.7	5.8%	n.a.	7.5	n.a.
1973-79	6.5	7.5	6.8	12.5%	9.5	n.a.
1979-89	7.1	7.3	5.5	14.7	10.3	n.a.
1989-2000	5.6	5.5	4.2	10.8	8.6	n.a.
2000-05	5.2	5.1	4.5	9.6	6.8	4.7%

* Hispanic category includes blacks and whites.
** 2006 uses seasonally adjusted data from 2006, quarter 1.

Source: Authors' analysis of BLS (2006a) data.

TABLE 4.3 Percentage-point change in unemployment rates 20 quarters after business cycle peaks

	1973q4 - 1978q4	1981q3 - 1986q3	1990q3 - 1995q3	2001q1 - 2006q1
Total	**1.1**	**-0.4**	**0.0**	**0.5**
Male	1.0	-0.1	-0.1	0.4
Female	1.0	-0.9	0.1	0.6
White	**0.8**	**-0.4**	**0.0**	**0.4**
Male	0.9	-0.2	-0.1	0.3
Female	0.7	-0.8	0.1	0.5
Black	**3.3**	**-1.0**	**-0.7**	**1.1**
Male	3.8	-0.5	-0.9	0.8
Female	2.6	-1.6	-0.4	1.4
Hispanic*	**0.6**	**1.0**	**1.0**	**-0.4**

* Seasonally adjusted data unavailable for Hispanics by gender.

Source: Authors' analysis of BLS (2006a) data.

TABLE 4.4 Unemployment rates over the current cycle by gender, race, and educational status (persons 25 years or older)

Educational status	2000	2001	2003	2005	Percentage-point change		
					2000-01	2001-03	2000-05
Total							
Less than high school	6.3%	7.2%	8.8%	7.6%	0.9	1.6	1.3
High school	3.4	4.2	5.5	4.7	0.8	1.3	1.3
Some college	2.9	3.5	5.2	4.2	0.6	1.3	1.3
College graduates	1.7	2.3	3.1	2.3	0.6	0.6	0.6
Men							
Less than high school	5.4%	6.4%	8.2%	6.4%	1.0	1.8	1.0
High school	3.4	4.3	5.7	4.6	0.9	1.2	1.2
Some college	2.7	3.4	5.4	3.9	0.7	1.2	1.2
College graduates	1.5	2.2	3.2	2.3	0.7	0.8	0.8
Women							
Less than high school	7.8%	8.6%	9.8%	9.7%	0.8	1.2	1.9
High school	3.5	4.0	5.2	4.8	0.5	1.3	1.3
Some college	3.0	3.6	4.9	4.5	0.6	1.5	1.5
College graduates	1.8	2.3	2.9	2.4	0.5	0.6	0.6
White							
Less than high school	5.6%	6.5%	7.8%	6.5%	0.9	1.3	0.9
High school	2.9	3.6	4.8	4.0	0.7	1.1	1.1
Some college	2.6	3.2	4.5	3.6	0.6	1.0	1.0
College graduates	1.6	2.1	2.8	2.1	0.5	0.5	0.5
Black							
Less than high school	10.7%	11.8%	13.9%	14.4%	1.1	2.1	3.7
High school	6.4	7.4	9.3	8.5	1.0	2.1	2.1
Some college	4.2	5.1	8.6	7.7	0.9	3.5	3.5
College graduates	2.5	2.7	4.5	3.5	0.2	1.0	1.0
Hispanic							
Less than high school	6.2%	7.4%	8.2%	6.2%	1.2	0.8	0.0
High school	3.9	4.5	5.9	4.5	0.6	0.6	0.6
Some college	3.3	3.8	5.8	4.1	0.5	0.8	0.8
College graduates	2.2	3.6	4.1	2.9	1.4	0.7	0.7
Unemployment rate, 25 years and older	3.0%	3.7%	4.8%	4.0%	0.7	1.1	1.0

Source: Authors' analysis of BLS (2006c) data.

FIGURE 4H Unemployment rates of foreign-born and native-born workers, 1994-2005

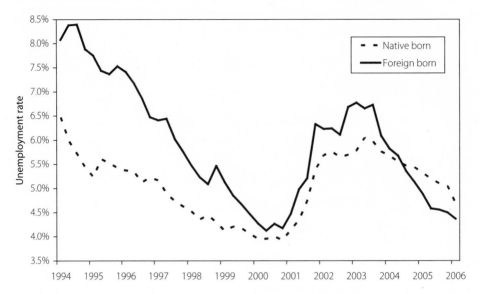

Source: Authors' analysis of BLS (2006c) data.

Over this time frame, there was less discrepancy across educational cohorts in the unemployment rates of men compared to women. By race, education made the least impact on unemployment rates for Hispanics and greatest for blacks when compared to whites. On average, college-educated blacks had an unemployment rate that was about 10 percentage points lower than those without a high school diploma. Another interesting finding in these data is that as educational attainment increases, the difference in unemployment rates by race lessens. Furthermore, tight labor markets reduced the variations in unemployment rates across races within educational cohorts.

In 2005, the unemployment rate for blacks with some college (7.7%) was much higher than the corresponding rates for whites and Hispanics. Across the board, the unemployment rates for blacks with less than a high school degree were extremely high and remained in the double digits even in the peak year of 2000.

As the debate over immigration policy heats up, another interesting dissection of unemployment rates is by native and foreign born workforces. **Figure 4H** gives this breakdown since 1994 (the extent of this data series). This series commenced during economic expansion and the tightening labor markets that followed the early 1990s recession and the relatively mild jobless recovery. As the robust and sustained expansion took hold, unemployment rates significantly declined for all workers. Interestingly, the measure of decline in these rates was much more pronounced for foreign-born workers. During the very tight

FIGURE 4I Wage declines of transitioning full-time workers and average unemployment rate

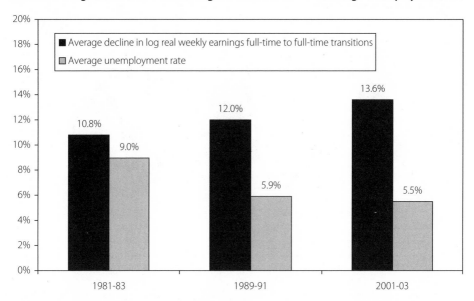

Source: Authors' analysis of BLS (2006c) and Farber (2005).

labor markets that prevailed in the late 1990s into 2000, enough jobs were created at a pace fast enough to provide opportunities for all who wanted to work. In 2000, when the technology "bubble" burst and led the economy into recession for most of 2001, rates increased at similar rates for both native and foreign-born workers. In 2003, when positive job growth was again realized, unemployment rates began to decline—as before, faster declines were experienced by foreign-born workers. As job growth became stronger throughout 2004-05, the unemployment rates of the foreign-born workforce fell below that of the native-born workforce.

As discussed later in this chapter, employment rates for those with less than a high school degree started increasing in the mid-1990s, a trend that persisted through the recession of 2001 and up to the current period, even as employment rates for those with a high school degree or more declined. The relatively strong labor demand for those with less education may be a partial explanation for the very low unemployment rates of the foreign-born workforce, as they disproportionately have less than a high school degree.

There are many measurable, as well as immeasurable, costs and consequences of job loss, mostly born by the displaced worker. **Figure 4I** examines real weekly earnings differences for displaced workers who made full-time-to-full-time employment transitions—in other words, workers who lost a full-time job but were re-employed in a full-time job. Even

FIGURE 4J Long-term unemployment as a share of total unemployment and the
unemployment rate, 1979-2006

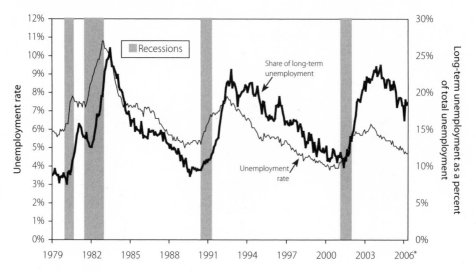

* Monthly data through April 2006.

Source: Authors' analysis of BLS (2006c) data.

as average unemployment rates have declined over these three periods, the wage cost for displaced workers has increased. Lower unemployment rates may signal that it is relatively easier to secure employment, but the cost of forgone wages has increased.

Long-term unemployment

While unemployment is difficult, a stint of long-term unemployment—six months or more of joblessness—may be devastating. Typically, after six months of being out of work, a worker has exhausted unemployment benefits and may have significantly or completely depleted savings. It is at this point that unemployment may have lasting effects, such as elevated levels of debt, diminished retirement and savings, or relocation from secure housing and communities to new, unfamiliar locations in order to find employment. **Figure 4J** charts unemployment rates and the share of those who have been unemployed long term. The most striking aspect of the figure is the unprecedented gap between the unemployment rate and long-term unemployment shares that emerged following the 2001 recession.

As Figure 4J shows, unemployment rates peaked right at the end of the "double-dip" recessions of the 1980s, which is consistent with all post-war recessions. However, this was not the case for the last two economic cycles. In addition, shares of long-term unemployment peaked much sooner in the 1980s and all other post-war recoveries compared to the two most recent ones. A closer look reveals how the last two cycles—both of which experienced "jobless" recoveries—have differed from historical measures.

FIGURE 4K Length of unemployment spells and the share of long-term joblessness associated with unemployment rates from 4.7% to 5.0%

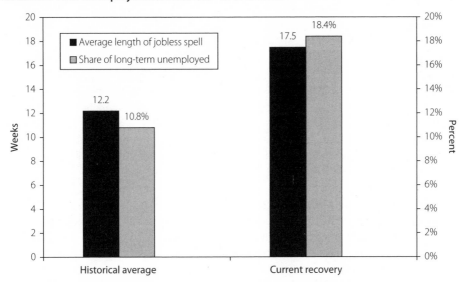

Source: Authors' analysis of BLS (2006c) data.

Excluding the last two cycles, since 1948 it took an average of 1.6 months into an economic recovery for unemployment rates to peak, and 8.3 months for long-term unemployment shares to peak. In other words, unemployment peaked very near the end of recessions, and long-term unemployment peaked shortly thereafter. The last two cycles have seen a different pattern emerge. Following the 1990-91 recession, it took 15 months for unemployment and 19 months for long-term unemployment to peak. The lag was even longer following the 2001 recession, when it took the unemployment rate 19 months and long-term unemployment 29 months to peak.

Following the 1990-91 recession, the unemployment rate increased more gradually, reaching a maximum of 7.8%. As the unemployment rate fell from 7.8% to 5.8%, long-term joblessness remained above 20% for 22 of those 29 months. This is the first instance since these data have been collected of high shares of long-term unemployment persisting despite relatively low and falling unemployment rates.

For the most recent economic cycle, the share of long-termers reached 20% 11 months into the recovery in October 2002. The share of long-term unemployed stayed above 20% for an unprecedented streak of 32 consecutive months. During those 32 months, the unemployment rate varied between 5.1% and 6.3%. The divergence of these two indicators is unmistakable in Figure 4J. The enormous gap that materialized after the 2001 recession represents an unambiguous break with precedent. It is clear that a significant share of the unemployed found it extremely difficult to secure employment following the 2001 recession.

Not only has the share of long-term unemployment been alarmingly high and persistent in this current business cycle, but the length of unemployment spells, as one would expect, has also increased. **Figure 4K** gives the historical and current recovery statistics for the average length of unemployment spells along with the share of long-term unemployed when the unemployment rate was from 4.7% to 5.0% (the range of unemployment rates over the past year). Historically, these relatively low unemployment rates were accompanied by unemployment spells that averaged just over 12 weeks and long-term unemployment shares of almost 11%. Over the current recovery, these average indicators were much elevated—average spells approached 18 weeks, and the long-term unemployment share averaged over 18%. Again, a clear break from historical trends is evident. A considerable share of unemployed workers has found it very difficult to find re-employment. Lackluster job growth—particularly the falloff in gross job gains as seen in Figure 4C—has certainly been a factor, along with the challenge faced by workers who have lost jobs in industries such as auto manufacturing in the "rust belt" areas of the United States.

Shifting shares of unemployment and long-term unemployment

As previously discussed, unemployment rates have been relatively low, but long-term unemployment has been historically high and not as responsive to unemployment declines. At any given time, unemployment and the subset of long-termers can be broken down into shares based on demographic characteristics. Generally, shares of both unemployment and long-term unemployment have shifted from less to more educated, from young to older workers, and from blue-collar to white-collar workers. **Table 4.5** offers such breakdowns over time, specifically the last three annual peaks along with the most recent annual data. Of course, for each demographic, the shares of the total workforce are similarly changing over time as the workforce has aged, and it has become more educated and more diverse by race and ethnicity.

As Table 4.5 indicates, as a share of total unemployment, long-term unemployment has increased substantially since 1979—from 8.6% to 19.6% in 2005. There is no doubt a plethora of factors have driven this increase, including, for example, an increase in dual-earner families, a more educated workforce, unemployment benefits, the mix of occupations in the economy, and the constant churning in the supply and demand of jobs.

Unemployment has always been disproportionably low for higher-educated workers. However, more recently, higher educational attainment is less of a bulwark against economic recessions. This phenomenon is conveyed in Table 4.5, which shows how the shares of unemployment and long-term unemployment have become less concentrated at the lower levels of education across time. For instance, those with less than a high school degree comprised 41.9% of unemployment and 39.3% of long-term unemployment in 1979. Both of these shares decreased considerably in 2005, to 27.0% and 24.1%. This decline, or "share shift," occurred at the same time that the share of the labor force comprised of workers with less than a high school degree decreased by approximately 50%. (Refer to educational attainment shares of the labor force at the bottom of Table 3.17 in Chapter 3 on wages for the distribution of the workforce by education.) Therefore, even as the share of unemployment and long-term unemployment fell for those with less education, in 2005, those shares were still above the share that they represent in the overall

TABLE 4.5 Shares of unemployment (U) and long-term unemployment (LTU) in peak years

	1979		1989		2000		2005	
	U	LTU	U	LTU	U	LTU	U	LTU
All groups	100.0%	8.6%	100.0%	9.8%	100.0%	11.4%	100.0%	19.6%
Education								
Less than high school	41.9%	39.3%	29.2%	29.0%	31.7%	29.5%	27.0%	24.1%
High school	33.6	37.1	41.6	42.7	34.0	35.2	34.3	34.3
Some college	16.9	14.4	17.9	15.2	22.1	21.1	24.8	24.6
College graduates	7.5	9.2	11.2	13.1	12.1	14.2	13.9	17.0
Age								
16-24	49.2%	30.7%	37.1%	18.1%	36.9%	23.6%	33.2%	21.7%
25-44	34.8	41.1	46.1	54.5	41.1	43.1	40.3	41.5
45+	16.0	28.1	16.7	27.4	21.9	33.2	26.5	36.8
Occupation								
Blue collar	n.a.	n.a.	36.4%	43.3%	32.3%	33.1%	30.4%	29.9%
Services	n.a.	n.a.	18.2	16.9	19.9	19.7	20.9	19.1
White collar	n.a.	n.a.	33.3	31.0	40.0	38.9	39.5	42.0
Gender								
Women	50.0%	40.8%	46.0%	32.0%	47.7%	44.3%	46.5%	43.7%
Men	50.0	59.2	54.0	68.0	52.3	55.7	53.5	56.3
Race								
Black	21.2%	29.9%	23.3%	29.2%	21.2%	27.9%	21.8%	28.4%
Hispanic	7.3	5.3	11.4	8.5	16.8	17.9	15.7	13.0
Other	1.8	1.8	3.0	2.7	5.4	6.6	6.2	7.8
White	69.6	63.0	62.3	59.5	56.6	47.6	56.3	50.8

Source: Allegretto and Stettner (2004).

FIGURE 4L Shares of long-term unemployment by education, 1979 and 2005

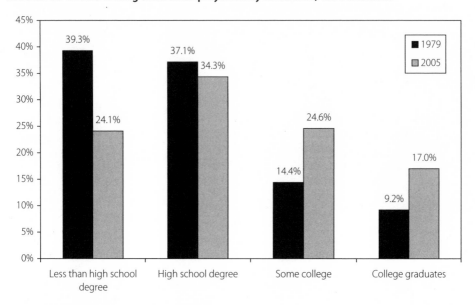

Source: Authors' analysis of Allegretto and Stettner (2004).

workforce. The converse is true for college graduates: their share of the workforce and of the unemployed has increased, but the latter to a much greater extent. Similar share shifting has occurred by age, occupation, gender, and race and is shown in the balance of Table 4.5. **Figure 4L** visually depicts these longer-term educational shifts—an 18 percentage-point swing from workers with a high school degree or less to those with at least some college.

The shifts in unemployment and long-term unemployment shares by education over the current cycle are also impressive. This shorter time span is less influenced by demographic changes and therefore reflects the changing risks faced by all workers regardless of education. Even in this shorter time span, from the last annual peak of 2000 to the most recent annual data from 2005, the distributional shift from the less-educated to the more-educated continued—for unemployment and more so for long-term unemployment (see **Figure 4M**). This trend may continue, as forces such as globalization subject more white collar and service industry jobs to off-shoring.

Underemployment

Overall unemployment and long-term unemployment capture important features of the labor market and its strengths and weaknesses. However, those statistics may fall short in explaining the extent of the underutilization of labor. Forever lost is the output from

FIGURE 4M Percentage-point change in shares of unemployment and long-term unemployment by educational attainment, 2000-05

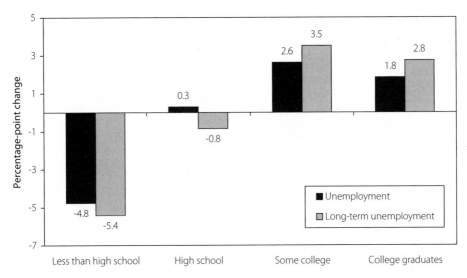

Source: Authors' anaylsis of Allegretto and Stettner (2004).

underutilized human resources, and the economic impact is far-reaching. Unemployment data include only workers who report that they are willing and able to work and have looked for work in the last four weeks; such data overlook workers who are not fully employed or who would like to be employed but are not actively seeking a job. A broader measure of underemployment in the economy is presented in **Table 4.6**. This alternative measure includes unemployed workers as well as: (1) those working part time but who want to work full time ("involuntary" part-timers); (2) those who want to work but have been discouraged from searching by their lack of success ("discouraged" workers); and (3) others who are neither working nor seeking work at the moment but who indicate that they want and are available to work and have looked for a job in the last 12 months. (The second and third categories together are described as "marginally attached" workers.)

Generally, the underemployment rate—like its major component, the unemployment rate—is countercyclical. As the economy expands or contracts, these rates decrease or increase, respectively. In 2003, one-tenth of the workforce was underemployed in some way, which represents a large amount of lost output. As the labor market tightening continued into 2006, underemployment has declined, although, like unemployment, this rate remains considerably higher than the 2000 rate when truly tight labor markets prevailed.

TABLE 4.6 Underemployment, 2000 to current period (in thousands)

	2000	2001	2003	2006q1
Underemployment				
Unemployed	5,703	6,755	8,791	7,069
Discouraged*	285	287	440	451
Other marginally attached*	855	1,006	1,026	1,053
Involuntary part time	3,137	3,593	4,542	4,061
Total underemployed	9,981	11,642	14,798	12,634
Civilian labor force	142,583	143,734	146,510	150,405
Underemployment rate**	7.0%	8.1%	10.1%	8.4%
Unemployment rate	4.0	4.7	6.0	4.7

* Marginally attached workers are persons who currently are neither working nor looking for work, but who indicate that they want and are available for a job and have looked for work in the last 12 months. Discouraged workers are the sub-set of the marginally attached who have given a job-market-related reason for not currently looking for a job.
** Total underemployed workers divided by the sum of the labor force plus discouraged and other marginally attached workers.

Source: Authors' analysis of BLS (2006c) data.

Employment

Many have speculated as to why employment rates declined following the 2001 downturn. Were these declines more cyclical (related to weak demand) or structural (voluntary) in nature? This section attempts to bring some clarity to this question. As with the prolonged time it took for jobs to rebound in this cycle, it has also taken a long time for depressed employment rates to bounce back. But, much of the data presented here, especially the most recent trends since the end of the jobless recovery (mid-2003), seems to indicate that the declines in participation and employment rates were, in large part, responses to lackluster demand and opportunity.

In this analysis we use data on employment rates as well as labor force participation rates. Generally, each measure tells the same story. Recall that labor force participation rates are the share of the working-age population that is either employed or unemployed. Employment rates measure the share of the working-age population that is employed, therefore the difference between the two is a measure of unemployment.

Employment rates arguably provide a better indicator of the extent of job market opportunity than do participation rates. Employment rates tend to get less attention than unemployment rates, although they are a particularly informative indicator during times of labor market weakness. Both of these measures are included in this analysis.

The long-run trend in participation increased from about 61% in the early 1970s to just over 66% in the late 1990s. But, as sometimes happens with economic data, the overall trend masks some very different trends by gender. Although attachment to the labor force for men

FIGURE 4N Annual labor force participation rate, 1973-2005

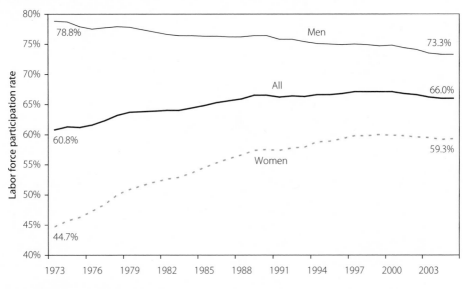

Source: Authors' analysis of BLS (2006c) data.

was lessening in those years, it was strengthening for women (**Figure 4N**). More recently, the rate changes for men and women have tempered. The subtleties of labor force attachment are revealed by looking at the employment rates by gender over the last three business cycles (counting, for argument's sake, the 1980s "double-dip" as a single cycle).

At any given time, cyclical and structural changes are occurring in the labor market. Employment rates are sensitive to economic downturns, even as longer term trends persist (**Figure 4O**). The contractions in employment rates that occurred around the 2001 recession were significant. The decline in the male rate was very similar to the rate pattern exhibited around the early 1990s downturn. The rate took longer to bounce back in the current cycle, but it clearly has. The rate decrease for women was more pronounced in terms of severity and duration throughout and following the 2001 recession. Only time will tell if this rate, which has been on a slight increase for the past two years, will rebound significantly in the future.

Interestingly, the employment rates of those 55 years of age and older defied any cyclical response to the 2001 recession. The rates for men, long on the decline, reversed course in 1993 and have continued upward ever since. The rates for women, which were relatively flat after the mid-1970s, also increased significantly from 1993 onward. These changing trends are illustrated in **Figure 4P**. There are several theories as to why these rates were insulated from the most recent downturn. First, most people get some portion of their health insurance coverage through their employer, and since health care costs have

FIGURE 4O Employment rates by gender, 1979-2006

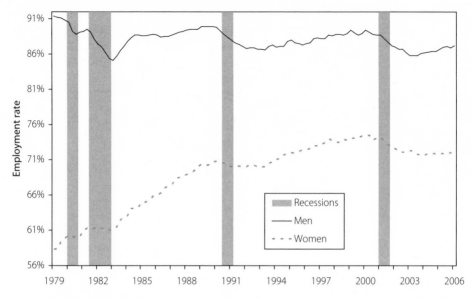

Source: Authors' analysis of BLS (2006c) data.

FIGURE 4P Annual employment rates 55 years and older, by gender, 1970-2005

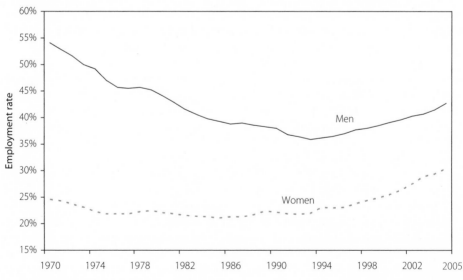

Source: Authors' analysis of BLS (2006c) data.

FIGURE 4Q Employment rates of young college graduates, 1979-2006

Source: Authors' analysis of BLS (2006c) data.

risen significantly, workers are working longer to cover them. Second, and related to the first theory, is the notion that Medicare is insufficient to cover health care costs. Finally, people also are working longer due to pension losses after the stock market crash.

One strong piece of evidence that supports the cyclical argument over the structural one is to look at employment rates of young college graduates. This cohort is expected to have very strong incentives and attachments to the labor market. **Figure 4Q** illustrates the employment rates of young college graduates (25-34 years old). Cyclical responses in this data series are evident, especially during the last two downturns. The rate fell precipitously throughout the 2001 recession until mid-2003 when the rate rebounded—which corresponded with positive job growth. Most recently, this pattern is tending to support evidence that the downturn in employment rates was a cyclical response to the lack of employment opportunity, even for our educated youth.

The decline in employment for college graduates also refutes other notions about the economy and recessions. Educational attainment, long held to insulate against economic recession, has been less effective for the last two downturns. This has also been pointed out in the analyses on unemployment and long-term unemployment. Moreover, the recent assertion that additional educational attainment that was posited as the key to strengthening the current economic recovery was also misguided. A closer look at employment rates by education throughout the current recovery are telling in this regard.

FIGURE 4R Change in employment rates by education 20 quarters after the 2001 peak

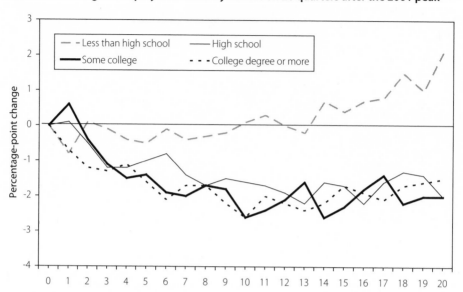

Source: Authors' analysis of BLS (2006c) data.

As shown in **Figure 4R**, employment rates for those without a high school diploma hardly faltered in the current cycle, while rates for those with a high school degree or more are still below peak levels. At the onset of the 2001 recession, employment rates for those with less than a high school degree were not as negatively affected as the employment rates for those at other levels of educational attainment. Moreover, the rates for those with less education began to trend upward just five quarters into the cycle, and surpassed peak levels 10 quarters into the cycle, while the rates for the other educational cohorts were still trending downward.

It has been posited that post-2001 labor force participation rate declines have been, as noted previously, primarily structural. Specifically, some analysts have stated that the rate declines were reflective of changes in the demographic makeup of the workforce. An exercise that incorporates age-sex cohort analysis shows that recent demographic changes cannot account for the decline in employment rates. This simulation incorporates 13 age cohorts by gender, resulting in 26 age-gender cohorts. By holding the age-gender participation rates constant, the variability in the actual rate due to demographic changes can be determined. This constructed measure allows the aggregate participation rate to vary only with actual changes in the population for each cohort.

Importantly, this simulation is sensitive to the date one picks at which to hold the age-gender participation rates constant. For this analysis, 1998 was chosen because it captures

FIGURE 4S Actual and simulated labor force participation rate (LFPR), 1998-2005

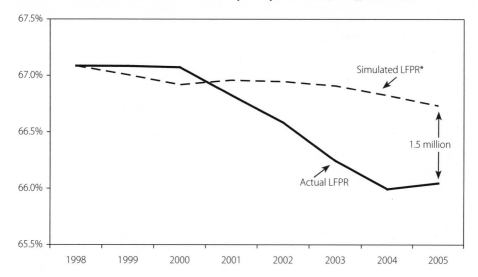

* Simulated LFPR holds within age and gender group participation rates constant at 1998 rates.

Source: Authors' analysis of BLS (2006c) data.

part of the economic expansion that occurred from the mid-1990s into 2000. The rates of 2000 could have been used, but a more conservative year was chosen because many think that the historically high rates attained in 2000 were an anomaly that resulted from the economic "bubble" that existed at that time.

Figure 4S shows the actual labor force participation rates against the simulated rates. The slight decline in the simulated rates from 67.1% to 66.7% from 1998 to 2005 may be attributed to demographic changes that occurred over that time. The much larger gap that emerged after 2000—when actual rates fell below the simulated rates—cannot be explained by demographic changes. The gap that steadily increased into 2004 held steady into 2005, representing approximately 1.5 million people that year. The falloff in labor force participation rates cannot be attributed to demographic changes—at this point it is impossible to definitively assert the rate downturn was primarily cyclical in nature. However, this analysis coupled with other analyses—such as those of the employment rates of young college graduates—leads one to believe it is quite probable that the lion's share of the decline in labor force participation was cyclical in nature, but only time will tell. Moreover, some portion of the 1.5 million missing from the labor force would add to the already 7 million unemployed and increase the unemployment rate.

TABLE 4.7 Nonstandard workers in the U.S. workforce

Work arrangement	1995	2001	2005
Regular part time	13.6%	13.3%	13.2%
Temp agency	1.0	0.9	0.9
On-call / day laborers	1.7	1.7	2.0
Regular self-employed	5.9	4.3	4.4
Independent contractor (wage & salary)	1.0	0.9	1.0
Independent contractor (self-employed)	5.7	5.5	6.5
Contract company employees	0.5	0.4	0.5
Direct hire temporaries	2.8	2.2	2.1
Standard workers	67.8%	70.7%	69.4%
All	100.0%	100.0%	100.0%

Source: Fisher, Ditsler, Gordon, and West (2006).

Nonstandard work

Many workers, consistently or at some point in their working lives, are employed in a non-standard work arrangement. Broadly defined, nonstandard work consists of employment arrangements that are not regular, full-time work. There are many reasons why a worker may not be employed on a full-time basis. On the supply side, many workers—students, older workers, workers with families—prefer employment that offers more flexibility than traditional 9-to-5 jobs. On the demand side, businesses might hire contingent workers in a multitude of capacities and for a variety of reasons. Some put workers directly on their payrolls but assign them to an internal temporary worker pool. Others hire on-call workers and day laborers. Employers also use temporary help agencies and contracting firms to obtain workers on a temporary basis, sometimes for long periods. Some businesses hire independent contractors to perform work that would otherwise be done by direct-hire employees. Hiring contingent workers also helps employers practice "just-in-time" employment strategies. Just-in-time employment allows firms to adjust labor the way that they traditionally adjusted inventory levels—cyclically with demand fluctuations. Retaining workers through economic downturns and hiring full-time permanent workers while testing the strength and sustainability of the upturns is now a cost that many employers are not willing or able to incur.

Table 4.7 shows the distribution of employment by type of work arrangement for three time periods. Roughly speaking, 1995 and 2005 are similar in that they are the fourth years following a recession. The 2001 data are from a survey that was administered in February 2001, therefore, these data likely reflect to a greater degree the peak distribution of work arrangements. These data are from the Contingent Work Supplement (CWS), which is a

FIGURE 4T Employment in temporary help industry as share of private employment, 1990-2006

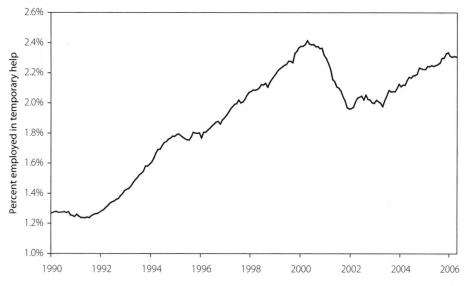

Source: Authors' analysis of BLS (2006b) data.

household survey of workers. One caveat here, the CWS almost certainly undercounts nonstandard work—in part because it does not account for a worker's second or third job. Therefore, the Current Employment Statistics (CES) survey of employers (which refers to jobs within a firm) is also used in this analysis.

In general, these data show a great deal of stability in standard/nonstandard work over the last decade, although there have been some subtle changes. During economic expansions, when unemployment falls and labor demand increases, the proportion of workers in nonstandard arrangements also tends to fall, as workers are able to find stable, full-time employment if they want it. This is borne out in the data, which reveals that the percentage of standard workers increased from 67.8% to 70.7% from 1995 to 2001.

There was little change in temporary help agency workers in Table 4.7, although there may be tradeoffs in direct-hire temporaries, temp agency hires, and independent contract hires. However, this is not the case if firm data or data on jobs are examined—which is reflected in **Figure 4T**. This figure shows employment in the temporary help industry as a share of private employment. When this data series was launched in 1990 the share of the workforce in the temporary help industry was 1.3%. Throughout the 1990s, the share of temporary help employment grew to 2.4% by 2000. After the stock bubble burst and then throughout the recession, this share fell precipitously to 2.0%. The temporary employment

FIGURE 4U Involuntary part-time employment as a percent of total employment

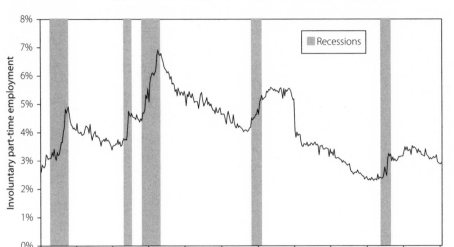

* 1994 CPS survey change.

Source: Authors' analysis of BLS (2006c) data.

share fluctuated throughout 2003, as businesses tested the reliability and resiliency of the recovery. As of April 2006, the percentage of workers employed in the temporary help industry rose to 2.3% as the economy picked up.

The data on part-time employment in Table 4.7 does not indicate much of a change from 1995 to 2005. However, **Figure 4U** illustrates a long term series on involuntary part-time employment from the monthly CPS. A survey change in 1994 accounted for the big decrease that year—data from before 1994 relied on those surveyed to determine whether they were voluntary or involuntary part-timers. The post-1994 surveys rely on additional implicit information to determine if respondents are actually available to work full time. Therefore, pre-1994 is not directly comparable to 1994 and beyond. But this series does offer insight into part-time employment and how it correlates with economic cycles.

Similar to other indicators, such as unemployment rates and shares of long-term un-employment (Figure 4J), part-time employment, as a share of total employment, increased during recessions and decreased during economic expansions. As with unemployment, it could be that the jobless recoveries that followed the last two recessions were accompanied with increased part-time employment shares well after the end of the recession. The 1994 survey change jump makes it hard to determine when this share peaked following the early 1990s recession, but it is clear that during the tightening of the labor market from the mid- to late 1990s, this share fell sharply. Part-time employment started to increase following

TABLE 4.8 Share of workers employed one year or more in their current job assignment

Work arrangement	1995	2001	2005
Regular part time	62.0%	63.0%	65.0%
Temp agency	24.4	27.0	33.7
On-call / day laborers	54.7	57.0	57.4
Independent contractor (wage & salary)	63.9	61.0	67.1
Contract company employees	50.9	55.0	65.2
Direct hire temporaries	49.0	50.0	47.1
Standard workers	81.0%	79.0%	80.0%

Source: Fisher, Ditsler, Gordon, and West (2006).

the bursting of the technology bubble in 2000. This share continued on a more volatile upward trend throughout the 2001 recession until it started a slight downward trend around late 2003. The tepid jobs recovery that didn't turn around until mid-2003, again, coincides with recent trends in this series.

The general trend in nonstandard work is toward more permanent nonstandard work or what is sometimes referred to as "perma-temping." Traditionally, the staffing of nonstandard workers was usually for short-time use—especially the use of temporary agencies and contract companies. However, the share of workers who were employed one year or more increased for most of the nonstandard work categories—refer to **Table 4.8**. For example, the share of contract company employees on the job at least a year increased from 50.9% to 65.2% over the last decade. The share for temp agency workers increased from 24.4% in 1995 to 33.7% in 2005. These types of work arrangements have become more permanent as outsourcing has become more prevalent.

Broken down along gender lines, women are represented disproportionately in nonstandard work, which may be due to the need for greater flexibility in their work schedules, especially for single mothers for whom workplace flexibility is extremely important. Gender breakdowns for the three survey years are shown in **Table 4.9**. The rates by gender for standard and nonstandard work have not changed much over time. The overall employment breakdown of nonstandard workers by gender in 2005 was 54.7% women and 45.3% men. Women were disproportionately represented as nonstandard workers—and they far exceed men in regular part-time employment. Of nonstandard workers, men tend to far outnumber women as self-employed independent contractors and contract company workers.

Nonstandard workers, in general, are not only often paid less (see the analysis of part-time workers in Chapter 3), but they are less likely to receive benefits from their employers and more likely to be uninsured. **Table 4.10** gives the source of health insurance for both types of workers, as well as two sub-sets of nonstandard work—temporary and part-time. Standard workers are much more likely to be insured and to be insured through employer-

TABLE 4.9 Share of workers by work arrangement and gender

Work arrangement	Percent of women employed		
	1995	2001	2005
All temporary workers	51.8%	49.7%	49.9%
Temp agency	52.8	58.9	52.8
On-call / day laborers	49.9	44.6	47.1
Direct hire temporaries	52.6	50.0	51.4
Independent contractor (wage & salary)	49.6	45.7	46.4
Independent contractor (self-employed)	29.7	33.9	33.5
Contract company employees	29.1	31.3	30.8
Regular part time	69.9	68.8	68.5
All nonstandard workers	55.9%	56.0%	54.7%
Standard workers	43.1%	44.5%	44.4%

Work arrangement	Percent of men employed		
	1995	2001	2005
All temporary workers	48.2%	50.3%	50.1%
Temp agency	47.2	41.1	47.2
On-call / day laborers	50.1	55.4	52.9
Direct hire temporaries	47.4	50.0	48.6
Independent contractor (wage & salary)	50.4	54.3	53.6
Independent contractor (self-employed)	70.3	66.1	66.5
Contract company employees	70.9	68.7	69.2
Regular part time	30.1	31.2	31.5
All nonstandard workers	44.1%	44.0%	45.3%
Standard workers	56.9%	55.5%	55.6%

Source: Fisher, Ditsler, Gordon, and West (2006).

provided health insurance. In 2005, 86.5% of standard workers were insured, compared to 72.0% of nonstandard workers. Of those percentages, 71.8% of standard workers were insured through their employer while just 20.8% of nonstandard worker were. Nonstandard workers were more likely to receive health insurance from a spouse or other family member's plan, but the rate at which nonstandard workers were uninsured was double that of standard workers in 2005. **Figure 4V** provides a visual breakdown of the 2005 data.

Lower access to employer-provided insurance was further exacerbated by lower take-up rates for nonstandard workers. The majority (61.1%) of nonstandard workers were not eligible for employer-provided insurance, and just one-in-five were insured by their employer's plan in 2005 (**Table 4.11**). In contrast, just 14.9% of standard workers were not

TABLE 4.10 Source of health insurance for standard and nonstandard workers, 1995, 2001, & 2005

	Own employer's health insurance	Spouse/family member plan	Other source of health insurance	Medicare/Medicaid/ other gov't source	Uninsured
1995					
Standard workers	74.0%	9.8%	3.4%	0.6%	12.3%
All nonstandard workers	20.3	37.8	10.3	4.2	27.3
Temporary workers	23.3	29.1	10.7	2.6	34.4
Part-time workers	18.0	43.3	9.2	5.0	24.5
2001					
Standard workers	73.9%	10.7%	3.0%	0.7%	11.7%
All nonstandard workers	21.3	39.0	10.5	5.3	24.0
Temporary workers	27.3	27.0	9.3	3.8	32.6
Part-time workers	18.2	45.1	9.8	6.1	20.7
2005					
Standard workers	71.8%	10.3%	3.5%	0.9%	13.5%
All nonstandard workers	20.8	34.7	10.8	5.8	28.0
Temporary workers	22.7	25.1	10.8	4.9	36.5
Part-time workers	18.8	40.3	9.7	6.5	24.7

Source: Fisher, Ditsler, Gordon, and West (2006).

FIGURE 4V Source of health insurance, 2005

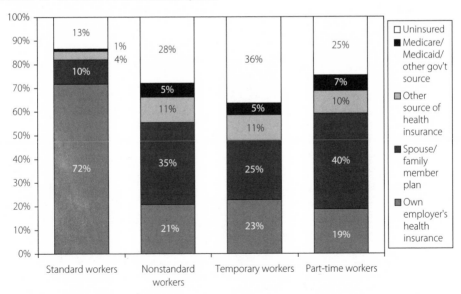

Source: Fisher, Ditsler, Gordon, and West (2006).

TABLE 4.11 Access to employer-provided health insurance, 1995, 2001, and 2005

Work arrangement	Insured by own employer plan	Eligible, but declined	Not eligible/ not offered
1995			
Standard workers	74.0%	11.3%	14.7%
All nonstandard workers	20.3	15.9	63.7
Temporary workers	23.3	11.9	64.8
Part-time workers	18.0	17.9	64.1
2001			
Standard workers	73.9%	12.9%	13.2%
All nonstandard workers	21.3	18.5	60.2
Temporary workers	27.3	13.2	59.5
Part-time workers	18.2	20.5	61.3
2005			
Standard workers	71.8%	13.4%	14.9%
All nonstandard workers	20.8	18.2	61.1
Temporary workers	22.7	15.2	62.0
Part-time workers	18.8	19.6	61.6

Source: Fisher, Ditsler, Gordon, and West (2006).

FIGURE 4W Access to employer-provided health insurance, 2005

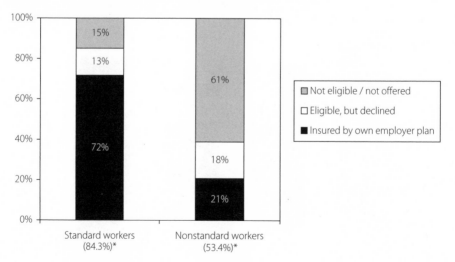

* Health insurance take-up rates in parenthesis.

Source: Fisher, Ditsler, Gordon, and West (2006).

TABLE 4.12 Access to employer-provided retirement plan, 1995, 2001 and 2005

Work arrangment	No plan available	Not eligible	Declined	Participates
1995				
Standard workers	27.9%	5.6%	3.3%	63.2%
All nonstandard workers	54.6	22.9	2.7	19.8
Temporary workers	52.5	26.5	2.5	18.5
Part-time workers	53.9	23.1	2.9	20.2
2001				
Standard workers	23.0%	5.7%	4.2%	67.2%
All nonstandard workers	48.0	23.5	3.9	24.6
Temporary workers	47.5	23.3	3.8	25.3
Part-time workers	46.9	25.1	3.9	24.1
2005				
Standard workers	25.0%	4.7%	4.6%	65.7%
All nonstandard workers	51.4	21.6	4.2	22.8
Temporary workers	53.8	21.7	3.3	21.1
Part-time workers	48.3	23.5	4.7	23.5

Source: Fisher, Ditsler, Gordon, and West (2006).

eligible, and 71.8% were insured through their employer. For the sub-set of temporary workers, the percent insured by their own employer plan jumped from 23.3% in 1995 to 27.3% in 2001 and fell again in 2005 to 22.7%. The reasons for ineligibility can include: too few work hours per week; employee has not worked at the job long enough; or the laws regarding temporary or contract employment arrangements. Many workers are precluded from benefits based on their work arrangement.

The problem of access to employer-provided health insurance for the nonstandard workforce is clear in **Figure 4W**. As the figure indicates, 85% of standard workers and 39% of nonstandard workers were eligible for employer-provided health insurance from their own employer. Furthermore, take-up rates for eligible standard and eligible nonstandard workers were 84.3% and 53.4%, respectively (located in parentheses in the figure). The two most common reasons for not enrolling were because workers had coverage from another source that was probably cheaper (or provided better coverage), or because the plan being offered was too expensive.

Retirement benefits were another fringe benefit that was harder to secure for nonstandard workers. **Table 4.12** provides a look at the access to job-based retirement plans by work arrangement. Standard workers, compared to nonstandard workers, were more likely to have a retirement plan available to them, and they were more likely to participate in those plans. About 70% of standard workers and 27% of nonstandard workers had access to

FIGURE 4X Access to job-based retirement plan, 2005

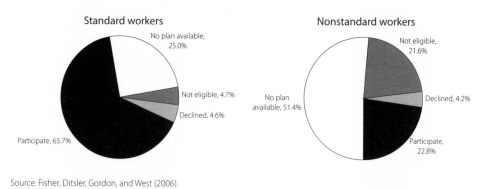

Source: Fisher, Ditsler, Gordon, and West (2006).

a retirement plan in 2005 (even if they didn't choose to participate). The percent of workers with no plan available dropped from 1995 to 2001, only to increase again in 2005 for both types of work arrangements. **Figure 4X** depicts access in 2005 to job-based retirement plans for standard and nonstandard workers.

Conclusion

The great American jobs machine is one of the most powerful mechanisms in our economy for achieving broadly based prosperity. But the faltering of that machine—as measured by the weakest jobs recovery on record—has left lingering adversity for workers and their families. It took 46 months to regain peak-level employment following the 2001 recession; in all previous recessions it took just 21 months on average. Recoveries the length of the current one usually have employment growth of around 10%—as of this writing, employment growth is just shy of 2% for this recovery. The lackluster jobs performance over this cycle resulted in lost output due to lower rates of employment. Worse for most workers is the fact that recent economic growth has not resulted in improved livings standards, due in part to the jobs situation.

Many economic indicators have responded positively to the end of the jobless recovery. For example, the unemployment rate reversed its upward trend, as did long-term unemployment shares, and the employment rate reversed its steady decline. As the analyses in this chapter have made clear, the retraction of labor that followed the 2001 recession was primarily cyclical and not structural. Most notably, the employment rate of young college graduates reversed a persistent downward trend that closely coincided with the positive job growth that began in mid-2003.

But on the other hand, even though some economic indicators have improved with the growth in jobs, many of these indicators have yet to regain the rates and levels attained during the last cyclical peak. For instance, although the decline in employment rates bottomed out in 2003 and reversed course, they are still below 2001 rates. As for unemployment rates, they have been improving, but they are relatively high compared to the 4.0% annual rate of 2000. This cycle has also had ongoing problems with unusually high shares of long-term unemployment.

Moreover, job growth has been too tepid to boost living standard for most workers—even as the economy expanded and labor productivity had posted some impressive gains over this recovery. Hopefully, workers will eventually find that the recent growth in output and strong worker productivity is making its way into the pockets of the workers who are responsible for such economic expansion in the first place.

CHAPTER 5

Wealth

Unrelenting disparities

Much of the preceding chapters has presented multifaceted discussions regarding wages and incomes. This chapter moves the discussion to an analysis of wealth, which includes both sides of the accounting ledger—assets and liabilities—or, net worth. As with the previous discussions concerning wages, there are enormous variations in wealth based on demographic characteristics such as gender, race, and household income. The skewed distribution of net worth is even greater than that of income or wages, both of which were presented in previous chapters.

Wealth is a vital component of a family's standard of living. Over the long term, families may try to accumulate wealth in order to finance education, purchase a house, start a small business, and/or fund retirement. In the short term, wealth—particularly financial assets such as checking account balances, stocks, and bonds—can help families cope with financial emergencies related to unemployment or illness. The level of wealth a family is able to accumulate determines how sufficiently it can smooth consumption when financial emergencies arise. Those families with little or no wealth may be financially devastated by any economic setback.

It is a challenge for middle- and lower-income families to accumulate ample wealth—especially when so many are in serious debt. These families may go without much needed necessities during hard financial times. Some debt, such as a mortgage, may be considered good debt, but may be hard to acquire. Other types of debt, such as the use of high-interest-bearing credit cards, may be much more problematic—especially when balances accrue in order to meet day-to-day living expenses.

There are several key findings that come out of this chapter. First, the skewed distribution of wealth has persisted, and it has become more concentrated at the top of the distribution over time. In the early 1960s, the average level of wealth held by the wealthiest fifth of all households was 15 times that of the overall median; by 2004 it was over

23 times. As would be expected, the distribution in the shares of wealth held by wealth class is very unequal. The share of all wealth held by the bottom 80% was just 15.3% in 2004—down from 19.1% in the early 1960s—and that 3.8% share of wealth shifted to the top 5% of households.

Second, the notion that a vast majority of American households are greatly invested in the stock market is refuted here. Less than half of all households hold stock in any form, including mutual funds and 401(k)-style pension plans. Moreover, of households that held stock, just 34.9% had stock holdings in excess of $5,000.

The ownership of stocks was particularly unequal. In 2004, the top 20% of stockowners held over 90% of all stocks, by value, while the bottom 80% of stockholders owned under 10%. Additionally, stocks are a bigger part of the asset portfolio for wealthier households. For those in the top 1% of the wealth distribution, stock assets made up over 21% of their total assets, while stocks consisted of just 4.8% of all assets for households in the middle fifth of the wealth distribution. While stock performance is very important, on a daily basis it does not significantly affect average households.

Home ownership is the most important asset for most American families. The increase in the wealth of average families generated by home ownership through means of home equity increases is vital. A remarkable and unprecedented surge in home ownership rates persisted from the mid-1990s to 2004. The slight decline in 2005 may have been in reaction to interest rate increases along with talk of a housing bubble. While the overall rate of home ownership is impressive, rates do vary considerably by income and race. Only about half of those in the bottom quarter of the income distribution own their homes, while 88.9% in the top quarter of the income distribution own homes. While black and Hispanic rates have been increasing, they still lag considerably behind that of whites.

Household debt has consistently trended upward, and it was over 130% of disposable personal income in 2005. As expected, debt-service burdens continued to plague lower-income families disproportionately, and they increased from 2001 to 2004. By 2004, it took about a fifth of income from a middle-income family to service their debt. Approximately one in four low-income households had debt-service obligations that exceeded 40% of their income, as did 13.7% of middle-income households. Moreover, the official report of debt by the Federal Reserve Board has undoubtedly understated serious financial hardships—akin to debt—incurred by households with high levels of financial insecurity. These households increasingly access loans and money through nontraditional or predatory lending institutions such as pawn shops and check-cashing centers.

Lastly, personal bankruptcy filings soared at the end of 2005 just before new stricter laws went into affect. For the year, nine out of every 1,000 adults declared personal bankruptcy. The opportunity to start anew through fair and reasonable bankruptcy laws is crucial for those who are faced with insurmountable debt. A large share of bankruptcy filings are preceded by the loss of employment, unmanageable medical bills, or divorce. Only time will tell how the new laws will affect the number of bankruptcy filings and ultimately how families will cope with large debt burdens.

TABLE 5.1 Distribution of income and wealth, 2004

	Distribution of:		
	Household income	Net worth	Net financial assets
All	100.0%	100.0%	100.0%
Top 1%	16.9	34.3	42.2
Next 9%	25.6	36.9	38.7
Bottom 90%	57.5	28.7	19.1

For detailed information on table sources, see Table Notes.

Source: Wolff (2006).

Net worth

The skewed distribution of net worth—assets minus debt—and its persistence are the main focus of this section. Net worth is the sum of a family's assets—real estate, checking and savings account balances, stock holdings, retirement funds (such as 401(k) plans and individual retirement accounts), and other assets—minus the sum of all of a family's liabilities—mortgages, credit-card debt, student loans, and other debts.

Changes in household wealth levels occur through new investments, returns on existing investments, savings, or inheritances. Net worth excludes assets in defined-benefit pension plans because workers do not legally own the assets held in these plans and thus do not necessarily benefit from improvements in the value of assets used to pay the defined benefit. (Their companies do benefit, however, because higher asset values lower the contributions companies have to pay to meet future defined benefits.) Nor do workers suffer financially if the underlying assets underperform expectations. For similar reasons, this analysis also excludes Social Security and Medicare from the net worth calculations (although the section projecting retirement income does include expected income from Social Security).

The inequitable distribution of wealth, which surpasses that of both wages and incomes, is central to this chapter. The skewed distributions of household income, net worth, and net assets seen in **Table 5.1** are unmistakable. In 2004 (the latest year available), the top 1% of households with the highest incomes received 16.9% of all income. These same households held 34.3% of all net worth and 42.2% of all net financial assets. At the other end of the distribution, the 90% of households with the lowest incomes received 57.5% of all income, but held just 28.7% and 19.1% of all net worth and net financial assets, respectively.

Growth in household net worth was greatly affected by the stock market crash of 2000. The slowdown in the growth of net worth from 2000 to 2005 compared to 1989 to 2000 was led by the rapid reduction in the value of stock—at an annual rate of -9.4% as shown in **Table 5.2**. The precipitous decline in the stock market due to the bursting of the bubble lasted from April 2000 until 2003 (see Figure 5E), and the subsequent recovery into 2004 helped to partially offset losses

TABLE 5.2 Growth of household wealth, 1949-2005

Type of wealth	Annual growth of net worth per household					
	1949-67	1967-73	1973-79	1979-89	1989-2000	2000-05
Total net worth*	2.6%	0.7%	0.6%	2.2%	3.0%	0.5%
Net financial assets**	2.7	-0.8	-0.2	2.5	4.1	-1.2
Net tangible assets***	2.1	4.1	2.2	1.6	0.5	4.7
Financial assets						
Stock	7.0%	-6.4%	-7.6%	3.5%	8.7%	-9.4%
Mutual funds	11.7	-6.4	-8.9	19.6	13.4	2.5
Stock and mutual funds	7.2	-6.4	-7.6	5.2	9.8	-5.6

* Includes all households, personal trusts, and nonprofit organizations.
** Financial assets less nonmortgage debt.
*** Consumer durables, housing, and land assets less home mortgages.

Note: Net financial assets includes a number of categories in addition to stocks and mutual funds. Therefore, the growth rates of stock and mutual funds do not sum to the growth rate of net financial assets.

Source: Authors' analysis of Federal Reserve Board (2006a) data and Bureau of Economic Analysis (2006) data.

FIGURE 5A Distribution of wealth by wealth class, 1983-2004

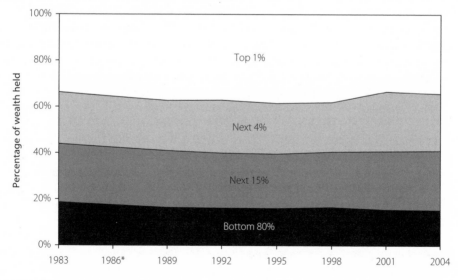

* See Figure Notes.
Source: Authors' analysis of Wolff (2006).

between 2001 and 2005. The increase in net tangible assets—driven by increased housing equity—also helped to keep annual growth of net worth in the positive range.

The unequal distribution of household wealth by wealth class has only become more inequitable over time. **Figure 5A** illustrates the stark inequality that persisted even during the boom years of the late 1990s. Since 1983, the top 1% of wealth holders consistently owned well over 30% of all wealth, and the bottom 80% of wealth holders, without exception, held under 20%. Those in the bottom 80% held 18.7% of all wealth in 1983, which decreased to just 15.3% in 2004, and the 3.4 percentage-point decrease was shifted to the top 20% of wealth holders.

Tables 5.3 and **5.4** provide a more detailed analysis of the distribution of wealth from 1962 to 2004. Table 5.3 shows that, in 2004, the top fifth of households held 84.7% of all wealth, while the middle fifth held a mere 3.8% (its lowest recorded share), and the bottom fifth actually had negative net worth—they owed 0.5% of all wealth. Over the 1962 to 2004 period, the top fifth increased their share of wealth by 3.7 percentage points, while the bottom four-fifths gave up that percentage.

The data in Table 5.4 illustrate how the absolute level of wealth changed over time for households by wealth class. From 2001 to 2004, the average wealth of the top 1% of households grew by $1.25 million, from $13.5 million in 2001 to nearly $14.8 million in 2004—a 3.0% annual increase. The average wealth of the middle 20% of households grew by 0.8% annually from $80,000 in 2001 to $81,900 in 2004. The annualized growth of median wealth was -0.2% between 2001 and 2004. The wealth of the poorest households (the bottom 20%), which had improved considerably from 1989 to 2001, saw a reversal of trend, and their wealth became more negative on average: -$11,400 in 2004, down from -$8,700 in 2001. Annualized growth for the top fifth was 2.1% compared to 1.5% for households in the bottom four-fifths of the wealth distribution.

A closer look at Table 5.4 reveals an increasing and persistent trend in the growth of inequality. The ratio of median-to-average wealth over time has been decreasing, down from 0.27 in 1962 to 0.18 in 2004, reflecting a faster increase in average wealth than median wealth. The increase in average wealth was driven by those at the top of the wealth distribution who have controlled greater shares of wealth since 1962.

Wealth inequality has persisted and gotten worse over time. The ratio of wealth of the top 1% to median wealth has grown over time and is shown in **Figure 5B**. In 1962, the top 1% of wealth holders had 125 times median wealth; that figure steadily rose and in 2004 the wealthiest had 190 times the wealth of the typical household (derived from Table 5.4).

Inequality also increased among the very wealthy between 1982 and 2004. **Figure 5C** shows the minimum, average, and maximum levels of wealth of the members of the Forbes 400, an annual list of the 400 wealthiest people in the United States. The figure shows wealth holdings on a log scale, which compresses large differences and allows the three lines to fit on the same graph. The gap between the wealthiest and the least wealthy members of the Forbes 400 grew significantly in the late 1990s—due in part to the run up in the stock market. As the stock market began to slide in 2000, the net worth of the very rich fell, but it resumed its upward trend in 2002 and continued into 2004. The average net worth of the Forbes 400 in 2004 was below its peak level hit in 1999. Overall, these data suggest that inequality—as defined by the ratio of maximum-to-average wealth—among the very

TABLE 5.3 Changes in the distribution of wealth, 1962-2004

Wealth class*	1962	1983	1989	1998	2001	2004	Percentage-point change:			
							1962-83	1983-89	1989-2001	2001-04
Top fifth	81.0%	81.3%	83.5%	83.4%	84.4%	84.7%	0.4	2.2	0.9	0.2
Top 1%	33.4	33.8	37.4	38.1	33.4	34.3	0.3	3.6	-4.0	1.0
Next 4%	21.2	22.3	21.6	21.3	25.8	24.6	1.2	-0.8	4.2	-1.2
Next 5%	12.4	12.1	11.6	11.5	12.3	12.3	-0.2	-0.5	0.7	0.0
Next 10%	14.0	13.1	13.0	12.5	12.9	13.4	-0.9	-0.1	-0.1	0.5
Bottom four-fifths	19.1%	18.7%	16.5%	16.6%	15.6%	15.3%	-0.4	-2.2	-0.9	-0.2
Fourth	13.4	12.6	12.3	11.9	11.3	11.3	-0.8	-0.3	-1.0	0.0
Middle	5.4	5.2	4.8	4.5	3.9	3.8	-0.2	-0.4	-0.9	-0.1
Second	1.0	1.2	0.8	0.8	0.7	0.7	0.2	-0.3	-0.1	0.0
Lowest	-0.7	-0.3	-1.5	-0.6	-0.4	-0.5	0.4	-1.2	1.1	-0.1
Total	100.0%	100.0%	100.0%	100.0%	100.0%	100.0%				

* Wealth defined as net worth (household assets minus debts).

Source: Wolff (2006).

TABLE 5.4 Changes in average wealth by wealth class, 1962-2004 (thousands of 2004 dollars)

Wealth class*	1962	1983	1989	1998	2001	2004	Annualized growth:			
							1962-83	1983-89	1989-2001	2001-04
Top fifth	$680.8	$1,001.9	$1,178.7	$1,305.8	$1,711.6	$1,822.6	1.8%	2.7%	3.2%	2.1%
Top 1%	5,622.8	8,315.2	10,547.9	11,825.1	13,537.8	14,791.6	1.9	4.0	2.1	3.0
Next 4%	890.2	1,375.4	1,522.1	1,670.2	2,616.4	2,676.7	2.1	1.7	4.6	0.8
Next 5%	416.1	598.2	655.4	722.5	999.9	1,054.7	1.7	1.5	3.6	1.8
Next 10%	235.1	323.0	366.1	399.7	523.0	576.3	1.5	2.1	3.0	3.3
Bottom four-fifths	$40.1	$57.5	$58.1	$65.1	$78.9	$82.5	1.7%	0.2%	2.6%	1.5%
Fourth	112.7	154.8	173.9	186.9	229.6	243.6	1.5	1.9	2.3	2.0
Middle	45.7	64.3	68.2	70.7	80.0	81.9	1.6	1.0	1.3	0.8
Second	8.0	14.5	11.9	12.9	14.9	14.4	2.9	-3.3	1.9	-1.0
Lowest	-6.1	-3.7	-21.3	-10.3	-8.7	-11.4	2.4	-33.9	7.2	-9.2
Median	$45.0	$63.3	$67.7	$70.3	$78.4	$77.9	1.6%	1.1%	1.2%	-0.2%
Average	168.2	246.4	282.3	313.2	405.5	430.5	1.8	2.3	3.1	2.0

* Wealth defined as net worth (household assets minus debts).

Source: Wolff (2006).

FIGURE 5B The ratio of the wealthiest 1% to median wealth in the U.S.

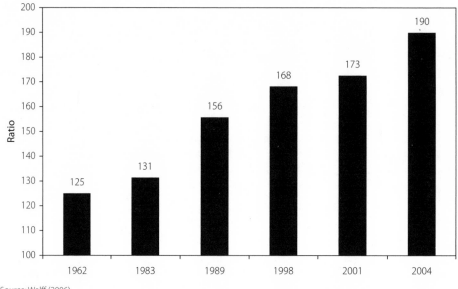

Source: Wolff (2006).

FIGURE 5C Annual net worth of "Forbes 400" wealthiest individuals

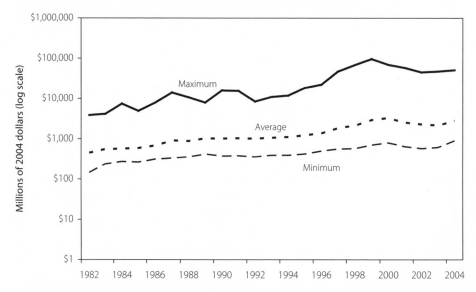

Source: Authors' analysis of Broom and Shay (2000) and Forbes (2006).

TABLE 5.5 Households with low net worth, 1962-2004 (percent of all households)

Net worth*	1962	1983	1989	1998	2001	2004	Percentage-point change:			
							1962-83	1983-89	1989-2001	2001-04
Zero or negative	23.6%	15.5%	17.9%	18.0%	17.6%	17.0%	-5.6	2.4	-0.3	-0.6
Less than $10,000*	34.3	29.7	31.8	30.3	30.1	29.6	-4.6	2.1	-1.7	-0.5

* Constant 1998 dollars.

Source: Wolff (2006).

top holders of wealth (above the level captured by the Survey of Consumer Finances, which, by design, excludes members of the Forbes 400) grew rapidly throughout the 1990s, before a slight reversal at the beginning of the 2000s.

Low net worth

An important feature of the wealth distribution is that a significant percentage of households have low net worth, and many have zero or negative net worth. These households are extremely vulnerable to financial distress and insecurity. **Table 5.5** reports the share of all households with zero or negative net worth or net worth less than $10,000. After substantial improvement from 1962 to 1983, these shares have shown small but consistent improvement since 1998. In 2004, 17.0% of all households had zero or negative net worth, while 29.6% had net worth of less than $10,000.

In terms of race, the experience of black households differed significantly from that of white households, an aspect of wealth distribution that will be discussed in more detail in the next section. The third panel of **Table 5.6** gives racial breakdowns for households with zero or negative net wealth. In 2004, more than twice the percentage of black households (29.4%) as white households (13.0%) had zero or negative net worth. The relative circumstances of black households improved substantially from 1989 to 1998, with a 13.3 percentage-point decline in households with zero or negative net wealth. However, the percent of black households with a zero or negative net worth increased from 1998 to 2001, jumping from 27.4% in 1998 to 30.9% in 2001 and not much improvement in 2004.

Racial divide

The distribution of wealth, by race, is profoundly unequal and the wealth racial gap is far larger than that of income (as shown in Chapter 1). The persistent and low relative wealth of blacks compared to whites is a function of the legacy of slavery, racism, and discrimination. While new laws, legislation, and progress in general have helped to level the playing field—it is

TABLE 5.6 Wealth by race, 1983-2004 (thousands of 2004 dollars)

Race	1983	1989	1992	1995	1998	2001	2004
Average wealth*							
Black	$54.2	$57.1	$61.3	$50.5	$67.5	$70.8	$101.4
White	$287.9	$340.6	$329.6	$300.4	$371.9	$496.8	$534.0
Black-to-white ratio	0.19	0.17	0.19	0.17	0.18	0.14	0.19
Median wealth							
Black	$5.5	$2.5	$13.9	$9.1	$11.6	$11.4	$11.8
White	$82.9	$98.4	$82.6	$75.6	$94.6	$113.5	$118.3
Black-to-white ratio	0.07	0.03	0.17	0.12	0.12	0.10	0.10
Households with zero or negative net wealth							
Black	34.1%	40.7%	31.5%	31.3%	27.4%	30.9%	29.4%
White	11.3%	12.1%	13.8%	15.0%	14.8%	13.1%	13.0%
Black-to-white ratio	3.0	3.4	2.3	2.1	1.9	2.4	2.3
Average financial wealth**							
Black	$27.3	$27.9	$34.9	$26.3	$43.6	$46.1	$61.5
White	$212.1	$257.5	$253.8	$233.6	$295.3	$394.3	$402.5
Black-to-white ratio	0.13	0.11	0.14	0.11	0.15	0.12	0.15
Median financial wealth							
Black	$0.0	$0.0	$0.2	$0.2	$1.4	$1.2	$0.3
White	$23.1	$31.2	$25.4	$22.4	$43.6	$44.9	$36.1
Black-to-white ratio	0.00	0.00	0.01	0.01	0.03	0.03	0.01

* Wealth defined as net worth (household assets minus debts).
** Financial wealth is liquid and semi-liquid assets including mutual funds, trusts, retirement, and pensions.

Source: Wolff (2006).

surely more equal than used to be the case—the historical legacy of the black economic experience shows up in profound wealth disparities. **Figure 5D** illustrates how non-whites fared in comparison to whites. Non-white income was 55.6% of white income, but non-white net worth was just 27.3% of white net worth—just about half the size of the income measure.

Table 5.6 presents an analysis of wealth by race. In 2004, the latest year available, the average black household had a net worth equal to just 19% of the average white household. The ratio fell to a mere 0.14 from 1998 to 2001 as black wealth increased just 5% compared to a 34% increase in white wealth.

The second section of Table 5.6 gives median wealth holdings for blacks and whites. The most striking aspect of these data is the extremely low level of median wealth of black households. In 2004, the median black household had a net worth of $11,800, or just 10% of the corresponding figure for whites. Decreases in median wealth for both races were what drove the decrease in the ratio from 1992 to 1995. The ratio decrease from 0.17 to

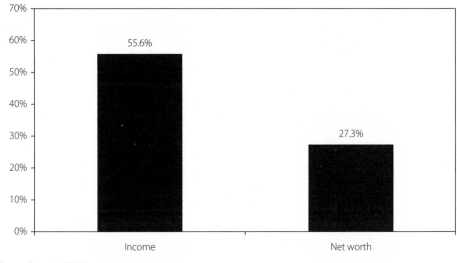

FIGURE 5D Share of income and net worth of non-whites compared to whites, 2004

Income: 55.6%

Net worth: 27.3%

Source: Bernstein (2006).

0.12 was due to the dynamic that black median wealth fell 34% while white median wealth fell 8%. The change in this ratio from 1998 to 2001 was due to a decrease in black median wealth and an increase in white median wealth. The ratio was unchanged in 2004 as both races had relatively similar increases in median wealth.

Black households were especially unlikely to hold financial assets such as stocks and bonds. In 2004, the average financial wealth of black households (as shown in Table 5.6, fourth panel) was only 15% of the average financial wealth for white households, an increase from 12% in 2001. The median financial wealth for blacks (as shown in the last panel of Table 5.6) was just $300, less than 1% of the corresponding figure for whites. The vast and lasting disparity in the distribution of wealth between blacks and whites is indicative of the lasting legacy of discrimination.

To summarize, the data on net worth reveal a highly unequal distribution of wealth by class, which has been further exacerbated by race. A significant share of the population has little or no net worth, while, over the last 40 years at least, the wealthiest 20% has consistently held over 80% of all wealth and the top 1% has controlled at least a third. There is no reason to believe these wealth disparities will lessen anytime soon.

Assets

The preceding section summarized the overall distribution of net worth—the sum of each household's assets and liabilities. This section focuses on the asset component of net worth. Households hold a variety of assets, from houses and boats to stocks and bonds. The distribu-

TABLE 5.7 Distribution of asset ownership across households, 2004

Wealth class	Percentage of all holdings of each asset:				
	Common stock excluding pensions*	All common stock**	Non-equity financial assets***	Housing equity	Net worth
Top 0.5%	29.5%	27.6%	38.8%	8.1%	25.3%
Next 0.5%	9.7	9.3	10.3	4.4	9.1
Next 4%	28.6	28.4	23.1	19.9	24.6
Next 5%	13.3	13.5	9.3	13.5	12.3
Next 10%	11.0	11.9	9.3	19.5	13.4
Bottom 80%	7.9	9.4	9.1	34.6	15.3
Total	100.0	100.0	100.0	100.0	100.0

* Includes direct ownership of stock shares and indirect ownership through mutual funds and trusts.
** Includes direct ownership of stock shares and indirect ownership through mutual funds, trusts, IRAs, Keogh plans, 401(k) plans, and other retirement accounts.
*** Includes direct ownership of financial securities and indirect ownership through mutual funds, trusts, and retirement accounts, and net equity in unincorporated businesses.

Source: Wolff (2006).

tion of assets among wealth classes, however, differs significantly by asset. Some assets, such as stocks and bonds, are highly concentrated; other assets, such as houses, are more widely held. The portfolio of wealth holdings varies with the amount of wealth. Wealthy households, for example, tend to have much of their wealth in stocks and bonds and other wealth-generating financial assets. Less-affluent households typically hold most of their wealth in housing equity.

Table 5.7 shows the distribution of several types of household assets in 2004 by wealth class. The top 5%, by wealth class, controlled well over half of all asset types except housing equity. Housing equity, compared to other assets, is more equitably distributed across wealth classes, but it is still skewed. The top 20%, by wealth class, held 65.4% of total housing equity, while the bottom 80% held just 34.6%. Also note that the bottom 80% in wealth class held just 7.9% of stock excluding pensions, and that share only increased to 9.4% when pensions were added.

Stocks

The stock market turned around in 2003 after a precipitous three year fall, although it is still no where near the highs associated with the run-up in stocks experienced at the end of the 1990s. As **Figure 5E** illustrates, the inflation-adjusted value of the Standard & Poor's 500 index of stocks increased 234% between 1990 and 2000, then fell almost 37% between 2000 and 2003. In 2004, a little more than half of all U.S. households had no stock holdings of any form, either direct (owning shares in a particular company) or indirect (owning shares through a mutual fund or through a 401(k)-style, defined-contribution pension plan), and, of those that did, almost two of three households had holdings less than $5,000. This

FIGURE 5E Growth of U.S. stock market, 1955-2005

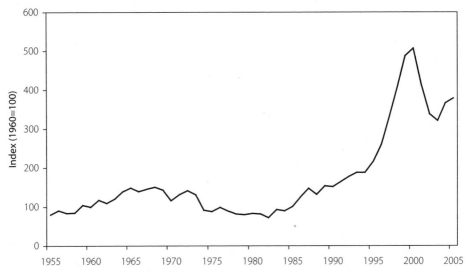

Source: Authors' analysis of the Economic Report of the President (2006) data.

fact contradicts the popular notion that the typical household is greatly invested in the stock market. Moreover, from 2001 to 2004 the share of households holding stock, particularly those holding more than a small amount, declined—the first decline since 1989. In 2004, the share of households with any stock holdings fell to 48.6% from 51.9% in 2001 as shown in **Table 5.8**. Furthermore, only 34.9% of Americans held stock worth more than $5,000, and this was down from 40.1% in 2001—the first decline in this share. The reality is that the typical household is not greatly affected by the volatility inherent in the stock market due to their overall lack of stock holdings.

The top panel of **Table 5.9** provides a more detailed description of the distribution of stock ownership by wealth class. Average holdings overall and for each wealth class decreased between 2001 and 2004. Recall that the stock market collapsed between 2000 and 2003, therefore the full impact was not evident by 2001. In 2004, the wealthiest 1% of households owned an average of almost $3.3 million in stocks—down from $3.8 million in 2001. By comparison, the average direct and indirect stock holdings of the middle 20% of households were small, at $7,500 in 2004 down from $12,800 in 2001, the largest percentage drop, by wealth class, over the period. Stock holding for those in the bottom 40% of households was just $1,400 in 2004, down from $2,000 in 2001.

These data confirm that stock holding is not that pervasive in the middle class. Of the $155,000 in average total assets held by the middle 20%, only $7,500 was in stock. Most of the assets for the middle class are in housing. Thus, fewer than 5% of all assets were in stock holdings for middle-class households versus just over 21% for those in the top 1%.

TABLE 5.8 Share of households owning stock, 1989-2004

Stock holdings	1989	1992	1995	1998	2001	2004
Any stock holdings						
Direct holdings	13.1%	14.8%	15.2%	19.2%	21.3%	20.7%
Indirect holdings	24.7	28.4	30.2	43.4	47.7	44.0
Total	31.7	37.2	40.4	48.2	51.9	48.6
Stock holdings of $5,000 or more*						
Direct holdings	10.0%	11.4%	12.3%	13.6%	14.6%	13.5%
Indirect holdings	16.9	21.5	22.7	32.2	36.8	31.0
Total	22.6	27.3	28.8	36.3	40.1	34.9

* Constant 1995 dollars.

Source: Wolff (2006).

Figure 5F (derived from Table 5.9) illustrates the distribution of stock market holding by wealth class in 2004. The top 1% owned 36.9% of all stock market holdings, while the next 9% owned 41.9%—hence, the top 10% of income holders owned close to 80% of stocks, while the bottom 90% owned just over 20%. **Figure 5G** (derived from Table 5.9) shows the persistent and imbalanced distribution of stock market wealth by class. Though there were some fluctuations in stock holding between the top 1%, the next 9%, and the next 10%, generally the top 20% by wealth class held approximately 90% of all stock, while the bottom 80% consistently held just 10% or less over the 1989-2004 period.

The unequal growth in stock wealth from 1989 to 2004 is illustrated by the step pattern shown in **Figure 5H** (derived from Table 5.9). There was almost no growth (0.5%) in stock market holdings for the bottom 40%. The middle 20% of households received only 1.2% of the rise in the overall value of stock holdings over the period. Over a third (34.4%) of the growth over the period went to the wealthiest 1% of households, while 42.7% of stock market growth went to the next 9% of households. In other words 77.1% of the growth in stocks went to the wealthiest 10%. This is slightly less than the share of total stock wealth for the top 10% in 1989, indicating that stock wealth became slightly more equal.

Stocks are also highly concentrated by household income. The high concentration of stock ownership means that the gains associated with the late 1990s stock boom were highly concentrated among those with the most income. Conversely, the losses from the bust years will also be concentrated among those with higher incomes. **Table 5.10** reports the share of all stock owned by households at different income levels in 2004.

Predictably, higher income households were much more likely to own stocks. Households with incomes at or above $250,000 represented just 2.5% of all households, of which 94.6% owned some form of stock, and they held 44% of all stock. Comparatively, the largest single share of households by income level (28.3%) had incomes at or between $25,000 and $49,999, but only 41.8% of those households were invested in stocks and their share of all stock was just 6.9%.

TABLE 5.9 Average household assets and liabilities by wealth class, 1962-2004 (thousands of 2004 dollars)

Asset type	Top 1%	Next 9%	Next 10%	Next 20%	Middle 20%	Bottom 40%	Average
Stocks*							
1962	$2,791.8	$142.8	$15.9	$5.1	$1.3	$0.3	$44.4
1983	1,812.7	117.0	14.0	5.3	1.8	0.5	32.1
1989	1,368.3	150.3	29.5	10.3	4.3	0.7	33.8
1998	2,926.5	337.8	92.1	31.9	10.7	1.9	83.2
2001	3,806.1	546.4	140.6	44.0	12.8	2.0	113.4
2004	3,276.5	413.4	105.6	31.3	7.5	1.4	89.0
All other assets							
1962	$3,037.1	$524.4	$249.2	$138.5	$75.0	$17.8	$151.5
1983	6,976.6	905.5	366.1	188.3	92.7	19.5	251.5
1989	9,696.6	995.5	393.5	215.0	103.3	22.4	297.9
1998	9,226.1	957.5	384.0	209.9	113.1	27.6	285.1
2001	10,079.2	1,302.4	467.6	250.2	121.1	28.3	350.2
2004	12,060.6	1,524.7	573.7	305.8	148.4	35.2	420.5
Total debt							
1962	$206.2	$40.4	$29.9	$30.9	$30.6	$17.2	$27.6
1983	474.1	78.9	57.0	38.8	30.2	14.5	37.2
1989	517.0	105.3	56.9	51.4	39.4	27.8	49.4
1998	327.5	121.6	76.4	54.9	53.0	28.2	55.1
2001	347.5	130.5	85.3	64.6	53.9	27.2	58.1
2004	566.8	174.2	103.8	93.8	74.1	34.4	79.1
Net worth							
1962	$5,622.8	$626.8	$235.1	$112.7	$45.7	$0.9	$168.2
1983	8,315.2	943.6	323.0	154.8	64.3	5.4	246.4
1989	10,547.9	1,040.6	366.1	173.9	68.2	-4.7	282.3
1998	11,825.1	1,173.6	399.7	186.9	70.7	1.3	313.2
2001	13,537.8	1,718.4	523.0	229.6	80.0	3.1	405.5
2004	14,770.4	1,764.0	576.3	243.4	81.8	2.2	430.5

* All direct and indirect stock holdings.

Source: Wolff (2006).

Households with incomes above $75,000 held 81% of all stock. The concentration of stocks within upper income levels holds true even for stocks in retirement plans, such as 401(k)s. The main difference between stock holdings in pension plans and other (direct) stock holdings is that pension assets are more evenly *distributed among high-income households*. While the highest-income group—households with an annual income above $250,000—controlled 56.4% of all publicly traded stock, these high earners owned 25.5%

FIGURE 5F Distribution of stock market holdings by wealth class, 2004

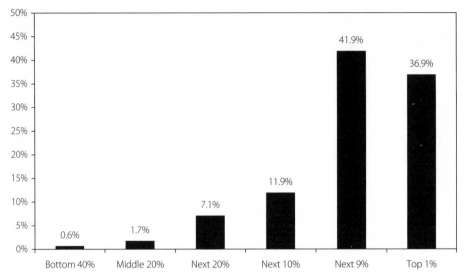

Source: Wolff (2006).

FIGURE 5G Distribution of stock market wealth by wealth class, 1989-2004

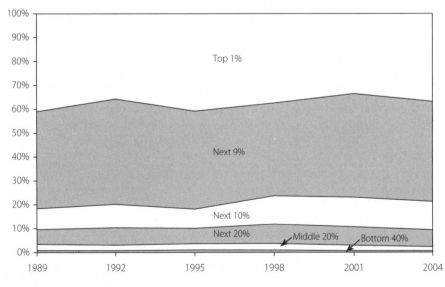

Source: Wolff (2006).

FIGURE 5H Distribution of growth in stock market holdings by wealth class, 1989-2004

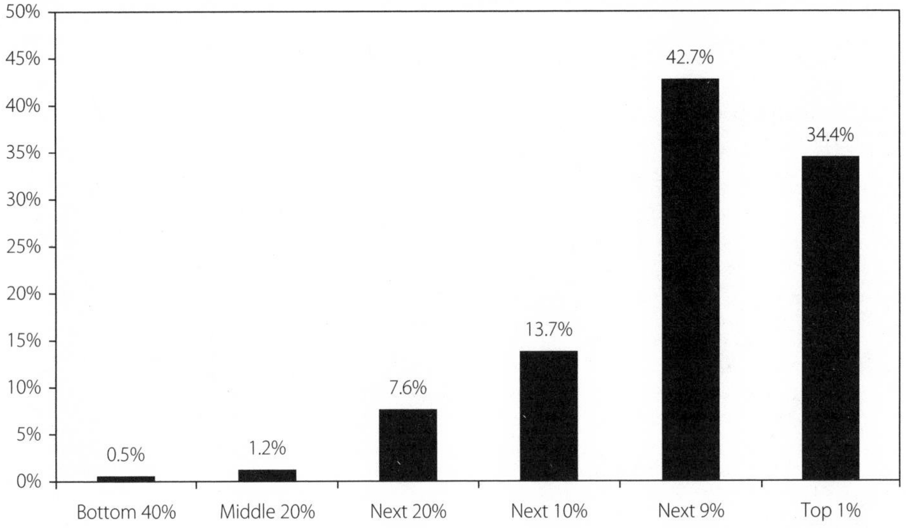

Source: Wolff (2006).

of stocks in pension plans, while households in the $100,000-$249,999 range own an even greater share (44.0%). At the same time, the bottom three-fourths of households—those with annual incomes of $74,999 or less—held only 20% of all stocks in pension plans (and only 15% of publicly traded stock).

The fallacy that all or even most American households are greatly invested in the stock market—either directly or indirectly through pension plans—is exposed in the above passages. To the extent that households are invested in the market, most households have little invested. For the most part, middle- to lower-income households depend almost solely on labor income to meet their financial obligations.

Home ownership
While much attention is paid to the ups and downs of the stock market, the fact is that housing equity is actually a far more important form of wealth for most households. The second section of Table 5.9, which shows the distribution of all non-stock assets by household wealth, makes this point indirectly. In 2004, the total value of all non-stock assets—comprised primarily of housing equity—held by the middle 20% of households was $148,400, almost 20 times larger than the average stock holdings for the same group ($7,500). While stock holding fell for all groups over the 2001-04 period, the category of "all other assets" increased for all wealth classes—due in large part to the run up in house prices and home equity over that period.

TABLE 5.10 Concentration of stock ownership by income level, 2004

Income level	Share of households	Percent who own	Percent of stocks owned:	
			Shares	Cumulative
Publicly traded stock				
$250,000 or above	2.5%	67.7%	56.4%	56.4%
$100,000-249,999	13.6	44.9	22.9	79.4
$75,000-99,999	9.4	32.4	5.6	84.9
$50,000-74,999	17.4	25.1	8.3	93.3
$25,000-49,999	28.3	12.8	4.7	98.0
$15,000-24,999	13.7	8.3	0.9	98.9
Under $15,000	15.2	4.6	1.1	100.0
All	100.0	20.7	100.0	
Stocks in pension plans*				
$250,000 or above	2.5%	79.4%	25.5%	25.5%
$100,000-249,999	13.6	75.1	44.0	69.6
$75,000-99,999	9.4	62.5	10.5	80.0
$50,000-74,999	17.4	49.4	10.8	90.8
$25,000-49,999	28.3	31.0	7.3	98.1
$15,000-24,999	13.7	12.1	1.3	99.4
Under $15,000	15.2	5.8	0.6	100.0
All	100.0	100.0	100.0	
All stocks**				
$250,000 or above	2.5%	94.6%	44.0%	44.0%
$100,000-249,999	13.6	86.6	29.2	73.2
$75,000-99,999	9.4	77.5	7.8	81.0
$50,000-74,999	17.4	62.5	9.9	90.9
$25,000-49,999	28.3	41.8	6.9	97.8
$15,000-24,999	13.7	19.6	1.2	98.9
Under $15,000	15.2	11.8	1.1	100.0
All	100.0	48.6	100.0	

* All defined contribution stock plans including 401(k) plans.
** All stock directly or indirectly held in mutual funds, IRAs, Keogh plans, and defined-contribution pension plans.

Source: Wolff (2006).

Census data shown in **Figure 5I** indicate that, in 2005, over two-thirds of households owned their own homes. Home ownership rates fluctuated within a fairly narrow band—64% to 66%—between the early 1970s and the late 1980s. However, ownership rates rose sharply and steadily from the early 1990s to 2004, when 69% of households were home-owners. Rates continued to rise, albeit at a slower pace, through the 2001 recession as low interest rates prevailed and home ownership dropped slightly in 2005 to 68.9% due, in part, to rising interest rates and, perhaps, to much talk of the existence of a housing bubble.

As with so many statistics presented throughout this text, home ownership rates are disparate demographically. **Table 5.11** presents data collected through the biennial

FIGURE 5I Average home ownership rates, 1965-2005

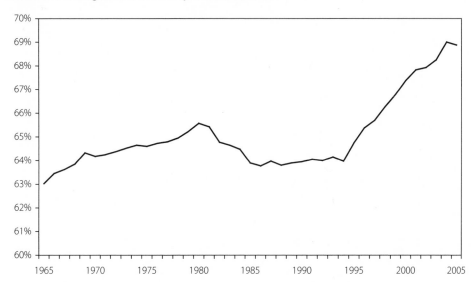

Source: Authors' analysis of U.S. Census Bureau (2005) data.

American Housing Survey, which show that home ownership rates vary considerably by race and income. Table 5.11 and **Figure 5J** show that, in 2005, white households were much more likely than black and Hispanic households to own their own homes—72.7% of white households were homeowners compared to 48.2% and 49.5% of black and Hispanic households, respectively. That Hispanics were slightly more likely than blacks to own their homes in 2005 was a reversal of trend. Even though a substantial racial divide exists for home ownership rates, all races have experienced increased rates of home ownership over time.

Table 5.11 also shows that 88.9% of households in the top 25% of the income distribution were homeowners, compared to just 49.0% of households in the bottom 25% in 2003 (the most recent data available by income). **Figure 5K** charts this information and illustrates that there is a lot of room for growth in home ownership rates, particularly for households at the bottom of the income distribution.

Retirement wealth and income adequacy

The concept of retirement adequacy is an important one. Expected retirement income is a key determinant of when (or even if) a worker will retire. A common test of retirement income adequacy is the ability in retirement to replace at least half of current income, based on expected pension, Social Security benefits, and returns on personal savings. **Table 5.12** shows the proportion of households that did not meet this test. In 2004 (the latest year for

TABLE 5.11 Home ownership rates by race and income

Race/income	Home ownership rates							Percentage-point change		
	1979	1989	1999	2001	2003	2005		1979-89	1989-99	1999-2005
All races	65.4%	64.0%	66.8%	67.8%	68.3%	68.9%		-1.4	2.8	2.1
White	68.4%	69.4%	70.5%	71.6%	72.1%	72.7%		1.0	1.1	2.2
Black*	44.4	42.9	46.3	47.7	48.1	48.2		-1.5	3.4	1.9
Hispanic	n.a.	40.3	45.5	47.3	46.7	49.5		n.a.	5.2	4.0
By income**										1999-2003
Top 25%	87.0%	84.5%	87.4%	88.0%	88.9%	n.a.		-2.5	2.9	1.4
Next 25%	72.3	68.6	73.1	73.4	74.6	n.a.		-3.6	4.5	1.5
Next 25%	56.2	56.3	57.8	59.7	60.5	n.a.		0.0	1.5	2.7
Bottom 25%	46.2	46.4	49.4	50.9	49.0	n.a.		0.2	2.9	-0.3

*   Black includes all non-white in 1979.
** Data only available through 2003.

Source: Authors' analysis of U.S. Census Bureau (2001, 2003, and 2005) data.

FIGURE 5J Home ownership rates by race, 1989-2005

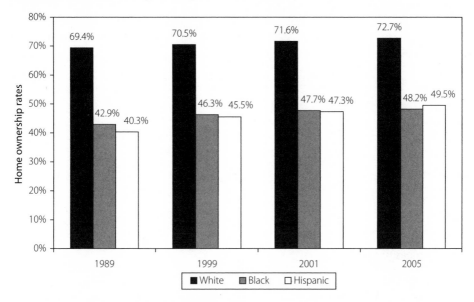

Source: Authors' analysis of U.S. Census Bureau (2003 and 2005) data.

FIGURE 5K Average rate of home ownership by income, 2003

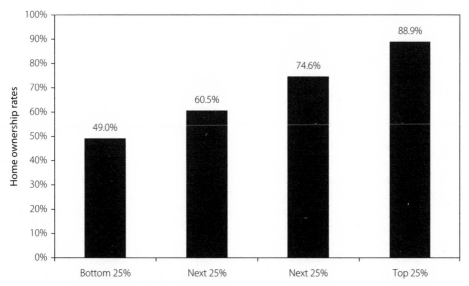

Source: Authors' analysis of U.S. Census Bureau (2005) data.

TABLE 5.12 Retirement income adequacy, 1989-2004

	Percent of households aged 47-64 with expected retirement income less than one half of current income					
					Percentage-point change	
Group	1989	1998	2001	2004	1989-2001	2001-04
All	30.5%	42.5%	28.1%	27.2%	-2.3	-0.9
By race/ethnicity*						
Non-Hispanic white	27.3%	40.3%	25.4%	24.1%	-2.0	-1.3
African American or Hispanic	42.1	52.7	40.0	39.0	-2.1	-1.0
By education**						
Less than high school	39.2%	48.6%	29.2%	46.6%	-10.0	17.4
High school degree	24.7	40.9	29.0	28.8	4.3	-0.2
Some college	18.8	42.4	30.1	34.7	11.3	4.6
College degree or more	20.8	40.7	25.4	21.2	4.6	-4.2
By family status						
Married couple	26.5%	37.3%	24.1%	26.6%	-2.4	2.5
Single male	22.6	62.4	26.5	29.0	3.9	2.5
Single female	43.8	45.0	39.0	27.7	-4.8	-11.3
By homeowner status						
Owns a home	24.9%	39.5%	25.1%	22.5%	0.2	-2.6
Renter	49.8	52.8	40.1	44.4	-9.7	4.3

* Asian and other races are excluded from the table because of small sample sizes.
** Households are classified by the schooling level of the head of household.

Note: A 7% real return on assets is assumed for financial wealth and net worth. Households are classified by the age of the head of household. Retirement income is based on marketable wealth holdings and all expected pension and Social Security benefits.

Source: Wolff (2006).

which data are available), 27.2% of households headed by someone age 47 to 64 expected retirement income to be *inadequate*.

Like other aspects of income and wealth, expected retirement adequacy was not uniformly distributed. African American or Hispanic households were more likely to have low incomes in retirement—39.0% will be unable to replace half of current income. Comparatively, 24.1% of white households were not expected to have adequate means in retirement.

Marked improvements were made over the 1998-2001 period for all the categories listed in Table 5.12, as the percent of households with inadequate expected retirement income fell. Some of those gains were lost between 2001 and 2004 as outcomes were mixed over this period.

Compared to earlier years, in 2004 having a college degree made a larger difference in expected retirement income—21.2% for households with a college degree or more were expected to have a retirement income of less than half their current income, com-

TABLE 5.13 Household debt by type, 1949-2005

	As a share of disposable personal income				All debt as a share of all assets	Mortgage debt as a share of real estate assets
	All debt	Mortgage	Home equity loans*	Consumer credit		
1949	33.2%	19.7%	n.a.	10.2%	6.4%	16.4%
1959	61.5	38.7	n.a.	17.1	10.4	26.0
1973	66.7	39.4	n.a.	19.7	12.8	26.8
1979	73.5	46.1	n.a.	19.8	13.9	28.0
1989	86.7	58.3	7.9%	19.2	15.5	33.9
2000	102.2	66.3	7.7	24.0	15.0	37.8
2005	131.8	95.8	11.6	24.2	18.6	40.1
Annual percentage-point change						
1949-59	2.8	1.9	n.a.	0.7	0.4	1.0
1959-73	0.4	0.0	n.a.	0.2	0.2	0.1
1973-79	1.1	1.1	n.a.	0.0	0.2	0.2
1979-89	1.3	1.2	n.a.	-0.1	0.2	0.6
1989-2000	1.4	0.7	0.0	0.4	0.0	0.4
2000-05	5.9	5.9	0.8	0.0	0.7	0.5

* Data for 1989 refer to 1990.

Source: Authors' analysis of Federal Reserve Board (2006a), Economic Report of the President (2006), and Economagic (2006) data.

pared to higher percentages for other education levels—this wasn't necessarily the case for other years.

Retirement adequacy varied little by family status in 2004, although there were significant changes from 2001 as more single males and substantially fewer single females had inadequate retirement income. Consequently there were large differences by homeowner status, as homeowners were much less likely to have inadequate retirement income.

Liabilities

Assets are one side of the balance sheet that tallies net worth; the other side is liabilities or debts. There is both "good" debt and "bad" debt; in and of itself, debt is not a problem for households. In fact, credit generally represents a tremendous economic opportunity for households, since they can use it to buy houses, cars, invest in education, and buy other big-ticket consumer goods and necessities that provide services over many years. Debt can also be used to cope with short-term economic setbacks such as unemployment or illness or to make important investments in education or small businesses. Debt becomes a burden only when required debt payments begin to crowd out other economic obligations or opportunities.

As **Table 5.13** indicates, in 2005 the total value of all forms of outstanding household debt was at its highest—18.6% of all assets. All debt, as a share of disposable personal income, was also at its highest at 131.8%. Mortgage debt, as a percent of disposable personal income, has greatly increased over time and was at its highest of 95.8% in 2005. Consumer credit debt (mostly credit card debt and auto loans) was almost one-quarter of total disposable income, but it has been fairly constant since 2000.

The historical trajectory of debt levels and the notable highs reached in 2005 are depicted in **Figure 5La**. The rate of growth in debt at the start of the new millennium was unprecedented—both for overall debt and for mortgage debt. All debt rose from about 20% of disposable personal income at the end of World War II to over 60% by the early 1960s. Overall debt levels then remained roughly constant through the mid-1980s, when they began to increase rapidly again. By 2005, overall debt was 30% more than disposable income. In 1947 mortgage debt was about 17% of all debt, but by 2005 that share had increased to 96%. As home ownership rates and home equity increased, so did home equity loans, as shown in **Figure 5Lb**. The steep growth rate in home equity loans indicates that households were increasingly spending their accumulated equity rather than saving it.

Aggregate debt is an important feature of the economy, but aggregate data do not describe the distribution of the debt. The distribution of debt (described in the third panel of Table 5.9) has some striking features. First, debt is more equally distributed than either assets or net worth. In 2004, for example, the average household in the top 1% had a net worth over 180 times greater than that of a household in the middle 20%. In the same year, however, the average debt held by the top 1% was about seven and a half times greater than the average for the middle 20%. Second, for typical households, debt levels were high compared to the value of assets. In 2004, the average outstanding debt of households in the middle 20% was $74,100 (typically mortgage debt plus credit card debt). This debt level was about 10 times greater than the corresponding $7,500 average for stock holdings and about 50% of the total value of all other assets which included the family home.

The growth in household debt by wealth level may be calculated by using data from Table 5.9. **Figure 5M** divides the total increase in debt between 2001 and 2004 among households at different points in the wealth distribution. (The approach here is identical to that used in Figure 5G, which looked at the distribution of growth in stock wealth.) Debt for the middle 20% grew by 19.5%, while the next 20% had the most growth in debt—28.2%. Debt held by the top 1% of households increased by 10.6% by comparison.

Debt service

As stated above, debt is not necessarily bad, and it is often essential. Debt may facilitate wealth creation, such as building equity on a purchased home or higher incomes due to educational investment. Debt does impose a financial burden on those who must repay it. Debt is a problem when the burden of repayment becomes overwhelming financially. Servicing debt may become harder in the near future as interest rates are currently on the rise. **Table 5.14** gives the average household financial obligations ratio for renters and homeowners. Obligations include the minimum required payments on outstanding debt (mortgage and consumer) plus automobile leases and rental payments, as a share of personal disposable income for selected years from 1980 through 2005.

As shown in Table 5.14, in the first quarter of 2006 minimum debt payments were the highest on record, and they totaled 17.6% of all household disposable income for home-

FIGURE 5La Mortgage debt as a percentage of disposable personal income, 1947-2005

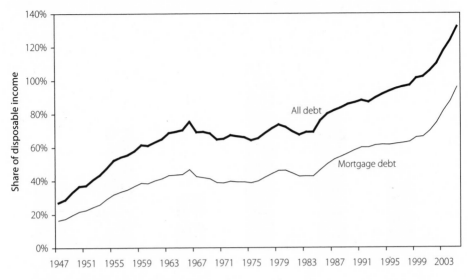

Source: Authors' analysis of Federal Reserve Board (2006a) data.

FIGURE 5Lb Debt (consumer credit and home equity loans) as a percentage of disposable personal income, 1947-2005

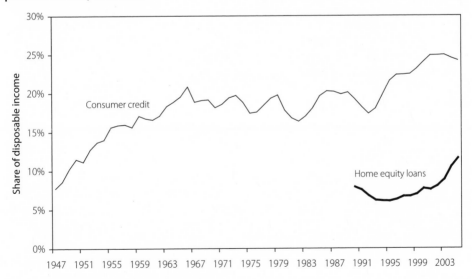

Note: Data for equity loans are unavailable prior to 1990.
Source: Authors' analysis of Federal Reserve Board (2006a) data.

FIGURE 5M Distribution of growth in debt, 2001-04

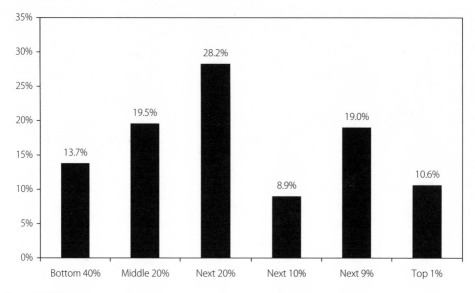

Source: Wolff (2006).

TABLE 5.14 Financial obligation ratio, 1980-2005 (as a percent of disposable personal income)

	Renters	Homeowners		
	Total	Total	Mortgage	Consumer
1980	24.2%	13.7%	8.3%	5.4%
1989	25.0	15.3	9.8	5.4
1995	26.2	15.0	9.6	5.4
2000	29.7	15.5	9.1	6.3
2005	24.8	17.2	10.8	6.4
2006*	24.3	17.6	11.4	6.2
Percentage-point change				
1980-89	0.8	1.6	1.5	0.1
1989-2000	4.8	0.2	-0.7	0.9
2000-05	-5.0	1.7	1.7	0.0

* Data refers to first quarter of 2006.

Source: Authors' analysis of Federal Reserve Board (2006b) data.

owners (6.2% consumer and 11.4% mortgage), while it was 24.3% for renters. Over the full period from 1980 to 2006, the financial service ratio is little changed for renters—falling from its 29.7% peak in 2000. For homeowners, the ratio increased from 13.7% in 1980 to 17.6% in 2006. Since 2000, the increase in this ratio for homeowners was mostly driven by mortgages. The sharp increase in home ownership (as discussed above) that started in the mid-1990s was impressive and it continued through the 2001 recession, fueled by low interest rates. But households are vulnerable to higher financial obligations if interest rates continue to increase.

This measure of financial obligations does not capture many additional costs incurred by low-income families that often have to turn to predatory lenders. Nontraditional lending services (such as pawn shops) and rapid-cash providers (such as non-bank check-cashing services) that charge extraordinary fees compared to traditional lending institutions constitute significant sources of "debt" for many low-income families.

A measure of household debt service by income percentile is given in **Table 5.15**. These calculations are a little different from those in Table 5.14. The debt service ratio is a narrower measure compared to the financial obligations ratio. This measure of debt service includes renters but does not include rental payments; it only includes debt payments on outstanding mortgage and consumer debt. In 2004, households in the top 10% spent 9.3% of their income meeting the minimum required debt payments, compared to 19.4% of income for middle income households—the highest percentage since 1989. Those at the top had the lowest debt service and the smallest increase over the 1989-2004 period. The bottom three-fifths of households saw the largest increases over the 1989-2004 period.

Hardship

Debt service payments equal to more than 40% of household income constitute a level of debt generally considered to represent economic hardship. **Table 5.16** takes a look at such hardship by income percentiles. For any given year, high debt burden was negatively associated with income level. In 2004, just 1.8% of households in the top 10%, compared to 27% in the lowest fifth of households, had high debt burdens. Note that data in this table include renters but not rental payments as debt, which suppresses these numbers.

Table 5.17 shows another measure of the impact of debt on economic hardship: the share of households, by income level, that were late paying bills. In 2004, about 9% of all households were 60 days or more late in paying at least one bill. Not surprisingly, the share of households behind on their bills was strongly related to income. Very few (0.3%) of the highest income group were late in paying bills, while 15.9% in the lowest income range were behind on at least one bill. Table 5.17 also illustrates a rise in the percentage of late-paying households between 2001 and 2004 for the lowest four-fifths of the income groups, while the top 20% had lower late-paying household percentages.

The ultimate indicator of debt-related difficulties is personal bankruptcy. New bankruptcy laws went into effect in October 2005 that made it more difficult and expensive for consumers to claim bankruptcy. As expected, there were record high bankruptcies filed before the stricter laws went into effect. **Figure 5N** graphs the rate of personal bankruptcies from 1980 through 2005. In 2005, nine out of every 1,000 adults declared personal bankruptcy. Research has shown that loss of employment, insurmountable medical bills, and/or divorce are leading causes for bankruptcy filings. The "fresh start" that bankruptcy grants will be harder to obtain regardless of reason.

TABLE 5.15 Household debt service as a share of household income, by income percentile, 1989-2004

Household income	1989	1992	1995	1998	2001	2004	Percentage-point change	
							1989-2004	2001-04
Top fifth								
Top 10%	8.7%	11.4%	9.5%	10.3%	8.1%	9.3%	0.6	1.2
Next 10%	15.7	15.5	16.6	16.8	17.0	17.3	1.6	0.3
Bottom four-fifths								
Fourth	16.9%	16.7%	17.9%	19.1%	16.8%	18.5%	1.7	1.7
Middle	16.3	16.1	15.6	18.6	17.1	19.4	3.1	2.3
Second	13.0	15.8	17.0	16.5	15.8	16.7	3.7	0.9
Lowest	14.1	16.4	19.1	18.7	16.1	18.2	4.1	2.1
Average	12.9%	14.4%	14.1%	14.9%	12.9%	14.4%	1.5	1.5

Source: Bucks, Kennickell, and Moore (2006).

TABLE 5.16 Share of households with high debt burdens, by income percentile, 1989-2004*

Percentile of household income	1989	1992	1995	1998	2001	2004	Percentage-point change	
							1989-2004	2001-04
Top fifth								
Top 10%	1.9%	2.5%	2.3%	2.8%	2.0%	1.8%	-0.1	-0.2
Next 10%	3.4	3.5	4.7	3.5	3.5	2.4	-1.0	-1.1
Bottom four-fifths								
Fourth	5.8%	8.2%	7.7%	9.8%	6.5%	7.1%	1.3	0.6
Middle	11.0	10.8	9.9	15.8	12.3	13.7	2.7	1.4
Second	14.5	16.0	18.0	18.3	16.6	18.6	4.1	2.0
Lowest	24.6	27.2	27.5	29.9	29.3	27.0	2.4	-2.3
Average	10.0%	11.5%	11.7%	13.6%	11.8%	12.2%	2.2	-1.4

* A high debt burden is a ratio of debt-to-income greater than 40%.
Source: Bucks, Kennickell, and Moore (2006).

TABLE 5.17 Share of households late paying bills, by income percentile, 1989-2004

Percentile of household income	1989	1992	1995	1998	2001	2004	Percentage-point change	
							1989-2004	2001-04
Top fifth								
Top 10%	2.4%	1.0%	1.0%	1.6%	1.3%	0.3%	-2.1	-1.0
Next 10%	1.1	1.8	2.8	3.9	2.6	2.3	1.2	-0.3
Bottom four-fifths								
Fourth	5.9%	4.4%	6.6%	5.9%	4.0%	7.1%	1.2	3.1
Middle	5.0	6.9	8.7	10.0	7.9	10.4	5.4	2.5
Second	12.2	9.3	10.1	12.3	11.7	13.8	1.6	2.1
Lowest	18.2	11.0	10.2	12.9	13.4	15.9	-2.3	2.5
Average	7.3%	6.0%	7.1%	8.1%	7.0%	8.9%	1.6	1.9

Source: Bucks, Kennickell, and Moore (2006).

FIGURE 5N Consumer bankruptcies per 1,000 adults, 1980-2005

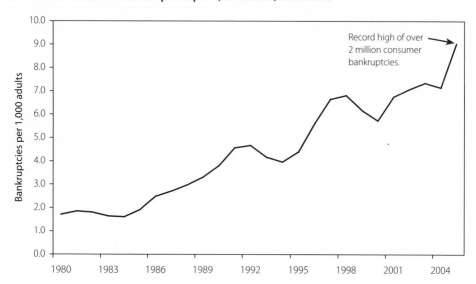

Source: Authors' analysis of American Bankruptcy Institute (2006) data.

Conclusion

The data presented here establish that the distribution of wealth is very unequal, much more so than the distribution of wages or incomes. The top 10% earned 42.5% of all household income but held 71.2% of all net worth in 2004. Recent changes in the tax codes, such as the reduction in the marginal income rates for the highest earners and reduced rates on dividends and capital gains, have exacerbated wealth concentration. A huge variation in levels of wealth held exists by wealth class. Average wealth held by the top 1% is close to $15 million while it is $81,000 for households in the middle-fifth of the wealth distribution. Strikingly, approximately 30% of households have a net worth of less than $10,000.

As the wealthiest continue to thrive, many households are left behind with little or nothing in the way of assets and often have significant debt. Approximately one in six households had zero or negative net wealth. These findings, like most economic statistics, vary by race—13.0% of white households compared to 29.4% of black households have zero or negative net wealth.

Median wealth of white households is 10 times that of African American households. Home ownership, an important asset and milestone of middle-class life in the United States, is out of reach for half of black and Hispanic households. Comparatively, 72.7% of white households are homeowners. Hence, race and other socioeconomic characteristics continue to be critical factors that exacerbate the skewed distribution of wealth in the United States.

A common misperception left over from the frenzied run up in stocks that occurred from the mid-1990s into 2000 is that most Americans are invested in the stock market. This is not, nor has it ever been, the case. More households are invested now than in the past, but it is still the case that just over half of all households are not invested in the stock market. As with other assets, the distribution of stock market holdings is concentrated at the upper end of wealth holders. The vast majority of stocks—approximately 80%—are held by the top 10% of wealth holders, while the bottom 40% of wealth holders own just 0.6% of all stocks.

Debt is on the increase, and since the new millennium, the rate of debt accumulation has soared. In 2005, debt exceeded disposable personal income by over 30%. Keeping up with financial obligations is becoming harder—burdens have always been relatively high for renters, and they have consistently trended upward for homeowners. If there is a significant downturn in house prices, as forecasted by many analysts, many homeowners may feel the pinch.

CHAPTER 6

Poverty
Rising over recovery as job market stalls

One of the most important challenges is discussing poverty in America is definitional. What, precisely, characterizes poverty in the U.S. economy? The government has an official definition, and while we devote some analysis to trends in this measure, it is widely considered to be an insufficient benchmark. The thresholds that designate official poverty status are far out-of-date, and the income definition omits both changes in American living standards and key factors regarding changes in tax policy that profoundly affect the living standards of the least advantaged.

Other work on how much income families need to make ends meet (see Allegretto 2005) suggests that *doubling* the poverty thresholds gets closer to income levels commensurate with realistic family budgets, and some of the analysis here uses this measure. We then turn to a much-improved poverty measure that incorporates more sources of both income and costs. Finally, we look at a measure of relative poverty, a definition that has many advantages over the absolute thresholds used in the rest of the chapter.

This research on definitions establishes some important facts about the extent and character of poverty in America:

- In 2005, 12.6% of the population, 37 million persons, including 13 million children, were poor.
- After falling steeply throughout the latter 1990s, poverty rates rose in the 2000-04 period, and this increase marks the first time that poverty rose through each of the first three years of a recovery; this trend offers a dramatic example of the narrowly shared benefits of the current recovery. (Poverty fell from 12.7% in 2004 to 12.6% in 2005, but the change was statistically insignificant.)
- The official poverty measure is out of date, and more valid measures show higher rates of poverty than the official measure.
- The 1990s, particularly the latter half of the decade, were a highly instructive period

for poverty policy. The combination of a full-employment job market and strengthened work supports proved to be a potent combination for lifting the incomes of many, though not all, poor families.

The last point is an important one in thinking about the steps policy makers need to take to diminish poverty amid the plenty in the U.S. economy. With both the economy and social policy pushing hard in the same direction, poverty was significantly reduced in the 1990s. The 2000s, by contrast, reveal a different picture. The policy levers from the earlier period were largely still in place, but the absence of full employment meant that a critical piece of the puzzle was missing, and poverty generally rose over these years.

The official poverty measure

The official poverty rate in 2005 (the latest data) was 12.6%, meaning that 37 million persons lived in families with incomes below the poverty threshold for their family size.

Like virtually every poverty analyst, we strongly believe that the official poverty statistics are inadequate to the task of determining who is poor in America. The thresholds used to determine poverty status were developed almost half a century ago, and have been updated only for inflation. Thus, they fail to show how changes in living standards over half a century are reflected in family expenditures. As the median income has risen over time, for example, the poverty thresholds have lagged behind, meaning that, by definition, the poor are falling ever further below the middle class. In 1960 the poverty line for a family of four was 48% of median family income; now it is 29%.

Spending patterns have changed over time, too. For example, thanks to both policy changes and evolving norms, more family members work in the paid labor market now than in the past, and so families are incurring greater work-related expenditures. Many analysts believe that such costs, most notably child care, should be subtracted from the income of working families when determining poverty.

Finally, the poverty measures fail to account for important changes in tax and transfer policy. Because official poverty status is determined using pretax income, the measure fails to capture the poverty-reducing impact of expansions in the earned income tax credit (EITC), a $40 billion wage subsidy program targeted at the working poor. Other objections include the failure to account for regional differences in the cost of living and the failure to count out-of-pocket expenditures on health care.

In short, the official measure is widely criticized for inadequately representing both needs and income. But would a more accurate measurement necessarily find a different poverty rate? For most analysts the answer is yes, and they further agree that the current measure understates poverty. In 2005, for example, a single parent with two children was poor if the family income (before taxes but counting cash transfers like welfare benefits) was below $15,735; for two parents with two children, the income threshold was $19,806. But detailed studies of family budgets, which take into account all expenses that families must incur to live in a safe and reliable manner, show income needs of about twice that amount.

Despite all these criticisms, the official measure is useful in studying poverty. First, it has a long history, and many informative time series using that metric. Second, while the

FIGURE 6A Poverty and twice poverty rate, 1959-2005

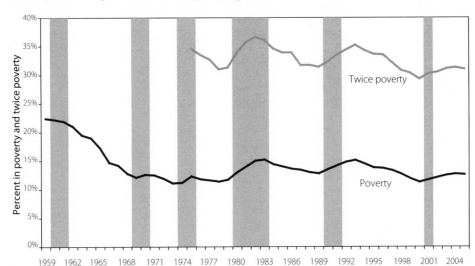

Note: Periods of recession are shaded.
Source: U.S. Census Bureau. For detailed information on figure sources, see Figure Notes.

official statistics omit many families whose incomes are arguably insufficient to meet their basic needs, the statistics still provide information about the most economically disadvantaged families. Third, by presenting poverty analysis alongside twice-poverty analysis (the share and number of persons with family incomes below twice the poverty threshold for their family types), we can present a more complete picture of the share of Americans facing income constraints.

Figure 6A and **Table 6.1** show the long-term trends in both poverty and twice poverty. The two trends are similar, although twice poverty tends to be slightly more responsive to the business cycle; this is probably the case because, as they move higher up the income scale, families tend to be more attached to the workforce and thus have incomes that are more responsive to the economic cycle. The large decline in poverty rates over the 1960s was due both to economic factors discussed below and the significant expansion of Social Security benefits, which helped reduce poverty among the elderly by 20 percentage points between 1959 and 1979.

Once this long slide ended in the early 1970s, poverty rates became more insensitive to economic expansions. For example, the table shows that poverty rates rose slightly, by about one point, between 1979 and 1989, while twice poverty was unchanged. The latter 1990s, however, serve as an instructive exception, one we investigate more closely later in the chapter. Poverty fell by 2.5 percentage points between 1995 and 2000, and twice poverty fell by 4.3 points.

TABLE 6.1 Percent and number of persons in poverty and twice poverty, 1959-2005

Year	Poverty rate	Number in poverty (000)	Twice poverty rate	Number in twice poverty (000)
1959	22.4%	39,490	n/a	n/a
1967	14.2	27,769	n/a	n/a
1973	11.1	22,973	n/a	n/a
1979	11.7	26,072	31.3%	69,849
1989	12.8	31,528	31.4	77,304
1995	13.8	36,425	33.6	88,810
2000	11.3	31,581	29.3	81,898
2005	12.6	36,950	31.0	90,872
Percentage-point changes				
1959-79	-10.7	-13,418	n/a	n/a
1979-89	1.1	5,456	0.1	7,455
1989-2000	-1.5	53	-2.1	4,595
1995-2000	-2.5	-4,844	-4.3	-6,911
2000-05	1.3	5,369	1.7	8,973

Source: U.S. Census Bureau.
For detailed information on table sources, see Table Notes.

Despite the relatively mild recession of 2001 (at least in terms of duration and GDP decline), poverty rose consistently from 2001 to 2004 (and was essentially unchanged in 2005). As can be seen in Figure 6A, poverty rose coming out of the early 1990s recession as well, though for just two years. Thus, the three-year increase in poverty from 2001 to 2004 is the longest in any recovery, a compelling example of the extent to which growth in this expansion is failing to reach those at the bottom of the income scale.

Racial and ethnic differences in poverty rates

Table 6.2 and **Figure 6B** show persistent differences in poverty rates by race and ethnicity. Given their lower income (see Chapter 1), poverty rates for minorities are consistently higher than those of whites. The rate for African Americans, for example, was at least three times that of whites through 1989. However, poverty among blacks and Hispanics was much more responsive than for whites to the faster and more broadly distributed income growth during the 1990s, and by 2000 the poverty rate for blacks was the lowest on record. The importance of this period of tight labor markets, and their poverty-reducing impact, is a theme we will return to throughout the chapter. Since the 2000 economic peak, the gap is again widening, at least for blacks.

Child and family poverty

Consistent research has made apparent the life-altering disadvantages of an economically

TABLE 6.2 Persons in poverty, by race/ethnicity, 1959-2005

Year	Total	White	Black	Hispanic
1959	22.4%	18.1%	n/a	n/a
1967	14.2	11.0	39.3%	n/a
1973	11.1	8.4	31.4	21.9%
1979	11.7	9.0	31.0	21.8
1989	12.8	10.0	30.7	26.2
1995	13.8	11.2	29.3	30.3
2000	11.3	9.5	22.5	21.5
2005	12.6	10.6	24.9	21.8
Percentage-point changes				
1959-79	-10.7	-9.1	n/a	n/a
1979-89	1.1	1.0	-0.3	4.4
1989-2000	-1.5	-0.5	-8.2	-4.7
1989-95	1.0	1.2	-1.4	4.1
1995-2000	-2.5	-1.7	-6.8	-8.8
2000-05	1.3	1.1	2.4	0.3

Source: U.S. Census Bureau.

FIGURE 6B Poverty rates by race/ethnicity, 1973-2005

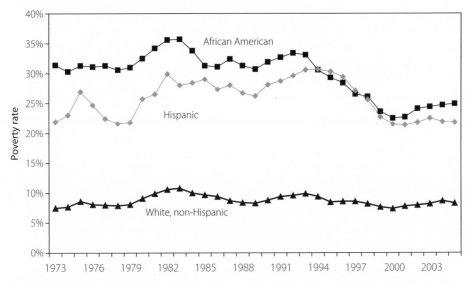

Source: U.S. Census Bureau.

TABLE 6.3 Percent of children in poverty, by race, 1979-2005

Year	Total	White	Black	Hispanic
Children under 18				
1979	16.4%	11.8%	41.2%	28.0%
1989	19.6	14.8	43.7	36.2
1995	20.8	16.2	41.9	40.0
2000	16.2	13.1	31.2	28.4
2005	17.6	14.4	34.5	28.3
Percentage-point changes				
1979-89	3.2	3.0	2.5	8.2
1989-2000	-3.4	-1.7	-12.5	-7.8
1989-95	1.2	1.4	-1.8	3.8
1995-2000	-4.6	-3.1	-10.7	-11.6
2000-05	1.4	1.3	3.3	-0.1
Children under 6				
1979	18.1%	13.3%	43.6%	29.2%
1989	22.5	16.9	49.8	38.8
1995	24.1	18.6	49.2	42.8
2000	17.2	14.1	32.9	28.9
2003*	20.1	16.6	39.4	32.3
Percentage-point changes				
1979-89	4.4	3.6	6.2	9.6
1989-2000	-5.3	-2.8	-16.9	-9.9
1989-95	1.6	1.7	-0.6	4.0
1995-2000	-6.9	-4.5	-16.3	-13.9
2000-03*	2.9	2.5	6.5	3.4

* Data for 2004 unavailable.
Source: U.S. Census Bureau.

deprived childhood. In 2005, 17.6% or about 13 million of the nation's children (persons less than age 18) were poor (**Table 6.3**). Again, rates are higher among minorities, with about a third of African American children and 28.3% of Hispanic children living in poverty.

Among children under six, for whom the damage inflicted by poverty is particularly severe, the rates are consistently higher than the overall child rates. The most recent available data, for 2003, reveal that about 20% of young children were poor that year, though the rate was almost double for black children.

After 2000, child poverty trended up after falling steeply, particularly for minorities, in the latter 1990s. Poverty among African American and Hispanic children fell by 10.7 and 11.6 percentage points from 1995 to 2000, with even faster declines among younger

TABLE 6.4 Family poverty, by race/ethnicity of family head and for different family types, 1959-2005

	Race/ethnicity of family head:				Families with children:	
					Married couples	Female head
	All	White	Black	Hispanic		
1959	18.5%	15.2%	n.a.	n.a.	n.a.	59.9%
1967	11.4	9.1	33.9%	n.a.	n.a.	44.5
1973	8.8	6.6	28.1	19.8%	n.a.	43.2
1979	9.2	6.9	27.8	20.3	6.1%	39.6
1989	10.3	7.8	27.8	23.4	7.3	42.8
1995	10.8	8.5	26.4	27.0	7.5	41.5
2000	8.7	7.1	19.3	19.2	6.0	33.0
2005	9.9	8.0	22.1	19.7	6.5	36.2
Percentage-point changes						
1959-73	-9.7	-8.6	n.a.	n.a.	n.a.	-16.7
1973-79	0.4	0.3	-0.3	0.5	n.a.	-3.6
1979-89	1.1	0.9	0.0	3.1	1.2	3.2
1989-2000	-1.6	-0.7	-8.5	-4.2	-1.3	-9.8
1989-95	0.5	0.7	-1.4	3.6	0.2	-1.3
1995-2000	-2.1	-1.4	-7.1	-7.8	-1.5	-8.5
2000-05	1.2	0.9	2.8	0.5	0.5	3.2

Source: U.S. Census Bureau.

children. The rate for black children in 2000—31.2%—is the lowest recorded rate for this group since these data were first collected in the mid-1970s. For Hispanic children, the large decline after 1995 brought them back to just above their 1979 rate.

Such numbers illuminate the distinction between trends and levels. The trend in sharply falling poverty rates was an unequivocal boon, yet even with these historic gains child poverty among minorities is still high.

Child poverty rates are fully a function of a family's income. **Table 6.4** shifts the unit of observation from persons to families, which in Census terminology refers to two or more persons related through blood, marriage, or adoption (i.e., one-person units are excluded). In general, family poverty rates are lower than poverty rates for persons, reflecting both the relatively high number of poor children and the inclusion of unrelated individuals in the person counts.

The patterns over time are similar to those shown in the previous tables, with consistently increasing rates of family poverty at business cycle peaks from 1973 to 1989. The poverty rates for African American families were essentially unchanged over these years, at about 28%. Over the 1990s, however, they fell by 8.5 percentage points; the 2000 rate of 19.3% is the lowest on record and marks the first time poverty for black families fell

TABLE 6.5 Average poverty gap, 1959-2005 (2005 dollars)

Year	Families	Years	Families
1959	$7,126	*Annual growth rates*	
1973	6,373	1959-73	-0.8%
1979	6,848	1973-79	1.2
1989	7,439	1979-89	0.8
1995	7,681	1989-2000	0.4
2000	7,732	1989-95	0.5
2005	8,125	1995-2000	0.1
		2000-05	1.0

Source: U.S. Census Bureau.

below 20%. Poverty among Hispanic families grew sharply, by 3.6 points, through 1995, but thereafter reversed course and fell even more quickly than it did for blacks; by 2000, Hispanics, too, posted the lowest rate on record.

Developments since 2000 provide a reminder that weak economic conditions since then have disproportionately hurt the least advantaged, the very groups who benefited most from the 1990s boom. Though family poverty was up across the board since 2000, two groups stand out: African Americans and single-mother families. Black families lost about two-fifths of the gains made over the latter 1990s boom, and poverty among mother-only families rose by more than three percentage points.

The depth of poverty

We now turn to two measures of the depth of poverty: the poverty gap and the share of the poor with incomes less than half the poverty threshold, i.e., the deeply impoverished.

Since a poverty threshold is a fixed-income level, families are considered poor whether they are one dollar or a thousand dollars below the poverty line. Thus, another useful way to gauge the depth of poverty is the "poverty gap": the average income deficit (the dollar gap between a poor family's income and its poverty threshold) experienced by poor families or individuals. For example, **Table 6.5** shows that, in 2005, the average poverty gap was about $8,000. This figure is the highest on record, meaning that poor families are, on average, poorer now than in earlier periods.

Figure 6C plots both family poverty rates and the average family poverty gap. Over the 1960s through the mid-1970s, both the poverty rate and the poverty gap declined, meaning that fewer families were poor and, of those who were, they were on average less poor over time. The strong labor market, along with the expansion of cash transfers over this period, including both Social Security (which significantly reduced the poverty of the elderly) and welfare benefits, contributed to these trends. As shown in Table 6.5, the average family poverty gap fell 0.8% annually over this period.

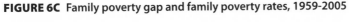

FIGURE 6C Family poverty gap and family poverty rates, 1959-2005

Source: U.S. Census Bureau.

Both family poverty and the poverty gap rose steeply over the recessionary period in the early 1980s, and, as shown in the figure, the two series diverged in the mid-1980s. In fact, the growth rates in the bottom section of the table reveal that the poverty gap has risen consistently over business cycle peaks. Thus, while the 1973 and 2000 poverty rates were about the same (8.8% in 1973 and 8.7% in 2000), the average poor family was over $1,300 (2005 dollars) worse off in the latter year.

The poverty gap series shows an interesting divergence from much of the data series observed thus far in that it shows no improvement over the latter 1990s. In fact, the average poor family was slightly worse off in 2000 than in 1995. This suggests that those families that exited poverty over this period were those whose incomes placed them closer to the poverty threshold, leaving behind the least well-off among the poor and raising the average poverty gap. **Figure 6D**, the share of the poor below half the poverty line, corroborates this interpretation. For a family of four with two children, this threshold amounted to just over $10,000 in 2005. After increasing from around 30% to around 40% through the 1980s, the share of the deeply poor has changed little, reinforcing the notion that the poor of today have lower average income levels than the poor in earlier periods.

To some extent, the trend toward poorer families within the poverty population is to be expected, given the strong shift of public policy toward work instead of cash assistance. The families most able to take advantage of both the strong labor market of the latter 1990s and the income supports tied to work, like the EITC, were likely to both

FIGURE 6D Percent of the poor below half the poverty line, 1975-2005

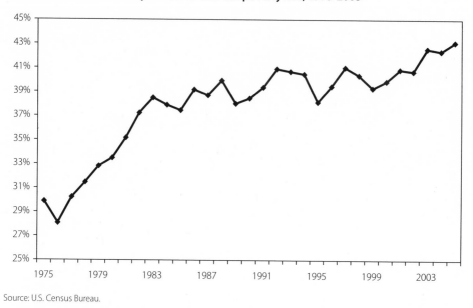

Source: U.S. Census Bureau.

climb out of poverty and do so from relatively close to the income threshold. Those left behind are probably the least likely to be able to take advantage of either a strong market economy or work-based supports.

That said, it is unsettling to recognize that, since 2000, both the poverty rate and the share below half poverty have been on the rise. In other words, since this last economic peak, more families are poor and average incomes are lower. Clearly, the anti-poverty momentum of the latter 1990s has disappeared.

Immigration and poverty

Immigration to America has led to a highly charged debate in recent years. One prevailing view of poverty suggests that immigrants are a main cause of the problem, but the data belie that claim. While it is true that some immigrants (though, as shown below, not naturalized citizens) have higher poverty rates than native-born persons, the trends are similar and, in fact, immigrant poverty rates fell three times faster over the 1990s than did rates for the native-born (see **Table 6.6** and **Figure 6E**). So, while more immigrants have joined the U.S. population, at least over this period (the only period for which the Census Bureau publishes such annual data), their likelihood of being poor has fallen.

However, it could still be the case that simply adding more immigrants, even with their diminished propensity toward poverty, boosts the overall poverty rate. A simple experiment shows this not to have occurred over this period. The share of the immigration popu-

TABLE 6.6 Poverty by place of birth, 1995-2005

	All	Native	Foreign born Total	Naturalized	Noncitizen
1995	13.8%	12.9%	22.2%	10.5%	27.8%
2000	11.3	10.8	15.4	9.0	19.2
2005	12.6	12.1	16.5	10.4	20.4
1995-2000	-2.5%	-2.2%	-6.8%	-1.5%	-8.6%
2000-05	1.3	1.3	1.1	1.4	1.2

Source: U.S. Census Bureau.

FIGURE 6E Poverty, native and foreign born, 1993-2004

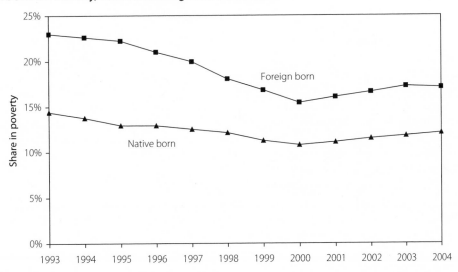

Source: U.S. Census Bureau.

lation increased from 9% to 12% between 1993 and 2004. Had the share remained constant at 9%, the overall poverty rate would have been 12.6% in 2004, instead of 12.7%. In other words, the decline in immigrant poverty almost fully offset the higher poverty effect of the growth of the immigrant population.

The table reveals another point that is particularly germane to the immigration debate. Part of the debate has revolved around whether immigration policy should smooth the path to citizenship for noncitizens, including undocumented immigrants. The data in the

TABLE 6.7 Likelihood of a one-year-old child being poor at least five of the next 10 years, by age and family characteristics

	Education of family head	
	Less than high school	High school or more
Female head of household		
White	63.0%	47.3%
African American	89.5	68.9
Two-parent family		
White	27.6%	16.7%
African American	55.6	33.3

Source: Stevens (1999).

table reveal that the poverty rate among noncitizens is consistently more than twice that for naturalized immigrants. Some of this big difference is likely attributable to different characteristics (e.g., immigrants from wealthier countries are more likely to be naturalized), relative skill levels between the two groups, and date of arrival. But even when we control for such factors, the significant differences in poverty rates remain, suggesting that naturalized citizens face certain economic advantages, such as in the job market, that give them a leg-up on noncitizens. The implication is that a smoother path to citizenship would help noncitizens become more integrated into the economy.

Characteristics associated with long spells of poverty

Thus far, the data presented have reflected cross-sectional snapshots of poverty status. While such data provide useful insights into trends in poverty and the related factors, they do not enable researchers to track the experiences of the same families over time. Using longitudinal data, we can learn more about poverty spells and their determinants. To what extent, for example, do families pass in and out of poverty, or are some family types more likely to be stuck at very low income levels? As the following data reveal, the characteristics that are associated with worse poverty outcomes—minority status, single motherhood, and educational status—are also associated with longer spells of poverty.

Table 6.7 shows that children in single-mother families are at high risk of lengthy poverty spells, measured here as the likelihood that a one-year-old child will be poor for at least five out of his or her first 10 years. This probability is particularly high for African American children of single mothers with less than a high school degree; these children have almost a 90% chance of spending at least five out of their first 10 years poor. Given the disadvantages associated with a childhood spent in extreme deprivation, such an alarmingly high likelihood of long-term poverty suggests that it is an important target for intervention (in fact, findings such as these have been influential in poverty debates, including welfare reform). The probability of lengthy spells drops for families headed by two parents and families headed by more highly educated persons. For a child born into a white family with two parents where the family head is at least a high school graduate, the likelihood of a long spell of poverty is 16.7%; for black families with the same characteristics, however, the chance of a long spell is 33.3%.

Alternative poverty measures

In the mid-1990s, a government-appointed panel convened by the National Academy of Sciences (NAS) was asked to update the way poverty is measured in America. The measure derived has many advantages over the official approach, and the Census Bureau has implemented a variety of versions of NAS recommendations. The key differences between the official measure and the Census publications of the NAS measures include the following:

- The NAS thresholds are based on actual expenditures on food, clothing, and shelter, and thus reflect increases in living standards.
- The NAS income measure is after-tax, and thus reflects the poverty-reduction effects of tax credits.
- NAS includes non-cash benefits in income (though it does not include the value of publicly provided health care).
- NAS deducts some work expenses, like child care expenditures for working families, from income.
- NAS subtracts out-of-pocket medical expenses, including premium payments.
- NAS factors in regional differences in the cost of living.

Using variants of these measures, the Census Bureau has generated a consistent time series back to 1999 of 12 different NAS-based approaches. For example, some measures account for geographical differences, while others do not.

A fundamental question is, do these improved measures generate lower or higher poverty rates relative to the official measure? **Figure 6F** illustrates the answer: the NAS measures (12 are included here) are uniformly higher than the official measure. On average over the period covered by the graph, the NAS rates are about one percentage point above the official rate, implying about 2.5 million more persons in poverty.

Another way to measure poverty—one with great intuitive appeal—tracks the poor while accounting for changes in prevailing income levels among the non-poor. Such measures are called "relative" in that they set the poverty threshold as a percent of the median income, which moves each year and typically rises in nominal terms.

The utility of this measure (the norm in international comparisons) is that it tells how the poor are faring relative to middle-income families. In fact, since the poverty line is adjusted only for inflation, anytime the median income grows in real terms, i.e., faster than inflation, the poor lose relative ground. As the next few figures reveal, this is precisely what occurred during the 1990s, when official poverty fell but relative poverty did not.

Figure 6G uses adjusted income measures much like those recommended by the NAS to compare relative poverty to absolute poverty. As has been shown above, absolute pov-

FIGURE 6F Poverty rates, official compared to National Academy of Sciences alternatives, 1999 to 2004

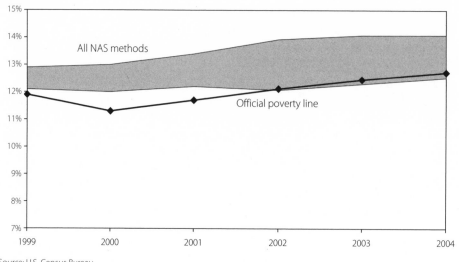

Source: U.S. Census Bureau.

FIGURE 6G Relative and absolute poverty, using adjusted income measures

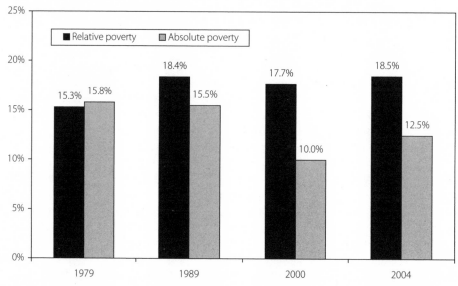

Source: Primus (2006) and authors' analysis of Census Bureau data.

erty fell fairly steeply in the 1990s, from 15.5% to 10.0% by this measure. But relative poverty fell only slightly, from 18.4% to 17.7%.

The reason for these different trends is that real median income rose in the 1990s (see Chapter 1), so the relative threshold of half the median was rising as well in real terms. The figure shows that in absolute terms the poor gained a great deal of ground. But in relative terms their incomes grew at about the same rate as middle incomes, and so the poor remained about the same distance from the middle class as before.

Because the relative measure tracks the social/economic distance between the poor and the middle class (in a way that absolute measures do not), it reveals the impact of changes in inequality on poverty. The share of the population that is poor in relative terms has hovered around 18% since the mid-1980s, showing that many more persons are poor in relative terms—their income is less than half the median—than in absolute terms. The fact that such a significant share of the population remains relatively distant from the mainstream is an important dimension of the poverty problem.

The one-two punch of full employment and pro-work policies

Much discourse regarding poverty reduction covers a range of ideas from strengthening anti-poverty programs, to creating greater incentives to work, to addressing perceived cultural shortcomings. While redistributive transfer programs are important poverty determinants, history also shows that one of the most effective anti-poverty programs is an economy that generates good jobs in a very tight labor market.

The U.S. economy has few institutions to strengthen the bargaining clout of the least advantaged. It is also an economy in which inequality affects most strongly the least-skilled. In the absence of greater union power or higher minimum wages, for example, it is particularly challenging for less-advantaged workers, including those with lower levels of education, to improve their living standards.

A tight labor market, however, such as the one that existed in the latter 1990s, is one of the best tools for lifting the wages and incomes of the least well off simply because there are more and better jobs available for the working poor in such periods. Moreover, this relationship has become even more important in the last decade, as poverty policy has become ever more focused on work in the paid labor market as the primary pathway out of poverty. Unfortunately, periods of full employment have been more the exception than the rule in recent decades.

The importance of full employment is at least threefold. First, tight labor markets force employers to bid up wages to get and keep the workers they need. Second, full employment helps to generate a more equitable distribution of growth, and thus helps to remove the wedge that inequality creates between overall growth and poverty reduction. Third, the demand for labor in a full employment economy draws persons into the job market (and extends the work hours of those already in the job market) who, under slack conditions, would be without work.

Table 6.8 relates some of the relevant indicators of strong (or weak) employment demand to poverty rates. Broadly speaking, in periods of fast productivity growth and tight job markets, poverty is diminished. This occurred in the 1960s, although another cause

TABLE 6.8 Changes in poverty rates and various economic indicators, 1959-2004

	Poverty rates	Productivity*	Unemployment	Inequality**	Low-wage growth***
1959-73	-11.3	2.8%	-0.6	-0.9%	n.a.
1973-89	1.8	1.3	0.4	10.6	-0.2%
1989-2000	-1.5	2.0	-1.3	4.0	1.0
1989-95	1.0	1.6	0.3	2.4	0.0
1995-2000	-2.5	2.5	-1.6	1.5	2.3
2000-04	1.4	3.5	1.5	0.6	0.4

Note: Poverty rates and unemployment are percentage-point changes; productivity and low-wage growth are annualized changes; inequality is percent change in Gini coefficient.
*   Nonfarm business sector.
** Gini coefficient.
*** 20th percentile real wage.

Source: U.S. Census Bureau, BLS, and authors' analysis.

for poverty's large drop in that decade was an increase in Social Security benefits that led to a decline in poverty rates among elderly persons. The 1980s were years of relatively low productivity growth, rising and generally high unemployment rates, and increasing inequality. This is a potent recipe for higher poverty rates, and poverty rose 1.8 points over those years.

The 1990s started much the same way, but the latter 1990s were a different story. Productivity growth was strong, accelerating more than one percent over the 1973-89 rate, meaning that the workforce was generating that much more output per hour each year. While it is a consistent belief among economists that higher productivity growth creates a path to higher living standards, in an era of greater inequality this relationship is strained. For that potential to be realized, other forces need to be in place to ensure an equitable distribution of income growth. In the latter 1990s, full employment played that role. The unemployment rate fell 1.6 points between 1995 and 2000, hitting 4.0% in 2000. The growth of inequality was diminished, as measured by the Gini coefficient, which grew 1.5% between 1995 and 2000, compared to 2.4% from 1989 to 1995. And, most critically, low wages (the real wage at the 20th percentile) grew at an annual rate of 2.3%, almost the same as productivity.

As shown in **Figure 6H**, this dynamic—tight labor markets helping to link the growth of low wages with productivity—has been missing from the economy for most of the past 30 years, and this is one key reason why poverty has been unresponsive to overall economic growth. Note, for example, that in the 2000s productivity growth reached 3.5%, a full point above the already impressive 1995-2000 pace. But unemployment rose in the recession of 2001, and by 2004 it remained above the full employment level of 2000. Lacking the pressure of tight labor markets, real growth in low wages slowed to 0.4% per year.

FIGURE 6H Real low-wage growth, productivity, and unemployment during three five-year periods

* 20th percentile hourly wage

Source: BLS and authors' analysis.

Getting it (mostly) right: poverty in the 1990s

The importance of tight job markets notwithstanding, even under the best macroeconomic conditions many poor families will need extra help. In the latter 1990s, for example, the push of welfare reform and the pull of the strong labor demand drew many single mothers into the job market. And for many of these women, full employment conditions helped generate significant wage gains in percentage terms. But even hourly wage gains of about a third, from around $6 to around $8 dollars an hour, do not provide enough income for these families to meet their basic consumption needs.

Fortunately, significant work supports—public benefits tied to work—were added or expanded over the 1990s. In the early 1990s, the highest benefit level under the EITC for a family with at least two children rose from about $1,700 to about $4,000 in 1995 dollars. The minimum wage was also increased in 1996/97, from $4.25 to $5.15 an hour.

Table 6.9 shows the impact of these policy changes by simulating the disposable (i.e., after tax and transfer) income for a single parent, one working at the minimum wage and one not working. The table strongly supports the observation that policy changes significantly improved the returns to work for low-income families. Note, for example, that in 1986 the gap in total disposable income between working and non-working families amounted to about $2,000. This is by no means an insignificant amount, but the difference more than tripled by 1996. Though the higher minimum wage was part of the difference,

TABLE 6.9 Earnings, taxes, and benefits under differing scenarios for work and marriage in 1986 and 1996 (1996 dollars)

| | Marriage and work scenario | | | | | |
| | 1986 | | | 1996 | | |
	Single parent does not work	Single parent works full time at minimum wage	Difference	Single parent does not work	Single parent works full time at minimum wage	Difference
Total earnings	$0	$9,820	$9,820	$0	$10,300	$10,300
Federal taxes: Social Security, Medicare, and income taxes other than EITC	0	-861	-861	0	-788	-788
Means-tested benefits, TANF (AFDC), and food stamps	8,459	2,578	-5,881	7,501	2,462	-5,039
Child care expense	0	-2,000	-2,000	0	-2,000	-2,000
Earned income tax credit	0	768	768	0	3,656	3,656
Child care support	0	159	159	0	1,000	1,000
Total "disposable" income	8,459	10,464	2,005	7,501	14,630	7,129
Government paid health insurance? (Medicaid)	Yes	No	Loses all coverage	Yes	Children under 15	Only adult loses coverage

Source: Ellwood (2000), Table 1.

the expansion of the EITC, from $768 to $3,656, was the most important change. Other income-lifting work supports added in the 1990s include publicly provided child care and the fact that children under 15 did not lose Medicaid coverage when their parents went to work in the low-wage labor market (though parents themselves often did lose coverage).

The previous table simulated the earnings of a minimum wage worker (versus a non-worker). Next we present evidence of actual advances made against poverty over the 1990s, thanks to the potent combination of tight job markets and pro-work public supports.

Poverty analyst Wendell Primus derived a poverty measure with many useful similarities to the concepts in the NAS measure discussed above. Primus's measure includes near-cash benefits, most notably food stamps, as well as the impact of taxes and work expenses. For an analysis of poverty in the 1990s, this method is particularly important because of the significant boost in the EITC in 1992.

As shown in **Table 6.10**, using this measure highlights the poverty-reducing effect of the expanded EITC, especially for families with children. Official poverty fell 3.5 percentage points for all persons over the 1990s and 6.1 points for children. The alternative measure fell even faster: 6.2 points for all and just under 10 points for children. Under the alternative measure, there were more poor children in 1992 but fewer in 2000. Changes in

TABLE 6.10 Alternative poverty measure, gains in the 1990s

	1992	2000	2004	*1992-2000*	*2000-04*
All					
Official	14.8%	11.3%	12.7%	-3.5%	1.4%
Alternative	17.5	11.3	12.5	-6.2	1.2
Children					
Official	22.3%	16.2%	17.8%	-6.1%	1.6%
Alternative	24.3	14.5	16.4	-9.8	1.9

Source: Tabulations provided by Wendell Primus.

TABLE 6.11 Income components of low-income single mothers with at least two children

	Income	Earnings*	Annual hours*	Public assistance	EITC
1979	$15,853	$6,708	804	$3,989	$350
1989	14,699	6,816	828	3,028	450
2000	16,775	10,108	1,191	905	1,981
2004	16,353	9,664	1,092	671	1,701
1979-89	-7.3%	1.6%	3.0%	-24.1%	28.7%
1989-2000	14.1	48.3	43.7	-70.1	340.1
2000-04	-2.5	-4.4	-8.3	-25.8	-14.1

* Refers to mothers' earnings and hours, not pooled across family.

Source: Authors' analysis of CPS data.

both measures over this period reflect the added work effort by low-income persons, but the expanded EITC is reflected only in the alternative measure. Primus estimates that this factor alone explains one-third of the difference in the changes in the two measures over the 1990s.

A good way to see these changes more closely is to track the income components of low-income single mothers. Their living standards have been particularly affected by changes in both market outcomes and poverty policy—such as welfare reform—over the last few decades. **Table 6.11** shows some of the big changes that occurred among low-income single mothers (those with incomes below twice poverty) between 1979 and 2004. The largest changes occurred over the 1990s, when income rose 14.1% (after falling 7.3% over the 1980s); this increase was driven by an almost 50% increase in real earnings and a huge jump in the EITC, by more than a factor of 4. The sharp decline in public assistance (cash transfers through welfare) was more than offset by these other factors.

FIGURE 6I Annual hours worked by low-income mothers, 1979-2004

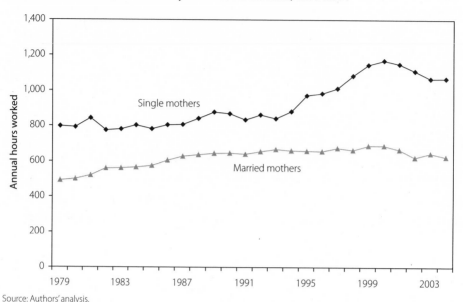

Source: Authors' analysis.

The rise in annual hours worked by single mothers is impressive. **Figure 6I** shows that the push of welfare reform predicated on work in the paid labor market, along with the pull of a higher minimum wage (increased in both 1996 and 1997) and the EITC expansion, led to a steep rise in hours worked. By contrast, the hours for low-income married mothers show no acceleration in the latter 1990s. Presumably, both groups of mothers faced the same economy, yet the policy changes were largely targeted at single mothers. The response was dramatic.

The 2000-04 data show an interesting reversal. Not only did income, earnings, and hours decline, as might be expected in a recession and a protracted jobless recovery, but public assistance and the EITC declined as well (food stamp receipt, not shown in the table, did increase over this period).

The decline in the EITC serves as a reminder that the tax credit is not necessarily counter-cyclical. The tax credit is structured so that the amount of the credit rises with income up to a certain point, flattens out for a range of income, and then begins to phase out. Since receipt is based on annual earnings, a person with relatively high earnings who loses her job over the course of the year can "back onto the schedule." However, those with low earnings who become unemployed will tend simply to lose much of the benefit. Analysis not shown here reveals that the loss of EITC benefits to low-income mothers was largely associated with job losses.

Taken together, this set of tables and figures provides insight into an anti-poverty strategy. Fast productivity growth (say, 2.5% per year or above) creates the potential

TABLE 6.12 Employment rates of 16-24-year-olds, not in school, high school or less, by race

| | African American | | White | |
	Men	Women	Men	Women
1989	57.8%	40.3%	79.6%	64.0%
1995	50.9	40.6	77.0	60.4
2000	52.2	52.1	78.1	65.8
2005	46.6	47.2	71.9	59.5
Percentage-point changes				
1989-2000	-5.7	11.8	-1.5	1.8
1995-2000	1.3	11.5	1.1	5.4
2000-05	-5.6	-4.9	-6.2	-6.3

Source: Authors' analysis of CPS data.

for increasing incomes and lower poverty rates. Full employment job markets create the pressure to ensure that this faster growth is broadly shared, i.e., to enforce productivity's potential boost to living standards. And expanded work supports, including the EITC and various other expenditure-replacing job supports (e.g., child care subsidies) help fill out the gap between what low-income families can earn and what they need to make ends meet.

However, not every group of disadvantaged workers prospered over the 1990s. Research has found that young African American men with no more than a high school degree were an exception to the trends described above. Apparently, the barriers these men face, including discrimination in key markets, keep them from rising with the others.

Table 6.12 shows the employment rates (the share of the population employed) for young (16-24-year-old) persons with no more than a high school degree (and no longer enrolled in school) by race and gender. Young black men with this profile fared particularly poorly. Over the 1990s, when many groups, including single mothers, were making significant labor market inroads, their employment rates fell about 6 percentage points. Even over the latter 1990s boom, their gains were trivial, especially compared with comparable black women. White men also fared poorly, but their levels of employment stayed well above those of young black men. Labor market opportunities for all these young workers contracted sharply over the 2000-05 period, with young black men losing another 5.6 percentage points of employment. By the end of this period, their employment rates were the lowest of all of the groups in the table. This is not to say that these men were totally unaffected by the potent anti-poverty combination of tight labor markets and generous work supports. In fact, in data not shown here, there is evidence that the families of these young persons experienced relatively strong income gains in the latter 1990s. For example, the poverty rate of young black men with the characteristics in the table fell about 6 points, from 30% to 24%, between 1995 and 2000 before heading back up to 30% by 2004.

TABLE 6.13 The impact of demographic and education changes on family poverty rates

	1969-79	1979-89	1989-2000	2000-04	1969-2000
Total demographic effect	0.5%	-0.2%	-0.6%	0.2%	-0.2%
Race	0.3	0.4	0.4	0.1	1.0
Education	-1.5	-1.2	-1.1	-0.1	-3.8
Family structure	2.0	0.7	0.4	0.2	3.0
Interaction	-0.2	-0.1	-0.2	-0.1	-0.5
Economic change	-1.1%	1.4%	-0.9%	1.2%	-0.6%
Growth	-1.7	-1.8	-2.1	0.6	-5.7
Inequality	0.7	3.2	1.2	0.7	5.1

Source: Author's analysis based on Danziger/Gottschalk (1995).

But the weak employment results suggest that this was the result of income gains of other family members. Their own economic fortunes were constrained by their multiple disadvantages.

A closer look at poverty's determinants

The previous section highlighted the synergistic impact of policy and growth in poverty reduction over the 1990s. But other factors are always in play, and other time periods are instructive as well. Table **6.13** shows the role played by each of a set of factors commonly associated with changes in poverty over the past 35 years.

The findings in the table underscore the importance of growth, which for this analysis is measured as average real income growth, and inequality, measured as the variance of the income distribution. But two other forces are shown to be significant as well: educational status and family structure. Educational upgrading played a consistent and relatively large poverty-reducing role over the period, a factor that has gotten short shrift in the national poverty debate. Conversely, family structure has been cited by many as a dominant force leading to higher poverty rates. In fact, though, its role has been smaller than that of overall growth, inequality, and education, and its impact has consistently diminished over time.

The most important points from the table are highlighted in the two panels of **Figure 6J**. Note that these figures focus exclusively on peak-to-peak comparisons. (We do not include the most recent period, 2000-04, because it is relatively short and had not peaked by 2004.) The first panel compares the diminishing impact of family structure to the consistently large (relative to other factors in the table) impact of education. By the latest full business cycle—that of the 1990s—educational upgrading subtracted 1.1 points from poverty, while family structure changes (largely the shift to mother-only families) added only 0.4 points.

FIGURE 6J Poverty determinants: impact on family poverty rates

Education and family structure

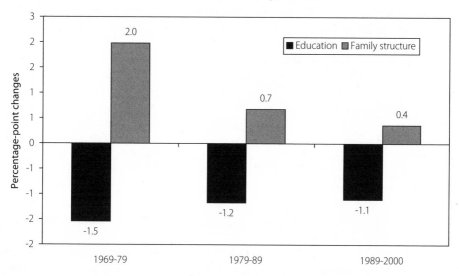

Growth and inequality

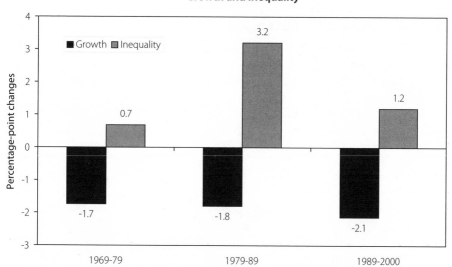

Source: Authors' analysis of Danziger and Gottschalk (1995).

While there are of course many important reasons to support the formation of two-parent versus one-parent families, these findings suggest that an educational upgrading strategy would have more of a poverty-reducing impact than one focused on changing family structure. At the very least, both strategies are important, yet recent low-income policy initiatives have focused more on encouraging marriage than on upgrading education.

The next panel of the figure looks at the economic variables of average real income growth and inequality. Both have the largest impacts of any single factors, with income growth lowering poverty by a total of 5.6 points and inequality increasing poverty by 5.1 points between 1969 and 2000. The time pattern of inequality's impact is notable: the 3.2-point increase in poverty over the 1980s attributable to the relatively large growth in inequality over this period is the single largest factor in any of the time periods reviewed here. Had inequality been stable over the 1980s, poverty would have fallen by two points instead of increasing by 1.2 points. The implication is that 5 million more persons were poor over the decade due to the skewed distribution of growth.

As noted, the 2000-04 period is not a long enough time frame to generate meaningful results from this type of analysis because the variables in question take time to evolve. However, it is notable that both slower growth and greater inequality led to higher poverty through 2004 (Table 6.13).

The importance of the economic variables, along with the heightened status of work in the paid labor market as a critical anti-poverty strategy, underscores the relevance of the low-wage labor market to poverty analysis. We turn to this analysis in the final section.

Role of the low-wage job market

Given the elevated role of work in the lives of poor and near-poor families, conditions in low-wage labor markets play an increasingly important role in evaluating progress against poverty. This section examines the characteristics of low-wage workers and their historical wage trends.

Table 6.14 looks at the characteristics of low-wage workers, defined the same way as in Table 3.7 (as the hourly wage that would lift a family of four above the poverty threshold, $9.60 an hour in 2005, given full-time, full-year work). Just under one-quarter of the workforce earned this wage level in 2005, and their average hourly wage was about $7.40, 41% of the average wage.

Comparing the percentages in the two columns reveals categories in which low-wage workers are overrepresented. Such workers are disproportionately female, minority, non-college-educated, and young. They also are more likely to work in low-wage industries such as retail trade and service industries, and less likely to work in durable manufacturing (non-durable manufacturing—the manufacture of things like food and apparel—pays much less than durable), transportation, finance and information services, and government. By occupation, low-wage workers are overrepresented in sales (e.g., cashiers) and services, where they staff the low-paying jobs such as security guards, food preparation, or home health aides in health services. They are least likely to be managers and professionals and significantly less likely to be covered by union contracts.

TABLE 6.14 Characteristics of low-wage workers, 2005 (Part 1 of 2)

	Low wage	Total workforce
Share of workforce	24.5%	100.0%
Number	29,275,894	119,587,366
Average wage	$7.36	$18.07
Gender		
Female	57.5%	47.8%
Male	42.5	52.2
Race/ethnicity		
White	56.5%	68.6%
African American	15.3	11.2
Hispanic	22.4	13.9
Asian	3.7	4.3
Other	2.2	1.8
Education		
Less than high school	22.9%	10.4%
High school	36.7	30.1
Associate's degree	6.9	9.8
Some college	24.7	20.1
College or more	8.8	29.6
Age		
18-25	37.6%	16.6%
26-35	21.4	23.9
35+	41.1	59.5
Industry		
Financial and information services	5.5%	9.6%
Manufacturing	8.8	12.7
Durable	4.8	8.1
Non-durable	3.9	4.6
Construction	4.6	6.9
Transportation and utilities	3.2	5.4
Services	52.4	43.8
Trade	21.3	14.8
Wholesale	2.1	3.3
Retail	19.2	11.6
Government	2.3	5.3
Other industries	2.0	1.3
Occupations		
Managers/professionals	11.3%	34.2%
Admin/office support	14.1	15.0
Blue collar	21.9	23.5
Services	35.3	16.1
Sales	15.6	10.4
Other occupations	1.8	0.7

Table continues

TABLE 6.14 Characteristics of low-wage workers, 2005 (Part 2 of 2)

	Low wage	Total workforce
Union status		
Non-union	93.7%	86.0%
Union	6.3	14.0
Family income		
Less than $25K	45.9%	28.6%
$25K-$50K	26.9	23.9
More than $50K	27.2	47.5

Source: Authors' analysis of CPS ORG data.

Some commentators have argued that we should worry less than we do about low-wage workers because many live in higher-income families. However, the final panel of Table 6.14 shows that while some low-wage workers—27.2%—live in families with income greater the $50,000, most reside in low- and low-middle-income families. Among the lowest-income families, those with less than $25,000, 45.9% are low-wage workers, compared to 28.6% in the total workforce.

The critical role of full employment is particularly germane in the low-wage labor market. **Figure 6K** makes this point by showing the impact on real wage growth of a one percentage-point decline in the unemployment rate. Note the steep downward staircase, particularly for men, revealing that those at the lower end get the biggest wage boost from tighter job markets. According to these results, based on data from 1973 to 2005, a year with lower unemployment leads to a 2% wage boost for low-wage men and a 1.5% boost for women. Compare this with the smaller gain to high-wage workers of well below 1%.

Figure 6L shows these dynamics in action, by tracking the pay of low-wage workers over time. Many of the wage-depressing factors discussed in Chapter 3 were in play throughout the 1980s, as wages fell for low-wage men and were relatively stagnant for women. The latter 1990s, however, a time when unemployment fell quickly to historically low levels, stand out as a period of real wage growth for low-wage workers and of significant progress against poverty.

The tail end of these series, when real low wages began to falter, is also instructive regarding the poverty-inducing effect of higher unemployment. The recession of 2001 was relatively mild in terms of gross domestic product, but the loss of full employment took a clear toll on low-wage growth (and also on poverty, up 1.4 points between 2000 and 2004, as shown in Table 6.1).

The final point in Figure 6L involves real wage levels. The straight line in the figure—the poverty-level wage needed to raise a family of four above poverty—serves as a benchmark against which to judge the adequacy of low-wage levels relative to what families need to make ends meet. With the earnings boost in the latter 1990s, low-wage males reached this benchmark, though women remained below it. But for most of the period,

FIGURE 6K Percent change in real wages with one-point decline in unemployment

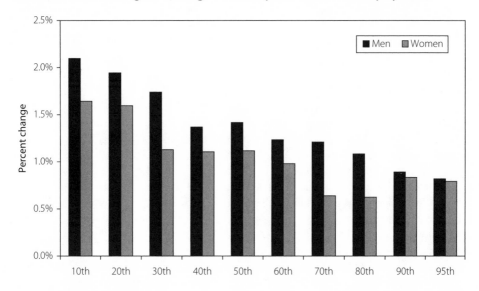

Source: Authors' analysis of CPS data.

FIGURE 6L Real hourly wages of low-wage workers

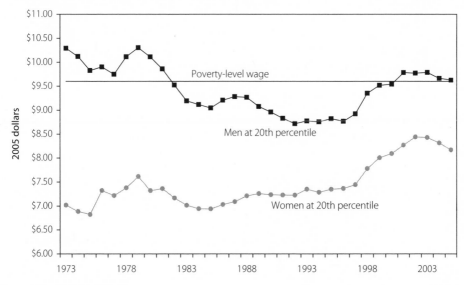

Source: Authors' analysis of CPS data.

20th percentile wages have lagged this benchmark, meaning that the universe of low-wage workers (i.e., including those earning below the 20th percentile) earned below the poverty-level wage. From a policy perspective, this gap underscores the need for wage subsidies and work supports that will help close the distance between what these workers earn and what they need.

Conclusion

While poverty amid plenty remains a serious problem in the American economy, our experiences over the past few decades are instructive. Policy changes have increased the reliance of low-income families on labor market income, wage subsidies (the EITC), and work supports like child and medical care. At the same time—in the latter 1990s—labor market conditions improved significantly as the job market tightened and provided some sorely lacking bargaining power for the least-well-paid workers. The combination of tight job markets and work supports did not reach everyone, such as black men without high school diplomas, but they proved to be a potent combination for poverty reduction.

Examined through this lens, the poverty problem (putting aside the inadequacies of the official measure) is in large part a function of the gap between the productivity of the workforce and the opportunities and incomes of those at the low end. Work support policies, though somewhat eroded through budget cuts (e.g., publicly provided health insurance is a target of both state and federal budget cutters), may generally remain in place, but the current recovery has not yet achieved the full employment conditions of the latter 1990s. Thus, the primary mechanism through which growth is distributed to low-income workers—a tight job market through which overall growth is broadly and fairly shared—is not fully in place, and poverty rates are rising.

CHAPTER 7

Regional analysis
Shared experiences, crucial differences

Previous chapters have focused exclusively on information of national scope. This chapter examines differences in the state of the economy in each of the nation's four regions. A regional focus is important because, in many ways, regional data more accurately represent the economy faced by workers in a particular area than do broad national data.

This chapter focuses on what happened to state labor markets in recent years. The contrast between the late 1990s and the early 2000s is sharp in most states. Expanding payrolls, full employment, and strong, broad-based wage growth were replaced by weak job growth, higher unemployment, and stagnating wages. Even though job growth has returned to most states, stagnant wage growth has turned to falling wages after adjusting for inflation.

Census regional definitions are used throughout this chapter. **Figure 7A** shows how the states are divided between the four Census regions: Northeast, Midwest, South, and West. While the division into these regions for economic purposes is not perfect (dividing such intertwined states as Pennsylvania and Maryland or New Mexico and Texas), they are useful in analyzing economic trends.

Just as national analysis can mask regional trends, regional analysis can mask state and local trends. Closer analysis for many states can be found in the state reports at http://www.earncentral.org/swx.htm.

The early 1990s slump versus the early 2000s slump

Twenty-two states had fewer jobs in 2001, when the economy officially went into recession, than in 2000. Even though the recession also ended in 2001, the country continued to lose jobs. By 2003, 34 states had fewer jobs than in 2000. In some states, the losses were severe. Michigan, for example, lost 264,000 jobs, or 5.7% of employment and North Carolina lost 144,000 jobs, or 3.7% of employment.

FIGURE 7A Census regions and divisions

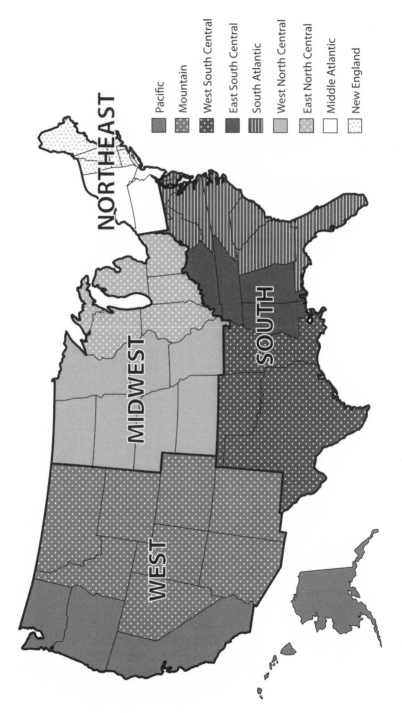

Pacific
Mountain
West South Central
East South Central
South Atlantic
West North Central
East North Central
Middle Atlantic
New England

NORTHEAST

SOUTH

MIDWEST

WEST

Source: U.S. Census Bureau.

The severity and geographic pervasiveness of the recent slump stand in contrast to the previous jobless recovery in the early 1990s, which disproportionately affected two areas of the country: the Northeast region and the state of California.

Job loss started early in the Northeast (**Figure 7B**)—every state in that region except Pennsylvania lost jobs between 1989 and 1990. No other state in the country lost jobs over that period—employment in the Midwest and South regions along with California grew by just under 3% and the remaining Western states (excepting California) saw robust job growth of over 4%.

The following year (1990 to 1991), job loss was more widespread, with just over half of the states losing jobs. The Northeast continued to suffer the worst, losing 3.7% of total nonfarm employment. Job growth slowed in Western states, but other than California and a slight loss in Oregon, all the Western states continued to add jobs.

The economic growth that followed the slump also took longer to take off in the Northeast and California. Between 1991 and 1992, only 10 states lost jobs—besides California, six were in the Census-defined Northeast and the other three were just to the southern border of that Census region (Delaware, Maryland, and the District of Columbia). The number of jobs in the Northeast didn't return to the 1989 peak until 1997, with employment in Rhode Island, Connecticut, and New York not returning to 1989 levels until 1999.

FIGURE 7B Annual regional employment growth, 1989-93

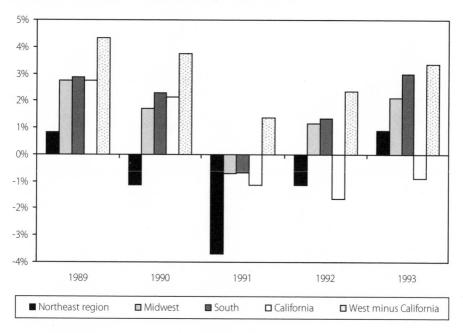

Source: Current Employment Statistics.

FIGURE 7C Unemployment rate by region, 1989-2005

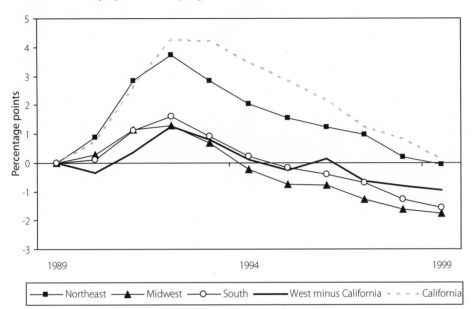

Source: Authors' analysis of Current Population Survey.

Not surprisingly given the job loss trends cited above, the unemployment rate rose earlier and higher in the Northeast and California, rising 3.7 percentage points between 1989 and 1992 in the Northeast and 4.2 points in California (**Figure 7C**). While other areas saw job losses and unemployment increases, the early 1990s "jobless recovery" was focused in the Northeast and California.

In contrast, the recent labor market slump was geographically pervasive. **Figure 7D** shows which states had more jobs three years after the two most recent recessions—in 1989 and in 2000. In 1992, 14 states had fewer jobs and 37 states had more than in 1989. In 2003, nearly the opposite was true: 34 states had fewer jobs and 17 had more. The 34 states were spread across the country unlike the geographic focus in the previous period.

Population shift

The 1990s saw a dramatic shift in population away from the Northeast and Midwest and toward the South and West. For example, while the Northeast states had 20% of the population in 1990, they only accounted for 4% of the growth in population over the next nine years (**Figure 7E**).

The Census Bureau divides population growth into six components: births, deaths, international migration, domestic migration, federal movement (the movement of federal

FIGURE 7D Job growth by state, 1989-92 and 2000-03

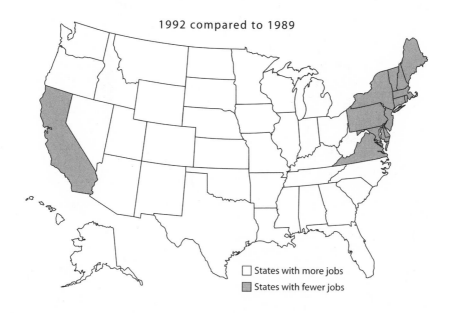

1992 compared to 1989

☐ States with more jobs
■ States with fewer jobs

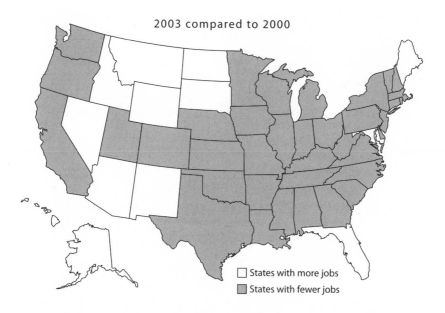

2003 compared to 2000

☐ States with more jobs
■ States with fewer jobs

Source: Authors' analysis of Current Population Survey.

FIGURE 7E Population growth

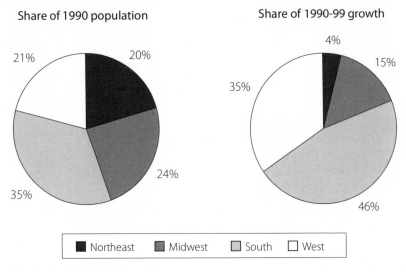

Share of 1990 population

Share of 1990-99 growth

Source: Authors' analysis of U.S. Census Bureau data.

employees such as military personal), and a statistical residual. Of these six, perhaps the most striking is domestic migration—the movement of people between states. For example, the Northeast region lost 3.0 million people to other areas, while the South gained 3.6 million people from other areas (**Figure 7F**).

All areas of the country gained significantly from international migration, especially California and the South. The Northeast relied the most heavily on immigration, being the only region that would have lost population without international migration.

Labor market slack

The national unemployment rate hit a 31-year low of 4.0% in 2000. This national trend was reflected throughout the states, all of which reached historically low unemployment in 2000. Twenty-eight states had unemployment below 4.0% and only one state (Alaska) had unemployment above 6.0%. By comparison, in 1989 (the economic peak prior to 2000), 13 states had unemployment above 6.0% and only nine states had rates below 4.0% (the national rate was 5.4%).

From 2000 to 2001 the unemployment rate of 16 states rose by 1 percentage point or more, mostly in those states affected strongly by manufacturing losses, including North Carolina, Michigan, Oregon, and Washington. By 2003, all but nine states had unemployment rates of 1 percentage point or more above their 2000 rates (**Figure 7G**).

In the Northeast and most South Atlantic states, the change in unemployment was

FIGURE 7F Domestic migration by region, 1990-99

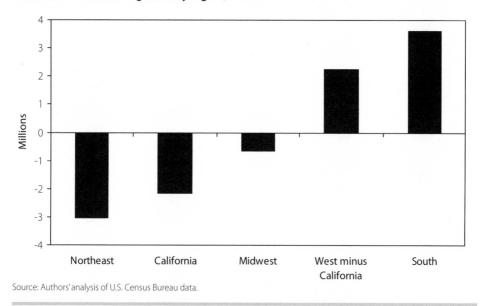

Source: Authors' analysis of U.S. Census Bureau data.

FIGURE 7G Unemployment rate by region, 1989-2005

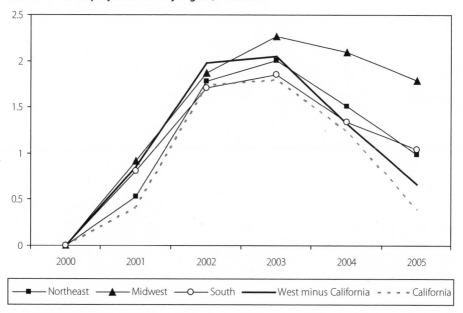

Source: Authors' analysis of Current Population Survey.

FIGURE 7H Long-term unemployment rate by region, 1989-2005

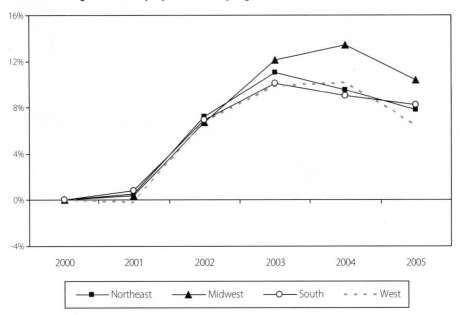

Source: Authors' analysis of Current Population Survey.

greater between 1989 and 1992, but in most of the rest of the country the increase in unemployment has been worse in the more recent period.

In 2003, unemployment rates started to fall again, although the improvement was less in the Midwest. The share of the unemployed that had been out of work for more than 26 weeks has remained high throughout the country, however (**Figure 7H**). Since state unemployment benefits usually run out at 26 weeks, the share of the unemployed without work for more than 26 weeks is a useful measure of the extent of the hardship caused by persistent joblessness. It is also a sign of weak demand and feeble job creation, since it shows that many workers are unable to leave unemployment for work.

Long-term unemployment rose considerably across the country between 2000 and 2003. For example, in the Midwest the long-term unemployment rate more than doubled. By 2005, despite job growth and falling unemployment rates, the long-term unemployment rates remained at least 6 percentage points above the 2000 rate in every region, with the Midwest remaining over twice the 2000 rate.

Another limitation of the unemployment rate is that it does not account for changes in the quality of employment. One aspect of job quality that has been declining in recent years is the availability of full-time employment. After declining in every state during the last half of the 1990s, the 2000 to 2003 period saw a rise in part-time employment in most states. Moreover, involuntary part-time work (meaning the part-time jobs held by workers who would take full-time work if it was available) increased in all but three states from 2000 to 2003. Both rates (part-time employment and involuntary part-time employment) have fallen since 2003, although they remain high in a number of states.

Manufacturing

The fortunes of the manufacturing industry have played a major role in regional differences in recent decades.

The Northeast's labor market troubles seem to have been very closely tied to its manufacturing sector. While other regions lost manufacturing jobs during the early 1990s slump, it was followed by a modest upswing until around 1998 when the manufacturing sector went into a downward spiral nationwide. The Northeast, on the other hand, lost manufacturing jobs every year through the present, except for a small increase in 1997. By 2005, the Northeast manufacturing sector was only two-thirds of what it was in 1990.

One of the key factors in the recent recession and jobless recovery was the travails of the manufacturing sector. Of the 34 states that had fewer jobs in 2003 than in 2000, 20 experienced job growth outside of manufacturing. For example, while Arkansas lost 14.2% of manufacturing jobs, all other industries grew by 2.1%.

While most states experienced job loss between 2000 and 2003 (and severe job losses in manufacturing), there was considerable variation among the states. As shown in **Figure 7I**, the level of job growth (or loss) by state correlates powerfully with each

FIGURE 7I Job loss by state (2000-03) compared to reliance on manufacturing employment in 2000

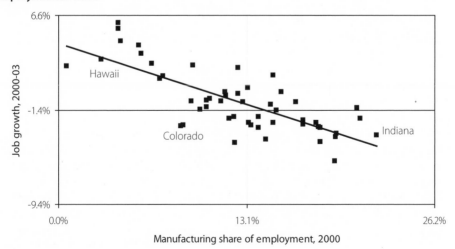

Source: Authors' analysis of Current Population Survey.

state's reliance on manufacturing. Given the severity of losses in this sector, it is not surprising to find such a strong relationship. In other words, what looks like regional variation is in many ways another measure of the importance of the decline of manufacturing in recent labor market trends.

The 21 states in the upper left quadrant of Figure 7I (e.g., Hawaii) are those with lower-than-average reliance on manufacturing and higher-than-average job growth. The 18 states in the lower right quadrant (e.g., Indiana) are those with higher-than-average reliance on manufacturing and lower-than-average job growth. The remaining 12 states cluster fairly close to the linear relationship suggested by the downward-sloping line. Colorado is one important example of a state that appears to be in opposition to this relationship between job loss and the manufacturing industry because it has a lower-than-average reliance on manufacturing and worse-than-average job loss (placing it in the lower left quadrant). However, while Colorado's manufacturing sector was only 8.6% of total employment, it suffered more than most sectors, with a decline of 18.3%, compared to losses of 1.3% in the remaining sectors.

The loss of manufacturing jobs, if not reversed, will have a significant impact on the living standards of working families. This is especially the case in those states that have relied heavily on the manufacturing industry. In Michigan, for example, the average weekly wage in manufacturing was $891 in 2005—27% above the average in the state's fastest growing industry (education and health services), which indicates a combination of lower hourly wages and scarcer full-time work in education and health services. In addition, manufacturing firms covered about 77% of their workers with health insurance, compared to 54% in education and health services.

Stagnant wage growth turns to falling wages

A weak labor market affects the living standards of working families directly when workers lose jobs or are unable to find work that pays well and provides adequate hours and benefits. Another impact of high unemployment is that workers have less bargaining power and wage growth can either decline or disappear.

Alternatively, full employment can lead to substantial wage gains as employers need to pay more to attract and retain workers. This was the case during the last half of the 1990s—from 1995 to 2000, low-wage workers in all but nine states saw annual real wage growth of 1% or higher.

Because wages are "sticky" (meaning they rarely fall in nominal terms), we wouldn't expect the weakened labor market of 2001 through 2003 to immediately result in dramatic wage declines. For the most part, the momentum of the latter 1990s fueled continued low- and median-wage growth. However, the effect of rising unemployment was noticeable wage growth slowed in most areas of the country as discussed in Chapter 1 (**Figures 7J and 7K**).

Again, there was regional variation. In the West North Central division (Midwestern states west of the Mississippi), for example, low-wage growth slowed from 3.1% annually from 1995 to 2000 to less than 1% annually from 2000 to 2003. There were some states, primarily in the Northeast, where wage growth was faster in the 2000 to 2003 period than between 1995 and 2000, but the overall picture was one of wage stagnation.

FIGURE 7J Growth in 20th percentile wages by division, 1995-2000, 2000-03, and 2003-05

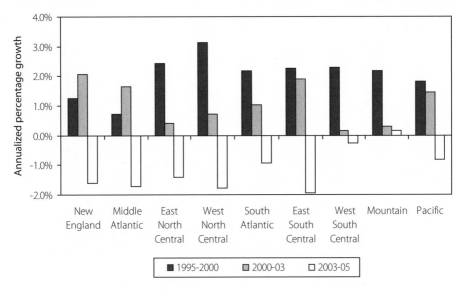

Source: Authors' analysis of CPS-ORG.

FIGURE 7K Growth in median percentile wages by division, 1995-2000, 2000-03, and 2003-05

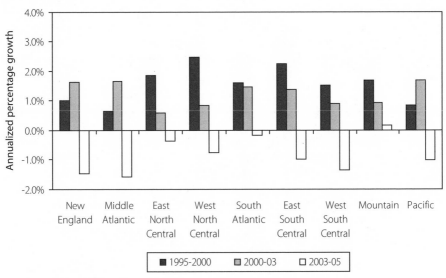

Source: Authors' analysis of CPS-ORG.

FIGURE 7L Value of federal minimum wage compared to share of workforce covered by higher state minimums

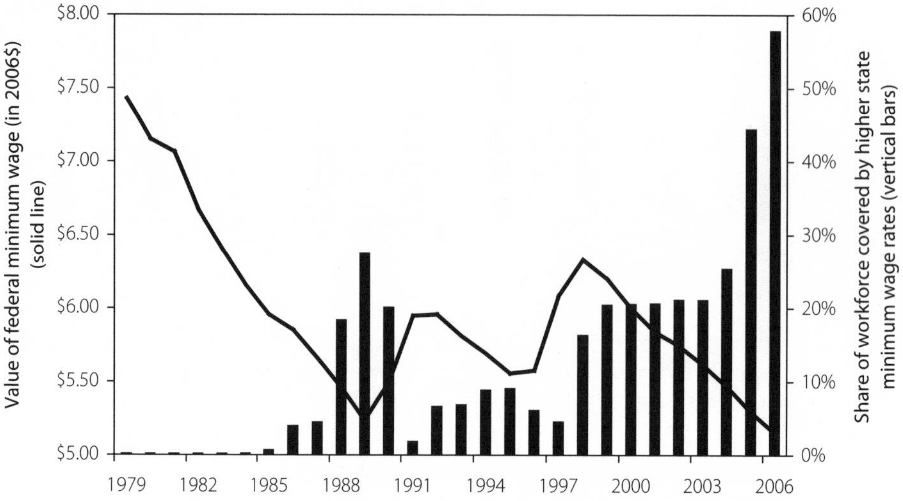

Source: Authors' analysis of CPS-ORG.

Two to three years after the 2001 recession, the momentum of the late 1990s ran out of steam and the result was that stagnant wage growth turned into falling real wages across most of the country. For example, low wages in the West North Central fell by an annual rate of 1.8% between 2003 and 2005. Even in the Northeast, where low- and median-wage growth sped up between 2000 and 2003 over the previous period, wage growth turned negative after 2003.

State minimum wages

The minimum wage is a key policy affecting the living standards of working families. The decline of the federal minimum wage in recent decades has had a very direct impact on workers, particularly for women in the workforce.

Previous analysis has focused exclusively on the federal minimum wage, but states have played an important role as well. By setting their own wage floors, states can alleviate the impact of federal neglect as well as account for regional differences in wage levels and the cost of living. For example, the Alaska minimum wage has been set above the federal rate for decades in recognition of the higher cost of living in that state.

From 1979 to 1989, the value of the federal minimum wage fell by 29.5%, from $7.23 to $5.09 (in 2005 dollars). In 1979, only one state (Alaska) had a higher minimum wage than the federal level. In response to inaction at the federal level, however, by 1989 there

TABLE 7.1 State minimum wages greater than the federal minimum wage, 2006

State	2006 state minimum wage	Planned 2007 state minimum wage	Planned 2008 state minimum wage
Alaska	$7.15	$7.15	$7.15
Arkansas	6.25 (effective 10/1/06)	6.25	6.25
California	6.75	7.50	8.00
Connecticut	7.40	7.65	7.65
Delaware	6.15	6.65	7.15
District of Columbia	7.00	7.00	7.00
Florida	6.40*	Inflation-adjusted	Inflation-adjusted
Hawaii	6.75	7.25	7.25
Illinois	6.50	6.50	6.50
Maine	6.75	6.75 (will increase to $7.00 on 10/1/07)	7.00
Maryland	6.15	6.15	6.15
Massachusetts	6.75	7.50	8.00
Michigan	6.95	6.95 (will increase to $7.15 on 7/1/07)	7.15 (will increase to $7.40 on 7/1/08)
Minnesota	6.15	6.15	6.15
New Jersey	7.15	7.15	7.15
New York	6.75	7.15	7.15
North Carolina	Federal level	6.15	6.15
Oregon	7.50*	Inflation-adjusted	Inflation-adjusted
Pennsylvania	Federal level	6.25 (will increase to $7.15 on 7/1/07)	7.15
Rhode Island	7.10	7.40	7.40
Vermont	7.25*	Inflation-adjusted	Inflation-adjusted
Washington	7.63*	Inflation-adjusted	Inflation-adjusted
Wisconsin	6.50	6.50	6.50

*State minimum wage adjusted annually for inflation.

Source: U.S. Department of Labor.

were 15 states with higher minimum wages and over one-fourth of the nation's workforce lived in states with minimum wages above the federal level (**Figure 7L**).

As of this writing, the federal minimum wage—fixed at $5.15—has not been raised since 1997. Once again, some states have stepped in and raised their minimum wage rates in the absence of a federal increase. The number of states with minimum wages higher than the federal level has quadrupled, from five in 1997 to 21 in 2004. The result of the action in the states on minimum wage lately is that over half of the nation's workforce is covered by minimum wages higher than the federal level for the first time (Figure 7L).

The wage levels set by the states range from $6.15 in Delaware, Maryland, and Minnesota to $7.63 in Washington state (**Table 7.1**). Voters in Oregon and Washington have passed ballot initiatives setting moderate annual adjustments to the state minimum wage to account for the rising cost of living. This policy ensures that the value of a minimum wage paycheck in those two states is not eroded by inflation.

Income inequality

While the type of detailed analysis on income inequality shown in Chapter 1 is not possible at the state level, recent analysis by EPI and the Center on Budget and Policy Priorities shows that the growth in income inequality has been widely spread throughout the country.

Income disparity between the top fifth of families and the poorest fifth of families grew in 39 states between the early 1980s and the early 2000s and did not decline significantly in any state. Even during the 1990s (a time of strong wage growth for low-wage workers), these two groups grew apart in almost half the states. The gap between high-income and middle-income families also grew in most states over the last 20 years.

The growth in income inequality among the states has been dramatic. In the early 2000s, the average income of the top fifth of families was over 6.4 times the average income of the bottom fifth of families in 32 states. No state had a gap that wide in the early 1980s.

CHAPTER 8

International comparisons
How does the United States stack up?

To this point we have examined a multitude of mostly domestic economic analyses positioned within a historical context. It is instructive to assess the relative position of the U.S. economy within the context of other similar international economies. This chapter examines international economies that face the same conditions as the United States with respect to trade, investment, technology, the environment, and other factors that shape economic opportunities. An international comparative approach provides an independent yardstick for gauging the strengths and weaknesses of the U.S. economy. In this chapter, the economic performance of the United States is compared to that of 19 other advanced, industrialized countries that, like the United States, belong to the Paris-based OECD, with an emphasis on the seven largest economies, called the G-7.

The performance of the U.S. economy—high productivity growth and relatively low unemployment—has many European policy, political, and economic analysts vying to emulate key features of the U.S. economy, including weaker unions, lower minimum wages, less-generous social benefit systems, and lower taxes. The international comparisons in this analysis can shed light on this ongoing debate about the advisability of exporting the "U.S. model."

Two dominant themes emerge from this chapter. First, while the United States is, on average, a very wealthy country, it also has a large variance in incomes between those at the top and the bottom of the income scale. Large variances in incomes make it difficult for economic growth to reach those at the bottom. Therefore, while it is true that many people in the United States are well-off, many are not. In fact, inequality is greater in the United States than in any of the other OECD countries. Moreover, inequality in the United States (along with the United Kingdom) has shown a strong tendency to rise, even as inequality was relatively stable or declining in most of the other OECD countries. Poverty and child poverty rates are the highest in the United States, as is the infant mortality rate. The de-emphasis on redistributive social policies only exacerbates the high levels of poverty and income inequality in the United States.

Second, many OECD countries with strong unions, worker protections, and higher taxes have caught up with, and in many cases, surpassed U.S. productivity while achieving lower unemployment rates. It is telling that so many European countries have been successful and productive within the more "rigid" European economic models. It is not a given that economies that have strong welfare states and labor protections are necessarily less productive and/or inferior to the economic model that characterizes the United States.

Incomes and productivity: the United States is less dominant

The standard of living in the United States has been among the highest in the world for the entire post-World War II period. **Tables 8.1** and **8.2** summarize data on the most common measure of living standards, per capita income (the total value of goods and services produced in the domestic economy per member of the population, which is therefore a pre-tax measure). Table 8.1 converts the value of foreign goods and services, measured in foreign currency, to U.S. dollars using market-determined exchange rates. A note of caution—because market exchange rates are based on short-term factors and are subject to substantial distortions from speculative movements and government interventions, comparisons based on exchange rates, even when averaged over a period of time such as a year, may yield unreliable and misleading results. Alternatively, purchasing-power parities are used in Table 8.2, and are explained in more detail below.

Referring to Table 8.1, in 1960, the United States had one of the highest standards of living among the 20 countries examined here, trailing only Switzerland, and it was well ahead of most of the European economies that were still rebuilding themselves after World War II. Per capita income grew rapidly in the United States in the 1960s and 1970s, but it rose nearly twice as fast—4.2% versus 2.2%—in the other OECD economies. In the 1980s and again in the 1990s, growth in per capita income decelerated sharply throughout most of the OECD countries, but it held at earlier levels in the United States. More recently growth in U.S. per capita income was just above average compared to the other rich countries. By 2004, per capita income in the United States was $39,728 per year, above the population-weighted average (excluding the United States) of $28,761, but below that of Japan ($42,146) and Norway ($42,832).

Using market exchange rates to convert the cost of goods and services in other countries to a U.S. value can, in some cases, give a misleading picture of relative standards of living. The relatively high level of income in Japan, for example, reflects fluctuations in market exchange rates in response to short-term international capital flows and other macroeconomic factors. However, this does not necessarily reflect long-term differences in national prices and the relative standard of living in Japan and the United States. In reality, prices vary considerably across countries. For example, land and housing prices are generally much lower in the wide-open United States, Canada, and Australia than they are in more crowded European countries and in Japan. To correct for this shortcoming, Table 8.2 uses an alternative set of criteria for converting the value of each country's goods and

TABLE 8.1 Per capita income using market exchange rates, 1960-2004 (2004 dollars)

Country	Per capita income*					Annual growth rates (%)			
	1960	1979	1989	2000	2004	1960-79	1979-89	1989-2000	2000-04
United States	$16,522	$24,914	$30,546	$37,721	$39,728	2.2%	2.1%	1.9%	1.3%
Japan	7,625	25,696	34,792	40,796	42,146	6.6	3.1	1.5	0.8
Germany**	9,117	16,959	20,244	25,225	25,823	3.3	1.8	2.0	0.6
France	8,713	16,409	19,813	23,882	24,826	3.4	1.9	1.7	1.0
Italy	5,461	13,732	17,322	20,300	20,912	5.0	2.3	1.5	0.7
United Kingdom	12,497	17,275	21,460	26,731	29,011	1.7	2.2	2.0	2.1
Canada	10,249	18,016	21,383	25,399	26,868	3.0	1.7	1.6	1.4
Australia	$8,344	$15,070	$18,174	$22,614	$24,592	3.2%	1.9%	2.0%	2.1%
Austria	8,322	17,101	20,624	26,397	27,358	3.9	1.9	2.3	0.9
Belgium	8,224	16,368	19,996	24,697	25,792	3.7	2.0	1.9	1.1
Denmark	12,560	22,735	26,085	32,719	33,595	3.2	1.4	2.1	0.7
Finland	5,683	16,203	22,150	25,413	27,578	5.7	3.2	1.3	2.1
Ireland	4,624	10,640	13,848	27,611	31,778	4.5	2.7	6.5	3.6
Netherlands	9,816	17,781	20,493	26,485	26,719	3.2	1.4	2.4	0.2
New Zealand	8,366	11,394	12,898	14,838	16,471	1.6	1.2	1.3	2.6
Norway	9,887	23,240	29,278	40,547	42,832	4.6	2.3	3.0	1.4
Portugal	2,518	6,288	8,472	11,358	11,250	4.9	3.0	2.7	-0.2
Spain	3,444	9,452	11,891	15,734	16,753	5.5	2.3	2.6	1.6
Sweden	10,057	20,783	25,377	29,760	31,927	3.9	2.0	1.5	1.8
Switzerland	22,843	29,271	34,660	37,237	37,007	1.3	1.7	0.7	-0.2
Average excluding U.S.	$8,402	$18,058	$22,860	$27,662	$28,761	4.2%	2.3%	1.8%	1.1%

* At the price levels and exchange rates of 2000 except for 1960, which is calculated at 1990 price levels and exchange rates.

** For all OECD data prior to 1991, Western Germany.

Source: Authors' analysis of OECD (1999, 2006a) data. For detailed information on table sources, see Table Notes.

TABLE 8.2 Per capita income using purchasing-power parity exchange rates, 1970-2004 (2004 dollars)

Country	Per capita income*					GDP index (United States = 100)				
	1970	1979	1989	2000	2004	1970	1979	1989	2000	2004
United States	$19,799	$24,914	$30,546	$37,721	$39,728	100	100	100	100	100
Japan	13,271	17,877	24,205	28,383	29,322	67	72	79	75	74
Germany	14,532	18,760	22,393	27,904	28,565	73	75	73	74	72
France	15,084	19,466	23,503	28,330	29,450	76	78	77	75	74
Italy	13,999	18,435	23,254	27,253	28,073	71	74	76	72	71
United Kingdom	14,703	18,037	22,407	27,911	30,292	74	72	73	74	76
Canada	16,726	21,684	25,736	30,571	32,338	84	87	84	81	81
Australia	$17,314	$19,791	$23,867	$29,697	$32,295	87	79	78	79	81
Austria	14,653	20,290	24,470	31,320	32,461	74	81	80	83	82
Belgium	14,761	19,283	23,557	29,096	30,385	75	77	77	77	76
Denmark	18,634	21,839	25,057	31,429	32,270	94	88	82	83	81
Finland	13,615	17,966	24,561	28,178	30,580	69	72	80	75	77
Ireland	8,968	12,103	15,753	31,408	36,148	45	49	52	83	91
Netherlands	17,129	20,857	24,038	31,066	31,340	87	84	79	82	79
New Zealand	16,368	17,350	19,638	22,593	25,079	83	70	64	60	63
Norway	15,786	22,682	28,575	39,574	41,804	80	91	94	105	105
Portugal	7,647	10,485	14,126	18,939	18,759	39	42	46	50	47
Spain	10,831	13,813	17,377	22,993	24,482	55	55	57	61	62
Sweden	17,882	20,701	25,277	29,643	31,801	90	83	83	79	80
Switzerland	24,381	26,035	30,829	33,120	32,916	123	104	101	88	83
Average excluding U.S.	$14,344	$18,388	$23,005	$28,059	$29,284	72	74	75	74	74

* At the price levels and PPP exchange rates of 2000.

Source: Authors' analysis of OECD (2006a) data.

services into U.S. dollars. These alternative exchange rates, known as purchasing-power parities (PPPs), are not based on international currency market exchange rates but, rather, on the price of buying an equivalent "basket" of goods and services in all countries. While calculation of PPPs presents many practical and conceptual problems, PPPs are a reasonable indicator of the relative price of consumption and arguably a better measure of relative living standards than market exchange rates.

When per capita income is measured on a PPP basis, as compared to market exchange rates, the United States also appears to provide an average standard of living that is well above that of the rest of the OECD economies, including those of the larger G-7 economies in the top panel. This ranking suggests that consumption goods (housing, food, transportation, clothing, and others) are generally cheaper in the United States than in the other economies, and these lower prices help to raise the standard of living in the United States relative to other "more expensive" economies. However, it is worth noting that PPPs do not account for the cost of non-market social goods, such as education, health care, or child care, which are much cheaper or completely covered by public spending in many European countries relative to the United States.

The pattern of growth in per capita income is similar regardless of whether PPPs or market exchange rates are used. For most of the economies examined in Table 8.1, growth in per capita income decelerated sharply in the 1980s. However, throughout the 1990s, about half of the economies experienced accelerated annual growth and half experienced decelerated annual growth from the previous decade. U.S. annual growth rates have steadily declined over the last three decades. This pattern also holds for Japan, France, Italy, Canada, Belgium, Portugal, and the overall average of OECD economies excluding the United States.

Figure 8A graphically illustrates annual per capita income growth rates for four time periods (data are from Table 8.1). Growth rates for the United States are compared to the average growth rates of all the other OECD countries. Annual growth rates were much higher, on average, for other OECD countries (4.2%) compared to the United States (2.2%) from 1960-79. From 1979-89, the growth rates of all other OECD countries (2.3%) slightly outpaced U.S. growth rates (2.1%). However for the next two time periods, growth rates of United States surpassed those of the OECD countries.

Table 8.2 also illustrates other nations' per capita income as a percentage of per capita income in the United States. For example, in 1970, Japan's per capital income was just 67% of that in the United States. By 2004, Japan's per capita income increased to 74% of the U.S. level. Switzerland's per capita income was greater than that in the United States in 1970, 1979, and 1989, but more recently in 2000 and 2004 per capita income in Switzerland fell behind that of the United States. Norway is the only country that had higher per capita income (using PPPs) than the United States in 2004.

The main determinant of an economy's current and future standard of living is the level and rate of productivity growth—the value of goods and services that the economy can produce, on average, in an hour of work. Productivity growth is a necessary component to increase living standards. Productivity is, therefore, the starting point in any explanation of differences in the level and growth of income across countries. **Table 8.3** presents other nations' productivity levels as a percentage of the U.S. level. Historically, the U.S. economy was far more productive than the OECD economies in our sample. For example,

FIGURE 8A Annual growth rates of per capita income using market exchange rates, 1960-2004 (2004 dollars)

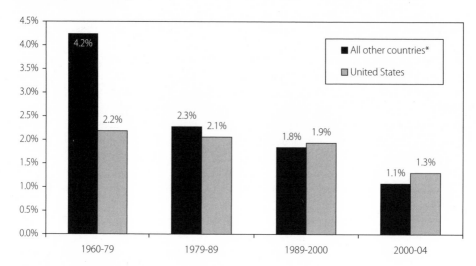

*Average of all countries listed in Table 8.2, not including the United States

Source: Authors' analysis of OECD (1999, 2006a) data.
For detailed information on all figures and sources see Figure Notes.

FIGURE 8B Productivity growth rates in G-7 countries

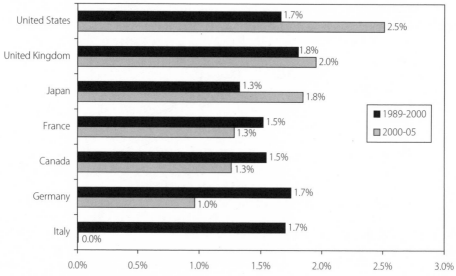

Source: Authors' analysis of OECD (2003a and 2005b) data.

TABLE 8.3 Relative productivity levels in the OECD, 1950-2004

Country	GDP per hour worked (United States = 100)					
	1950	1973	1980	1990	1995	2004
United States	100	100	100	100	100	100
Japan	15	47	55	68	72	73
Germany	39	76	88	94	104	92
France	46	77	88	103	106	107
Italy	43	83	97	104	115	92
United Kingdom	61	64	70	74	80	87
Canada	85	86	88	85	86	80
Australia	72	69	72	71	73	77
Austria	–	–	–	–	–	91
Belgium	59	85	102	110	113	113
Denmark	60	81	89	94	97	90
Finland	35	60	64	74	80	86
Ireland	–	46	58	74	83	104
Netherlands	59	92	106	112	113	100
New Zealand	–	81	71	65	63	59
Norway	57	79	101	115	128	125
Portugal	19	40	–	44	50	53
Spain	25	56	69	82	87	76
Sweden	58	79	83	81	84	88
Switzerland	86	96	101	95	86	82
Average excluding U.S.	41	68	78	85	91	86

Source: Authors' analysis of OECD (2003c and 2005b) data.

in 1950, the United States produced more than six times more goods and services in an hour as compared to Japan and over twice as much in an hour as France. However, by 2004, five OECD economies matched or exceeded U.S. productivity—Norway (125%), Belgium (113%), France (107%), Ireland (104%), and the Netherlands (100%).

The pattern of productivity growth summarized in **Table 8.4** closely resembles that of per capita income. The first key feature of productivity growth is the dramatic slowdown after the mid-1970s: growth was much more rapid in the 1960s than it was in the 1980s and 1990s. In fact, other countries had closed the gap with U.S. productivity to a great extent by 1995 (the non-U.S. average being 91% of U.S. productivity, with three other G-7 countries having higher productivity than the United States), but faster U.S. productivity growth over the last 10 years has widened the productivity gap.

Figure 8B illustrates data from Table 8.4 for the two time periods: 1989-2000 and 2000-05. Growth rates were fairly similar for the 1989-2000 period across these G-7 coun-

TABLE 8.4 Labor productivity growth per year in OECD, 1960-2005

Country	1960-73	1973-79	1979-89	1989-2000	2000-05
United States	2.6%	0.3%	1.2%	1.7%	2.5%
Japan	8.4	2.8	2.8	1.3	1.8
Germany	4.5	3.1	1.4	1.7	1.0
France	5.3	2.9	2.5	1.5	1.3
Italy	6.4	2.8	1.9	1.7	0.0
United Kingdom	4.0	1.6	1.8	1.8	2.0
Canada	2.5	1.1	1.0	1.5	1.3
Australia	3.0%	2.5%	1.1%	2.0%	0.8%
Austria	5.9	3.1	2.4	2.5	1.8
Belgium	5.2	2.7	2.4	1.6	1.2
Denmark	3.9	2.3	1.3	2.4	2.0
Finland	5.0	3.2	3.4	2.9	1.9
Ireland	4.8	4.3	4.1	3.7	3.1
Netherlands	4.8	2.6	1.6	1.4	0.9
New Zealand	2.1	-1.1	1.9	0.7	1.0
Norway	3.8	2.7	1.0	2.7	2.7
Portugal	7.5	0.5	2.2	2.1	0.4
Spain	5.9	2.8	2.7	1.4	0.4
Sweden	3.7	1.4	1.8	2.8	2.0
Switzerland	3.3	0.8	0.4	0.3	0.8

Source: Authors' analysis of OECD (1998, 2003a, and 2005a).

tries—the range was 1.3% to 1.8%. More recently, U.S. productivity growth has rebounded and is significantly above the other countries' rates.

Traditionally, economists have excused the relatively lower U.S. productivity up to the 1990s by arguing that it is much harder to lead than to follow, to innovate than to imitate. In this view, productivity growth was faster outside the United States because other economies were engaged in a constant game of catch-up in which they rapidly assimilated technological improvements pioneered in the United States. While this view may have made sense as late as the 1960s or 1970s, the data on productivity levels in Table 8.3 suggest otherwise after that point. As early as 1980, several European economies had matched or exceeded U.S. productivity levels, and many others had narrowed the gap considerably. By 1995 there were six nations with higher productivity levels. The fact that so many European countries have had productivity levels at or above U.S. levels for a decade or two suggests that these countries' comprehensive welfare and collective-bargaining systems have not stymied income growth or improvements in economic efficiency relative to the more free-market-oriented United States. It is not yet well understood why U.S. productivity has exceeded that of other countries since 1995. It may partially be due to different measures (the United States adjusts its computer output for quality while other countries do not). The differences seem to go beyond investment in information technology because U.S. investments since 2000 have been slight. It seems unlikely that these other countries have seen their productivity growth impeded by their "social model" post-1995, but not before then.

Some economists have also dismissed the evidence of high European productivity levels as simply a by-product of high European unemployment rates. These economists argue that low-productivity workers find jobs in the low-unemployment United States, thus pulling down the average productivity level of the U.S. economy. Indeed, in Europe, which generally has higher unemployment rates than the United States, low-productivity workers are less likely to work and therefore don't pull down average productivity levels. But this argument still has several flaws. First, three European economies in Table 8.3 that had 2004 productivity levels above the U.S. level—Ireland, the Netherlands, and Norway—actually had *lower* unemployment rates than the United States. (See Table 8.11, which shows that in 2004 the unemployment rate was 4.5% in Ireland, 4.6% in the Netherlands, and 4.4% in Norway.) The very low unemployment rates in these countries did not prevent them from achieving high productivity levels. Second, in the United States in the late 1990s, even as the unemployment rates of low-skill workers fell to historic depths, productivity growth accelerated. Third, in high-unemployment European economies, an important share of unemployed workers had mid to high levels of formal education. (See, for example, Table 8.12 and the related discussion.) This suggests that average productivity would not be significantly affected in a negative way if unemployed workers became employed.

Table 8.5 combines 2004 data from Table 8.3 and 8.21 to illustrate how productivity levels would potentially change if currently unemployed workers in each country were included in the workforce and each had zero productivity—this is an extreme but conservative assumption. The adjusted productivity levels are calculated by assuming that in those countries where unemployment rates exceed that of the United States, the unemployed are employed but produce no output. In France, for example—a country that in 2004 had high unemployment (9.6%) and productivity equal to 107% of the U.S. level—adjusted productivity is calculated by subtracting the U.S. unemployment rate of 5.5% from France's 9.6% unemployment rate, which leaves 4.1%. Next, to obtain adjusted productivity, subtract the 4.1% from the initial productivity level of France: 107 - 4.1 = 102.9. Hence, France's adjusted productivity was 102.9 (rounded to 103 in Table 8.5)—which is still above the U.S. level. This analysis shows that the high unemployment rate in France does not explain their high productivity level relative to the United States. It is also worth noting that France achieved its relatively high productivity even as it lowered the standard workweek to 35 hours. Thus, adjusting for differences in unemployment did not alter the basic conclusion that a number of advanced countries now have higher productivity levels than the United States.

Of the five countries that had productivity levels higher than the United States in 2004, all of them had adjusted productivity levels higher than U.S. levels. The adjusted productivity of Spain—which had an unemployment rate of 10.9%—fell the most, from a relative productivity level of 76% of the U.S. level to an adjusted level that is 70% of the U.S. level.

TABLE 8.5 Productivity and unemployment rates in OECD, 2004

Country	Productivity (US=100)	Unemployment rate	Adjusted Productivity*
United States	100	5.5%	–
Japan	73	4.7	73
Germany	92	9.5	88
France	107	9.6	103
Italy	92	8.0	89
United Kingdom	87	4.7	88
Canada	80	7.2	78
Australia	77	5.5%	77
Austria	91	4.8	92
Belgium	113	7.9	110
Denmark	90	5.4	90
Finland	86	9.0	82
Ireland	104	4.5	105
Netherlands	100	4.6	101
New Zealand	59	3.9	60
Norway	125	4.4	126
Portugal	53	6.7	52
Spain	76	10.9	70
Sweden	88	6.4	87
Switzerland	82	4.4	83

* Assumes unemployment above the U.S. rate corresponds to employed workers with no ouput.

Source: Authors' analysis of OECD (2005b) data.

Employment and hours worked: differing labor/leisure preferences

The per capita income figures in Tables 8.1 and 8.2 appear, at face value, to be at odds with the international estimates of productivity levels in Table 8.3. Per capita income in the United States—the value of goods and services produced annually per person—is generally much higher relative to the other OECD economies than is the U.S. productivity level (i.e., the value of goods and services produced in one hour of work in the United States). These differences between per capita income and productivity levels stem from two important differences across countries: the share of the total population employed and the average number of hours worked each year by those with jobs.

The U.S. economy employs a greater share of its working-age population, and its workers work, on average, more hours per year than workers in any other rich, industrialized economy. This additional work raises per capita income in the United States relative to other economies with roughly similar productivity levels but lower levels of employment and lower average annual hours worked. Supporters of the U.S. model have long argued that the ability of the United States to generate a greater volume of work, whether mea-

TABLE 8.6 Employment rates in OECD countries

	1979	1989	2000	2004	Percentage-point change		
					1979-89	1989-2000	2000-04
Male							
United States	73.8%	72.5%	71.9%	69.2%	-1.3	-0.6	-2.7
Japan	78.2	75.1	72.5	69.6	-3.1	-2.6	-2.9
Germany*	69.8	65.9	61.7	57.8	-3.9	-4.2	-3.9
France	69.6	61.2	59.0	58.7	-8.4	-2.2	-0.3
Italy	66.3	59.9	56.5	57.1	-6.4	-3.4	0.6
United Kingdom	74.5	70.4	67.5	66.9	-4.1	-2.9	-0.6
Canada	74.3	71.7	68.3	68.6	-2.6	-3.4	0.3
Australia	75.3%	72.1%	68.7%	68.8%	-3.2	-3.4	0.1
Netherlands	74.3	65.1	71.9	71.0	-9.2	6.8	-0.9
Sweden	73.7	70.9	64.3	63.1	-2.8	-6.6	-1.2
Female							
United States	47.5%	54.3%	57.7%	56.0%	6.8	3.4	-1.7
Japan	45.7	47.4	46.4	45.5	1.7	-1.0	-0.9
Germany*	38.4	39.7	44.6	44.6	1.3	4.9	0.0
France	40.5	41.2	43.9	45.7	0.7	2.7	1.8
Italy	27.3	28.6	30.5	34.2	1.3	1.9	3.7
United Kingdom	45.3	49.7	52.5	53.5	4.4	2.8	1.0
Canada	45.6	53.9	56.1	58.3	8.3	2.2	2.2
Australia	40.7%	48.8%	52.6%	53.8%	8.1	3.8	1.2
Netherlands	29.2	37.4	52.2	54.0	8.2	14.8	1.8
Sweden	57.2	61.7	56.1	56.1	4.5	-5.6	0.0

* For all BLS data prior to 1999, Western Germany.

Source: Authors' analysis of BLS (2005) data.

sured in terms of number of jobs or hours of work, is an essential feature of the U.S. model. To address this contention, this section takes a closer look at international employment rates, average hours worked, and unemployment rates.

The United States did, indeed, employ a greater share of its working-age population (men and women combined) than seven of the other nine countries listed in **Table 8.6**. In 2004, the United States employed 69.2% of its male working-age population—third only to the Netherlands (71.0%) and Japan (69.6%). That same year, 56.0% of women were employed in the United States—third to Canada (58.3%) and Sweden (56.1%). Employment rates may vary because of differences across economies in school enrollment rates for adults, early retirement rates, and women's non-market responsibilities, especially child care.

Table 8.6 shows a different pattern over time for employment rates of men and women. Generally, among working-age men, employment rates have been falling since 1979. There

TABLE 8.7 Average annual hours worked in OECD, 1979-2004

| | 1979 | 1989 | 2000 | 2004 | Change in hours | | |
					1979-89	1989-2000	2000-04
United States	1,861	1,878	1,858	1,824	17	-21	-33
Japan	2,126	2,070	1,821	1,789	-56	-249	-32
Germany	1,758	1,589	1,443	1,426	-169	-147	-17
France	1,755	1,608	1,496	1,441	-147	-112	-55
Italy	1,697	1,654	1,613	1,585	-43	-41	-28
United Kingdom	1,815	1,782	1,701	1,669	-32	-81	-32
Canada	1,800	1,770	1,768	1,751	-30	-2	-17
Australia	1,904	1,870	1,855	1,816	-34	-15	-40
Austria	–	–	1,582	1,550	–	–	-32
Belgium	–	1,612	1,545	1,522	–	-67	-23
Denmark	–	1,466	1,467	1,454	–	1	-13
Finland	1,870	1,803	1,750	1,736	-67	-53	-13
Ireland	–	1,919	1,688	1,642	–	-231	-46
Netherlands	–	1,452	1,368	1,357	–	-84	-11
New Zealand	–	1,832	1,817	1,826	–	-15	9
Norway	1,514	1,440	1,380	1,363	-74	-60	-17
Portugal	–	1,867	1,691	1,694	–	-176	3
Spain	2,022	1,822	1,815	1,799	-199	-7	-16
Sweden	1,530	1,565	1,625	1,585	34	60	-40
Switzerland	–	–	1,603	1,556	–	–	-47
Average excluding U.S.	1,874	1,774	1,656	1,628	-90	-116	-28

Source: Authors' analysis of OECD (2005b) data.

were large decreases in male employment rates over the 1980s. The reduction continued throughout the 1990s and less so in the first part of the new decade. Among working-age women, employment rates rose between 1979 and 1989 in every country, and increased substantially in Canada, the Netherlands, and Australia. From 1989 to 2000, all countries, most exceptionally the Netherlands (14.8), had increases in female employment rates, with the exception of Sweden (-5.6) and Japan (-1.0). Employment rates for women decreased for two countries from 2000 to 2004—the United States with -1.7 and Japan with -0.9 decline—but remained the same or increased for the other 18 countries.

Table 8.7 is a listing of average annual hours worked in OECD countries. In 2004, workers in the United States worked, on average, more hours per year (1,824 hours) than workers in any of the other countries except New Zealand. The historic leader in annual hours worked—Japan—worked fewer hours than the United States (1,789 hours compared to 1,824 hours) in 2004. Japan has reduced average hours worked by 16% between 1979 and 2004. Workers in Norway and the Netherlands worked the fewest hours per year.

TABLE 8.8 Per capita income compared to OECD average

| | Per capita income (OECD average=100) | Difference from OECD average attributed to: | | |
		Productivity	Hours worked per person	Labor utilization
United States	130.2%	11.7%	15.2%	3.2%
Japan	96.8	-18.2	9.1	5.9
Germany	93.6	11.1	-11.4	-6.1
France	99.9	27.0	-13.2	-13.9
Italy	90.3	9.6	-2.9	-16.5
United Kingdom	100.9	-3.3	3.6	0.6
Canada	104.2	-11.0	7.6	7.6
Australia	106.6%	-8.1%	12.0%	2.7%
Denmark	105.2	7.7	-8.7	6.2
Finland	100.1	-5.4	8.4	-3.0
Ireland	119.4	20.0	0.2	-0.7
Netherlands	93.3	4.6	-18.2	6.9
New Zealand	81.0	-33.4	9.1	5.2
Norway	132.7	47.2	-23.0	8.5
Portugal	59.3	-46.2	2.5	3.0
Spain	84.7	-16.2	28.8	-28.0
Sweden	101.9	2.9	-1.1	0.1

Source: Bivens (2006).

The data on employment rates and average hours worked suggest that more of the U.S. population (as a share of the U.S. working population) contributes more hours to GDP than was the case in most other OECD countries. European nations, on the other hand, chose to take their productivity gains in the form of reduced hours—through shorter workweeks, longer vacations, and earlier retirements. This is an explicit policy choice—France, for example, reduced its workweek from 39 to 35 hours in January 2000.

The calculations in **Table 8.8** help to reconcile the differences between the United States and the other economies' productivity levels on the one hand, and their per capita income levels on the other. The last three columns in Table 8.8 break down the variation in per capita income that diverges from the OECD average of 100. For example, the per capita income in the United States was 130.2% of the OECD average of 100. Therefore, per capita income in the United States was 30.2% higher than the OECD average. The 30.2% is further broken down by productivity, hours worked per person, and labor utilization (employment-to-population ratio). For the United States, 11.7% of the 30.2% of per capita income above the OECD average was attributable to higher productivity, 15.2% to more hours worked per person, and 3.2% to slightly higher employment rates. Portugal had the lowest per capita income—59.3% of the

TABLE 8.9 Work and leave policies in weeks in the OECD

Country	Full-time employees		
	Average annual work	Statutory minimum vacation	Actual holiday and vacation
United States	46.2	0.0	3.9
Japan	–	–	–
Germany	40.6	4.0	7.8
France	40.7	5.0	7.0
Italy	41.1	4.0	7.9
United Kingdom	40.8	4.0	6.6
Canada	–	–	–
Australia	–	–	–
Austria	39.5	5.0	7.3
Belgium	40.3	4.0	7.1
Denmark	39.4	5.0	7.4
Finland	38.9	4.0	7.1
Ireland	43.9	4.0	5.7
Netherlands	39.6	4.0	7.6
New Zealand	–	–	–
Norway	37.0	4.2	6.5
Portugal	41.9	4.4	7.3
Spain	42.1	4.4	7.0
Sweden	36.0	5.0	6.9
Switzerland	42.6	–	6.1

Source: Alesina, Glaeser, and Sacerdote (2005).

OECD average, or, put differently, Portugal's per capita income was 40.7% less than the OECD average. The -40.7% divergence from the OECD average of 100 can mostly be attributed to a -46.2% productivity gap. Norway's per capita income is 132.7% of the OECD average; their productivity difference was the highest (47.2%), but they also had the lowest hours worked per person (-23.0% of the OECD average). The basic lesson of these employment and hours data is that a significant portion of the apparently higher standard of living in the United States comes not from working more efficiently than other comparable economies, but simply from more people working and doing so for more hours.

An important complement to work is leisure. **Table 8.9** reveals one important reason for international differences in hours worked—generous annual vacation policies in Europe. Again, these data show that U.S. workers worked more than workers in other countries. U.S. full-time workers averaged 46.2 weeks of work per year—followed by Ireland (43.9) and Switzerland (42.6). Full-time workers in Sweden and Norway worked the least—36 and 37 weeks per year, respectively.

In Europe, the statutory minimum vacation was four to five weeks per year (shown in column 2). Interestingly, the United States has no statutory vacation time. Employers are free to offer vacations or not. Perhaps even more revealing is the actual amount of holiday and vacation time taken. On average, full-time U.S. workers get just under four weeks of paid holiday and vacation time. For Europeans, actual holiday and vacation time exceeds statutory vacation minimums by several weeks. For instance, the statutory minimum in Italy was four weeks, but the actual time taken was just under eight weeks. It seems the labor/leisure decision in Europe is structurally different than in the United States.

The capacity of the U.S. economy to sustain high employment rates is an important economic accomplishment. **Table 8.10** puts U.S. job creation into historical and international context. The table shows the annual employment growth rate in 20 OECD economies over three periods: 1979-89, 1989-2000, and 2000-04. Australia (2.4%) had the highest annual growth rate in employment from 1979 to 1989. The United States, at 1.7%, was above the OECD average of 0.8%, but was lower than four other countries. During this period only Ireland (-0.5%) had a negative annual growth rate in employment. During the 1990s, the United States again had better than average growth (1.4% versus the average of 1.0%), but six countries had as-strong-or-better annual growth rates in employment—most notably Ireland at 3.8%.

From 2000 to 2004, the United States had lower-than-average growth rates in employment—0.4% versus the average of 0.7%. The United States was in recession for most of 2001 and a subsequent jobless recovery continued into 2003—therefore job creation was tepid (see Chapter 4). Eleven countries had equal or higher annual growth rates in employment compared to the United States from 2000 to 2004, with Spain leading the list with high annual increases of 3.8% over this period.

Table 8.11 reports the unemployment rate in 20 OECD countries for 1979, 1989, 2000, and 2004. Over the late 1990s, many OECD countries experienced falling unemployment rates. The jobless rate remained low in the United States in 2000 (4.0%), and eight other countries had rates below 5%—Switzerland (2.7%), the Netherlands (2.9%), Norway (3.4%), Austria (3.7%), Portugal (4.1%), Ireland (4.3%), Denmark (4.4%), and Japan (4.7%). In 2004, unemployment rates in 13 countries were worse than they were in 2000. For that same year, nine countries had unemployment rates lower than the 5.5% U.S. rate.

Table 8.12 assesses an important claim about the causes of higher unemployment rates in some European countries; specifically, the claim by some economists that Europe's labor market institutions—such as strong unions, high minimum wages, and generous benefits—have priced less-skilled workers out of jobs. If this were the case, one would expect the unemployment rates of less-educated workers and better-educated workers to be relatively close to one another in the United States, where relatively weak unions, low minimum wages, and poor benefits would have less of an effect on the employment prospects of less-educated workers (in other words, where compensation can fall so as to promote more jobs for the less-skilled). Conversely, one would expect the unemployment rates of less-educated and better-educated workers to be relatively farther apart in Europe, where labor market institutions would, by conventional thinking, disproportionately hurt job creation for less-educated workers. Yet the data in Table 8.12 run completely counter to this expectation.

TABLE 8.10 Employment in OECD countries, 1979-2004

	Employment (thousands)				Employment change (thousands)			Annual growth rate (%)		
	1979	1989	2000	2004	1979-89	1989-2000	2000-04	1979-89	1989-2000	2000-04
United States	98,824	117,342	136,891	139,252	18,518	19,549	2,361	1.7%	1.4%	0.4%
Japan	54,790	61,280	64,460	63,290	6,490	3,180	-1,170	1.1	0.5	-0.5
Germany	26,120	27,469	36,236	35,876	1,349	8,767	-360	0.5	2.6	-0.2
France	21,392	21,842	23,698	24,259	450	1,856	561	0.2	0.7	0.6
Italy	20,057	20,833	20,874	22,146	776	41	1,272	0.4	0.0	1.5
United Kingdom	25,080	26,549	27,058	27,845	1,469	509	787	0.6	0.2	0.7
Canada	10,669	12,986	14,759	15,950	2,317	1,773	1,191	2.0	1.2	2.0
Australia	6,079	7,715	8,990	9,578	1,636	1,275	588	2.4%	1.4%	1.6%
Austria	3,051	3,342	3,743	3,732	291	401	-11	0.9	1.0	-0.1
Belgium	3,660	3,670	4,093	4,139	10	423	47	0.0	1.0	0.3
Denmark	2,439	2,610	2,692	2,689	171	82	-3	0.7	0.3	0.0
Finland	2,246	2,494	2,326	2,356	248	-168	29	1.1	-0.6	0.3
Ireland	1,151	1,099	1,664	1,829	-52	565	165	-0.5	3.8	2.4
Netherlands	4,821	6,065	7,758	7,990	1,244	1,693	232	2.3	2.3	0.7
New Zealand	1,262	1,532	1,808	2,017	270	276	209	2.0	1.5	2.8
Norway	1,862	2,014	2,246	2,258	152	232	12	0.8	1.0	0.1
Portugal	3,854	4,377	4,997	5,087	523	620	91	1.3	1.2	0.4
Spain	12,109	12,558	15,425	17,875	449	2,867	2,451	0.4	1.9	3.8
Sweden	4,180	4,442	4,159	4,213	262	-283	54	0.6	-0.6	0.3
Switzerland	3,095	3,704	4,089	4,185	609	385	96	1.8	0.9	0.6
Average excluding U.S.	25,621	27,912	30,387	30,414	2,219	2,697	231	0.8%	1.0%	0.7%

Source: Authors' analysis of OECD (2006b) data.

TABLE 8.11 Unemployment rates in the OECD, 1979-2004 (percent of civilian labor force)

| Country | Standardized unemployment | | | |
	1979	1989	2000	2004
United States	5.8%	5.3%	4.0%	5.5%
Japan	2.1	2.3	4.7	4.7
Germany	2.7	5.6	7.8	9.5
France	5.3	9.1	9.5	9.6
Italy	5.8	9.7	10.4	8.0
United Kingdom	4.7	7.1	5.4	4.7
Canada	7.5	7.5	6.8	7.2
Australia	6.1%	6.0%	6.3%	5.5%
Austria	–	–	3.7	4.8
Belgium	9.1	7.4	6.9	7.9
Denmark	–	6.8	4.4	5.4
Finland	6.5	3.1	9.8	9.0
Ireland	–	14.7	4.3	4.5
Netherlands	5.8	6.6	2.9	4.6
New Zealand	–	7.1	6.0	3.9
Norway	2.0	5.4	3.4	4.4
Portugal	–	5.2	4.1	6.7
Spain	7.7	13.9	11.3	10.9
Sweden	2.1	1.5	5.6	6.4
Switzerland	–	–	2.7	4.4
Average excluding U.S.	4.2%	6.6%	7.0%	7.1%

Source: Auhtors' analysis of OECD (2001e, 2003b and 2005) data.

The unemployment rate for workers with less than a high school education in the United States in 2003 was almost three times higher than the rate for college-educated workers—only Austria (4.0), Germany (3.5), and Belgium (3.1) had higher ratios. The ratio of high school-to-college unemployment rates was 1.8 in the United States, which was higher than all the other countries except Finland (2.1), Germany (2.0), and Belgium (1.9). Thus, Europe's strong labor market institutions do not appear to have priced less-skilled workers out of the market. If anything, the European institutions appear to be associated with substantially *lower* relative unemployment rates for less-educated workers.

TABLE 8.12 Unemployment rates in the OECD by education level, 2003

	Unemployment rate			Ratio of:	
Country	Less than high school	High school	College	Less than high school/ college	High school/ college
United States	9.9%	6.1%	3.4%	2.9	1.8
Japan	6.7	5.4	3.7	1.8	1.5
Germany	18.0	10.2	5.2	3.5	2.0
France	12.1	7.5	6.1	2.0	1.2
Italy*	9.0	6.4	5.3	1.7	1.2
United Kingdom	6.9	3.9	2.4	2.9	1.6
Canada	10.9	6.5	5.2	2.1	1.3
Australia	7.0%	4.3%	3.0%	2.3	1.4
Austria	7.9	3.4	2.0	4.0	1.7
Belgium	10.7	6.7	3.5	3.1	1.9
Denmark	7.2	4.4	4.7	1.5	0.9
Finland	11.1	9.2	4.3	2.6	2.1
Ireland	6.3	2.9	2.6	2.4	1.1
Netherlands*	3.8	2.2	2.1	1.8	1.0
New Zealand	4.9	2.9	3.5	1.4	0.8
Norway	3.9	3.6	2.5	1.6	1.4
Portugal	5.7	5.1	4.9	1.2	1.0
Spain	11.2	9.5	7.7	1.5	1.2
Sweden	6.1	5.2	3.9	1.6	1.3
Switzerland	6.1	3.3	2.9	2.1	1.1
Average excluding U.S.	9.7%	6.4%	4.5%	2.2	1.4

* Data for Italy and Netherlands are from 2002.

Source: Authors' analysis of OECD (2004a, 2005b) data.

Workers' wages and compensation: some getting ahead, some falling behind

The vast majority of workers in the OECD countries examined here rely heavily on their wages and other work-related benefits for their economic security and well-being. The level, growth, and distribution of wages and benefits are important economic indicators that provide insight into international differences and similarities. **Table 8.13** shows the inflation-adjusted annual growth rates of worker compensation (wages plus fringe benefits) in the private sector. Keep in mind that real wage growth stagnation or decline hampers any standard of living improvements. The first detail to notice is that growth rates vary considerably across countries and across time. In the 1980s, the United States put in the

TABLE 8.13 Real compensation growth per year in the OECD, 1979-2005

Country	1979-89	1989-2000	2000-05
United States	-0.2%	0.8%	1.7%
Japan	1.3	0.3	0.1
Germany	0.9	0.8	-0.5
France	1.1	0.2	0.9
Italy	1.3	0.7	0.5
United Kingdom	1.5	1.9	3.4
Canada	0.5	1.2	0.4
Australia	0.0%	1.0%	0.6%
Austria	1.6	1.2	0.3
Belgium	1.2	1.6	0.6
Denmark	0.5	1.1	1.1
Finland	3.1	1.5	1.9
Ireland	1.3	1.7	1.4
Netherlands	-0.3	0.6	1.0
New Zealand*	-1.0	3.3	2.1
Norway	0.4	1.7	2.3
Portugal	-0.6	3.4	1.1
Spain	1.7	1.3	0.2
Sweden	1.0	2.4	2.5
Switzerland	1.3	0.8	0.6
Average excluding U.S.	1.1%	0.9%	0.7%

* For New Zealand 2000-05 is 2000-03.

Source: Authors' analysis of OECD (2003a and 2005a) data.

fourth-worst performance, with average compensation *falling* about 0.2% per year—way below the average *increase* of 1.1%. The U.S. average from 2000 to 2005 was 1.7%, well above the OECD average of 0.7% in real compensation growth. Four countries fared better than the United States, most notably Norway with 2.3% growth. Note also that Germany had negative real compensation growth from 2000-05.

The most extensive international data on compensation covers a narrower group of workers—production workers in manufacturing (representing between 12% and 22% of employed workers) for whom there is more extensive data, which allows us to examine compensation growth that excludes the very high earners. It is often mistakenly thought that U.S. manufacturing's lack of international competitiveness is due to prohibitively high labor costs relative to other countries. **Table 8.14** shows that even in 1979 that wasn't always the case, and in 2004 it was less so. Table 8.14 compares hourly compensation in manufacturing in OECD countries to the corresponding levels in the United States. National compensation rates were converted into U.S. dollars using market exchange rates

TABLE 8.14 Relative hourly compensation of manufacturing production workers, 1979-2004, (U.S. = 100)

Country	Using market exchange rates				Using purchasing-power parity			
	1979	1989	2000	2004	1979	1989	2000	2004
United States	100	100	100	100	100	100	100	100
Japan	60	88	112	95	56	63	78	76
Germany	124	123	120	147	101	121	133	127
France	85	88	78	103	69	86	93	91
Italy	78	101	70	88	100	109	94	83
United Kingdom	63	74	85	107	69	79	89	92
Canada	87	103	84	92	94	101	101	96
Australia	83	87	73	100	76	82	96	99
Austria	88	99	97	122	86	105	115	110
Belgium	131	108	102	129	92	109	120	118
Denmark	117	102	111	146	84	84	107	104
Finland	83	118	99	132	70	91	109	111
Ireland	55	68	65	95	59	74	73	76
Netherlands	126	105	98	133	101	111	115	117
New Zealand	51	53	40	56	61	59	61	57
Norway	114	128	115	150	77	96	112	110
Portugal	19	21	23	30	34	37	38	34
Spain	59	63	54	74	66	76	79	78
Sweden	125	122	102	123	88	95	102	98
Switzerland	117	117	107	131	89	97	95	95
Average excluding U.S.	82	93	92	105	77	88	95	93

Source: Authors' analysis of BLS (2001 and 2005) data.

(columns 2-5) and purchasing-power parity (columns 6-9). Market exchange rates reflect the relative value of American goods, services (including labor), and assets in international markets; therefore, the compensation figures here capture the relative costs to an employer of hiring U.S. labor and thus reflect aspects of competitiveness. In 1979, seven countries had manufacturing compensation rates above the U.S. level. By 2004, 11 countries did. From 1979 to 2004, manufacturing compensation converged closer to the U.S. average. In 1979, 1989, and 2000 the U.S. compensation level was above the OECD average, but by 2004, the U.S. compensation level fell below that of the OECD average.

In terms of purchasing-power parities (which better reflect the ability of the compensation levels in each country to guarantee a specific standard of living), U.S. workers fared better than most of the other countries in the earlier periods. In 1979, manufacturing com-

TABLE 8.15 Annual growth in real hourly compensation in manufacturing in the OECD, 1979-2004

	1979-89		1989-2000		2000-04	
Country	All employees	Production workers	All employees	Production workers	All employees	Production workers
United States	0.1%	-0.7%	1.1%	0.1%	2.6%	1.8%
Japan	1.8	1.4	1.7	2.0	1.0	0.4
Germany	2.5	2.1	2.1	1.5	0.6	0.1
France	1.9	2.1	1.5	1.1	1.8	1.5
Italy	1.0	1.8	0.3	-0.3	0.5	-0.2
United Kingdom	3.0	1.8	2.1	1.5	2.2	2.8
Canada	0.3	0.1	0.0	0.7	0.0	0.0
Australia	–	0.6%	–	1.5%	1.7%	3.0%
Austria	–	2.1	–	1.4	-	0.3
Belgium	1.3%	1.4	1.0%	1.9	1.6	0.6
Denmark	1.4	-0.1	0.9	2.6	2.6	1.3
Finland	–	3.2	–	2.8	–	2.7
Ireland	–	1.9	–	1.7	–	2.6
Netherlands	1.4	0.5	1.4	1.0	1.7	1.6
New Zealand	–.	-0.8		0.8	-	0.5
Norway	1.0	0.9	1.9	1.6	2.7	2.2
Portugal	–	1.5	–	1.7	–	0.5
Spain	–	1.3	–	1.5	–	1.3
Sweden	1.1	0.9	1.8	1.4	2.5	1.2
Switzerland	–	1.3	–	0.2	–	0.7
Average excluding U. S.	1.9%	1.5%	1.6%	1.3%	1.2%	1.0%

Source: Authors' analysis of BLS (2006e) and OECD (2006b) data.

pensation on a PPP basis was highest and about the same in the United States, Germany, Italy, and the Netherlands.

The OECD average increased between 1979 and 2000—signaling a contraction of the compensation gap—rising from just 77% to 95% of the U.S. level. By 2004, manufacturing compensation in the United States (100) had fallen behind that of Germany (127), Belgium (118), the Netherlands (117), Finland (111), Austria (110), Norway (110), and Denmark (104). Italy was even with and surpassed the United States in 1979 and 1989, but has been slipping ever since—down to 83 in 2004.

Table 8.15 looks more carefully at the growth of real hourly compensation in manufacturing. Growth in compensation was determined on a purchasing-power basis over the periods 1979-89, 1989-2000, and 2000-04. The table examines growth in compensation over the three periods separately for all manufacturing employees and for production workers only. During the 1980s, the United States, at just 0.1% per year, had one of the lowest rates of growth in hourly compensation in manufacturing among OECD countries where data were available. Among U.S. production workers in the 1980s, real hourly compensation actually fell 0.7% per year, compared to average growth in the other advanced economies of 1.5% per year. Production worker compensation also fell in New Zealand (-0.8% per year), and Denmark (-0.1% per year), but rose in every other country examined here. Between 1989 and 2000, the United States again turned in one of the worst performances in compensation growth for all production workers—with a 0.1% per year growth rate (only Italy was lower at -0.3%). Outside the United States, hourly compensation for production workers grew 1.3% on average per year.

The beginning of the new millennium saw U.S. compensation growth surpass OECD averages for both overall manufacturing and production workers. The 2.6% growth rate of U.S. manufacturing workers was well above the OECD average of 1.2%. Several other countries had large increases in annual compensation growth rates for all manufacturing employees, including Norway (2.7%), Denmark (2.6%), and Sweden (2.5%). Compensation increases were less, in most cases, for production workers. Italy (-0.2%) and Canada (0.0%) posted the lowest growth in compensation for production workers from 2000 to 2004. The United States (1.8%) was above the average of 1.0% growth for production workers, but that rate was far below the 2.6% growth for all U.S. employees in manufacturing. This disparity signals that non-production manufacturing workers are faring much better than their production counterparts.

The large gap in the growth rates in hourly compensation for all manufacturing employees (which includes both production and non-production white-collar and supervisory workers) and the negative-to-stagnant growth rates for production workers in the United States through the 1980s and 1990s were other manifestations of growing wage inequality in the United States.

The majority of manufacturing workers are production workers. The wide disparity between growth in production workers' wages and wages overall means that manufacturing supervisors and other, non-production workers' wages have far outpaced production workers' wages. In short, the hourly compensation data suggest that manufacturing compensation grew more slowly and more unequally in the United States than it did in other OECD countries over the 1979-2000 period. While it is good news that wage growth was positive in the United States for both total manufacturing and production workers over the 2000-04 period, the disparity in those growth rates is telling.

Household income and inequality: higher incomes and inequality in the United States

To this point, much of the data presented has been on an individual or per capita basis. For example, the per capita income figures in Tables 8.1 and 8.2 were economy-wide, annual averages. Averages, such as these, may be deceiving because they mask inequalities and the fact that economic outcomes can strongly diverge for different populations within a na-

TABLE 8.16 Household income inequality in the OECD

| Country | Gini coefficient | | Change in Gini coefficient | | Ratio of 90th to 10th percentile |
	1989	2000	Percent change	Point change	
United States	0.338	0.368	8.2%	0.030	5.4
Japan	0.315	–	–	–	4.2
Germany	0.257	0.252	-2.0	-0.005	3.2
France	0.287	0.288	0.3	0.001	3.5
Italy	0.303	0.333	9.0	0.030	4.5
United Kingdom	0.336	0.345	2.6	0.009	4.6
Canada	0.281	0.302	7.0	0.021	4.0
Australia	0.304	0.311	2.3%	0.007	4.3
Austria	0.227	0.260	12.7	0.033	3.2
Belgium	0.232	0.277	16.2	0.045	3.3
Denmark	0.254	0.257	1.2	0.003	3.2
Finland	0.210	0.247	15.0	0.037	2.9
Ireland	0.328	0.323	-1.5	-0.005	4.6
Netherlands	0.266	0.248	-7.3	-0.018	3.0
Norway	0.231	0.251	8.0	0.020	2.8
Spain	0.303	0.340	10.9	0.037	4.8
Sweden	0.218	0.252	13.5	0.034	3.0
Switzerland	0.307	0.274	-12.0	-0.033	3.4
Average excluding U.S.	0.285	0.281	4.4%	0.017	3.8

Source: Smeeding (2006) and Luxembourg Income Study (2006a).

tion. This section moves the discussion into the arena of inequality and the distribution of income across different economies. Because individuals make important decisions about employment and consumption as part of a family or broader household, much of the analysis in this section will examine household data.

Table 8.16 uses two measures of household income inequality for OECD countries. The first inequality measure is the Gini coefficient, an inequality measure that ranges from zero (perfect equality of income across households) to one (all income is concentrated at the very top of the income distribution). In 1989 and 2000 the United States had the highest Gini coefficient and both were well above the OECD averages. Finland had the least amount of inequality with Gini coefficients of 0.210 in 1989 and 0.247 in 2000. Gini coefficients increased over the two time periods for all countries, except Germany, Ireland, the Netherlands, and Switzerland.

The second measure in Table 8.16 is the "90-10 ratio," which measures how many times more income a household in the 90th percentile has compared to a household in the

FIGURE 8C Relative income comparisons in the OECD*

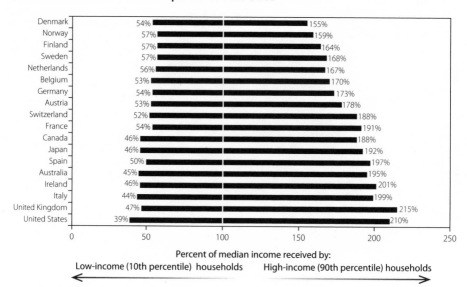

Percent of median income received by:
Low-income (10th percentile) households   High-income (90th percentile) households

* The gap between the income of the top 10% and the bottom 10% of households.

Source: Smeeding (2006).

10th percentile. The higher the ratio, the more inequality exists. Again, the U.S. ratio was the highest and much higher than the OECD average ratio. The countries with the least amount of inequality by this measure were Norway and Finland. Whether measuring inequality by Gini coefficients or 90-10 ratios, the United States exhibits the greatest degree of inequality. The next two figures build on the inequality analysis.

Figure 8C shows the income spread in each nation between the 90th and 10th household income percentiles expressed as ratios of the nation's median (50th percentile) income. In the United States, a household in the 10th percentile of the income distribution received just 39% of the income of the median household (the household exactly in the middle of the income distribution). In the other 17 economies, the 10th percentile household received between 44% (Italy) and 57% (Finland, Norway, and Sweden) of their median national income. At the other extreme, the 90th percentile household in the United States made 210% of U.S. median income, a level surpassed only by the United Kingdom (215%). Denmark (155%) and Norway (159%) are well below the OECD average of 171%. Consequently, the ratio of the 90th to the 10th percentile is largest for the United States (5.4) and smallest for Norway (2.8) and Finland (2.9).

Figure 8D compares low- and high-income households of each nation to the median in the United States, an analysis that also accounts for differences in the absolute standard of living across countries. Low-income (10th percentile) households in the United States made only 39% of the U.S. median income in 2000. It is interesting to note that, although

FIGURE 8D Share of U.S. median income received by low- and high-income OECD households, 2000*

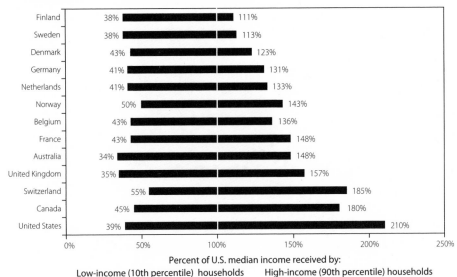

Percent of U.S. median income received by:

Low-income (10th percentile) households ← → High-income (90th percentile) households

* These relative income measures compare the gap between the top 10% and the bottom 10% of household income in each country to the U.S. median income in purchasing-power-parity terms.

Source: Smeeding and Rainwater (2001) and Smeeding (2006).

the United States has higher incomes than other countries, those at the 10th percentile in the United States have income levels comparable to those of low-income households in countries that are less wealthy than the United States. Four countries—Australia, the United Kingdom, Finland, and Sweden—had household income at the 10th percentile, close to the 39% of the U.S. median. To the extent that these countries provide more social and economic support to their citizens than the United States, these numbers provide a somewhat incomplete comparison regarding the living standards of low-income people. Further in this chapter are figures regarding transfers and social spending, specifically regarding child poverty (Figures 8G and 8H) and health care (Figure 8I). Not surprisingly, high-income households were much better off in the United States (210% of the median income) than in the rest of the countries. The next closest was Switzerland, where high-income households were 185% of the U.S. median.

Figures 8E and **8F** show historical distributions of the top decile and the top 0.1% income shares. For the United States, both of these shares fell from 2000 to 2003. This time frame encompassed the stock market collapse of 2000 and the 2001 recession that was followed by a lengthy jobless recovery well into 2003. Since 2003 both of these shares have rebounded and continued their upward trend. This reversal signifies that the decrease in shares at the start of the 2000s was cyclical and not due to a structural shift.

FIGURE 8E Top decile income share in France and in the United States

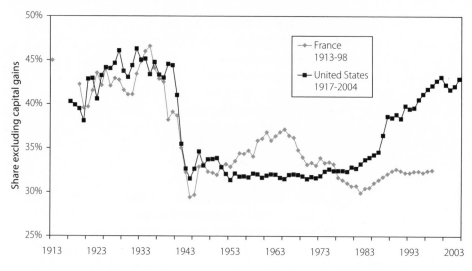

Source: Piketty and Saez (2001).

FIGURE 8F Top 0.1% family income share in France, the United States, and the United Kingdom

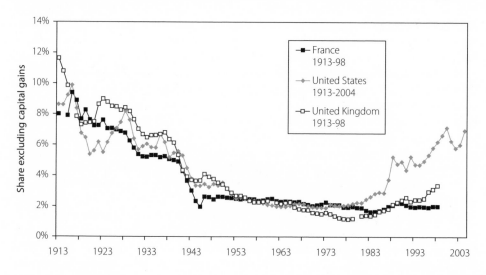

Source: Piketty and Saez (2001).

The top-decile income share was larger in France than in the United States, for the most part, after World War II until the late 1970s but generally tracked the U.S. trend. However, the U.S. top-decile share of income rocketed upward to close to an all-time high in 2000, at 44%. France's top-decile income share held steady over the last 20 years and was lower at the end of the period than in the 1960s.

A look at the top 0.1% income share (Figure 8F) shows a similar pattern, although the post-World War II fall was not as drastic as in Figure 8E. There was a steady decline in the top 0.1% income share for all three countries (France, United States, and United Kingdom) from 1913 through World War II until the mid-1980s. In 1998, the top 0.1% income share was 2.0% in France; this percentage had been somewhat stable and slightly decreasing since the 1940s. The top 0.1% income share was 3.3% in 1998 for the United Kingdom, and it had been trending upward since the late 1970s. For the United States, the top 0.1% income share was 7.4% in 1998—this share increased enormously from the late 1970s to 1998. Both of these figures illustrate the income inequality that exists in developed countries and how it has worsened much more in the United States relative to France or the United Kingdom.

Poverty: the United States has highest levels

Many would argue that it isn't how well off the affluent are in a society that matters most of all, but how the most vulnerable fare in a society that is the relevant measure of societal well-being. So far we have shown that the United States has relatively high per capita income accompanied with a significant degree of inequality. Moreover, the large inequality gap in the United States is associated with higher levels of poverty relative to a majority of the OECD countries because economic growth does not reach the poor. **Table 8.17** summarizes international data on poverty rates. Following the standard methodology for international comparisons, the table defines the poverty rate as the share of households that received 50% or less of the median income in each country. In the United States, this threshold amounted to an income that was much higher than the official poverty rate (see Chapter 6). (Figure 8D, which compares the income of the 10th percentile household in each country to the U.S. median income, provides an indication of the absolute standard of living of low-income families across the OECD countries.)

Like the official U.S. definition of poverty, the poverty rates in Table 8.17 take into account cash transfers and are adjusted for family size, but unlike the U.S. definition, they also account for taxes and tax credits. The United States, with 17.0% of its total population living in poverty, had the highest level of overall poverty among the 17 countries examined here. Ireland (16.5%) and Australia (14.3%) followed the United States. The United States was also unique in that it had the highest rate of child poverty (21.9%) and the third-highest rate of elderly poverty (24.7%). Finland (5.4%), Norway (6.4%), and Sweden (6.5%) had the lowest overall poverty rates.

It is informative to know how much of a difference transfers make regarding outcomes such as poverty. **Figure 8G** illustrates this difference in child poverty rates before and after taxes and transfers. As mentioned, the data in Table 8.17 are post-transfer (some of the rates in Table 8.17 do not exactly match those in Figure 8G because of varying reference years; see Table and Figure Notes). The pre-transfer OECD average child poverty rate (excluding

TABLE 8.17 Poverty rates in OECD countries, 2000

Country	Poverty line (50% of median)		
	Total poverty	Children	Elderly
United States	17.0%	21.9%	24.7%
Germany	8.3	9.0	10.1
France	8.0	7.9	9.8
Italy	12.7	16.6	13.7
United Kingdom	12.4	15.3	20.5
Canada	11.4	14.9	5.9
Australia	14.3%	15.8%	29.4%
Austria	7.7	7.8	13.7
Belgium	8.0	6.7	16.4
Denmark	9.2	8.7	6.6
Finland	5.4	2.8	8.5
Ireland	16.5	17.2	35.8
Netherlands	7.3	9.8	2.4
Norway	6.4	3.4	11.9
Spain	14.3	16.1	23.4
Sweden	6.5	4.2	7.7
Switzerland	7.6	6.7	18.4

Source: Luxembourg Income Study (2006b) data.

the United States) was 21.1%—which declined by over 10 percentage points post-transfer to 10.7%. The U.S. rate was 26.6% pre-transfer and only fell by 4.7% to 21.9% after transfers. The usual suspects—Denmark (2.4%), Finland (2.8%), Norway (3.4%), and Sweden (4.2%)—had the lowest incidence of post-transfer childhood poverty.

Whereas Figure 8G illustrates the predictive relationship of transfers on child poverty, it does not have information about spending levels. **Figure 8H** builds on the analysis of childhood poverty by further examining the incidence of child poverty in relation to social expenditures. The diagonal line in Figure 8H illustrates that countries that had higher social expenditures, as a percentage of GDP, also had lower poverty rates among children. The negative relationship between social expenditures and child poverty is clearly evident. The United States stands out as the country with the lowest expenditures and the highest child poverty rate. The paucity of social expenditures addressing high poverty and growing income inequality in the United States is not due to a lack of resources—high per capita income and high productivity make it possible for the United States to afford social welfare spending. Although strong growth in the United States benefited low-wage workers and their families, inequality has continued to rise. In the United States, growth has generally

FIGURE 8G Child poverty rates before and after taxes and transfers, 2000

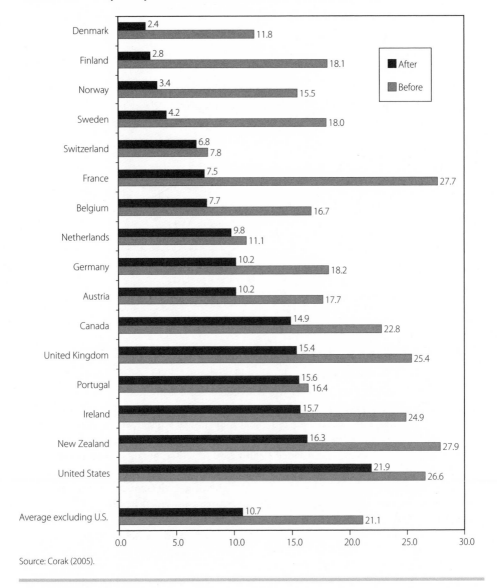

Source: Corak (2005).

not been shared equally in terms of wages paid by firms or through redistributive social policies. These and other relatively low expenditures on social welfare, such as health care, are implicated in the high poverty rates in the United States.

FIGURE 8H Social expenditure versus child poverty

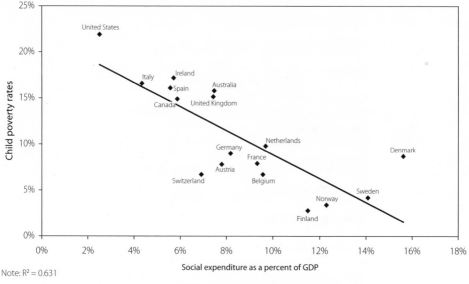

Note: R² = 0.631

Source: Authors' analysis of OECD (2004b) and Luxembourg Income Study (2006b) data.

Health care: a problem of distribution in the United States

One of the most pressing issues in the United States is health care. The United States spends more on health care and has worse average outcomes than all our OECD coun-tries. Americans who have adequate health insurance are provided good health care. But in the United States, many people have no health insurance whatsoever. For the most part, Americans rely on either private health insurance—through an employer or through di-rect purchase—or government-provided health care. In 2004, about 16% of people in the United States did not have any form of health care insurance coverage. As Chapter 3 points out, the incidence of employer-provided health care has been decreasing. At the same time, the government has been cutting back on government-provided health care. Moreover, these cutbacks are happening as the price of purchasing health care on the market is out of the realm of possibility for most low- to middle-income workers, let alone those who are among the unemployed or disenfranchised. This section takes a look at health care spend-ing and outcomes across OECD countries.

Figure 8I illustrates the amount of public and private expenditures on health care as a percentage of GDP. The United States spent more on health care per capita than any of the other countries. In total, the United States spent 15.0% of its GDP on health care—Switzer-land (11.6%) and Germany (11.1%) were second and third in spending. The countries that spent the least were Ireland (7.4%), Austria (7.5%), and Finland (7.5%). Strikingly, it was only in the United States that private expenditures were greater than public expenditures on

FIGURE 8I Public and private expenditures on health care spending, 2003 (percent of GDP)

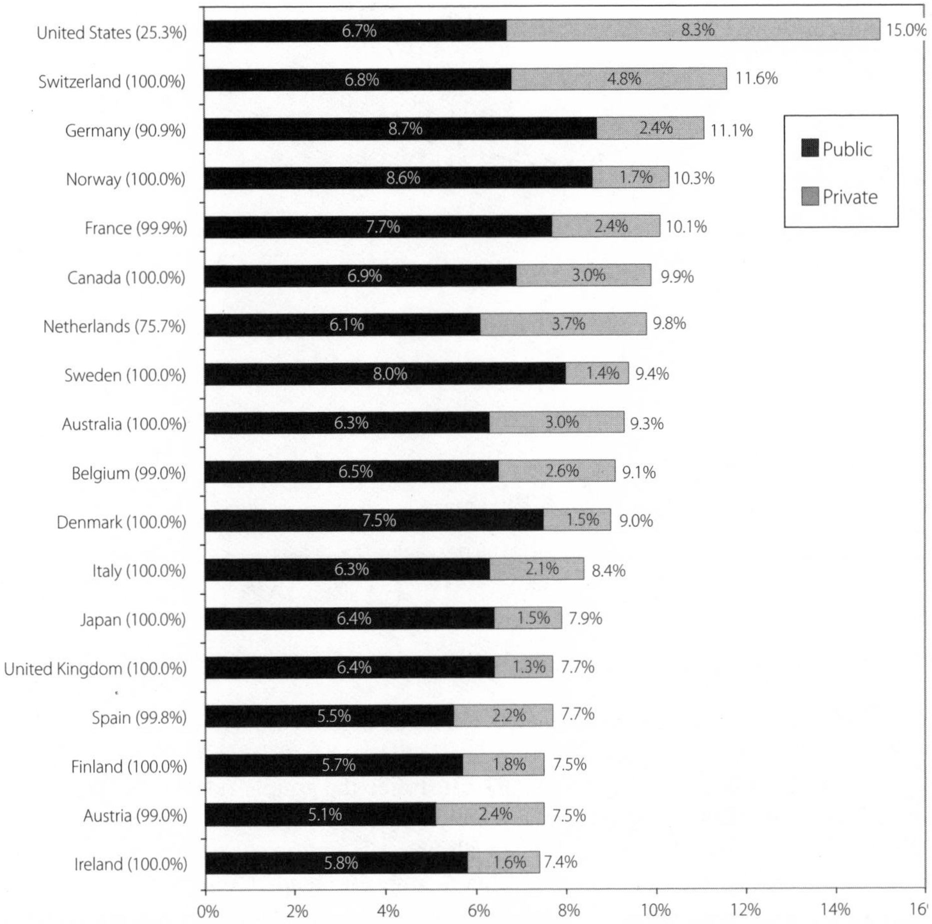

Country	Public	Private	Total
United States (25.3%)	6.7%	8.3%	15.0%
Switzerland (100.0%)	6.8%	4.8%	11.6%
Germany (90.9%)	8.7%	2.4%	11.1%
Norway (100.0%)	8.6%	1.7%	10.3%
France (99.9%)	7.7%	2.4%	10.1%
Canada (100.0%)	6.9%	3.0%	9.9%
Netherlands (75.7%)	6.1%	3.7%	9.8%
Sweden (100.0%)	8.0%	1.4%	9.4%
Australia (100.0%)	6.3%	3.0%	9.3%
Belgium (99.0%)	6.5%	2.6%	9.1%
Denmark (100.0%)	7.5%	1.5%	9.0%
Italy (100.0%)	6.3%	2.1%	8.4%
Japan (100.0%)	6.4%	1.5%	7.9%
United Kingdom (100.0%)	6.4%	1.3%	7.7%
Spain (99.8%)	5.5%	2.2%	7.7%
Finland (100.0%)	5.7%	1.8%	7.5%
Austria (99.0%)	5.1%	2.4%	7.5%
Ireland (100.0%)	5.8%	1.6%	7.4%

Legend: ■ Public ■ Private

Note: Percentage of population covered by public health care spending appears in parentheses by the country name.

Source: OECD (2004b) data.

health care. Overwhelmingly, for the other OECD countries, public expenditures on health care accounted for the majority of overall spending on health.

Located in parenthesis next to each country in Figure 8I is the percentage of people with health coverage provided by public health care spending. In Austria, where a mere 5.1% of its GDP was spent on public health care, 99% of people there were covered. Comparatively, the United States spent 6.7% of its GDP on public health care, but just 25.3% of people were covered.

FIGURE 8J Life expectancy at birth and health spending per capita, 2003

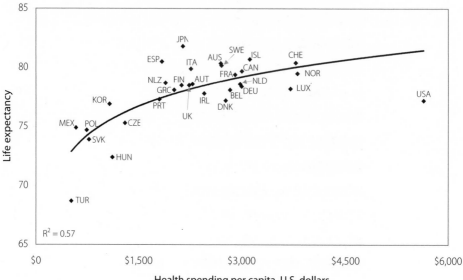

Note: See the Figure Notes section at the end of the book for a guide to the country abbreviations.

Source: OECD (2005c) data.

Of course, health spending is not the whole of health care. An essential question is: What is the relationship across countries between health care spending and outcomes? Based on OECD data, **Figure 8J** illustrates the simple relationship between life expectancy at birth and per capita health care spending. Higher per capita health care spending is generally associated with a higher life expectancy—as is indicative of the positive slope of the line. However, this relationship tended to be less pronounced at higher per capita spending. The United States was a clear outlier. It had the highest per capita health care spending, but its life expectancy was lower than that of any of the OECD countries analyzed in this chapter except Denmark. The United States and Denmark had the same life expectancy (77.2 years), but the United States spent twice as much as Denmark on health care.

Another important health outcome is infant mortality rates. As **Figure 8K** indicates, in 1979 infant mortality rates (per 1,000 live births) were very high for many OECD countries. The highest rates were in Italy (15.4), the United Kingdom (14.8), and Austria (14.7). Moreover, the lowest rates at that time were Sweden (7.5), Finland (7.6), and Japan (7.9)—all of which were higher than the highest rates in 2003. Hence, all countries made significant progress in reducing infant mortality between 1979 and 2003. As with life expectancy, the U.S. infant mortality rate—while it decreased nearly 50% from 1979 to 2003—was the highest amongst these OECD countries in 2003. In

FIGURE 8K Infant mortality, per 1,000 live births

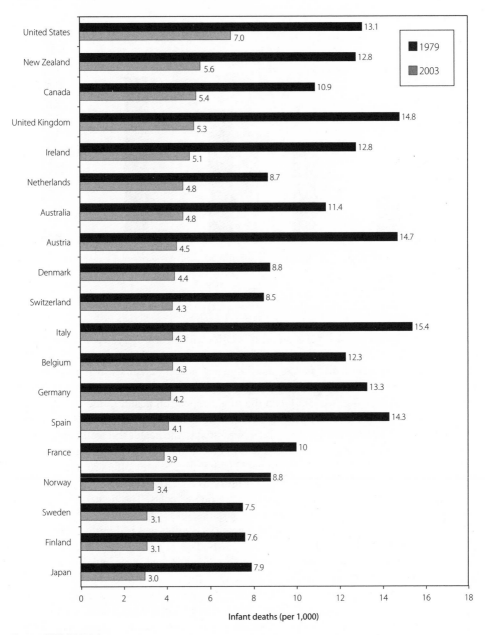

Infant deaths (per 1,000)

Source: OECD (2005c) data.

FIGURE 8L Percent going without needed health care due to costs

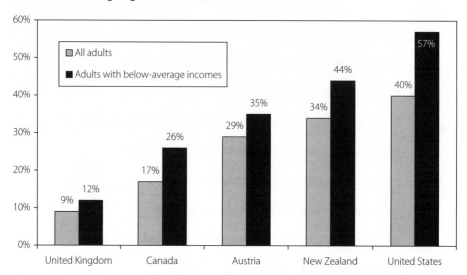

Source: Commonwealth Fund (2004).

2003, Japan (3.0) had the lowest infant mortality rate, while Italy, Spain, and Austria decreased their rates by approximately 70% during this period.

Although there are many factors that influence health outcomes, it is clear that the distribution of health care goes a long way in explaining the differences in the health outcomes described here—especially given the money spent on health in the United States. Many in the United States enjoy premier health care while others have none. Compared to the United States, other countries are more committed to the health and well-being of their citizens through more universal coverage and more comprehensive health care systems.

The Commonwealth Fund International Health Policy Survey offers some insight into health care costs and health care received. **Figure 8L** charts responses to a survey question of whether adults went without needed care due to costs. The lighter bars included the responses from all surveyed adults and the darker bars represent the responses from adults with below-average incomes. Forty percent of adults surveyed in the United States reported they went without needed care due to costs. This percentage increased to 57% for the respondents with below-average incomes. For all adults and those with below-average income, survey respondents in the United Kingdom reported the lowest incidence of forgone needed health care due to costs. This is true despite the fact that the United Kingdom spent a relatively low 6.4% of its GDP on public health that covered 100% of its citizens. All of the other countries surveyed had a smaller share than the United States in the overall and low-income populations that went without health care because of costs, even though the United States spends a larger share of its income on health care.

Evaluating the U.S. model

The United States is clearly one of the richest, most productive economies in the world. However, compared to other advanced economies, our more market-driven model yields highly varied results regarding the living standards of our citizens. We have more inequality, higher poverty rates, an expensive-yet-underperforming health care system, and workers who work more than European workers and have far fewer paid days off.

Supporters of the U.S. economic model generally acknowledge the relative inequality in the United States but argue that our model provides greater mobility, stronger job growth, and greater dynamism than do more interventionist economies. Conversely, the argument goes, the economies that have less flexibility and greater labor protections suffer under such a regime. The evidence, however, provides little support for this view. As the data reviewed in this chapter reveal, there is a wide diversity of economic outcomes, and many "interventionist" economies do as well or better than the United States on some key macroeconomic measures, from productivity to job growth, to poverty and health care.

Due to the highly unequal distribution of income in the United States, low-wage workers and low-income households are almost universally worse off in absolute terms than their low-wage, low-income counterparts in other, less-affluent OECD countries. Furthermore, as discussed in Chapter 2, the United States has less mobility than several of its European counterparts.

The U.S. success in employment creation is often exaggerated. U.S. job growth rates since 2000 were lackluster by its own historical standards and far worse than several other OECD countries with various kinds of labor market institutions. From 2000 to 2004, unemployment rates generally increased for most OECD countries. However, half of the countries had unemployment rates lower than in the United States in 2004. Perhaps most importantly, the pattern of unemployment rates in OECD countries was completely inconsistent with the idea that labor market institutions had priced less-educated workers out of jobs—the "flexible" U.S. labor market had the highest relative unemployment rate for less-educated workers among all the OECD countries.

In the United States, it is possible to work full-time, full-year and still live in poverty. In the United States, poverty and child poverty rates are the highest of all the countries studied. How can it be that the wealthiest country in the world—the United States—has such appallingly high child poverty rates? Certainly, part of the explanation has to be the lack of policy focus to alleviate such problems in the United States.

The U.S. health care system, which hinges greatly on employer-provided health care, is clearly underperforming. Despite much higher expenditures compared to other countries, the United States still has the highest infant mortality rates and lowest life-expectancy rates of all the other developed countries studied here. The problem, once again, is distributional in nature. Those with the resources in our country have access to world-class health care; those without are often left behind.

Another mistake made by those who advocate for the U.S. model is to ignore the different preferences for labor and leisure between the United States and Europe. Institutionally, European countries have mandated vacation time for their workers, whereas the United States has not. In essence, some countries have chosen to translate their higher levels of productivity into more leisure, while the United States has tended to use such efficiency gains to boost consumption of goods. As a result, Americans work a great deal more than their European counterparts. Hence, while it is true that the United States is one of the richest countries, as measured by per capita income, half of that advantage is due to more hours worked. Moreover, U.S. productivity no longer leads the OECD, even after adjusting for unemployment.

Given these caveats, along with the lack of correlation between a given model and particular outcomes, countries should not assume that the highly deregulated, high-inequality U.S. model is the most successful economic model. Other countries with much less inequality and more regulated markets have relatively impressive macroeconomic outcomes, while others have mixed outcomes (France, for example, has higher productivity levels than the United States, yet much higher unemployment). Moreover, unlike the United States, many of the citizens in other countries have a deep respect for the role of the government in their lives, and they look at the U.S. model with a more jaundiced view than policy makers touting the U.S. model.

Appendix A

This appendix explains the various adjustments made to the U.S. Census Bureau's March Current Population Survey (CPS) data and the methodology used to prepare the data in the tables discussed on the following pages.

The data source used for our analyses of family incomes and poverty is the March CPS microdata set. Each March, approximately 60,000 households are asked questions about their incomes from a wide variety of sources in the prior year (the income data in the 2005 March CPS refer to 2004). For the national analysis in Chapter 1, we use the data relevant to the year in question.

In order to preserve the confidentiality of respondents, the income variables on the public-use files of the CPS are top-coded, i.e., values above a certain level are suppressed. Since income inequality measures are sensitive to changes in the upper reaches of the income scale, this suppression poses a challenge to analysts interested in both the extent of inequality in a given time period and the change in inequality over time. We use an imputation technique, described below, that is commonly used in such cases to estimate the value of top-coded data. Over the course of the 1990s, Census top-coding procedures underwent significant changes, which also must be dealt with to preserve consistency. These methods are discussed below.

For most of the years of data in our study, a relatively small share of the distribution of any one variable is top-coded. For example, in 1989, 0.67% (i.e., two-thirds of the top 1%) of weighted cases are top-coded on the variable "earnings from longest job," meaning actual reported values are given for over 99% of those with positive earnings. Nevertheless, the disproportionate influence of the small group of top-coded cases means their earnings levels cannot be ignored.

Our approach has been to impute the average value above the top-code for the key components of income using the assumption that the tails of these distributions follow a

Pareto distribution. (The Pareto distribution is defined as $c/(x^{(a+1)})$, where c and a are positive constants that we estimate using the top 20% of the empirical distribution (more precisely, c is a scale parameter assumed known; a is the key parameter for estimation). We apply this technique to three key variables: income from wage and salary (1968-87), earnings from longest job (1988-2000), and income from interest (1968-92). Since the upper tail of empirical income distributions closely follows the general shape of the Pareto, this imputation method is commonly used for dealing with top-coded data (West, undated). The estimate uses the shape of the upper part of the distribution (in our case, the top 20%) to extrapolate to the part that is unobservable due to the top-codes. Intuitively, if the shape of the observable part of the distribution suggests that the tail above the top-code is particularly long, implying a few cases with very high income values, the imputation will return a high mean relative to the case where it appears that the tail above the top-code is rather short.

Polivka (1998), using an uncensored dataset (i.e., without top-codes), shows that the Pareto procedure effectively replicates the mean above the top-code. For example, her analysis of the use of the technique to estimate usual weekly earnings from the earnings files of the CPS yields estimates that are generally within less than 1% of the true mean.

As noted, the Census Bureau has lifted the top-codes over time in order to accommodate the fact that nominal and real wage growth eventually renders the old top-codes too low. For example, the top-coded value for "earnings from longest job" was increased from $50,000 in 1979 to $99,999 in 1989. Given the growth of earnings over this period, we did not judge this change (or any others in the income-component variables) to create inconsistencies in the trend comparisons between these two time periods.

However, changes made in the mid- and latter 1990s data did require consistency adjustments. For these years, the Census Bureau both adjusted the top-codes (some were raised, some were lowered; the new top-codes were determined by using whichever value was higher: the top 3% of all reported amounts for the variable, or the top 0.5% of all persons), and used "plug-in" averages above the top-codes for certain variables. "Plug-ins" are group-specific average values taken above the top-code, with the groups defined on the basis of gender, race, and worker status. We found that the Pareto procedure was not feasible with unearned income, given the empirical distributions of these variables, so for March data (survey year) 1996 forward we use the plug-in values. Our tabulations show that, in tandem with the procedure described next regarding earnings, this approach avoids trend inconsistencies.

The most important variable that we adjust (i.e., the adjustment with the largest impact on family income) is "earnings from longest job." The top-code on this variable was raised sharply in survey year 1994, and this change leads to an upward bias in comparing estimates at or around that year to earlier years. (Note that this bias is attenuated over time as nominal income growth "catches up" to the new top-code, and relatively smaller shares of respondents again fall into that category.) Our procedure for dealing with this was to impose a lower top-code on the earnings data that we grew over time by the rate of inflation, and to calculate Pareto estimates based on these artificial top-codes. We found that this procedure led to a relatively smooth series across the changes in Census Bureau methodology.

For example, we find that, while our imputed series generates lower incomes among, say, the top 5% of families (because we are imposing a lower top-code) in the mid-1990s, by the end of the 1990s our estimates were only slightly lower than those from the unadjusted Census data. For 2001 forward we do not have any top-code adjustments.

Table 1.1: We decompose the growth of average family income in the following manner (all monetary values are in real terms). We begin with log changes in family income over the relevant time periods—this is the value to be decomposed between annual hours, hourly wages, and other (non-labor) income. For example, in Table 1.1, this equals 13.2% for the lowest fifth over the 1995-2000 period. Family earnings grew 24.1% over this period, and we multiply this value by earnings/income averaged over the two years. For this period, that ratio is 0.525. This result represents the earnings contribution (12.7%). In order to decompose this value further into the wage and hours shares, we use weights derived from their growth over the period as shown in the table. The wage share, 1995-2000, is thus computed as $(9.5\%/(9.5\%+14.6\%))*12.7\%$, or 5.0%, where 9.5% and 14.6% are the log growth rates of annual hours and annual earnings. The share of income growth attributed to the change in "other" is derived by multiplying its growth over the period by the ratio of other/income, again averaged over the two years (note that for the lowest fifth, this is simply one minus the 0.525 value noted above). It is the nature of this type of log decomposition that if the "other" category is a relatively large share of the total, the decomposition will not perfectly sum to the total, but this is not the case here.

Tables 1.20–1.21: The source for these tables is the March CPS datasets described above. The analysis focuses on married-couple families with children, spouse present, where both spouses were between 25 and 54 years of age. The distributional analysis places 20% of families, not persons, in each fifth.

The annual hours variable in the March data is the product of two variables: weeks worked per year, and usual hours per week. Since allowable values on the latter variable go up to 99, this product can be over 5,000. Such values are clearly outliers, and we decided to exclude cases with annual hours greater than 3,500, which led to the exclusion of between 2% and 5% of cases over the years of our analysis.

For the analysis of income with and without wives earnings in Table 1.21, we create separate quintile cutoffs for the distributions with and without wives' earnings.

Table 6.11: The methodology for this decomposition is taken from Danziger and Gottschalk (1995, Chapter 5). The change to be explained is the difference in poverty rates between t_0 and t_1. We first isolate the effect of average income growth by assigning the average growth between the two time periods to all families in t_0 and recalculate the poverty rate (we adjust each family's poverty line for the increase in the CPI over this period). This procedure holds the demographic composition and the shape of the income distribution constant in t_0 while allowing incomes to grow equally for all families. Thus, the difference between this simulated poverty rate and the actual t_0 poverty rate is attributable to the growth in average income.

We repeat this exercise for each demographic group in t_0 (we use three family types: married couples, female headed families, and persons living alone (a small residual group of male-headed families is included with married couples, since it was too small to sepa-rate out), two races—white and non-white—and three education categories of the fam-ily head—less than high school, high school and some college, and college or more). By weighting each of these simulated t_0 rates by their t_1 population shares, we can simulate a t_0 poverty rate that reflects the average income growth and demographic composition of t_1. The difference between this simulated rate and the one discussed in the above paragraph gives the contribution of demographic change over the time period. Finally, since this second simulated rate incorporates the mean growth and demographic change between the two periods, but not the change in the shape of the distribution, the difference between this second simulated rate and the actual rate for t_1 equals the change in poverty rates attribut-able to changes in inequality over the two periods.

Appendix B

This appendix provides background information on the analysis of wage data from the Current Population Survey (CPS), which is prepared by the U.S. Census Bureau for the Bureau of Labor Statistics (BLS). Specifically, for 1979 and beyond, we analyze microdata files provided by the BLS that contain a full year's data on the outgoing rotation groups (ORG) in the CPS. (For years prior to 1979, we use the CPS May files; our use of these files is discussed below.) We believe that the CPS ORG files allow for a timely, up-to-date, and accurate analysis of wage trends keeping within the familiar labor force definitions and concepts employed by BLS.

The sampling framework of the monthly CPS is a "rolling panel," in which households are in the survey for four consecutive months, out for eight, and then back in for four months. The ORG files provide data on those CPS respondents in either the fourth or eighth month of the CPS (i.e., in groups four or eight, out of a total of eight groups). Therefore, in any given month the ORG file represents a quarter of the CPS sample. For a given year, the ORG file is equivalent to three months of CPSs (one-fourth of 12). For our analysis, we use a sample drawn from the full-year ORG sample, the size of which ranges from 160,000 to 180,000 observations during the 1979 to 1995 period. Due to a decrease in the overall sample size of the CPS, the ORG was shrunk to 145,000 cases from 1996 to 1998, and our current sample comes in at about 170,000 cases.

Changes in annual or weekly earnings can result from changes in hourly earnings or from more working time (either more hours per week or weeks per year). Our analysis is centered around the hourly wage, which represents the pure price of labor (exclusive of benefits), because we are interested in changing pay levels for the workforce and its subgroups. We do this to be able to clearly distinguish changes in earnings resulting from more (or less) work rather than more (or less) pay. Most of our wage analysis, therefore, does not take into account that weekly or annual earnings may have changed because of longer or shorter working hours or lesser or greater opportunities for employment. An exception to this is Table 2.1, where we present annual hours, earnings, and hourly weighted wages from the March CPS.

In our view, the ORG files provide a better source of data for wage analysis than the traditionally used March CPS files. In order to calculate hourly wages from the March CPS, analysts must make calculations using three retrospective variables: the annual earnings, weeks worked, and usual weekly hours worked in the year prior to the survey. In contrast, respondents in the ORG are asked a set of questions about hours worked, weekly wages, and (for workers paid by the hour) hourly wages in the week prior to the survey. In this regard, the data from the ORG are likely to be more reliable than data from the March CPS. See Bernstein and Mishel (1997) for a detailed discussion of these differences.

Our sub-sample includes all wage-and-salary workers with valid wage and hour data, whether paid weekly or by the hour. Specifically, in order to be included in our sub-sample, respondents had to meet the following criteria:

- age 18-64;
- employed in the public or private sector (unincorporated self-employed were excluded);
- hours worked within the valid range in the survey (1-99 per week, or hours vary—see discussion below); and,
- either hourly or weekly wages within the valid survey range (top-coding discussed below).

For those who met these criteria, an hourly wage was calculated in the following manner. If a valid hourly wage was reported, that wage was used throughout our analysis. For salaried workers (those who report only a weekly wage), the hourly wage was their weekly wage divided by their hours worked. Outliers, i.e., persons with hourly wages below 50 cents or above $100 in 1989 CPI-U-X1-adjusted dollars, were removed from the analysis. Starting from year 2002, we use CPI-RS-adjusted dollars instead. These yearly upper and lower bounds are presented in **Table B-1**. CPS demographic weights were applied to make the sample nationally representative.

The hourly wage reported by hourly workers in the CPS is net of any overtime, tips, or commissions (OTTC), thus introducing a potential undercount in the hourly wage for workers who regularly receive tips or premium pay. OTTC is included in the usual weekly earnings of hourly workers, which raises the possibility of assigning an imputed hourly wage to hourly workers based on the reported weekly wage and hours worked per week. Conceptually, using this imputed wage is preferable to using the reported hourly wage because it is more inclusive. We have chosen, however, not to use this broader wage measure, because the extra information on OTTC seems unreliable. We compared the imputed hourly wage (reported weekly earnings divided by weekly hours) to the reported hourly wage; the difference presumably reflects OTTC. This comparison showed that significant percentages of the hourly workforce appeared to receive negative OTTC. These error rates range from a low of 0% of the hourly workforce in the period 1989-93 to a high of 16-17% in 1973-88, and persist across the survey change from 1993 to 1994. Since negative OTTC is clearly implausible, we rejected this imputed hourly wage series and rely strictly on the hourly rate of pay as reported directly by hourly workers, subject to the sample criteria discussed above.

TABLE B.1 Wage earner sample, hourly wage upper and lower limits, 1973-2005

Year	Lower	Upper
1973	$0.19	$38.06
1974	0.21	41.85
1975	0.23	45.32
1976	0.24	47.90
1977	0.25	50.97
1978	0.27	54.44
1979	0.30	59.68
1980	0.33	66.37
1981	0.36	72.66
1982	0.39	77.10
1983	0.40	80.32
1984	0.42	83.79
1985	0.43	86.77
1986	0.44	88.39
1987	0.46	91.61
1988	0.48	95.40
1989	0.50	100.00
1990	0.53	105.40
1991	0.55	109.84
1992	0.57	113.15
1993	0.58	116.53
1994	0.60	119.52
1995	0.61	122.90
1996	0.63	126.53
1997	0.65	129.54
1998	0.66	131.45
1999	0.67	134.35
2000	0.69	138.87
2001	0.71	142.82
2002*	0.70	140.05
2003*	0.72	143.26
2004*	0.74	147.06
2005*	0.76	152.10

* Upper limit adjusted by CPI-RS.

Source: Authors' analysis.

For tables that show wage percentiles, we "smooth" hourly wages to compensate for "wage clumps" in the wage distributions. The technique involves creating a categorical hourly wage distribution, where the categories are 50-cent intervals, starting at 25 cents. We then find the categories on either side of each decile and perform a weighted, linear interpolation to locate the wage precisely on the particular decile. The weights for the interpolation are derived from differences in the cumulative percentages on either side of the decile. For example, suppose that 48% of the wage distribution of workers by wage level are in the $9.26-9.75 wage "bin," and 51% are in the next higher bin $9.76-10.25. The weight for the interpolation (in this case the median or 50th percentile) is (50-48)/(51-48) or 2/3. The interpolated median equals this weight, times the width of the bin ($.50), plus the upper bound of the previous bin ($9.75), or $10.08 in this example.

For the survey years 1973-88, the weekly wage is top-coded at $999.00; an extended top-code value of $1,923 is available in 1986-97; the top-code value changes to $2,884.61 in 1998-2005. Particularly for the later years, this truncation of the wage distribution creates a downward bias in the mean wage. We dealt with the top-coding issue by imputing a new weekly wage for top-coded individuals. The imputed value is the Pareto-imputed mean for the upper tail of the weekly earnings distribution, based on the distribution of weekly earnings up to the 80th percentile. This procedure was done for men and women separately. The imputed values for men and women appear in **Table B-2**. A new hourly wage, equal to the new estimated

TABLE B.2 Pareto-imputed mean values for top-coded weekly earnings, and share top coded, 1973-2005

| | Share | | | Value | |
| | Percent hours | | | | |
Year	All	Men	Women	Men	Women
1973	0.11%	0.17%	0.02%	$1,365	$1,340
1974	0.16	0.26	0.01	1,385	1,297
1975	0.21	0.35	0.02	1,410	1,323
1976	0.30	0.51	0.01	1,392	1,314
1977	0.36	0.59	0.04	1,384	1,309
1978	0.38	0.65	0.02	1,377	1,297
1979	0.57	0.98	0.05	1,388	1,301
1980	0.72	1.23	0.07	1,380	1,287
1981	1.05	1.82	0.10	1,408	1,281
1982	1.45	2.50	0.18	1,430	1,306
1983	1.89	3.27	0.25	1,458	1,307
1984	2.32	3.92	0.42	1,471	·1,336
1985	2.78	4.63	0.60	1,490	1,343
1986	0.80	1.37	0.15	2,435	2,466
1987	1.06	1.80	0.20	2,413	2,472
1988	1.30	2.19	0.29	2,410	2,461
1989	0.48	0.84	0.08	2,710	2,506
1990	0.60	1.04	0.11	2,724	2,522
1991	0.71	1.21	0.17	2,744	2,553
1992	0.77	1.28	0.22	2,727	2,581
1993	0.86	1.43	0.24	2,754	2,580
1994	1.25	1.98	0.43	2,882	2,689
1995	1.34	2.16	0.43	2,851	2,660
1996	1.41	2.27	0.46	2,863	2,678
1997	1.71	2.67	0.65	2,908	2,751
1998	0.63	0.98	0.25	4,437	4,155
1999	0.71	1.12	0.21	4,464	4,099
2000	0.83	1.38	0.24	4,502	4,179
2001	0.92	1.46	0.34	4,477	4,227
2002	0.91	1.44	0.33	4,555	4,252
2003	1.07	1.69	0.40	4,546	4,219
2004	1.19	1.90	0.42	4,611	4,195
2005	1.30	2.02	0.51	4,623	4,264

Source: Authors' analysis.

value for weekly earnings, divided by that person's usual hours per week, was calculated.

In January 1994, a new survey instrument was introduced into the CPS; many labor force items were added and improved. This presents a significant challenge to the researcher who wishes to make comparisons over time. The most careful research on the impact of the survey change has been conducted by BLS researcher Anne Polivka (1996, 1997). Interestingly, Polivka does not find that the survey changes had a major impact on broad measures of unemployment or wage levels, though significant differences did surface for some sub-groups (e.g., weekly earnings for those with less than a high school diploma and those with advanced degrees, the unemployment rate of older workers). However, a change in the reporting of weekly hours did call for the alteration of

TABLE B.3 Share of wage earners assigned an hourly wage from imputed weekly hours, 1994-2005

Year	Percent hours vary
1994	2.0%
1995	2.1
1996	2.4
1997	2.4
1998	2.5
1999	2.4
2000	2.4
2001	2.5
2002	2.5
2003	2.5
2004	2.7
2005	2.7

Source: Authors' analysis.

our methodology. In 1994 the CPS began allowing people to report that their usual hours worked per week vary. In order to include non-hourly workers who report varying hours in our wage analysis, we estimated their usual hours using a regression-based imputation procedure, where we predicted the usual hours of work for "hours vary" cases based on the usual hours worked of persons with similar characteristics. An hourly wage was calculated by dividing weekly earnings by the estimate of hours for these workers. The share of our sample that received such a wage in the 1994-2005 period is presented in **Table B-3**. The reported hourly wage of hourly workers was preserved.

BLS analysts Ilg and Hauzen (2000), following Polivka (1999), do adjust the 10th percentile wage because "changes to the survey in 1994 led to lower reported earnings for relatively low-paid workers, compared with pre-1994 estimates." We make no such adjustments for both practical and empirical reasons. Practically, the BLS has provided no adjustment factors for hourly wage trends that we can use—Polivka's work is for weekly wages. More importantly, the trends in 10th percentile hourly wages differ from those reported by Ilg and Hauzen for 10th percentile weekly earnings. This is perhaps not surprising, since the composition of earners at the "bottom" will differ when measured by weekly rather than hourly wages, with low-weekly earners being almost exclusively part-timers. Empirically, Ilg and Hauzen show the unadjusted 50/10 wage gap jumping up between 1993 and 1994, when the new survey begins. In contrast, our 50/10 wage gap for hourly wages falls between 1993 and 1994. Thus, the pattern of wage change in their data differs greatly from that in our data. In fact, our review of the 1993-94 trends across all of the deciles shows no discontinuities whatsoever. Consequently, we make no adjustments to account for any effect of the 1994 survey change. Had we made the sort of adjustments suggested by Polivka, our measured 1990s' fall in the 50/10 wage gap would be even larger and the overall pattern—falling 50/10, rising 90/50, and especially the 95/50 wage gaps—would remain the same.

When a response is not obtained for weekly earnings, or an inconsistency is detected, an "imputed" response is performed by CPS using a "hot deck" method, whereby a response from another sample person with similar demographic and economic characteristics is used for the nonresponse. This procedure for imputing missing wage data appears to bias between union and nonunion members. We restrict our sample to the observations with non-imputed wages only for union wage premium analysis (Table 3.34).

Demographic variables are also used in the analysis. Starting in January of 2003, individuals are asked directly if they are Spanish, Hispanic, or Latino categories. Persons who report they are Hispanics also may select more than one race. For consistency purpose, our race variable comprises four mutually exclusive categories across years:
• white, non-Hispanic;
• black, non-Hispanic;
• Hispanic, any race;
• all others.

In January 2003, the CPS used the 2002 Census Bureau occupational and industry classification systems, which are derived from the 2000 Standard Occupational Classification (SOC) system and the 2002 North American Industry Classification System (NAICS). The new classification system creates breaks in existing data series at all levels of aggregation. Since we have built in "old" and "new" industry and occupation systems in our underline 2000-02 data, we use year 2000 as a break point to create consistent analysis with the "old" code for pre-2000 analysis and the "new" code for post-2000 analysis.

Beginning in 1992, the CPS employed a new coding scheme for education, providing data on the respondent's highest degree attained. The CPS in earlier years provided data on years of schooling completed. The challenge to make a consistent wage series by education level is to either make the new data consistent with the past or to make the old "years of schooling" data consistent with the new, educational attainment measures. In prior versions of *The State of Working America*, we achieved a consistent series by imputing years of schooling for 1992 and later years, i.e., making the "new" consistent with the "old." In this version, however, we have converted the "old" data to the new coding following Jaeger (1997). However, Jaeger does not separately identify four-year college and "more than college" categories. Since the wages of these sub-groups of the "college or more" group have divergent trends, we construct pre-1992 wages and employment separately for "four-year college" and "advanced." To do so, we compute wages, wage premiums, and employment separately for those with 16, 17, and 18-plus years of schooling completed. The challenge is to distribute the "17s" to the 16 years (presumably a four-year degree) and 18-plus years (presumably advanced) groups. We do this by using the share of the "17s" that have a terminal four-year college degree, as computed in the February 1990 CPS supplement that provides both education codings: 61.4%. We then assume that 61.4% of all of the "17s" are "college-only" and compute a weighted average of the "16s" and 61.4% of the "17s" to construct "college-only" wages and wage premiums. Correspondingly, we compute a weighted average of 38.6% (or 1 less 61.4%) of the "17s" and the "18s" to construct advanced "wages and wage premiums." Distributing the "17s" affects each year differently depending on the actual change in the wages and premiums for "17s" and the changing relative size of the "17s" (which varies only slightly from 2.5% of men and women from 1979 to 1991).

We employ these education categories in various tables in Chapter 3, where we present wage trends by education over time. For the data for 1992 and later, we compute the "some college" trends by aggregating those "with some college but no degree beyond high school" and those with an associate or other degree that is not a four-year college degree.

Table notes

Introduction

1   *Productivity growth and living standards.* See various tables throughout *The State of Working America.*

2   *Changes in real incomes, annual hours, and earnings among middle-income families.* Authors' analysis of March CPS data.

3   *Income inequality in the late 1990s vs. the early 2000s.* Pikettty and Saez (2003) updated to 2006. Available at http://elsa.berkeley.edu/~saez/.

4   *Employment, wage, benefit, and income trends for young workers and families.* Author's analysis of CPS-ORG and U.S. Census Bureau (2006). Also see Tables 1.7 and 3.21 and Figures 3Q and 3R.

5   *Annual earnings of 25-29-year-olds, by education.* Authors' analysis of PUMS data.

Chapter 1

1.1   *Real family income growth by income fifth.* Authors' analysis of March CPS data; see Appendix A for explanation.

1.2   *Income inequality, boom and bust.* Pikettty and Saez (2003), updated to 2006. Available at http://elsa.berkeley.edu/~saez/.

1.3   *Median family income.* U.S. Census Bureau, Historical Income Tables, Families, Table F-5.

1.4   *The growth of real median family income and productivity.* U.S. Census Bureau, Historical Income Tables, Families, Table F-5 and BLS for non-farm business productivity growth.

1.5   *Annual family income growth for the middle fifth, unadjusted and adjusted for family size.* The unadjusted (for family size) values come from Census Income Table F-3; however, instead of using the deflator CPI-U-RS (the standard deflator in this edition), we use CPI-U in order to maintain greater consistency with the growth rates labeled "adjusted for family size." These values are derived by dividing family income by the poverty threshold for that family size, which is deflated using the CPI-U (Census Table F-21).

1.6   *Median family income by race/ethnic group.* Census homepage, Historical Income Tables, Families, Table F-5.

1.7   *Median family income by age of householder.* Census homepage, Historical Income Tables, Families, Table F-11.

1.8   *Median family income by family type.* Census homepage, Historical Income Tables, Families, Table F-7.

1.9   *Shares of family income going to income fifths and to the top 5%.* Census homepage, Historical Income Tables, Families, Table F-2.

1.10   *Real family income by income group, upper limit of each group.* Census homepage, Historical Income Tables, Families, Table F-1.

1.11   *Average real income levels, by income group, and shares of growth accruing to each group.* CBO (2005) data, Effective Federal Taxes Rates 1979 to 2003, Table 1-C.

1.12   *Gini coefficients: After-tax income and consumption inequality.* Johnson et al. (2005).

1.13   *Effective federal tax rates for all households, by comprehensive household income quintile.* CBO (2005) data, Effective Federal Taxes Rates 1979 to 2003, Table 1-A.

1.14   *Effective federal tax rates for all households, by comprehensive household income quintile.* Authors' analysis of CBO (2005) data, Effective Federal Taxes Rates 1979 to 2003, Tables 1-A and 1-C.

1.15   *Effective tax rates for selected federal taxes.* CBO (2005) data, Effective Federal Taxes Rates 1979 to 2003, Table 1-A.

1.16   *Federal and state/local revenue as a share of GDP.* NIPA Tables 1.1.5, 3.2, and 3.3.

1.17   *Composition of federal and state/local tax revenue, by progressive and regressive components.* NIPA Tables 3.2 and 3.3.

1.18   *Effective tax rates and the impact of Bush tax changes.* Data provided by Robert McIntyre, Institute on Taxation and Economic Policy.

1.19   *Distribution of families and persons by income level.* Authors' analysis of Census homepage, Historical Income Tables, Families, Table F-23; bottom panel from unpublished Census Bureau data provided by Jack McNeil and Charles Nelson.

1.20   *Sources of income by income group and distribution of income types.* Based on tabulations from the Urban-Brookings Tax Policy Center Microsimulation Model (version 0305-3A) provided by Peter Orzag.

1.21   *Shares of market-based personal income by income type.* From NIPA Table 2.1. Capital gains data are from the Internal Revenue Services Statistics on Income series and include gains as well as losses. See http://www.irs.gov/taxstats/article/ 0,,id=115033,00.html. The capital gains data for 2005 are an estimate based on the growth in CBO forecasts for capital gains from 2004 to 2005.

1.22   *Shares of income by type and sector.* Based on NIPA Table 1.13 (available in June 2006). The "corporate and business" sector includes "corporate" and "rest of world." Capital income consists of profits, and net interest. The "government/ nonprofit" sector includes the household, non-profits, government enterprise, and general government sectors. The capital income in this sector is the interest and rent earned plus the surplus of government enterprises.

1.23   *Corporate sector profit rates and shares.* Uses corporate income from NIPA Table 1.13. Corporate income is corporate profits (with IVA and CCAdj) plus net interest. Compensation is line 10. "After-tax profit rates" account for a tax rate based on the quotient of taxes on corporate income and applied to capital income, as previously defined. Corporate capital data are from the BEA series, the Current-Cost Net Stock of Private Nonresidential Fixed Assets. This is updated to 2005 based on growth in Flow of Funds data on tangible assets. The "capital-output ratio" is corporate capital divided by capital income.

1.24   *Annual hours of work, husbands and wives, age 25-54, with children, by income fifth.* Authors' analysis of March CPS data, see Appendix A.

1.25   *Real income growth of prime-age, married couple families with children, and wives' contribution.* Authors' analysis of March CPS data, see Appendix A.

Chapter 2

2.1   *Intergeneration wealth transmission, parents to children.* Charles and Hurst
       (2003), Table 2.

2.2   *Share of young adults remaining in poorest fifth, by cohort and race.* Corcoran
       and Matsudaira (2006), Table 9.

2.3   *Family income mobility over three decades.* Bradbury and Katz (2002), Table
       A1.

2.4   *Income mobility for white and black families; percent moving from the bottom
       25% to the top 25% and vice versa.* Hertz (2003), Table 9.

Chapter 3

3.1   *Trends in average wages and average hours.* Productivity data are from the BLS
       and measure output per hour in the non-farm business sector. The wage-level data
       are based on the authors' tabulations of March CPS files using a series on annual,
       weekly, and hourly wages for wage and salary workers (the sample definition in
       the CPS-ORG wage analysis is used; see Appendix B). The weekly and hourly
       wage data are "hour weighted," obtained by dividing annual wages by weeks
       worked and annual hours worked. The 1967 and 1973 values are derived from
       unpublished tabulations provided by Kevin Murphy from an update of Murphy
       and Welch (1989). Their values include self-employment as well as wage and
       salary workers. The values displayed in this table were bridged from CPS 1979
       values using the growth rates in the Murphy and Welch series. Hours of work were
       derived from differences between annual, weekly, and hourly wage trends.

3.2   *Growth in private-sector average hourly wages, benefits, and compensation.*
       These data are computed from the NIPA tables, which are available online.
       "Wages and salaries" are calculated by dividing wage and salary accruals (Table
       6.3) by hours worked by full-time and part-time employees (Table 6.9). "Total
       compensation" is the sum of wages and salaries and social insurance. Social
       insurance is total compensation (Table 6.2) minus the sum of volunteer benefits
       (sum of health and non-health benefits; see Table 6.11) and wages and salaries.
       "Benefits" is the difference between total compensation and wages and salaries.
       These data were deflated using the NIPA personal consumption expenditure (PCE,
       chain-weighted) index, with health insurance adjusted by the PCE medical care
       (chained) index. These data include both public- and private-sector workers.

       The BLS Employer Costs for Employee Compensation (ECEC) data provide
       cost levels for March for private-industry workers. We categorize wages and
       salaries differently than BLS, putting all wage-related items (including paid

leave and supplemental pay) into the hourly wage. Benefits, in our definition, include only payroll taxes, pensions, insurance, and "other" benefits. The sum of wages and salaries and benefits makes up total compensation. It is important to use the current-weighted series rather than the fixed-weighted series because composition shifts (in the distribution of employment across occupations and industries) have a large effect. Employer costs for insurance are deflated by the medical care component of the CPI-U-RS. All other pay is deflated by the CPI-U-RS for "all items." Inflation is measured for the first quarter of each year.

3.3   *Hourly and weekly earnings of private production and nonsupervisory workers.* BLS Current Establishment Survey data. Available online. Deflated using CPI-U-RS.

3.4   *Wages for all workers by wage percentile.* Based on analysis of CPS wage data described in Appendix B.

3.5   *Wages for male workers by wage percentile.* Based on analysis of CPS wage data described in Appendix B.

3.6   *Wages for female workers by wage percentile.* Based on analysis of CPS wage data described in Appendix B.

3.7   *Distribution of total employment by wage level.* Based on analysis of CPS wage data described in Appendix B. The poverty-level wage is calculated using the preliminary estimate of the four-person weighted average poverty threshold in 2005 divided by 2,080 hours which is 9.60. This figure is deflated by CPI-U-RS to obtain the poverty-level wage levels for other years. The threshold is available at the Census Web site. We calculated more intervals than we show but aggregated for simplicity of presentation (no trends were lost).

3.8   *Distribution of white employment by wage level.* See note to Table 3.7. These are non-Hispanic whites.

3.9   *Distribution of black employment by wage level.* See note to Table 3.7. These are non-Hispanic blacks.

3.10 *Distribution of Hispanic employment by wage level.* See note to Table 3.7. Hispanics may be of any race.

3.11 *Growth of specific fringe benefits.* Based on ECEC data described in note to Table 3.2.

3.12 *Change in private-sector employer-provided health insurance coverage.* Based on tabulations of March CPS data samples of private wage-and-salary earners ages 18-64 who worked at least 20 hours per week and 26 weeks per year. Coverage is defined as being included in an employer-provided plan where the employer paid for at least some of the coverage.

3.13   *Employee health insurance contribution requirements and employee cost shares,*
        1992-2005. Data are from Lettau (2004, 49), Wiatrowski (2004), and from the
        National Compensation Survey. Kaiser Family Foundation data are from Kaiser
        Family Foundation (2005).

3.14   *Inequality of employer-provided health insurance participation and cost, 2003.*
        Data are from Lettau (2004, 48).

3.15   *Change in private-sector employer-provided pension coverage.* These data are
        from the March CPS on pension coverage using the sample described in the note
        to Table 3.12.

3.16   *Dimensions of wage inequality.* All of the data are based on analyses of
        the CPS-ORG data described in Appendix B. The measures of "total wage
        inequality" are natural logs of wage ratios (multiplied by 100) computed from
        Tables 3.5 and 3.6. The exception is that the 1979 data for women are 1978-
        80 averages. This was done to smooth the volatility of the series, especially
        at the 10th percentile. The "between group inequalities" are computed from
        regressions of the log of hourly wages on education categorical variables (high
        school omitted), experience as a quartic, marital status, race, and region (4).
        The college/high school and high school/less-than-high-school premiums are
        simply the coefficient on "college" and "less than high school" (expressed
        as the advantage of "high school" over "less than high school" wages). The
        experience differentials are the differences in the value of age (calculated from
        the coefficients of the quartic specification) evaluated at 25, 35, and 50 years.
        "Within-group wage inequality" is measured as the root mean square error from
        the same log wage regressions used to compute age and education differentials.

3.17   *Real hourly wage for all by education.* Based on tabulations of CPS wage
        data described in Appendix B. See Appendix B for details on how a consistent
        measure of education was developed to bridge the change in coding in 1992.

3.18   *Real hourly wage for men by education.* See note to Table 3.17.

3.19   *Real hourly wage for women by education.* See note to Table 3.17.

3.20   *Educational attainment of workforce employment.* Based on analysis of CPS
        wage earners. The data are described in Appendix B. The categories are as
        follows: "less than high school" is grade 1-12 or no diploma; "high school/
        GED" is high school graduate diploma or equivalent; "some college" is
        some college but no degree; "associate college" is occupational or academic
        associate's degree; "college B.A." is a bachelor's degree; and "advanced degree"
        is a master's, professional, or doctorate degree.

3.21   *Hourly wages of entry-level and experienced workers by education.* Based on
        analysis of CPS wage data described in Appendix B.

3.22   *Hourly wages by decile within education groups.* Based on analysis of CPS
        wage data described in Appendix B.

3.23   *Decomposition of total and within-group wage inequality.* All of the data are from
        the ORG CPS data sample described in Appendix B. "Overall wage inequality" is
        measured as the standard deviation of log wages. "Within-group wage inequality"
        is the mean square error from log wage regressions (the same ones used for Table
        3.16). "Between-group wage inequality" is the difference between the overall
        and within-group wage inequalities and reflects changes in all of the included
        variables: education, age, marital status, race, ethnicity, and region.

3.24   *Hourly wage growth by gender, race/ethnicity.* Based on analysis of CPS wage
        data described in Appendix B.

3.25   *The gender wage ratio.* Wages and ratio are based on 50th percentile from
        Tables 3.5 and 3.6.

3.26   *Impact of rising and falling unemployment on wage levels and wage ratios.*
        The unemployment rate is from BLS. Wage data are based on analysis of
        quarterly CPS wage data (see Appendix B). The "simulated effect of change
        on unemployment" was calculated by regressing the log of nominal wages on
        lagged wages, unemployment, productivity growth, and seasonal dummies
        for each included percentile, by gender. Using these models, wages were
        predicted given a simulated unemployment rate series where in one case
        the unemployment rate maintained its 1979 level through the third quarter
        of 1987 (preventing its actual increase), and in the other case maintained its
        1995 level through the fourth quarter of 2000 (preventing its actual decrease).
        "Unemployment contribution to change" shows the wage simulated by the
        model in the final quarter of the simulation period compared to the actual wage.

3.27   *Employment growth by sector.* Employment levels by industry are from the BLS
        Current Establishment Survey (CES). Compensation by industry is from the
        BLS Employer Costs for Employee Compensation (ECEC) series for March
        2006 (Table 10 for private sector workers). Compensation for certain industries
        is based on NIPA data for compensation per full-time equivalent worker.
        College intensity by industry is computed form the CPS-ORG data described in
        Appendix B.

3.28   *Annual pay of expanding and contracting industries.* These data reflect the
        average (annual) wages, benefits, and compensation of the net new employment
        in each period based on changes in industry composition. The employment data
        are payroll counts from the BLS establishment survey and the pay data are from
        NIPA (calculated per payroll employee). The pay of the net new employment is
        a weighted average of the pay by industry where the weights are the changes in
        each industries employment share over the time period.

3.29   *Source of rising manufacturing trade deficit by country/region and factor intensity.* This is an update of Cline (1997), Table 4.3, p. 188, presented in Bivens (2006).

3.30   *Trade-deficit-induced job loss by wage and education level.* This is an update of Scott et al. (1997), Tables 1 and 2, presented in Bivens (2006).

3.31   *Share of Mexican and other immigrants in workforce.* Data in Figure 1 from Borjas and Katz (2006) and authors' computations of the CPS for 2000 and 2005.

3.32   *Percent distribution of educational attainment of immigrants.* Table 2 in Borjas and Katz (2006).

3.33   *Union wage and benefit premium.* Employment cost index pay-level data for March 2005 in *Employer Costs for Employee Compensation,* Table 10, for private industry: ftp://ftp.bls.gov/pub/special.requests/ocwc/ect/ececqrtn.pdf.

3.34   *Union wage premium by demographic group.* "Percent union" is tabulated from CPS-ORG data (see Appendix B) and includes all those covered by unions. "Union premium" values are the coefficients on union in a model of log hourly wages with controls for education, experience as a quartic, marital status, region, industry (12) and occupation (9), and race/ethnicity, and gender where appropriate. For this analysis we only use observations that do not have imputed wages. This is because the imputation process does not take union status into account and therefore biases the union premium toward zero. See Mishel and Walters (2003).

3.35   *Union premiums for health, retirement, and paid leave.* Based on Table 4 in Mishel and Walters (2004), which draws on Buchmueller, DiNardo, and Valletta (2001).

3.36   *Union impact on paid leave, pension, and health benefits.* Based on Table 3 in Mishel (2003) which draws on Pierce (1999b), Tables 4, 5, and 6.

3.37   *Effect of declining union power on male wage differentials.* This analysis replicates, updates, and expands on Freeman (1991), Table 2. The analysis uses the CPS-ORG sample used in other analyses (see Appendix B). The year 1978, rather than 1979, is the earliest year analyzed because we have no union membership data in our 1979 sample. The "union wage premium" for a group is based on the coefficient on collective bargaining coverage in a regression of hourly wages on a simple human capital model (the same one used for estimating education differentials, as described in note to Table 3.16), with major industry (12) and occupation (9) controls in a sample for that group. The change in union premium across years, therefore, holds industry and occupation composition constant. "Percent union" is the share covered by collective bargaining. Freeman's analysis assumed the union premium was unchanged over time. We allow the union premium to differ across years so changes in the union effect are driven by changes in the unionization rate and the union wage premium. The analysis compares the change in the union effect on relative wages to the actual change in relative wages (regression-adjusted with simple human capital controls plus controls for other education or occupation groups).

3.38   *Union wage premium for subgroups.* Based on Table 2 in Mishel and Walters (2003), which draws on Gundersen (2003), Table 5.1 and Appendix C, and Card (1991), Table 8.

3.39   *Illustration of impact of unions on average wages of high school graduates.* Based on Table 5 in Mishel and Walters (2003).

3.40   *Value of the minimum wage.* Historical values of minimum wage from Shapiro (1987, 19). Deflated using CPI-U-RS.

3.41   *Characteristics of workers affected by potential federal minimum wage increase to $7.25 by 2008.* From Fox (2006).

3.42   *Impact of lower minimum wage on key wage differentials among women.* The impact of the change in the minimum wage since 1979 is based on comparing the actual changes from 1979 to simulated wage distributions in 1989 and 1997 where the real value of the minimum wage in 1979 is imposed on the data. This analysis is based on the CPS-ORG data described in Appendix B. The simulated microdata are obtained by setting the hourly wages of those in the "sweep" (earning between the current minimum wage and the 1979 value) at the 1979 value (inflation-adjusted by CPI-U-RS) of the minimum wage. Those earning less than the legislated minimum wage were assigned a wage at the same proportionate distance to the 1979 level as they were to the existing minimum. In 1997, the existing minimum was based on a weighted average by month of the prevailing minimum of $4.75 for nine months and $5.15 for three months. The counterfactual returns to education were estimated on the simulated microdata with a simple human capital model and compared to the actual change (based on the same model) presented in Table 3.17. The other wage differentials are based on logged differentials computed from the actual and simulated microdata. The shares earning less than the 1979 minimum are computed directly from the data.

3.43   *Distribution of potential minimum wage gains and income shares by fifth for a proposed federal increase to $7.25 by 2008.* Authors' analysis of CPS-ORG data.

3.44   *Use of computers at work.* Card and DiNardo (2002).

3.45   *Executive annual pay.* The 1992-2005 data are from a *Wall Street Journal/ William M.* Mercer survey (of 350 large industrial and service companies) of CEO compensation. "Realized direct compensation" includes salary, bonus, gains from options exercised, value of restricted stock at grant, and other long-term incentive award payments. The average compensation for 1989 is backed out of the 1995 data by extrapolating the 1989-95 trend in the Pearl Meyer/*Wall Street Journal* data.

3.46   *Average CEO compensation.* Based on Bebchuk and Grinstein (2005), Table 1.

3.47   *CEO pay in advanced countries.* Total CEO compensation in dollars and the ratio of CEO to production-worker pay are from Towers Perrin (1988, 2003, and 2005).

3.48   *Effect of changing occupational composition on wages and education.* This is a shift-share analysis based on the changes in the employment shares of 754 occupations as projected in the most recent BLS projections (Hecker 2006). The education intensities, training requirements, and median annual wage for each occupation are available at ftp://ftp.bls.gov/pub/special.requests/ep/OPTDData/.

Chapter 4

4.1   *Employment to population percentages, actual and simulated.* Data are taken from Schmitt (2005). "Good" jobs pay at least $16 per hour (in constant 2004 dollars); have health insurance that is fully or partially paid by the employer; and a pension plan in which the employee participates. "Bad" jobs pay less than $16 per hour (in constant 2004 dollars); offer no paid health insurance; and do not have a pension plan in which the employee participates. The sample is all 18-to-64-year-old employees, including the incorporated self-employed.

4.2   *Unemployment rates.* BLS (2006c), Table A-1.

4.3   *Percentage-point change in unemployment rates 20 quarters after business cycle peaks.* Monthly seasonally adjusted unemployment data are from BLS (2006a), Tables A-1 and A-2. Data analysis is from the peak of the recession to the current quarter.

4.4   *Unemployment rates over the current cycle by gender, race, and educational status (persons 25 years or older).* Data are taken from BLS (2006c) and Table A-4.

4.5   *Shares of unemployment (U) and long-term unemployment (LTU) in peak years.* Data are taken from an unpublished update of Allegretto and Stettner (2004). Occupational categories do not sum to 100% because those in Armed Forces and those who did not report an occupation were left out.

4.6   *Underemployment.* Data taken from BLS (2006c), Table A-12. Discouraged workers are individuals not in the labor force who wanted a job, had searched for work in the previous year, or were available to work but were not actively searching for work because of discouragement over job prospects. "Other marginally attached" individuals are in identical circumstances, but are not actively searching for work for reasons other than discouragement, including family responsibilities, school or training commitments, or ill health or disabilities. "Involuntary part-time" workers cite "economic reasons" for working fewer than 35 hours per week.

4.7   *Nonstandard workers in the U.S. workforce.* Nonstandard work refers to any work arrangement other than employment in a full-time, full-year wage and salary job. Data are from Fisher et al. (2005), and from unpublished updates of that work provided to the Economic Policy Institute by the Iowa Policy Project.

4.8   *Share of workers employed one year or more in their current job assignment.* See note to Table 4.7.

4.9   *Share of workers by work arrangement and gender.* See note to Table 4.7.

4.10   *Source of health insurance for standard and nonstandard workers.* See note to Table 4.7.

4.11   *Access to employer provided health insurance.* See note to Table 4.7.

4.12   *Access to employer provided retirement plan.* See note to Table 4.7.

Chapter 5

5.1   *Distribution of income and wealth.* Unpublished analysis of Survey of Consumer Finances (SCF) data prepared in April 2006 by Edward Wolff for the Economic Policy Institute.

5.2   *Growth of household wealth.* Net worth and asset data are from the Federal Reserve Bank (2006a), Table B.100, p. 94. Nonprofit organizations, a small component judging from the breakout on tangible assets, were included because the Federal Reserve does not give breakouts for financial assets. Data were converted to real dollars using the CPI-RS. The number of households is based on Census Bureau (2005), Table HH-1. We used the number of families in 1950 for the number of families in 1949.

5.3   *Changes in the distribution wealth.* See note to Table 5.1.

5.4   *Changes in average wealth by wealth class.* See note to Table 5.1.

5.5   *Households with low net wealth.* See note to Table 5.1.

5.6   *Wealth by race.* See note to Table 5.1.

5.7   *Distribution of asset ownership across households.* Financial wealth is liquid and semi-liquid assets including mutual funds, trusts, retirement, and pensions. It does not include assets such as vehicles, primary residence, or other real estate investments. Also see note to Table 5.1.

5.8   *Share of households owning stock.* See note to Table 5.1.

5.9   *Average household assets and liabilities by wealth class.* See note to Table 5.1.

5.10   *Concentration of stock ownership by income level.* See note to Table 5.1.

5.11   *Home ownership rates by race and income.* Authors' analysis of BLS data from the American Housing Survey. Data for home ownership by race and for all Americans are taken from Housing Vacancy Survey (2005), Tables 13 and 20, Bureau of Census (2001, 2003, and 2005). Other yearly data are taken from the American Housing Survey. Average home ownership rates by income quintile estimated using ownership rates and population shares by discrete income categories. These data are taken from American Housing Survey, Bureau of Census (1999, 2003, and 2005), Tables 3-12 and 4-12.

5.12   *Retirement income adequacy.* See note to Table 5.1.

5.13   *Household debt by type.* Disposable personal income is personal income less tax and like tax payments. Personal taxes include income, estate and gift, and personal property taxes and motor vehicle licenses. Like-tax payments include passport fees, fines and forfeitures, and donations. Data are from the Federal Reserve Board (2006b) and Economagic (2006).

5.14   *Financial obligation ratio.* Federal Reserve Board (2006b). The financial obligation service (FOS) burden adds automobile lease payments, rental payments on tenant-occupied property, homeowners' insurance, and property tax payments to the debt service ratio. The homeowner mortgage FOS includes payments on mortgage debt, homeowners' insurance, and property taxes, while the homeowner consumer FOS includes payments on consumer debt and automobile leases. Annual averages of seasonally adjusted quarterly data available at http://www.federalreserve.gov/releases/housedebt/default.htm. See note to Table 5.12 for disposable personal income definition.

5.15   *Household debt service as a share of income by income percentile.* Data are taken from Bucks, Kennickell, Moore (2006), Table 14, p. 34.

5.16   *Share of households with high debt burdens by income percentile.* Data are taken from Bucks, Kennickell, Moore (2006, Table 14, 35).

5.17   *Share of households late paying bills by income level.* See note to Table 5.15.

Chapter 6

6.1   *Percent and number of persons in poverty and twice poverty.* Census homepage, Historical Poverty Tables, Persons, Tables 2 and 5.

6.2   *Persons in poverty by race/ethnicity.* See note to Table 5.1.

6.3   *Percent of children in poverty by race.* Census homepage, Historical Poverty Tables, Persons, Table 3. Data on children under six are from FERRET Poverty Table 1 for 2003 and from P-60 poverty publications for earlier years.

6.4   *Family poverty by race/ethnicity of family head and for different family types.* Census homepage, Historical Poverty Tables, Persons, Table 4.

6.5   *Average poverty gap.* Recent years from detailed Census tables, such as http:// pubdb3.census.gov/macro/032005/pov/new28_001_01.htm for 2004. Prior to 1987, data are from annual Census P-60 poverty reports.

6.6   *Poverty by place of birth.* Census homepage, Historical Poverty Tables, Persons, Table 23.

6.7   *Likelihood of a 1-year-old child being poor at least five of the next 10 years, by age and family characteristics.* Stevens (1999).

6.8   *Changes in poverty rates and various economic indicators.* For "poverty rates" see note to Table 6.1; for "productivity" see BLS, measures of output per hour in the non-farm business sector; for "per capita income" see NIPA Table 2.1; for "unemployment" see BLS, monthly CPS; for Inequality, or Gini coefficient, see U.S. Census Bureau, Historical Income Tables, Families, Table F-4, and note to Figure 1I; low-wage growth, authors' analysis of hourly wages as described in Appendix B.

6.9   *Earnings, taxes, and benefits under differing scenarios for work and marriage.* Ellwood (2000), Table 1.

6.10   *Alternative poverty measure, gains in the 1990s.* Official measures, Census homepage, Historical Poverty Tables, Persons, Tables 2 and 3. Alternative: unpublished tabulations provided by Wendell Primus.

6.11   *Income components for low-income single mothers with at least two children.*
Authors' analysis of March CPS data. 'Low income' refers to below twice the
poverty threshold.

6.12   *Employment rates of 16-24-year-olds, not in school, high-school or less, by
race.* Authors' analysis of CPS data.

6.13   *The impact of demographic and educational changes on family poverty rates.*
See Appendix A.

6.14   *Characteristics of low-wage workers.* Authors' analysis of CPS-ORG data; see
Appendix B.

Chapter 7

7.1   *State minimum wages greater than the federal minimum wage.* U.S. Department
of Labor. Note: as of this writing, a number of states currently have minimum
wage increases under consideration.

Chapter 8

8.1   *Per capita income, using market exchange rates.* At the price level and exchange
rates of 2000, except 1960, which is calculated at 1990 exchange rates and
corrected for conversion differences using IFS data. GDP per capita for 1960
is from OECD (1999, Table 20, 146), converted to 2004 dollars (from 1990
dollars in original) using a GDP deflator constructed using data from the Bureau
of Economic Analysis (2006, Table 1.1.4) available online at http://www.bea.
doc.gov. GDP per capita for the other years is taken from OECD (2006a, Table
A9, 332-33 and online at www.sourceoecd.org) converted to 2004 dollars (from
2000 dollars in original) by a GDP deflator constructed using data from the
Bureau of Economic Analysis (2006a, Table 1.1.4). Population for 1960 for all
other OECD countries with the exception of Germany, and 1970 for Germany, is
from the Penn World Table (2006), http://pwt.econ.upenn.edu. Data for Germany
refers to Western Germany prior to 1991 for this and all following OECD
sourced tables. Population-weighted averages excluding the United States
computed using annual national population data from OECD (2005a), *Annual
National Accounts, Volume 1*, available at www.sourceoecd.org.

8.2   *Per capita income, using purchasing-power-parity exchange rates.* At the price
level and PPP exchange rates of 2000. GDP per capita for all years is taken
from OECD (2006a), *National Accounts: Main Aggregates, Volume 1,* Table
B7, p. 338, converted to 2004 dollars (from 2000 dollars in original) using
a constructed GDP deflator that applied data from the Bureau of Economic

Analysis (2006), Table 1.1.4, http://www.bea.doc.gov. Population-weighted averages, excluding the United States, were computed using annual national population data from OECD (2005a).

8.3 *Relative productivity levels in the OECD.* GDP data taken from the OECD (2005b), Table D.2. GDP per capita table indexed relative to U.S. data for the same year. Data adjusted for PPP by source. The methodology has two levels. The first level involves converting annual snapshots of GDP per hour worked into PPP-adjusted GPD per hour worked. The second level involves creating a time series using the converted PPP GPD per hour worked. Population-weighted averages excluding the United States computed using annual population data from the OECD (2003c), for 1980 to 2002. For 1950, 1960 population data was used to calculate the population-weighted average excluding the United States for 1950. The population data for 1960 is from the Penn World Table, http://pwt.econ.upenn.edu (2006). Of this Penn World population data, for Germany, the data are for 1970, while for all the other OECD countries represented in Table 8.3 the data are for 1960.

8.4 *Labor productivity growth per year in the OECD.* Business sector. For the 1960-73 column, data are for earliest available year: 1961 for Australia and Ireland; 1962 for Japan and the U.K.; 1964 for Spain; 1965 for France and Sweden; 1966 for Canada and Norway; 1967 for New Zealand; 1969 for the Netherlands; and 1970 for Belgium. The data in the first two columns are taken from OECD (1998), Annex Table 59, p. 284, and begin in 1960 or earliest available year: 1961 for Australia and Ireland; 1962 for Japan and the U.K.; 1964 for Spain; 1965 for France and Sweden; 1966 for Canada and Norway; 1967 for New Zealand; 1969 for the Netherlands; and 1970 for Belgium. Data from 1979 to 2005 were taken from OECD (2005a), Annex Table 12, p. 217. Quarters 1 through 3 are real for 2005, while quarter 4 is an estimate used to calculate 2005. Population-weighted averages excluding the United States computed using annual population data from OECD (2005a).

8.5 *Productivity and unemployment rates in the OECD.* This table is constructed from data in Tables 8.3 and 8.11. For further details on sources, see notes for Tables 8.3 and 8.11.

8.6 *Employment rates in OECD countries.* Employment rates taken from BLS (2005), Table 4, ftp://ftp.bls.gov/pub/special.requests/ForeignLabor/flslforc.txt. Employment rates calculated from total employment as a percentage of working-age population. For Germany, 1979 and 1989 data are for Western Germany; 2000 and 2002 data are for Germany. Data for Germany and France for 2004 are for 2003 for both men and women.

8.7   *Average annual hours worked in the OECD.* OECD (2005b), Table F. Hours
        are calculated as the total number of hours worked over the year divided by the
        average number of people employed. The data are intended for the comparison
        of trends over time.

8.8   *Per capita income compared to OECD average.* Unpublished analysis of OECD
        data prepared in April 2006 by L. Josh Bivens for the Economic Policy Institute.

8.9   *Work and leave policies in weeks in the OECD.* Data on minimum statutory
        vacation from Alesina et al. (2005). http://www.eiro.eurofound.eu.int/2004/03/
        update/tn0403104u.html.

8.10   *Employment in OECD countries.* All data are taken from OECD (2006), civilian
        employment tables. Population-weighted averages excluding the United States
        computed using annual population data from the OECD (2005a).

8.11   *Unemployment rates in the OECD.* Data for 1979 are from OECD (2001a),
        Table A, p. 208. Data for 1989, 2000 are from OECD (2003b), Basic
        Structural Statistics table, p. 268. Data for 2004 are from OECD (2005b),
        Table 9, p. 299. According to the OECD, in so far as possible, these data
        have been adjusted to ensure comparability over time and to conform
        to the guidelines of the International Labor Office (ILO). All series are
        benchmarked to labor-force-survey-based estimates. In countries with annual
        surveys, monthly estimates are obtained by interpolation/extrapolation and
        by incorporating trends in administrative data, where available. The annual
        figures are then calculated by averaging the monthly estimates (for both the
        unemployed and the labor force). For countries with monthly or quarterly
        surveys, the annual estimates are obtained by averaging the monthly or
        quarterly estimates, respectively. For several countries, the adjustment
        procedure used is similar to that of the Bureau of Labor Statistics, U.S.
        Department of Labor. For European Union (EU) countries, the procedures
        are similar to those used in deriving the Comparable Unemployment Rates
        (CURs) of the Statistical Office of the European Communities. Minor
        differences may appear mainly because of various methods of calculating
        and applying adjustment factors, and because EU estimates are based on the
        civilian labor force. For Germany, Western Germany data are used for 1979
        and 1989. Population-weighted averages excluding the United States are
        obtained using annual population data from the OECD (2005a).

8.12   *Unemployment rates in the OECD by education level.* Unemployment rates
        measures using OECD's standardized unemployment rate. OECD describes
        educational categories as: "Less than upper secondary," "upper secondary," and
        "tertiary" OECD (2005b, Table D, 250-52). For Germany, data is for Eastern and
        Western Germany. Data for Italy and the Netherlands are from 2002 from OECD
        Employment Outlook, (2004b, Table D, 306-08). Population-weighted averages

excluding the United States computed using annual population data from the OECD (2005a).

8.13   *Real compensation growth per year in the OECD.* Compensation per employee in the business sector. Nominal compensation per employee in the business sector is from OECD (2005a), Annex Table 11, including New Zealand, which contains data only up to 2003. The data were deflated by changes in consumer prices from OECD (2003a), Annex Table 16, p. 220 and online for 2001 to 2003 Consumer Price Changes figures. For Germany, growth rate reported uses data for Western Germany for 1979-91 and data for Germany for 1992 to 2004. Current data for New Zealand was unavailable. Population-weighted averages excluding the United States computed using annual population data from the OCED (2005a).

8.14   *Relative hourly compensation of manufacturing production workers.* Index of hourly compensation costs for production workers in manufacturing from BLS (2001 and 2005), Table 1. Population-weighted averages excluding the United States computed using annual population data from the OECD (2005a). In the OECD, between 1979 and 2004, 12% to 23% of workers were in manufacturing. Data are from the BLS (2005), http://www.bls.gov/fls/flshcindnaics.htm.

8.15   *Annual growth in real hourly compensation in manufacturing in the OECD.* Compensation for all workers in manufacturing is hourly compensation in manufacturing, on a national currency basis, from BLS (2006d), Table 8.1. The hourly compensation in manufacturing data refer to employees (wage and salary earners) in Belgium, Denmark, Italy, and the Netherlands, and to all employed persons (employees and self-employed workers) in the other countries. Compensation for production workers is hourly compensation costs in national currency for production workers in manufacturing from BLS (2006d), Table 4. Data are deflated using consumer price indexes derived from OECD (2006b), Table 16. Population-weighted averages excluding the United States computed using annual population data from the OECD (2005a).

8.16   *Household income inequality in the OECD.* For each country, the latest year available is used. Data for the Gini coefficients and the percentile ratios are taken from Smeeding (2006), Figure 1. Gini coefficients are based on incomes that are bottom coded at 1% of disposable income and top coded at 10 times the median disposable income. Gini coefficient for Japan is calculated from 1993 Japanese Survey of Income Redistribution. Averages excluding the United States calculated as simple averages. Ratio of 90th to 10th percentiles is from LIS (2006a).

8.17   *Poverty rates in OECD countries.* Data represent annual snapshots of poverty
in the OECD countries. Poverty data for the total population, children, and the
elderly are taken from Luxembourg Income Study Web site (2006). All data for
2000, except as follows: 2002 for Switzerland, 1999 for Netherlands, Poland,
and the U.K.; 1997 for Denmark; 1994 for Australia and France. All data are
based on household-level analysis.

Figure notes

Introduction

A   *Real wages and productivity growth.* Analysis of Tables 3.1, 3.4, and 3.17.

B   *Job growth in the current business cycle compared with previous cycles.* Data are taken from BLS (2006c).

C   *Number of months to regain peak level employment after a recession, current and prior business cycles.* Data are taken from BLS (2006c).

D   *Changes in the employment rate.* Actual employment rates are taken from BLS (2006c). Simulated rates are calculated holding each age and gender cohort employment rates constant at 1998 rates. The population variable changes within each group and a new simulated employment rate shows the changes of demographic shifts in the population.

E   *Share of capital income in the corporate sector.* Data from Table 1.23.

F   *Annual wages of "some college" workers who entered labor force in 1970.* Authors' analysis of PUMS data.

G   *Annual wages of workers with some college attendance (less than a degree) by age.* Authors' analysis of PUMS data.

Chapter 1

1A   *Real income growth: 1990s boom vs. post-2000 expansion.* Census homepage, Historical Income Tables, Families, Table F-1.

1B   *Components of middle income changes.* Table 1.1.

1C   *Years it took for median family income to regain prior peak.* Census homepage, Historical Income Tables, Families, Table F-5, and www.nber.org for recession dates.

1D   *Real median family income.* Table 1.3.

1E   *Productivity and real median family income growth.* Table 1.3 and BLS nonfarm business productivity.

1F   *Ratio of black and Hispanic to white median family income.* Table 1.6.

1G   *Africa American/white income ratio, actual and simulated holding unemployment constant at 2000 level.* We regressed the black/white income gap on unemployment rate (in logs, including four lags), the lagged value of the dependent variable and a dummy for an intercept shift in 1994. We then model the effect on the racial income gap of holding unemployment constant at its 2000 level of 4%.

1H   *Impact of a one-point increase in unemployment on median family income, by age.* The figure sows the coefficients on the unemployment rate from a regression of the change in the log of real median family income for families headed by persons within the age brackets shown in the figure (plus a constant).

1I   *Real family income growth by quintile.* Census homepage, Historical Income Tables, Families, Table F-3. 1947 data provided by Census Bureau.

1J   *Ratio of family income of top 5% to lowest 20%.* See Figure 1I.

1K   *Low-, middle-, and high-income growth.* Table 1.10.

1L   *Family income inequality, Gini coefficient.* Census homepage, Historical Income Tables, Families, Table F-4.

1M   *The share of income going to the top 1%, including capital gains.* Pikettty and Saez (2003) updated to 2006. Available at http://elsa.berkeley.edu/~saez/.

1N   *Income share, top 0.01%, by income source.* Pikettty and Saez (2003) updated to 2006. Available at http://elsa.berkeley.edu/~saez/.

1O   *Growth in real household income.* Table 1.11.

1P   *Consumption inequality among children.* Same source as Table 1.12.

1Q   *Change in income shares by income percentile, pre- and post-tax.* Table 1.11.

1R   *The value of the Bush tax cuts by income class.* Table 1.18.

1S   *Share of capital income.* This is based on Congressional Budget Office data on the Share of Corporate Income Tax Liabilities (which is derived from the Share of capital income) presented in Table 1B.

1T   *Capital shares in the corporate sector.* Annual data developed for Table 1.23.

1U   *Before and after-tax return to capital.* Annual data developed for Table 1.23.

1V   *Top-five officers' total pay relative to corporate profits.* From Bebchuk and Grinstein (2005).

1W   *Average weekly hours compared to family work hours.* Authors' analysis of March CPS data as described in Appendix A.

Chapter 2

2A   *Intergenerational income persistence, sons and daughters.* Lee and Solon (2006), Tables 1 and 2.

2B   *Likelihood that low-income son ends up above various percentiles.* Unpublished data provided by Gary Solon.

2C   *Intergenerational mobility.* Aaronson and Mazumder (2005), Table 1.

2D   *Intergenerational mobility, role of education.* Blandon (2004).

2E   *Income position of the entering class at top colleges and community colleges.* Carnevale and Rose (2004), Table 3-1.

2F   *College completion by income status and test scores.* Fox, Connelly, and Snyder (2005), Table 21.

2G   *Intergeneration earnings mobility in six countries.* Solon (2002).

2H   *Intergenerational mobility: Percent of sons and daughters in lowest fifth, given fathers in lowest fifth.* From Jäntti et al. (2006) Tables 12 and 13.

2I   *Real median income growth, cohorts, age 30-50.* Authors' analysis of Census homepage, Historical Income Tables, Families, Table F-11.

2J   *The share of families staying in the top fifth.* See Table 2.3.

Chapter 3

3A   *Changes in productivity and hourly wages, benefits, and compensation.* Productivity measured as output per hour in the non-farm business sector. Compensation and wages as measured in Table 3.2. Pensions and insurance measured as in Table 3.11.

3B   *Changes in productivity and hourly wages, benefits, and compensation.* Productivity measured as output per hour in the non-farm business sector. Annual wages are from table 3.1. Median wage is from Table 3.4. Hourly wage for production, non-supervisory workers is from Table 3.3.

3C   *Hourly wage and compensation growth for production/non-supervisory workers.* See note to Table 3.4. Hourly compensation was estimated based on multiplying hourly wages by the ratio of compensation to wages for all workers in each year. The compensation/wage ratio is drawn from the NIPA data used in Table 3.2. The compensation/wage ratio for 2005 was set equal to 2004's level plus the change between 2004 and 2005 in the comparable ratio in the ECEC (Table 3.11).

3D   *Changes in real hourly wages for men by wage percentile.* See note to Table 3.5.

3E   *Changes in real hourly wages for women by wage percentile.* See note to Table 3.6.

3F   *Share of workers earning poverty-level wages, by gender.* See note to Table 3.7.

3G   *Share of workers earning poverty-level wages, by race/ethnicity.* See notes to Tables 3.8, 3.9, and 3.10.

3H   *Private-sector employer-provided health insurance coverage.* See note to Table 3.12.

3I   *Share of pension participants in defined-contribution and defined-benefit plans.* Buessing and Soto (2006).

3J   *Men's wage inequality.* Based on ratios of wages by decile in annual data presented in Table 3.5.

3K   *Women's wage inequality.* Based on ratios of wages by decile in annual data presented in Table 3.6.

3L   *95/50 percentile wage inequality.* Based on ratios of wages by percentile presented in Tables 3.5 and 3.6.

3M   *College/high school wage premium.* Differentials estimated with controls for experience (as a quartic), region (4), marital status, race/ethnicity, and education, which are specified as dummy variables for less than high school, some college, college, and advanced degree. Estimates were made on the CPS ORG data as described in Appendix B, and presented in Table 3.16.

3N   *Productivity and hourly compensation growth.* Average hourly productivity and compensation are for the non-farm business sector and available from the BLS web site (see major sector productivity and cost index). The compensation series is deflated by the CPI-U-RS. The median compensation of female, male, and all workers is derived by multiplying the compensation/wage ratio (based on the NIPA data discussed in the note to Table 3.2 and Figure 3C) by the real median wage series for each in Tables 3.4, 3.5, and 3.6.

3O   *Entry-level wages of male and female high school graduates.* See note to Table 3.21.

3P   *Entry-level wages of male and female college graduates.* See note to Table 3.21.

3Q   *Health and pension coverage for recent high school graduates.* Computed from the same data as used in Tables 3.12 and 3.15.

3R   *Health and pension coverage for recent college graduates.* Computed from the same data as used in Tables 3.12 and 3.15.

3S   *The gender wage ratio by percentile.* The gender wage ratio is calculated by dividing the female wage by the male wage at the respective wage level. See note to Tables 3.5 and 3.6 for wage derivations.

3T   *Unemployment.* The unemployment rate is available at the BLS Web site (see Current Population Survey).

3U   *Share of intermediate inputs supplied by imports.* Update of Feenstra and Hanson (2001) presented in Bivens (2006).

3V   *Employment in software and computer services and retail software investment.* From Bivens and Price (2006).

3W   *Union membership in the United States.* Hirsch and Macpherson (1997) and BLS (Employment and Earnings).

3X   *Real value of the minimum wage.* Series compiled by authors and deflated using CPI-U-RS.

3Y   *Minimum wage as percentage of average hourly earnings.* Calculated from values of minimum wage (Table 3.40) and average hourly earnings (Table 3.4).

3Z   *Ratio of CEO to average worker pay.* Calculated by dividing the CEO average annual pay (see note to Table 3.45) by production non-supervisory workers' average annual pay (hourly average multiplied by 2,080 multiplied by the compensation/wage ratio discussed in note to Table 3.2). The production non-supervisory worker's average hourly pay is available online from the BLS (see Current Establishment Survey). CEO pay for the pre-1995 period based on the Pearl Meyers/*Wall Street Journal* survey scaled to the level of the Mercer CEO pay in 1995 (meaning the data rely on the levels of Mercer in 1995 and the growth between earlier years and 1995 as shown in the Pearl Meyer data).

3AA   *Shares of earnings among top 1% of earners.* Schwabish (2006).

Chapter 4

4A   *Number of months for employment to regain peak level following recession.* Data are taken from BLS (2006c).

4B   *Employment growth, 61 months after peak.* Data are taken from BLS (2006c).

4C   *Gross job gains and losses.* Seasonally adjusted data from 1990q2 to 1992q2 are from Faberman (2004) and data from 1992q3 to 2005q3 are from BLS (2006a). Gross job gains and gross job losses are expressed as rates by dividing their levels by the average of employment in the current and previous quarters. This provides a symmetric growth rate. These data are Business Employment Dynamics data and are from the administrative records of the regularly collected establishment employment data (Quarterly Census of Employment and Wages program). This program is a quarterly census of all establishments under state unemployment insurance programs, representing about 98% of employment on non-farm payrolls.

4D   *Percent change in employment 61 months after business cycle peak, by industry.* Monthly seasonally adjusted data are from BLS (2006b), Table B-1.

4E   *Employment changes for all private-sector industries and IT-producing industries.* Unpublished update of Allegretto (2005). BLS payroll employment data, by industry, were used to determine IT-producing industry employment levels. The compilation of IT-producing industry employment follows from Sandra Cooke's methodology in the *Digital Economy 2003*. This grouping represents IT workers across industries. IT-producing industries are those that produce, process, or transmit information goods and services as either intermediate demand (inputs to production of other industries) or as final products.

4F   *Actual and simulated share of good jobs.* See note to Table 4.1.

4G   *Unemployment rate and its trend.* Unemployment data and authors' calculation for trend of annual unemployment data (using Hodrick–Prescott filter with power 2 in Eviews) from BLS (2006c).

4H   *Unemployment rates of foreign-born and native-born workers.* Data from BLS (2006c). Seasonally adjusted using the X-12 adjustment.

4I   *Wage declines of transitioning full-time workers and average unemployment rate.* Data for log change in weekly earnings after a full-time to full-time transition are taken from Farber (2005), Figure 10. Unemployment rates are taken from BLS (2006c).

4J   *Long-term unemployment as a share of total unemployment and the unemployment rate.* Data are from BLS (2006c).

4K   *Length of unemployment spells and the share of long-term unemployment associated with unemployment rates from 4.7% to 5.0%.* Unemployment from 4.7% to 5.0% during the past year is compared with the characteristics of that level of unemployment prior to this recovery. Data are taken from BLS (2006c).

4L   *Shares of long-term unemployment by education.* See note to Table 4.5.

4M   *Percentage-point change in shares of unemployment and long-term unemployment by educational attainment.* See note to Table 4.5.

4N   *Annual labor force participation rate.* Data are from BLS (2006c), Table A-2.

4O   *Employment rates by gender.* Data are from BLS (2006c).

4P   *Annual employment rates 55 years and older by gender.* Data are taken from BLS (2006c).

4Q   *Employment rates of young college graduates.* Authors' calculation of employment rates for 25-35 year olds from BLS (2006c) micro data. Data seasonally adjusted using the STAMP adjustment.

4R   *Change in employment rates by education.* Data are taken from BLS (2006c).

4S   *Actual and simulated labor force participation rates.* Actual LFPRs are taken from BLS (2006c). Simulated rates are calculated holding each age and gender cohort LFPR constant at 1998 rates. The population variable changes within each group and a new simulated LFPR shows the changes of demographic shifts in the population. For more discussion and a contrary view see Aaronson et al. (2006).

4T   *Employment in temporary help industry as share of private employment.* Data are from BLS (2006b).

4U   *Involuntary part-time employment as a percent of total employment.* Data are from BLS (2006c).

4V   *Source of health insurance.* See note to Table 4.7.

4W   *Access to employer provided health insurance.* See note to Table 4.7.

4X   *Access to job-based retirement plan.* See note to Table 4.7.

Chapter 5

5A   *Distribution of wealth by wealth class.* Data derived from Table 5.1. Data for 1986 calculated by taking half of the difference between 1983 and 1989 and adding it to 1983 to get a linear approximation.

5B   *The ratio of the wealthiest 1% to median wealth in the United States.* Data derived from Table 5.4.

5C   *Annual net worth of "Forbes 400" wealthiest individuals.* Data for 1982 to 2001 adapted from Broom and Shay (2000, Table 2, 15); updated to 2000 and 2001 by Broom and Shay (via personal correspondence). Data for 2000 through 2004 are from Forbes.com (2006), Forbes 400 list.

5D   Share *of income and net worth of non-whites compared to whites.* Data from Bernstein (2006). Available online at http://www.epi.org/content.cfm/webfeatures_snapshots_20060315.

5E   *Growth of U.S. stock market.* Standard & Poor's Composite Index from Economic Report of the President (2006, Table B-96, 392), deflated by the CPI-RS (Table B-62).

5F   *Distribution of stock market holdings by wealth class.* Data derived from Table 5.9.

5G   *Distribution of stock market wealth by wealth class.* Data derived from Table 5.9.

5H   *Distribution of growth in stock market holdings by wealth class.* Data derived from Table 5.9.

5I   *Average home ownership rates.* Yearly average of data published by the U.S. Census Bureau, Housing Vacancy Survey (2005), Historical tables, Table 14, home ownership rates for the U.S. and regions.

5J   *Home ownership rates by race.* Data from Table 5.11.

5K   *Average rate of home ownership by income.* Data from Table 5.11.

5La   *Debt as percentage of disposable personal income.* See note to Table 5.13.

5Lb   *Debt as percentage of disposable personal income.* See note to Table 5.13.

5M   *Distribution of growth in debt.* Calculated from Table 5.9.

5N   *Consumer bankruptcies per 1,000 adults.* Data on consumer bankruptcies from the American Bankruptcy Institute Web page (2006), U.S. Bankruptcy Filings table. Data on adult population from the Economic Report of the President (2006), Table B-35, http://www.gpoaccess.gov/eop/. Bankruptcies per 1,000 adults calculated from above data.

Chapter 6

6A   *Poverty and twice-poverty rates.* See note to Table 6.1.

6B   *Poverty rates by race/ethnicity.* See note to Table 6.1.

6C   *Family poverty gap and family poverty rates.* See notes to Table 6.4 and 6.5.

6D   *Percent of the poor below half the poverty line.* Census homepage, Historical Poverty Tables, Table 5, Table 22.

6E   *Poverty, native and foreign born.* Table 6.6.

6F   *Poverty rates, official compared to National Academy of Sciences alternatives.* U.S. Census Bureau, Alternative Poverty Estimates, Table B3.

6G   *Relative and absolute poverty, using adjusted income measures.* Relative measures: authors' analysis of March CPS data. Poverty threshold is defined as 50% of median income; equivalence scale is square root of family size. Absolute measure is from unpublished tabulations provided by Wendell Primus.

6H   *Real low-wage growth, productivity, and unemployment during three five-year periods.* Productivity and unemployment from BLS, low-wage growth from CPS-ORG series described in Appendix B.

6I   *Annual hours worked by low-income mothers.* Table 6.11.

6J   *Poverty determinants: Impact on family poverty rates.* Table 6.13.

6K   *Percent change in real wages with one-point decline in unemployment.* Authors' analysis of CPS-ORG data. Phillips curve model regresses nominal wage changes on the gender-specific unemployment rate and CPI-RS inflation with one wage (with inflation coefficient constrained to equal one). We include a dummy for post-1995 intercept shift, as in Katz and Krueger (1999). Models for low-wage women include nominal minimum wage when it is significant.

6L   *Real hourly wages of low-wage workers.* Wages are based on analysis of CPS wage data as described in Appendix B. The poverty-level wage is the hourly wage that, at full-time, full-year work, would lift a family of four above the poverty line. This equals $960 in 2005 dollars.

Chapter 7

7A   *Census regions and divisions.* U.S. Census Bureau.

7B   *Annual regional employment growth.* BLS, available online (see Current Employment Statistics survey).

7C   *Unemployment rate by region.* Authors' analysis of basic CPS data.

7D   *Job growth by state.* BLS, available online (see Current Employment Statistics survey).

7E   *Regional population growth.* U.S. Census Bureau. http://wwwcensusgov/popest/estimatesphp.

7F   *Domestic migration by region.* http://wwwcensusgov/popest/estimatesphp.

7G   *Unemployment rate by region.* Authors' analysis of basic CPS data.

7H   *Long-term unemployment rate by region.* Authors' analysis of basic CPS data.

7I   *Job loss by state, compared to reliance on manufacturing employment in 2000.* Authors' analysis of BLS data, available online (see Current Employment Statistics survey).

7J   *Growth in 20th percentile wages by division.* Based on analysis of CPS wage data as described in Appendix B.

7K   *Growth in median percentile wages by division.* Based on analysis of CPS wage data as described in Appendix B.

7L   *Value of federal minimum wage compared to share of workforce covered by higher state minimums.* U.S. Department of Labor. Note: As of this writing, a number of states currently have minimum wage increases under consideration.

Chapter 8

8A   *Annual growth rates of per capita income using market exchange rates.* At the
price level and exchange rates of 2000 except for 1960 which is at 1990 exchange
rates. Market exchange rates were used instead of PPP due to the availability of the
data, but it is important to note that growth rates across countries are comparable
using either PPP or market exchange rates. See note to Table 8.1.

8B   *Productivity growth rates.* See note to Table 8.4.

8C   *Relative income comparisons in the OECD.* Data are from Smeeding (2006),
Figure 1.

8D   *Composition of low and high incomes to U. S. median.* Data taken from
Smeeding and Rainwater (2001) and Smeeding (2006), Figure 2. Household
income at the 10th and 90th percentiles in each country is compared to median
income. For France, Australia, Denmark, Norway, and Switzerland, data are
represented as percent of overall U.S. 1997 medium equivalent income in
purchasing-power-parity terms. For the United States, Germany, the United
Kingdom, Canada, Belgium, Finland, the Netherlands, and Sweden, data are
represented as percent of U.S. 2000 median equivalent income in purchasing-
power-parity terms. Income inequality measured as disposable household
income per equivalent adult. Averages excluding the United States calculated as
simple averages.

8E   *Top decile income share in France and in the United States.* Data for France is
not available for 1914-18 and extends to 1998 while data for the United States
begins in 1917 and has been updated to extend to 2002. Data are taken from
Piketty and Saez (2001), Figure 19. Authors' computations based on income tax
returns (France: see Piketty (2001), Table A1, pp. 90-100); U.S.: see Piketty and
Saez (2001), Table A1, pp. 90-100).

8F   *Top 0.1% income share in France, the United States, and the United Kingdom.*
Data are taken from Piketty and Saez (2001), Figure 21. Piketty and Saezs'
computations are based on income tax returns (France: see Piketty (2001, Table
A1, 99-100); U.S.: see Piketty and Saez (2001, Table A1, 99-100); U.K.: see
Atkinson (2001). Data for the United States have been updated by Piketty and
Saez to extend to 2002.

8G   *Child poverty rates before and after taxes and transfers.* Data taken from Corak
(2005) Figure 7, available at http://www.unicef-icdc.org/publications/pdf/
iwp_2005_01.pdf. Poverty rates defined as 50% of median household income of
each country. Data for Austria, Belgium, and Denmark are for 1997, and data for
Netherlands and United Kingdom are from 1999. All other countries are for 2000.

8H   *Social expenditures vs. child poverty in the OECD.* Data on child poverty taken from Luxembourg Income Study Web site (2006b) and are taken for the latest year possible and for the 50th percentile. Data are all for 2000 except for Australia and France (1994), Denmark (1997), United Kingdom, and The Netherlands (1999), and Switzerland (2002). Data for social expenditure is calculated from OECD (2004) Annex Table B6. $R^2 = 0.6311$. The data for the chart only appears in the Web version, not in the book itself. Social expenditure is calculated by subtracting out pensions and health benefits from public social expenditure.

8I   *Public and private expenditures on health care spending.* Data taken from OECD (2004b). Data for Japan, United Kingdom, Australia, and Belgium are from 2002.

8J   *Life expectancy at birth and health spending per capita.* Data taken from OECD (2005c). Variations in GDP per capita may influence *both* life expectancy and health expenditure per capita. Many other factors, beyond national income and total health spending, also need to be taken into account to explain variations in life expectancy across countries. Country codes are as follows: AUS = Australia, AUT = Austria, BEL = Belgium, CAN = Canada, CZE = Czech Republic, DNK = Denmark, FIN = Finland, FRA = France, DEU = Germany, GRC = Greece, HUN = Hungary, ISL = Iceland, IRL = Ireland, ITA = Italy, JPN = Japan, KOR = South Korea LUX = Luxembourg, MEX = Mexico, NLD = Netherlands, NZL = New Zealand, NOR = Norway, POL = Poland, PRT = Portugal, SVK = Slovakia (Slovak Republic), ESP = Spain, SWE = Sweden, CHE = Switzerland, TUR = Turkey, GBR = United Kingdom, and USA = United States.

8K   *Infant mortality, per 1,000 live births.* Data taken from OECD (2005c). Some of the international variation in infant and neonatal mortality rates may be due to variations among countries in registering practices of premature infants (whether they are reported as live births or not).

8L   *Percent going without needed health care due to costs.* Data taken from Schoen and Osborn (2004).

Bibliography

Aaronson, D. and Mazumder, B. 2005. "Intergenerational Economic Mobility in the U.S., 1940 to 2000" Federal Reserve Bank of Chicago. WP 2005-12.

Aaronson, Stephanie, Bruce Fallick, Andrew Figura, Jonathan Pingle, and William Wascher. 2006. *The Recent Decline in Labor Force Participation and Its Implications for Potential Labor Supply, Division of Research and Statistics.* Board of Governors of the Federal Reserve System. <http://www.brookings.edu/es/commentary/journals/bpea_0603bpea_aaronson.pdf>

Alesina, Alberto F., Glaeser, Edward L., and Sacerdote, Bruce. 2005. "Work and leisure in the U.S. and Europe: Why so different?" Discussion paper no. 5140. Washington, D.C.: Center for Economic and Policy Research.

Allegretto, Sylvia, and Stettner, Andy. 2004. "Educated, experienced, and out of work." Unpublished update of Issue Brief #198. Washington, D.C.: Economic Policy Institute.

Allegretto, Sylvia. 2005. "The aftermath of the tech bubble." *JobWatch.* Washington, D.C.: Economic Policy Institute. <http://jobwatch.org/email/jobwatch_20050805.html>. Unpublished update 2006.

American Bankruptcy Institute. 2006. *Annual, Total Business and Non-business Bankruptcy Filings.* Alexandria, Va.: American Bankruptcy Institute.

Blanden, Jo. 2004. "International evidence on education and intergenerational mobility." CEE conference paper. Centre for the Economics of Education, LSE. <http://cee.lse.ac.uk/conference_papers/15_10_2004/jo_blanden.pdf>

Bernstein, Jared. 2006. "Minority wealth gap: Net worth gap twice that of income." *EPI Economic Snapshot*. Washington, D.C.: Economic Policy Institute. <http://www.epi.org/content.cfm/webfeatures_snapshots_20060315>

Bivens, Josh. 2006. Unpublished analysis of OECD data. Washington, D.C.: Economic Policy Institute.

Borjas, George J., and Lawrence F. Katz. 2005. "The evolution of the Mexican-born workforce in the United States." National Bureau of Economic Research, Working Paper No. 11281. Cambridge, Mass.: NBER.

Bradbury, Katharine, and Jane Katz. 2002. "Women's labor market involvement and family income mobility when marriages end." Federal Reserve Bank of Boston. *New England Economic Review,* Q4, pp. 41-74.

Buessing, Marric, and Mauricio Soto. 2006. "The state of private pensions: Current 5500 Data." Center for Retirement Research *Issue in Brief*, February 2006, No. 42.

Buchmueller, Thomas C., DiNardo, John E., and Valletta, Robert G. 2001. "Union effects on health insurance provision and coverage in the United States." National Bureau of Economic Research, Working Paper No. 8238. Cambridge, Mass.: NBER.

Bucks, Brain K., Arthur B. Kennickell, and Kevin B. Moore. 2006. "Recent changes in U.S. family finances: Evidence from the 2001 and 2004 Survey of Consumer Finances." *Federal Reserve Bulletin.* January. <http://www.federalreserve.gov/pubs/bulletin/2006/financesurvey.pdf>

Broom, Leonard, and William Shay. 2000. "Discontinuities in the distribution of great wealth: Sectoral forces old and new." Paper prepared for the Conference on Saving, Intergenerational Transfer, and the Distribution of Wealth held by the Jerome Levy Economics Institute at Bard College, June 7-9, 2000.

Card, David. 1991. "The effect of unions on the distribution of wages: Redistribution or relabelling?" Working Paper No. 287. Princeton, N.J.: Department of Economics, Princeton University.

Card, David, and John E. Dinardo. 2002. "Skill biased technological change and rising wage inequality: some problems and puzzles." National Bureau of Economic Research, Working Paper No. W8769. Cambridge, Mass.: NBER.

Carnevale, Anthony P., and Stephen J. Rose. 2003. *Socioeconomic Status, Race/Ethnicity, and Selective College Admissions.* A Century Foundation Paper.

Chapman, Jeff, and Liana Fox. 2006. *The Wage Effects of Minimum Wage Increases,* Washington, D.C.: Economic Policy Institute.

Cline, William R. 1997. *Trade and Income Distribution.* Washington, D.C.: Institute for International Economics.

Charles, K. and Hurst, E. 2003. "The Correlation of Wealth Across Generations." *The Journal of Political Economy,* Vol. 111, No. 6 (Dec.), Research Library Core pg. 1,155 University of Chicago 2002.

Corak, Miles. 2005. "Principles and practicalities for measuring child poverty in rich countries." LIS working paper no. 406. Luxembourg: Luxembourg Income Study.

Economagic. 2006. *Economic Time Series.* Washington, D.C.: Economagic.com. <http://www.economagic.com>

Economic Report of the President. *Annual.* Washington, D.C.: U. S. Government Printing Office.

Ellwood, D. 2000. "Anti-poverty policy for families in the next century." *The Journal of Economic Perspectives.* Vol. 14, No. 1, pp. 187-98.

Farber, Henry S. 2005. "What do we know about job loss in the United States? Evidence from the displaced workers survey, 1984-2004." Working Paper #498. Princeton, N.J.: Industrial Relations Section, Princeton University. <http://www.irs.princeton.edu/pubs/pdfs/498.pdf>

Faberman, Jason. R. 2004. "Gross jobs flows over the past two business cycles: Not all 'recoveries' are created equal." Working Paper no. 372. Washington, D.C.: Bureau of Labor Statistics, Office of Employment and Unemployment Statistics. <http://www.bls.gov/ore/pdf/ec040020.pdf>

Federal Reserve Board. 2006a. *Flow of Funds Accounts of the United States: Annual Flows and Outstanding.* Washington, D.C.: Board of Governors of the Federal Reserve System. <http://www.federalreserve.gov/releases/Z1/Current/data.htm>.

Federal Reserve Board. 2006b. *Household Debt Burden.* Washington, D.C.: Board of Governors of the Federal Reserve System. <http://www.federalreserve.gov/releases/housedebt/default.htm>

Fisher, Peter S. Ditsler, Elaine Colin Gordon, and David West. 2006. *Nonstandard Jobs, Substandard Benefits.* The Iowa Policy Project, unpublished update February 2006. <www.iowapolicyproject.org/2005_reports_press_releases/051201-nonstdjobs.pdf>

Fox, M. A., B. A. Connolly, and T. D. Snyder. 2005. *Youth Indicators 2005: Trends in the Well-Being of American Youth.* Washington, D.C.: U.S. Department of Education. National Center for Education Statistics. Table 21. <http://nces.ed.gov/pubs2005/2005050.pdf>

Freeman, Richard. 1991. "How much has de-unionization contributed to the rise in male earnings inequality?" National Bureau of Economic Research, Working Paper No. 3826. Cambridge, Mass.: NBER.

Gundersen, Bethney. 2003. *Unions and the well-being of low-skill workers.* George Warren Brown School of Social Work, Washington University. Ph. D. dissertation

Hecker, D. E. 2005. "Employment outlook: 2002–14: Occupational Employment Projections to 2014." *Monthly Labor Review.* Vol 128., No 11 (Nov.).Washington D.C.: Department of Labor.

Hertz, Tom. Forthcoming. "Rags, Riches and Race: The Intergenerational Economic Mobility of Black and White Families in the United States." In *Unequal Chances:Family Background and Economic Success,* edited by Samuel Bowles, Herbert Gintis, and Melissa Osborne. New York and Princeton: Russell Sage and Princeton University Press.

Jäntti, Markus, Bernt Bratsberg, Knut Röed, Oddbjörn Raaum, Robin Naylor, Eva Österbacka, Anders Björklund, and Tor Eriksson. 2006. "American exceptionalism in a new light: A comparison of intergenerational earnings mobility in the nordic countries, the United Kingdom, and the United States." Discussion Paper No. 2006:1938. Institute for the Study of Labor.

Johnson D., Smeeding T., and Boyle Torrey B. 2005. "Economic inequality through the prisms of income and consumption." *Monthly Labor Review.* April 2005. Washington, D.C.: U.S. Department of Labor, Bureau of Labor Statistics.

Katz, Lawrence F., and Krueger, Alan G. 1999. "The high pressure U.S. labor market of the 1990s." *Brookings paper on Economic Activity.* 1999, No. 1, pp. 1-65. Washington, D.C.: Brookings Institute.

Kaiser Family Foundation and The Health Research and Educational Trust. 2005. *Employer Health Benefits 2005: Annual Survey.* Menlo Park, Calif.: Kaiser Family Foundation.

Lee, C., and Solon, G. 2005. "Trends in intergenerational income mobility." NBER Working Paper No. 12007. Washington, D.C. <http://www.nber.org/papers/w12007>

Lettau, Michael. 2004. "New statistics for health insurance from the National Compensation Survey." *Monthly Labor Review.* August 2004. Washington, D.C.: U.S. Department of Labor, Bureau of Labor Statistics.

Luxembourg Income Study. 2006a. *Income Inequality Measures*. Luxembourg: Luxembourg Income Study. <http://lisweb.ceps.lu/keyfigures/ineqtable.htm>

Luxembourg Income Study. 2006b. *Relative Poverty Rates for the Total Population, Children and the Elderly*. Luxembourg: Luxembourg Income Study. <www.lisproject.org/keyfigures/povertytable.htm>

Mazumder, B. 2005. "Fortunate sons: New estimates of intergenerational mobility in the United States using social security earnings data." *Review of Economics and Statistics*. Vol. LXXXVII, No. 2, pp. 235–55.

Organization for Economic Cooperation and Development. 1998. *Economic Outlook*. Paris: OECD.

Organization for Economic Cooperation and Development. 1999. *National Accounts of OECD Countries. Main Aggregates Volume I. 1960-1996*. Paris: OECD.

Organization for Economic Cooperation and Development. 2001. *Employment Outlook*. June 2001. Paris: OECD.

Organization for Economic Cooperation and Development. 2003a. *Economic Outlook*. Paris: OECD. <http://www.oecd.org/dataoecd/5/47/2483871.xls>

Organization for Economic Cooperation and Development. 2003b. *Employment Outlook*. Paris: OECD. <www.sourceoecd.org>

Organization for Economic Cooperation and Development. 2003c. *OECD Science and Technology: Towards a Knowledge Based Economy*. Paris: OECD. <http://www1.oecd.org/publications/e-book/92-2003-04-1-7294/Annex_tables_excel/Dt2_e.xls>

Organization for Economic Cooperation and Development. 2004a. *Employment Outlook*. Paris: OECD.

Organization for Economic Cooperation and Development. 2004b. *Health Data*. Paris: OECD. <www.oecd.org/health/healthdata>

Organization for Economic Cooperation and Development. 2005a. *Economic Outlook*. Paris: OECD. <http://www.oecd.org/dataoecd>

Organization for Economic Cooperation and Development. 2005b. *Employment Outlook*. Paris: OECD. <http://www.oecd.org/dataoecd/36/30/35024561.pdf>

Organization for Economic Cooperation and Development. 2005c. *Health Data*. Paris: OECD. <www.oecd.org/health/healthdata>

Organization for Economic Cooperation and Development. 2006a. *National Accounts of OECD Countries, Main Aggregates Volume I, 1970-2004*. Paris: OECD.

Organization for Economic Cooperation and Development. 2006b. *National Accounts of OECD Countries, Comparative Tables Volume I, 1970-2004*. Paris: OECD.

Piketty, Thomas. 2001. "Income inequality in France, 1901-1998." Discussion Paper No. 2876. Washington, D.C.: Center for Economic and Policy Research.

Piketty, Thomas, and Saez Emmanuel. 2001. "Income inequality in the United States, 1913 to 1998." Working Paper No. 8467. Washington, D.C.: National Bureau of Economic Research. <http://www.nber.org./papers/w8467>

Penn World. 2006. *Penn World Table*. <http://pwt.econ.upenn.edu>

Pierce, Brooks. 1999. "Compensation inequality." Office of Compensation and Working Conditions, Department of Labor, Working Paper No. 323.

Schoen, Cathy, and Osborn, Robin. 2004. "Primary care and health system performance: Adults' experiences in five countries." *Health Affairs*. Web exclusive, October 28, 2004. The Commonwealth Fund. <http://www.cmwf.org/publications/publications_show. htm?doc_id=245178>

Schmitt, John. 2005. "How Good is the Economy at Creating Good Jobs?" Washington, D.C.: Center for Economic and Policy Research. <http://www.cepr.net/publications/labor_markets_2005_10.pdf>

Scott, Robert E., Thea Lee, and John Schmitt. 1997. *Trading Away Good Jobs: An Examination of Employment and Wages in the U.S., 1979-94*. Briefing Paper. Washington, D.C.: Economic Policy Institute.

Settersten, Richard A., Jr., Frank F. Furstenberg, and Ruebn G. Rumbaut. 2005. *On the Frontier of Adulthood: Theory, Research, and Public Policy*. Chicago: University of Chicago Press.

Shapiro, Isaac. 1987. *No Escape: The Minimum Wage and Poverty*. Washington, D.C.: Center on Budget and Policy Priorities.

Schwabish, Johnathon A. 2006. "Earnings inequality and high earners: Changes during and after the stock market boom of the 1990s." Congressional Budget Office Working Paper Series. Washington, D.C.: Congressional Budget Office.

Smeeding, Timothy, and Lee Rainwater, 2001. "Comparing living standards across nations: Real incomes at the top, the bottom, and the middle." Luxembourg Income Study Working Draft Paper. Luxembourg: Luxembourg Income Study.

Smeeding, Timothy M. 2006. "Poor people in rich nations: The United States in comparative perspective." *Journal of Economic Perspective,* Vol. 20, No. 1, pp. 69-90.

Solon, Gary. 2002. "Cross-country differences in intergenerational earnings mobility." *Journal of Economic Perspectives*, Vol. 16, No. 3, pp. 59-66.

Stevens, Ann Huff, 1999. "Climbing out of poverty, falling back in: Measuring the persistence of poverty over multiple spells." *Journal of Human Resources,* Vol. 34, No. 3, pp. 557-88.

Towers Perrin. Annual. *Worldwide Total Remuneration.* <www.towersperrin.com>

U.S. Department of Commerce, Bureau of the Census. 2001. *American Housing Survey.* <http://www.census.gov/hhes/www/housing/ahs/ahs01/ahs01.html>

U.S. Department of Commerce, Bureau of the Census. 2003. *American Housing Survey.* <http://www.census.gov/hhes/www/housing/ahs/ahs03/ahs03.html>

U.S. Department of Commerce, Bureau of the Census. 2005. *Housing Vacancy Survey. Housing Vacancies and Homeownership Annual Statistics.* Washington, D.C.: U.S. Government Printing Office.

U.S. Department of Commerce, Bureau of Economic Analysis. 2006a. *National Economic Accounts.* <http://www.bea.doc.gov/bea/dn/nipaweb/SelectTable.asp?Selected=N>

U.S. Department of Commerce, Bureau of Economic Analysis. 2006b. *National Income and Product Accounts* <http://www.bea.gov/bea/dn/nipaweb/index.asp>

U.S. Department of Labor, Bureau of Labor Statistics. 2001. *International comparisons of hourly compensation costs for production workers in manufacturing, 1997-2000.* Washington, D.C.: Bureau of Labor Statistics. <ftp://ftp.bls.gov/pub/special.requests/ForeignLabor/supptab.txt>

U. S. Department of Labor, Bureau of Labor Statistics. 2005. *Comparative civilian labor force statistics, ten countries, 1959-2004.* Washington, D.C.: Bureau of Labor Statistics. <ftp://ftp.bls.gov/pub/special.requests/ForeignLabor/flslforc.txt>

U.S. Department of Labor, Bureau of Labor Statistics. 2006a. *Business Employment Dynamics.* Washington, D.C.: U.S. Government Printing Office. <http://www.bls.gov/ces/home.htm>

U.S. Department of Labor, Bureau of Labor Statistics. 2006b. *Current Employment Statistics.* Washington, D.C.: U.S. Government Printing Office. <http://www.bls.gov/ces/home.htm>

U.S. Department of Labor, Bureau of Labor Statistics. 2006c. *Current Population Survey.* Washington, D.C.: U.S. Government Printing Office. <http://www.bls.gov/cps/home.htm>

U.S. Department of Labor, Bureau of Labor Statistics. 2006d. *Employer Cost for Employee Compensation Historical Listing.* Washington, D.C.: Bureau of Labor Statistics. <http://www.bls.gov/pub/special.requests/ocwc/ect/ececqrt.pdf>

U. S. Department of Labor, Bureau of Labor Statistics. 2006e. *International Comparison of Hourly Compensation Costs for Production Workers in Manufacturing, 1975-2004.* Washington DC: Bureau of Labor Statistics. <ftp://ftp.bls.gov/pub/special.requests/ForeignLabor/prodsuppt07.txt>

Wiatrowski, William J. 2004. "Medical and retirement plan coverage: Exploring the decline in recent years." *Monthly Labor Review*, August. U.S. Department of Labor, Bureau of Labor Statistics.

Wolff, Edward. 2006. Unpublished analysis of Survey of Consumer Finances data prepared in 2006 for the Economic Policy Institute.

Index

D

E

About EPI

The Economic Policy Institute was founded in 1986 to widen the debate about policies to achieve healthy economic growth, prosperity, and opportunity. Today, despite rapid growth in the U.S. economy in the latter part of the 1990s, inequality in wealth, wages, and income remains historically high. Expanding global competition, changes in the nature of work, and rapid technological advances are altering economic reality. Yet many of our policies, attitudes, and institutions are based on assumptions that no longer reflect real world conditions.

With the support of leaders from labor, business, and the foundation world, the Institute has sponsored research and public discussion of a wide variety of topics: globalization; fiscal policy; trends in wages, incomes, and prices; education; the causes of the productivity slowdown; labor market problems; rural and urban policies; inflation; state-level economic development strategies; comparative international economic performance; and studies of the overall health of the U.S. manufacturing sector and of specific key industries.

The Institute works with a growing network of innovative economists and other social science researchers in universities and research centers all over the country who are willing to go beyond the conventional wisdom in considering strategies for public policy.

Founding scholars of the Institute include Jeff Faux, former EPI president; Lester Thurow, Sloan School of Management, MIT; Ray Marshall, former U.S. secretary of labor, professor at the LBJ School of Public Affairs, University of Texas; Barry Bluestone, Northeastern University; Robert Reich, former U.S. secretary of labor; and Robert Kuttner, author, editor of *The American Prospect*, and columnist for *Business Week* and the *Washington Post* Writers Group.

For additional information about the Institute, contact EPI at 1333 H St. NW, Suite 300, Washington, DC 20005, (202) 775-8810, or visit www.epi.org.

About the authors

LAWRENCE MISHEL is president of the Economic Policy Institute and was the research director from 1987 to 1999. He is the co-author of the previous versions of *The State of Working America*. He holds a Ph.D. in economics from the University of Wisconsin, and his articles have appeared in a variety of academic and non-academic journals. His areas of research are labor economics, wage and income distribution, industrial relations, productivity growth, and the economics of education.

JARED BERNSTEIN joined the Economic Policy Institute as a labor economist in 1992 and is currently the director of the Living Standards Program. Between 1995 and 1996, he held the post of deputy chief economist at the U.S. Department of Labor, where, among other topics, he worked on the initiative to raise the minimum wage. He is co-author of six previous editions of *The State of Working America* and co-author (with Dean Baker) of the book *The Benefits of Full Employment*. He specializes in the analysis of wage and income inequality, poverty, and low-wage labor markets, and his writings have appeared in popular and academic journals. Dr. Bernstein holds a Ph.D. in social welfare from Columbia University.

SYLVIA ALLEGRETTO joined the Economic Policy Institute in 2003 after receiving her Ph.D. in economics from the University of Colorado at Boulder. Her areas of interest include income inequality, family budgets, unemployment, unions, and collective bargaining. She is co-author of the EPI book *How Does Teacher Pay Compare?* This is her second edition as a co-author of *The State of Working America*.